D0103369

Indi'n Humor

Lee Marmon (Laguna Pueblo), "White Man's Moccasins."
(Courtesy of Lee Marmon)

Indi'n Humor,

Bicultural Play in Native America

Kenneth Lincoln

New York   Oxford
OXFORD UNIVERSITY PRESS
1993

Oxford University Press

Oxford   New York   Toronto
Delhi   Bombay   Calcutta   Madras   Karachi
Kuala Lumpur   Singapore   Hong Kong   Tokyo
Nairobi   Dar es Salaam   Cape Town
Melbourne   Auckland   Madrid

and associated companies in
Berlin   Ibadan

Copyright © 1993 by Oxford University Press, Inc.

Published by Oxford University Press, Inc.,
200 Madison Avenue, New York, New York 10016

Oxford is a registered trademark of Oxford University Press

Library of Congress Cataloging-in-Publication Data
Lincoln, Kenneth.
Indi'n humor : bicultural play in native America / Kenneth Lincoln.
    p.   cm.
Includes bibliographical references and index.
ISBN 0-19-506887-4
1. Indians of North America—Humor.   2. American wit and humor.
3. American literature—Indian authors—History and criticism.
I.   Title.   E98.H77L56   1993   970.004'97—dc20   91-15666

9 8 7 6 5 4 3 2 1

Printed in the United States of America
on acid-free paper

For Paula Gunn Allen
who taught me
the humor beyond hurt

Acknowledgments

Among several hundred who helped in some way, the following deserve special mention. Paula Allen joked with me when the going got tough. Vee Salabiye teased me through a local purge into writing the book. Vine Deloria, Jr., first catalogued "Red Humor" in *Custer Died For Your Sins* and later told me some choice ones. Alfonso Ortiz showed me a special part of the Pueblo Southwest where every sunrise brings a smile. Al Logan Slagle taught me about comic angles into reality. Rebecca Tsosie never wavered in her warm support, and Mark Monroe kept a family sense of humor through hard times. My brother Richard, Hal Marienthal, Alan Dunn, Hal Pruett, Karin Jones, Reed Wilson, Laura Coltelli, and my UCLA colleagues brought me back to finish the book when I was down for the count.

Dozens of scholars responded to my inquiries about tribal language and laughter. J. Anthony Paredes sent many letters, more jokes. Calvin Bedient trained his hawkeye on the fine points of the arguments, and William Gleason was ever careful in his editorial suggestions, as well as assisting with the bibliography. My graduate students in American Indian Studies patiently endured long classroom hours of talk about Indi'n humor. Rachel, my daughter, has continued to be a comic blessing; and Jeannine Johnson stood by me when I had no laughter left.

To all these extended family I say *A-hó!* and *Mitakuye oyasin.*

Some of this material appeared in earlier versions in *Caliban* 3 (1987); *Kenyon Review* 9 (Winter 1987); Laura Coltelli, ed., *Native American Literatures* (Pisa: Servizio Editoriale Universitario, 1989); the Native American Series for poets (Los Angeles: UCLA, American Indian Studies Center, 1978, 1984, 1987); *Pacific Historical Review* 56 (Spring 1987); *San Francisco Chronicle,* 11 March 1990; *Spring* 49 (1989); *MELUS* 16 (Fall 1989–1990); and *Storia Nordamericana* 5 (1988).

Los Angeles   K.L.
June 1991

Contents

Indi'n Humor

(Pre)amble

INTERVIEWER: "Why do you suppose that Indian humor has been so little recognized by the majority culture? And so little understood?"

MOMADAY: "It's probably been kept a secret. It's one of the strongest elements of language within Indian cultures. . . . Humor is really where the language lives, you know. It's very close to the center, and very important."

N. SCOTT MOMADAY, in Charles L. Woodard, *Ancestral Voice*

"Indians? It's a good thing they weren't looking for Turkey."

VINE DELORIA, JR.

On the eve of the New World quincentennial, Euroamericans are rediscovering the "Indian" they created by mistaken cartography, then idealized to dispossess, and all but annihilated by military conquest. For American "Indians" a five-hundred-year holocaust exploded in the slipstream of Christopher Columbus. His wake vaporized 97 percent of the 75 to 100 million natives in the Western Hemisphere. Pre-Columbian, indeed, signifies a Native American world not discovered, but decimated.

Yet some 2 million diverse "Indians" survive today and tribally control 53 million acres of reservation lands in the United States. Every twenty years or so, given an oil shortfall or another frontier revival, we rediscover them, while America enters a new coming-of-age crisis. Today the concerns seem to be ecology, the peace imperative, global power realignments, and the nagging question of national roots for a country essentially composed of immigrant exiles who keep drifting west. So the Pueblo farmer, the Hopi pacifist, the Iroquois statesman, and the Cherokee gentleman come into soft media focus, along with

Princess Tekakwitha (the canonized martyr) and Pocahontas (everyone's grandmother) next to the high gloss of a Rambo Sioux warrior and a drugged-out Yaqui shaman—these "Indian" phantasms shadow the intercultural ironies of red–white history and salt American Indian humor. Why—better, how—have Native Americans outlasted half a millennium of assault on two thousand indigenous cultures in the West? To be sure, it is not by casting themselves as victims, crucified in the name of the true cross. It is not in lamenting dispossession under the banner of Manifest Destiny, or in pitying themselves reserved through the odd idealism of our simultaneously obliterating and conserving national resources ("reserves" of virgin timber, wild animals, and Indians seem more accurately tourist prisoner-of-war camps). The noble savage, the "poor Indian," the stoic warrior, the libidinous princess, the dogged squaw, the medicine witch, the cigar-store totem, the tearful ecologist, and the rainmaking shaman—these humorless stereotypes, ludicrous in themselves yet permeating American culture today, have been invented by non-Indians for roundabout reasons. Generally, they circle the messy aftermath of abuses of America's natives and nature-at-large, while advertisers continue to turn tricks and make bucks. Our "fine feathered friends" serve as the miner's canary of Western cultural devastation, as Felix Cohen noted forty years ago in the *Handbook of Federal Indian Law*. If they go, so do we.

What do Indians make of a summer 1990 issue of *People Weekly*, featuring Louise Erdrich, the Chippewa writer, trimmed with German-Indian silver jewelry and a jay feather in her borsolino, as one of "The 50 Most Beautiful People in the World," along with Michelle Pfeiffer and Tom Cruise? What do they think of Siouxie and the Banshees, a British punk band, or the Mazda "Navajo" Jeep? After a decade of Hollywood antipathy toward Westerns with redskins, how do they react to the sudden spate of Rambo-Sherlock-Hiawatha films—Kevin Costner's *Dances with Wolves,* Robert Redford's *Dark Wind* and *Peltier,* and John Fusco's *Incident at Oglala* and *Thunderheart?* The last features a half-Indian detective investigating murders on a reservation, only to discover his ancestral roots (spun off from the success of Tony Hillerman's Jim Chee fictions and Stephen King's *Pet Sematary?*). Fusco, working with Robert De Niro and recently "adopted" by Pine Ridge Sioux, told an interviewer that the script "deals with the ongoing oppression and attempted genocide of the Indian culture, as well as the exploitation of the earth."[1] Is this filmic news?

Indians generally respond to these gold-rush crusades with sharp humor, a good dose of sarcasm, resigned laughter, and a flurry of ironic "rez" (reservation) jokes that travel the Moccasin Telegraph like wildfire. They laugh hard and deep among themselves and grimace around whites, exorcising the pain, redirecting their suffering, drawing together against the common enemy—cultural ignorance. They hold out for a day when the newcomers will settle down as natives in the Americas.

This study tries to relay that complex of Indian humor to non-Indians. The approach borrows from the millennia-old tribal legacies of Trickster, an antiheroic comic teacher and holy fool, to fashion a new image of the surviving Indian as comic artist more than tragic victim, seriously humorous to the native core. There are many variants, hundreds of tribal points of view, thousands of differing styles and opinions on the subject. My own argument for tribal comic wisdom takes heart from the *heyoka,* or sacred clown, vision on the western high plains, among the Lakota where I grew up in Nebraska—*the power to make live* and *the power to destroy,* as imaged in the wooden bowl of sky water and the thunder-and-lightning bow. The powers to heal and to hurt, to bond and to exorcise, to renew and to purge remain the contrary powers of Indian humor, Lakota-based, tribally binding, universally human. They are specific to Native Americans, idiosyncratic to contemporary tribal cultures in renaissance today, imperative to their continuance—as well as to our own intercultural understandings of the Americas.

Indi'n Humor focuses on ethnic literary humor, from jokes in bars and at meetings and in kitchens; to the quieter wit of old wise people; to historical ironies still salting intercultural politics; to the outrageous license of holy fools in mythic times and at contemporary Indian ceremonies; to the written literature of the Native American renaissance that began in the late 1960s. "For a country so rich in native humor," John Lowe stresses, "we have a paucity of truly analytical treatments of it, and in fact *no* book that deals *exclusively* with ethnic humor exists, except for jokebooks or anthologies."[2] So what crops up in *The Complete Book of Ethnic Humor* under "American Indian," but more of the timeworn slurs: "Virgin Squaw: A wouldn't Indian"; or ho-ho, "Meanwhile back on the reservation, an Indian maiden did a naked rain dance and made the Creeks rise."[3]

Aside from culture-specific studies that dimple anthropology, American Indian humor remains a mystery, if not an oxymoron, to many: "A book on *what?*" people reply in disbelief to my research. W. W. Hill's

Navajo Humor (1943) may be a minor pioneering classic in the Southwest, but who has perused Julian Steward's doctoral dissertation, "The Ceremonial Buffoon of the American Indian," tucked away in a scholarly journal?[4] In response to my survey of scholars, J. Anthony Paredes, chairman of the Anthropology Department at Florida State University, wrote to me of his master's thesis under W. W. Hill at the University of New Mexico in 1964, "Plains Indian Clowns: A Typological Study." He mentioned Steward's doctoral dissertation (read by how many others? Professor Paredes wondered). Along with several letters and some tribal jokes, he added another "somewhat obscure reference" to James Howard's "The Dakota Heyoka Cult."[5] And yet, he conceded, most people are probably interested in the jokes as living cultural quips. "The best thing I can do in responding to your questionnaire," Professor Paredes wrote me, "is send you some of the best jokes I recall."

The person who pestered me to write this book, Velma Salabiye, UCLA's Navajo librarian, has told me the best jokes, and she wields her sense of humor as daily survival. There seems to be a cultural perspective behind the individual persona. "A Navajo who can 'see' and express the humor of situations is highly cherished and appreciated as a family member, a guest, a visitor, or a fellow worker," Gary Witherspoon explains. "Navajo humor emphasizes wit and is often very subtle. At the basis of this humor are creative thought and creative expression."[6] When a Navajo child laughs out loud for the first time, the parents invite extended kin to a "first laugh" rite, where the child symbolically gives salt and bread to all. This crystalline cut of daily sustenance, good humor, and grace ensures lifelong generosity as a facet of Navajo tribalism. "Eat bread and salt and speak the truth," goes a related Slovakian proverb.

Trying to teach me a simple Navajo greeting, *Ya-ah-teeh!*, Vee Salabiye bantered a Navajo language-training phrase, translated "The goat fell in the mud." Navajos laughed about driving into Gallup, New Mexico, to see the cowboy-and-Indian movie *A Distant Trumpet*. Indians would line up to hear a line from Monument Valley that the movie's star, Troy Donahue, could not translate: "Just like a snake, you crawl in your own shit."

Charlie Hill keeps the Moccasin Telegraph humming with one-liners on and off "The Tonight Show." The first English immigrants, he snaps, were illegal aliens—"Whitebacks, we call 'em." Hill imagines the Algonkians asking innocently, "You guys gonna stay long?" His

Custer jokes are not printable ("Look at all those f——ing Indians!"—
a barroom nude painting of Custer's last words). A Sioux fast-food
chain: "Pups on a Pole." Getting the "munchies" while watching
"Lassie" on the tube, Hill's Sioux roommate ate the landlady's dog.

Telling or penning a joke is risky business. Thus "literate" here
means "verbally skilled," in or out of the great tradition—and crafting
a good joke, telling a comic story, or simply conveying one's humor
may be the highest verbal (and transverbal) interactive art of all. Indeed,
as Freud implied, joking is a kind of daily cultural poetry. Paula Gunn
Allen wrote in response to my questionnaire on Indian joking: "Not to
make too much of it, but humor is the best and sharpest weapon we've
always had against the ravages of conquest and assimilation. And while
it is a tiny projectile point, it's often sharp, true and finely crafted."[7]
"What's three feet high and a mile long?" she tossed in among half a
dozen other quips: "A Pueblo Grand Entry."

Pueblos are not especially tall people among Native Americans, contrary to the high-cheekboned Sioux stereotype. Their ceremonial entries
go way back in time (several millennia at least) and include immensely
complex clan and cultural kinship systems. To catch the joke, there's
still no substitute for common sense and quick wit. "Understanding the
form and pressure of, to use the dangerous word one more time, natives'
inner lives," Clifford Geertz writes, "is more like grasping a proverb,
catching an allusion, seeing a joke—or, as I have suggested, reading a
poem—than it is like achieving communion."[8] "Spits straight up,"
goes the Japanese proverb, "learns something." This may be concretely
Japanese on a lotus-blossom day in Kyoto, but I suspect it's translatable
across cultures and climates. The specific here encodes the universal
integer. "We were poor as Job's turkey during the Depression," my
daughter's great-grandmother would say. About three thousand years of
Jewish and Christian history glance off that allusion to Job's trials. The
turkey seems more recently American, where émigrés from everywhere
began "as poor as poor can be," survived that, and prospered to give
thanks. And "there goes the neighborhood," Native Americans are said
to have said at Plymouth Rock. The humor (and hurt) of these intercultural discoveries make up the subject of this book.

Indi'n Humor addresses multiple disciplines, overlaps special in-
terests, and responds to intercultural questions. Methodologically
mixed, the approach is a breed of its own. There is no ideal reader, but
more a heterogenous audience of mixed opinions, cultural frictions,

varying motives, and incalculable differences about humor in literature and in life. My approach is associative, interdisciplinary, and phenomenological—ever suspicious of arrogating closure. I trust specific investigation, distrust academic overkill. My models in associative particularity—from Lao-tsu and Heraclitus long ago, through Bachelard and Heidegger a century back, to such as Kristeva and Geertz today—move my thoughts *toward* awareness, as they caution respect of the contextual field and illuminate the luminous details in the critical foreground. I do not write to exhaust the subject or to silence the reader, but to startle, or to disturb, or otherwise to trigger interactive dialogues. William Carlos Williams, the doctor–poet, first freed my scholarly attentions from pseudo-grids and proved the virtue of close attention, careful inquiry, and empathic probing. Dickinson, Yeats, Heaney, and other poets continue to convince me to focus closely and feel truly and trust the big picture to come through the fine particulars. Novelists like Toni Morrison or Vladimir Nabokov, Louise Erdrich or Ron Hansen, strike me as no less closely focused or clearly tuned. So *Indi'n Humor* takes its cues from literary craftspeople. It is less about criticism than culture, more in search of imaginative spark than speculative certainty. My critics will badger the lack of systematic tidiness. So be it. I'd rather not squeeze the sap from living thoughts—choose to activate the data, not to co-opt the cultures. This approach is open response, not a closed case. *Caveat lector*.

I have included personal experiences as data, along with sociocultural scaffolding, literary theory, and textual analysis. Books record lives, simply said; they are not made up of thin air or of information merely retrieved from research files. And it would be folly to think our models and methods will not be revised, reversed, or reinvented as they become public property. Thus this study presumes no closure. It broadens literary context to include speaking people and lived situations, as well as recent theoretical constructions and deconstructions, in dialogue with American Indian verse and current popular fiction. Clifford Geertz calls for systematically modest assertions that place the whole realistically in context for what it is: here a non-Indian scholar advancing what he knows, guesses, and proposes about American Indian humor, comparative cultures, even nativist gender studies. The target is literature; the scope, intercultural and broadly humanist. The discussions include readers' tastes and tendencies. The focus remains words per se, as spoken and written by American Indians or advanced about them by non-Indians.

Indi'n

> For me the language is an odd brand of English, mostly local, mostly half-breed spoken by the people around me, filled with elegance and vulgarity side by side, small jokes that are language jokes and family jokes and area jokes, certain expressions that are peculiar to that meeting of peoples who speak a familiar (to me) laconic language filled with question and comment embedded in a turn of phrase, skewing of diction, a punning, cunning language that implies connections in diversity of syntax and perception, the oddness of how each of us seems and sees.
>
> PAULA GUNN ALLEN, "Autobiography of a Confluence"

Buffalo Bill Cody respectfully added the adjective "American" to "Indian" in his Wild West Show a hundred years ago. Rubrics such as "Native American" and "First American" advance academic ways of glossing what differing tribal peoples generically call "Indi'n."[9] This contracted spoken icon, idiosyncratic of pan-tribal dialects, comes from the people with a purpose. Sociolinguistics helps sharpen the contrary argument's edge. Wsevolod W. Isajiw speaks of an ethnic "double boundary" drawn from both "within" a group and "without."[10] That is, "ethnicity" is *inter*cultural, something like counterreflective mirrors, where "in-group" and "out-group" are seen (and joked about) from both sides.

Tribal societies have named themselves variations on "the people" for millennia. For the past five hundred years, the Euroamerican outsider has spoken roughshod over native names, from the misnomer "Indian" down to today's advertising icons. Labeling or, more accurately, misnaming some 75 to 100 million pre-Columbian natives glossed as "Indians" initiated a Euroamerican process of mistranslating and stereotyping that has persisted for centuries, Tzvetan Todorov argues in *The Conquest of America* (1984). Roger Williams in *A Key into the Languages of America* (1643) catalogued Euroamerican names imposed *on* American natives: "*Natives, Salvages, Indians, Wild-men* (so the *Dutch* call them *Wilden*)." Native languages were brushed aside, along with their speakers. *"Abergeny men, Pagans, Barbarians, Heathen"* came to signify "the other" as aboriginal enantiomorph, at once inversely noble and savage, given shifting predispositions on the advancing Western frontier. Richard Bernheimer's *Wild Man in the Middle Ages* (1952) investigates the mythic imagining that preceded—indeed, precluded—cultural integrity to be granted "Native" America. Euroamericans transposed cathedral gargoyles onto American Indians, as easily as calling them savage children or consorts of Satan. So in the beginning Indians were most wildly "other," as today they remain misunderstood, the West's noble icon and sentimental native.

The word "Indi'n," with its dialectal elision, crosses the first boundary between native tribal peoples and immigrant Euroamericans. America is not India, we all know by now, and these tribal aborigines are nominally not In-*di*-ans. They do not spell or speak themselves as such; by inverse relation to "proper" English, indeed, they collate dialectally across a continent as differing peoples with hundreds of cultural tongues. "Since dialect, at least to the oppressor, is part and parcel of the negative stereotype," John Lowe notes, "pride in dialect constitutes inversion, transforming an oppressive signifier of otherness into a pride-inspiring prism, one which may be used for the critical inspection of 'the other' " ("Ethnic Humor" 448). Anthony Mattina predicates a pan-Indian spoken, even written, English that stretches from Colville Reservation oral narratives to Leslie Silko's 1977 novel *Ceremony*: "I don't think it would be an overgeneralization to state that Red English is a pan-Indian phenomenon, with various subdialects, of course."[11] Thus, to capsulize the point, in their own dialects of "Red English," American Indians identify themselves apart from Euroamerican others.[12] Their own varieties of spoken English are separatist, to a certain extent, as the reservation land base of 53 million acres remains set apart from mainstream America. From northern plains to southwestern deserts, from coastal forests to the Smokies, the pan-tribal term is spoken as "Indi'n." It is an interesting twist on an old misnomer, "Indians," as the pan-tribal word has been taken in and turned around. Such dialectal inversion—and ritual transformation—lie at the heart of Indi'n humor.

Nationalist definitions further distinguish red from white cultures. Lakota and Navajo, for example, represent two of the largest Indian "domestic dependent nations," as federally defined. Historically, these are tribal complexes in extended language families bonded over vast time and place. A dozen or more major language families extend far across native North America, and some five hundred distinct tongues pool locally to differentiate cultures among particular tribes. In *A Breeze Swept Through* (1987), Luci Tapahonso writes with an idiomatic twist of serving her Navajo uncle American coffee:

> I sit down again and he tells me
>   some coffee has no kick but
>   this one is the one.
>   It does it good for me.

> I pour us both a cup and
>   while we wait for my mother,
>   his eyes crinkle with the smile
>   and he says
>   yes, ah yes, this is the very one
>   (putting in more cream and sugar)

> So I usually buy Hills Brothers coffee
>   once or sometimes twice a day
>   I drink a hot coffee and

>   it sure does it for me.

>   ("Hills Brothers Coffee")

A more specific focus funnels down to a regional band: the Oglala Sioux of Pine Ridge, near my hometown; or Shungopavi village on the Hopi Second Mesa for Mike Kabotie; or Antelope clan at Acoma for Simon Ortiz. These enclaves within tribes remain identifiable by spoken dialects, products of cultural place and local history. In the poem "Yaadi La," for example, Tapahonso tells a "la-di-da" Coyote story of marital betrayal with a slant on standard English, not to mention a microcourse in Navajo:

> she fed the kids fried potatoes and spam and they watched TV.
> later her sister came over, she said, he's gone, huh?
>   ma'ii' alt'aa dishii honey, i won't do it again 'aach' eeh
>   noo dah diil whod. (old coyote was probably saying
>   in vain: honey, i won't do it again.)
> they just laughed and drank diet pepsi at the kitchen table.

>   . . .

> he came home the next evening and handed her his paycheck
> signed. the kids brought in his sacks of clothes and sat

back down to watch the flintstones. he sat at the table
and said i deserve everything you do to me.
    you're just too good for me.
she kept on washing dishes then she asked: ruthie's
    nits' aa' yooyeelwod? (she has run away from you?)

she sat awhile not saying anything then went out to get
some wood. she called her sister up saying:
    ma'ii nadza! want to go to town tomorrow?
    'ayoo shibeeso holo, hey! (coyote's back
    and I have money to blow now!)

'inda ma'ii nachxoogo tloodi nagha jiin'.
(they said the coyote walked around outside that night pouting.)

Such literary use of the spoken Indi'n word—an English sometimes
mixed with tribal and regional inflections—frames this study in what
Geertz calls "local knowledge" of the people's own understandings.
Indian idiomatic play points toward a trickster's tolerance for deviance
and a survivalist's native humor.

The straightest local passage into tribal particulars leads through family and extended kin. When asked about his father's most distinguishing
trait, the Kiowa Pulitzer Prize–winning novelist and poet N. Scott
Momaday replied: "My father had a very well-developed sense of
humor. And he loved to 'kid,' to use the term. When he was in such a
mood, and that was very often, he would smile in a particular way. He
would break into a smile and sort of squint his eyes. That's the first
gesture that I remember."[13] And from the other perspective, Freud
suggests, the infant's primal smile (turning satisfied from a mother's
breast) may signal the "first gesture" toward biological and familial
bonds that evolve and constellate as cultural humor. "The whole damn
tribe is one big family," John (Fire) Lame Deer says of the Sioux at
Rosebud, South Dakota.[14] Tongue here inflects hearth and home. Joking crackles from kitchen to toolshed, with humor truly the "permitted
disrespect" of sibling rivalry or motherly affection or fatherly teasing or
cousin cudgeling. And in this case, literature is a record of personal
definitions from psychosocial perspectives.

"What's the Indi'n definition of a papoose?" a Navajo friend asks
me. "A consolation prize for a chance on a blanket." Ethnicity comes
through cultural self-definition and biological given, individual epis-

temology and collective history. As Werner Sollors contests in *Beyond Ethnicity* (1986), the written word is a sign of spoken heritage through both "consent" and "descent."

Characters

> Yet the Indian is actually a very human person—humorous, sexy, sensitive, touchy and quick-tempered, a great gossip and practical joker, a born mimic, a politician from infancy, and an incorrigible lover of human society.
>
> STANLEY VESTAL, "The Hollywooden Indian"

With no small irony, regional dialects of red English bond hundreds of tribes across their own iconic buckskins, as do other English dialects in India or Africa today. "I don't think it would be an overgeneralization," Anthony Mattina considers, "to state that Red English, with various dialects of course, is a pan-Indian phenomenon, roughly analogous to Black English" ("Mythography" 139). Racial and regional inflections of an emerging common tongue now extend worldwide, since perhaps half of humanity speaks some variant of English. More than half the books and three-quarters of the world's mail are written in English.[15] The Chinese are learning English several hours a day on television and radio in order to "modernize" and interact with the rest of the world. European communities all trade in English. Global English dialects, almost languages in themselves (black English from the streets of Harlem to those of Johannesburg), constitute intercontinental lingua francas, regardless of one's politics.

New forms of English are redefining the tongue rapidly for all of us. The black novelist John Wideman describes how his ancestors created "verbal icons" from standard American speech, playing poetically with the spoken slippage: "Africans took English sounds and with variation in tempo, rhythm, tone and timbre transformed them."[16] Within these speech patterns lay the metrics, textures, and lyrics of cultural literacy. "What makes a work 'Black'?" Toni Morrison poses.[17] "The most valuable point of entry into the question of cultural or racial distinction, the one most fraught, is its language—its unpoliced, seditious, confrontational, manipulative, inventive, disruptive, masked and unmasking

language." This is pure Trickster poetics. "I am a Black woman poet,"
Lucille Clifton defines herself in *Contemporary Poets* (1980), "and I
sound like one":

girls
first time a white man
opens his fly
like a good thing
we'll just laugh
laugh real loud my
black women

children
when they ask you
why is your mama so funny
say
she is a poet
she don't have no sense

("Admonitions")

Across cultures and gender chasms, the black poet Jay Wright musically
mixes African, Caribbean, and American voices in his verse. "This is my
mitote, / batoco, areito, / my bareitote. / This is my bareitote, / areito,
batoco, / my a-ba-mitote. / Corre, corrido navideño." ("Rhythm,
Charts and Changes"). Literature rises from speech, patterns the daily
inflections, and codifies a people's dialogue with itself. And humor
alchemizes this emic speech into ethnic music, as with the three whor-
ing muses of Toni Morrison's novel *The Bluest Eye*: "From deep inside,
her laughter came like the sound of many rivers, freely, deeply, mud-
dily, heading for the room of an open sea."[18] Such a literate tradition of
black dialectal humor courses through Langston Hughes's novel *Not
Without Laughter* (1930) and his collection of short stories, *Laughing to
Keep from Crying* (1952), as it spices his "Jesse B. Semple" dialogues
in postwar America.

Hanay Geiogamah, the Kiowa dramatist, instructs the actors for *Body
Indian*, which premiered in 1972 at New York's La Mama Experimental
Theater Club by the American Indian Theater Ensemble:

1. Lines must be delivered in a clipped fashion, a kind of talk characterized
by a tendency to drop final *g* ("goin' "), to jam words together ("lotta"), to
add a grammatically superfluous final *s* ("mens"), to leave a hiatus between a

final and an initial vowel ("a old one"), and (in women's speech particularly) to lengthen vowels inordinately ("l——ots"). In no way whatever is anything negative or degrading intended; this is simply the way the characters in this play speak English. The actors should be warned against overplaying this "Indian" speech. It should never become garbled and unclear.[19]

As a Kiowa playwright listens closely in order to dramatize tribal talk, so could literary critics and social historians pay more attention to red English in America and, beyond that, to the dialogics and poetics of humor that define peoples among themselves. Differences are where we start to listen. "Rather than changing the way Indians talk," Mattina defends the nonstandard dialects of red English, "I advocate educating those who hear Indians talk. This is an old problem, plenty discussed with reference, for example, to Black English. Some will die thinking that Reds and Blacks better talk the way we do, by God; some will die shaking their heads" (*Golden Woman* 9).

Writers today are carving a Native American renaissance from regional dialects of red English—its concise dictions, distinctive inflections, loping rhythms, iconic imagery, irregular grammar, reverse twists on standard English, and countless turns of coiling humor. As Geiogamah says, no negative slur is here intended—"this is simply the way" tribal people speak, even joke. "Thus, even in the most sacred of the ceremonies," Leslie Silko deduces from Emory Sekaquaptewa's remarks on clowns punning in English, "traditional Hopis see no reason not to use an English word to get a laugh, a laugh being their sacred duty and a part of the whole overall ceremony."[20] Serious men make good *koshares,* or clowns, the Hopi say, for in their language the word for "clowning" means "to make a point." A "smile is sacred," adds one elder in the film documentary *Hopi Songs of the Fourth World* (1988).

Tribe to tribe, Indians speak distinct inflections of red English with regional senses of humor.[21] Listen to N. Scott Momaday's fictional voices in peyote prayers spoken at the Holiness Pan-Indian Rescue Mission in Los Angeles:

Henry Yellowbull: "Be with us tonight. Come to us now in bright colors and sweet smoke. Help us to make our way. Give us laughter and good feelings always. . . ."

Cristobal Cruz: "Well, I jes' want to say thanks to all my good frens here tonight for givin' me this here honor, to be fireman an' all. This here shore is

a good meetin', huh? I know we all been seein' them good visions an' all, an'
there's a whole lot of frenhood an' good will aroun' here, huh? . . ."

Napoleon Kills-in-the-Timber: "Great Spirit be with us. We gone crazy for
you to be with us poor Indi'ns. We been bad long time 'go, just raise it hell
an' kill each others all the time. An' that's why you 'bandon us, turn your
back on us. Now we pray to you for help. Help us! We been suffer like hell
some time now. . . ."

Ben Benally: "Look! Look! There are blue and purple horses . . . a house
made of dawn. . . ."[22]

These southwestern, California, and northern and southern plains voices
sketch prayers to the spirits in cross-tribal red English. Speech patterns
in this text tend to be glottal, end-stopped, or truncated in noun–verb
clusters. In plain English, talk is to the point, terse. Verbs crop up
sporadically, and adjectives are spare, adverbs even sparser. Subjects
and verbs don't always agree. The rarified tenses—conditional, pas-
sive, perfect—seldom surface, and auxiliary verbs fade out. As with
Tosamah's invocational mix of "conviction, caricature, and callousness" in *House Made of Dawn*, there appears a great deal of linguistic "code switching," even dialect swapping. Framing devices shift
within voices: "Good evening, blood brothers and sisters, and welcome, welcome. Gracious me, I see lots of new faces out there tonight.
Gracious me! May the Great Spirit—can we knock off that talking in
the back there?—be with you always" (*HMD* 86).

So differences in culture register as separate tongues within a polyglot
English. Considering that Navajo, a language of thirteen distinct tenses,
corresponds little with the Latin grammar imposed on Germanic-based
and French-overlaid English, and that Hopi in effect has *no* verb tenses
as we know them, it seems no surprise that Indi'n English invents itself
as distinct from the mainstream schoolings, European origins, and class
proprieties of America. Vincent Crapanzano catches a pointillist cadence in a Navajo description of New York City: "Big. Many cars.
Everything over my eyes."[23] In Sioux country farther north, Marnie
Walsh sketches "Bessie Dreaming Bear" of Rosebud, South Dakota, in
Voices from Wah'Kon-Tah (1960):

we all went to town one day
went to a store

bought you new shoes
red   high heels

aint seen you since

This is the native grammar (and humor) of lived situations.[24]

Terrain

> Ethnic humor has always formed a significant part of the world of
> American folklore and culture, partly because it provides pleasure,
> and partly because of its connection with mythical concepts of
> aggression, struggle, and our national passion play and ritual,
> "Americanization." Humor, moreover, is absolutely central to our
> conception of the world. Despite this fact, we tend to become
> suddenly solemn when we begin to write, particularly for scholarly
> journals and books. To be funny indicates a lack of seriousness.
> Perhaps for this reason, histories and studies of ethnicity, assimila-
> tion, and ethnic literature have frequently ignored a vital aspect of
> their subject; for although minorities have often entered into full
> citizenship through long and arduous struggle, this procedure has
> sometimes been both shortened and sweetened when they have
> made up their minds to enter laughing.
>
> JOHN LOWE, "Theories of Ethnic Humor"

Just a note on method: we do what we do. My approach angles from an
American studies perspective, leans toward an ethnic studies persua-
sion, confesses an American Indian studies prejudice, and claims a
northern plains predisposition. We are who we are, after all, and best to
foreground this from the start. Most basically, my analysis works with
American culture as its focus, moving on a path of "focused wandering," as Howard Norman says the Cree speak of travel between villages. That is, the study designates goals and getting to them, all the
while exploring along the way. Method is not a lockstep mode or an end
in itself; theory goes in service of practice ("the sway of usage," Martin
Heidegger says in his 1971 study *On the Way to Language*). This means
that the rooted "target" moves with the dialogue.

   So *Indi'n Humor* tracks regional dialects of "red English" pan-tribally in a Euroamerican setting. The approach comes up interdisciplinary

with a literary bias, starting with the English minim, the *syllable* of most basic sound and meaning. This acoustic minimalism begins as a phonetic or even musical process, at first listening for the sounds an "other" makes or doesn't make, as the case may be, where silence shapes speaking. Cultural parameters determine how speakers and listeners size up one another. Crapanzano says in *The Fifth World of Forster Bennett,* "The Navajo don't talk much, and even for a Navaho Forster is quiet. His monotone makes him a master of understatement. Most white men, Gene tells me, think he's stupid and most Navajos consider him intelligent" (105).

In the beginning I'm uncritically "-etic," listening from the outside in. As the listening goes along cultural lines, I slowly find myself bridging into the "-emic" insider's illusion that I know what's going on, or at least I flatter myself so, given a choice comic morpheme. This illusion soon dissolves. For *syllable* leads to syllable, building "words" in literary sequences, and eventually a *syntax* or phrasing starts to establish a "line" (rhythm, pitch, tone, cadence in the rippling of the phonemes). Where the sentence ends or the line breaks, pauses, or enjambs (ends but goes on) opens a set of syntactic questions about form—which leads to a third consideration: *structure.* Why do two lines make a couplet in Roberta Whiteman's *Star Quilt*? or five sliding beats blank verse in James Welch's *Riding the Earthboy 40*? or five shaped paragraphs an essay in Vine Deloria, Jr.'s *Custer Died For Your Sins*? or so many chapters a novel in N. Scott Momaday's *House Made of Dawn*? What dictates the Navajo pause in a Coyote telling, the clown's hop in the Pueblo kiva, the curve of the horizon from a Lakota vision pit on the mountain? How do crafted differences, in short, compose a whole beyond themselves?

This kind of reflection leads into a fourth problem: *style*—how we do what we do. Is it the whole or the motion of the parts that targets our attention? What is the connection between product and process? Is Charlie Hill, the Indian comedian, continuously funny on stage, or is he funny only when we laugh? How does his "humor" encompass the particular one-liners that delight red and/or white audiences? Is Gerald Vizenor's hilarious video starring Charlie Hill, *Warriors of Orange* (1984), a clever bunch of Indi'n jokes or a "comic form" as Northrop Frye would define such? Does dancer or dance define the dancing movement? Perhaps style is the figure in cultural motion, and structure maps its going along. Style may be a way of describing what specifies the cultural process we're caught up in—the personality of the maker, the character of the experience experienced. This preamble is clearly stamped with the author's personality and "style," in imagined dialogue with an absent reader.

But then things get complicated: What *gives* character or shape to personal experience? As culturally bound integers in time and space, don't we stylists "project" meaning onto things, aside from their inherent thingness? We "read" (into) things. And this is where cultural metaphors go to work, simile on one side (conceptual signs) and symbol hip-deep in things on the other (icons that speak beyond themselves). So this appears to be where undertone and overtone make the syllable or single note a harmonic (or disharmonic) chord. For the social scientist, these chromatics present symbolic registers of culture, the synchronic moments when we hear what's been going on diachronically for centuries with a people. For the aesthetician, it's harmony; for the humorist, the rippling interplay of time, space, and people across differences.

If syntax seems in some way analogous to a lyric line or narrative sequence (moment by moment in timed space—the pacing of a joke), and structure composes the whole, as style is the more or less magic differential between Mozart and Mahler, then simile-to-symbol constitutes that subterranean complex of hidden thirds, fourths, half-tones, and sliding notes that give tone and texture to a text. It's the bubble behind the joke about to burst. In *Insight and Outlook,* Arthur Koestler describes this as "in"-sight that comes "out" to look. Freud sees it as a crafted "release" in joking, and Mary Douglas details the "permitted disrespect" of contextual codes that key such artistic release. Indians tell me it's what makes the fun funny, the clown with the bent arrows comic at a Sun Dance, or blackface "Jesse Jackson" *katsinas* jokable in orange wigs at Hopi ceremonies the year I started this study. Joking appears, in short, as culture-in-action. The cultural anthropologists, from Frazer, Boas, and Sapir, to Turner and Geertz, have much to tell us about how we read meanings into things. Indi'n humor, since it is so little discussed yet so widely acknowledged among tribes, projects a perfect inner circle or play-sphere, in Johan Huizinga's sense, to gauge how we read one another across the Buckskin Curtain.

So lastly, I ask, what is the *sense* in all this? Why am I doing what I do, and to what end; and why did "others" basically so not do, or do a bit, or do so differently? Does it mean anything culturally significant or measurable, beyond my own personal interest? Might it make a difference in anyone's life? Should it be fun? These thorny questions of intention, use, and personal reward will never be answered to anyone's satisfaction. They seem in the fullest sense ultimate and irresolvable; but it pays to ask them at the end-of-the-beginning as a conditional check on how syllable led to syntax, to structure, to simile/symbol, to style, to sense. Theoreticians might periodically question both means and ends as self-reflexive "suckholes" (Cree freezing quicksand).

Those cautions look back on how I thought I wrote this book—and now begin revising with a multitude of readers in mind, from Bakersfield to Boston to Rattlesnake Butte. We should never forget that we, the *see-ers* here (writer/reader), are see*ing* the *seen* (my pretext/our context/your text)—and that on the other side native "seers" peer back at us. Seeing is intercultural dialogue, especially when an Anglo writes about Indi'n humor. The ideal translator would be a breed of both, and many of the new Indian writers are just that, bicultural ethnographers. Such American "native" translators chart a process of symbolic interaction for all of us, a phenomenology of subjects and objects in kinetic tension going back centuries. We play seriously at understanding things, scientifically and humanistically. Surety and speculation need not conflict. Hence, a due measure of humility—and humor—is called for. "Historians have found the first treaty the United States government ever signed with the Indians," says Frank Marcus, the Taos Pueblo fire chief. "It states that the Indians can keep their land 'for as long as the river runs clear, the buffalo roam, the grass grows tall, and the mountains stand proud—or ninety days, whichever comes first.' "[25]

1

Red/White American

Everything is funny as long as it is happening to somebody else.
WILL ROGERS

Back Home

By the late 1960s, I had read *Black Elk Speaks*—a strangely troubling, still visionary story by John Neihardt about my northern plains home. During my last semester in graduate school, a Japanese-American friend lent me a new novel, *House Made of Dawn,* by a Kiowa writer as yet unknown (Momaday's Pulitzer was a few months away). Then in the spring of 1969 *Playboy* published "Anthropologists and Other Friends," from Vine Deloria, Jr.'s outrageously titled *Custer Died For Your Sins.* The line was borrowed from a bumper sticker to goad missionaries. The *Playboy* essay was illustrated with a casually dressed contemporary Indian pinned in a specimen box. I read it in the city engineer's drafting room in Alliance, Nebraska, where I worked during college vacations. Alliance rednecks didn't consider Indians funny or literate; my callow stereotypes shattered.

Little did I know of Scott Momaday's resonant sense of humor (in a month he would buy me a hamburger on Berkeley's Telegraph Avenue). Nor was I aware that Nick Black Elk, along with Joe Chips, had been *heyokas,* or sacred Sioux clowns, around my hometown. And I discovered that Deloria, a Standing Rock Sioux, not only was a skilled lawyer and satiric writer, but had been a Lutheran divinity student for four years. He was now publishing in an all-American glossy *on Indian humor!* I had a few things to learn.

Indians do laugh a lot.[1] Kitchen to back porch, tribal council to national caucus, the tribal "cement" of the pan-Indian movement today

21

comes through Indi'n humor. Deloria says: "When a people can laugh at themselves and laugh at others and hold all aspects of life together without letting anybody drive them to extremes, then it seems to me that that people can survive."[2] This humor is both traditional and contemporary, tribal and geopolitical.

Not only do Indians bond and revitalize, scapegoat and survive through laughter, but they draw on millennia-old traditions of Trickster gods and holy fools, comic romance and epic boast. There is, and always has been, humor among Indians—and some five hundred tribal variants in the contiguous United States, locally indigenous to climate and geography, genetics and history. Daniel Brinton, in *The Myths of the New World,* crowned the ubiquitous antihero, "Trickster," the year of the 1868 Red Cloud Treaty. S. G. F. Brandon, in *A Dictionary of Comparative Religions* (1970), sees this lawless comic figure as the "mythological portrayal of a kind of surd-factor," an original radical as clown of the creation, who proves both diverse and common across global cultures.[3] While "the" Trickster is pan-Indian, and some forms of libidinous humor surface in many tribal creation myths (from African Ananse to Chinese Monkey King), Wichikapache remains specifically a Cree fool of the Canadian North who teaches survival through error. Wakdjungkaga, a near relative in northeastern Nebraska, breaks all the Winnebago rules to prove them. Pueblo *koshares* in the Southwest drink urine and bathe in dung to stretch the limits of the gods, inversely to relieve ceremonial tension (these spirits have no human limits). The Iroquois false-face creator in the Northeast illustrates the doublings of reality through true and false twins; and Navajo Ma'ii, or Coyote Old Man, helps both to re-create the Southwest as "first-born" creator *and* to rearrange or decreate it a bit. Always messing around, he is a comic "changing" spirit who continues the shape shiftings, just as the Mother Earth herself, Changing Woman, rejuvenates a cyclical world "with grace and beauty" (so goes the ideal formula for aging among the Navajo).

The particularities here are not easy to assimilate for non-Indians, steeped in the American work ethic, plain moral styles, and a Puritan exclusion of humor from serious or sacred sites (as I grew up anyway). Specifics are not exactly intertribal. Navajo and Sioux and Hopi and Crow and Chippewa aren't much unified on anything but resistance to Anglo encroachment, as Deloria notes, considering the frequency of jokes about Columbus and Custer. Still, this study focuses on the ethnic glue of Indi'n humor. Some of the broader continuities and overlaps should dispel the antimyth that Indians have no humor. The tribal specifics of cases over time and terrain indicate just the opposite. Indians laugh with special significance among themselves—from the traditional Blackfeet Dung Suitor to James Welch's farting horse in *Winter in the Blood* (1974), from puckish Cheyenne jumping mice to shifty-eyed Paiute ravens, from pigeon-toed Chumash coyotes all the way to Louise Erdrich's lyric feminist humor in modern fiction and Momaday's wise-cracking peyote priest, Tosamah, in *House Made of Dawn* (1968). To unify, to purge, to regenerate, Northrop Frye says in *Anatomy of Criticism* (1957), is to enact the muses of spring, the three fates of the comic spirit. These remain particularly *native* to America, Indian in origin, perhaps universally human. "One of the best ways to understand a people," Deloria writes, "is to know what makes them laugh" (*Custer* 146). Indi'n humor may well be an undiscovered index to America's first peoples.

In 1931, the year that John Neihardt listened to Nick Black Elk, Constance Rourke heard our national character in a distinctly "American" humor.[4] Rourke felt that American humor tapped resilient and liberated resources, a frontier courage to face "west" toward the uncharted, the wild, the Indian in America. Out west, Vine Deloria, Jr.'s premises in *Custer Died For Your Sins* anticipate the audacity (and red humor) of his second tract, the claim that our native *God Is Red* (1973). Deloria's own work and life natively show that law, religion, literature, social science, and the comic spirit *can* have a common axis in Indi'n humor—an integrative spirit from Indian America—and reach a reading public outside academia. No stranger to theory or humor, Deloria writes and thinks with the best of quick-shot, trick-riding, literary marksmen. The art of his native humor provides telling examples of Freud's "economy" of release in dreams, jokes, and poetry. "What did you call this country before Columbus?" the Indian buff recycles the quip in *Custer*. "Ours." It's a good thing Columbus wasn't "looking for Turkey," Deloria testified in the Omaha federal court hearings on the 1868 Red Cloud Treaty.

A submerged, then "released," comic voice speaks here for "the people." Americans-at-large these days are still looking for what to call this country: Is it finally ours, "*we* the people," as Iroquis means? How united or divided do we remain in a pluralist democracy? What do "natives" among us have to say about communality and continuity?

Deloria's red wit is honed by a *human* science, candid and engaging— real things lie at stake, cultural and self-definitional at the heart of matters. Johan Huizinga calls such the agon or ludic contest of "play." All this can be tapped, if not measured, in Indi'n humor.

History holds some intercultural texts worth resurrecting. "Let us examine the facts," Corn Tassel exhorts "brother warriors" when whites come to "the forest's edge" in 1785 to draw up a treaty with the Cherokee for peace (and land). Having invaded in the dead of night and driven the tribes into the woods, now whites want to "talk of the law of nature and the law of nations," Corn Tassel notes wryly, "and they are both against you."[5] Observing that whites arrogantly expect Indians to adopt white laws, religion, manners, and customs, Corn Tassel urges the Cherokee to consider the "good effect of these doctrines," if any, rather than "hearing you talk about them, or reading your papers." Talk's cheap. Indians already have law, religion, manners, and customs that make them Cherokee. If whites want Indians to farm as they do, "May we not, with equal propriety, ask, why the white people do not hunt and live as we do?" Corn Tassel's contrary logic carries the appeal of plain talk with an ironic dialogical twist: we are *not* "your slaves. We are a separate people!" Indian nations have been free-standing for millennia. Still, the "great God of Nature" has placed two peoples "in different situations," Corn Tassel says. The best treaty here would be drawn from coexistent cultural tolerance; xenophobic arrogance makes no sense in either direction. Nature has stocked white lands "with cows, ours with buffalo; yours with hog, ours with bear; yours with sheep, ours with deer." Your God has given whites the "advantage," Corn Tassel concedes with no little irony, since "your cattle are tame and domestic while ours are wild and demand not only a larger space for range, but art to hunt and kill them." The comic binocularity here—one profile straight-faced in the "facts," the other side strategic in the survivalist "art" of humor—carries the argument for Corn Tassel two centuries later, historical conquest notwithstanding.

Homo ludens, Huizinga argues, is *Homo* at his best—and *she's* even better-humored, feminists like Paula Gunn Allen (*The Sacred Hoop* [1986]) and Rayna Green (*That's What She Said* [1984]) reply with an Indi'n twist. "What do you do for poison oak?" a student in a large auditorium once asked Mabel McKay, the Cache Creek Pomo elder, interviewed as a native healer. "Calamine Lotion," she shot back. When a middle-aged Stanford woman asked for "spirit" tips on how

Mabel stayed so youthful, the medicine woman suggested dying her hair.[6] Louise Erdrich's richly humorous fictions set feminist arts into ludic play beside the writings of James Welch and N. Scott Momaday, suggesting "humorous" gender differences to be respected among Indians. Whereas Euroamerican women have sought equality for a century, tribal women were seldom disenfranchised in their cultures. The great majority of pre-Columbian tribes, perhaps 90 percent, seem to have been matrilocal.[7] Rather than "stealing" back the language, as Alicia Ostriker sees feminists like Adrienne Rich doing to break into mainstream American poetry,[8] literary Indian women like Paula Gunn Allen may simply be voicing their native birthright. "Being a woman cannot be demonstrated, it must be felt," Hélène Cixous contends; "it must make itself felt, it is the experience of a pleasure." But just what do French feminists like Cixous and Kristeva mean by *jouissance,* and can we translate the concept toward ethnic feminist humor? "When one talks woman to you, you must *respond* and respond as if to an accusation," Cixous challenges today's reader.[9] Are these defensive lines equally drawn by Native American feminists parting the Buckskin Curtain?

Humor tacitly, if not openly, declares "the other" game to be played *with.* "Play, then, is a preliminary or divertive surface-life," Max Eastman theorizes, "in which success is fun, but failure funny."[10] From a cyclical comic perspective, no one loses if they still play the game. In addition to survival and renewal, a comic vision in these terms can be amicably competitive, even pleasurably engaging. Deloria counts coup (to touch the enemy in plains battle) most sharply on those he has most hope for—anthros, clerics, Congress, curious readers—as *Custer Died For Your Sins* sets up the comic realism of cultural confrontations. The potshots make both sides think, if disagreeably, then finally dialogically. Between Indians and whites, this friction reconstitutes an exchange beyond satiric diatribe, for a change. In *We Talk, You Listen* (1970), Deloria writes with acerbic bite on treaty violations, and historical debate takes yet another turn.

Such jibes spark serious play, a form of public teasing to raise Indian–white issues. Teasing is key to Indian bonding, Deloria notes; it serves as a daily check-and-balance on tribal norms. The word "teasing," as we know it in Western terms, comes from the Anglo-Saxon *taesan* ("pull" or "pluck"). It once meant to raise a nap on cloth; now it means to annoy and/or entertain by aggressively focusing play toward extended kin. So tribal teasing, pan-Indian style with red English, targets issues with an attention that roughs its audience affectionately, Indian-to-white. We "permit" the disrespect, Mary Douglas argues, as something of a familial or social agreement. It's a way of circling pain, according to Freud, of encompassing reality's "threat" to the ego by using that very threat to *open* an audience to its common, if not bonding, values. "One" may tease oneself in an existential or academic vacuum, but as with most things human, a cultural "other" makes it more fun; and three draws a crowd. Henri Bergson, in "Rire" (1899), adds that laughter goes in need of an echo.

So when Deloria quotes Custer shouting "Take no prisoners!" at the Little Big Horn, or cites AIMsters (American Indian Movement stalwarts) chanting "We Shall Overrun" in the 1970s, or warns Black Panthers against playing "Cowboys and Blacks"—this red satirist is inviting "the others" to joust and to interact with Native America. Historically, "whites" invaded "reds" with enslaved "blacks" (not to mention indentured "browns" and "yellows"). The native castles— roundhouses, wickiups, tipis, igloos, hogans—were sacked, good "goods" stolen, all but 3 percent of the population exterminated, the remaining few "reserved" for posterity as endangered species. "Indian giver" is probably the worst joke in our popular lexicon, appearing as a term of xenophobic guilt that inverts historical fact. An entire hemisphere was taken, not to be given back, and remnant Indians survive in reserves. Carter Camp, the Osage AIM warrior, recalls that staples were always critical at the Wounded Knee military occupation in 1973— ammunition, cigarettes, and especially toilet paper went in short supply. So "thank God" for those six little missionary churches in the hamlet and all the stacks of shiny new Bibles printed on rice paper!

There's a bite in this Indi'n humor. George Custer (who got what glory he was after) offers reverse scapegoat release for Indian bitterness, beyond the pain of historical statistics, body counts, present-day poverty, and continued suffering. Warriors grow "too old to muss the custard anymore," Deloria puns on Custer's folly. The triple play Custer/mustard/custard reduces this "hero" to flatulent flan (as generally known, "too old to cut the mustard" is an old midwestern crack about "breaking wind"). At a literary level, Deloria's syllabic nonsense frees the mind from too much sense. The pun distances personal emotions from wounded honor, scalp-taking, our losses, their betrayals, not to mention fears of aging and death. Like the redness of blood, or jokes about failure, dying remains a universal for all human beings (the last joke?). So Indian–white tragedies can be alchemized through the alembic of modern red humor; intercultural differences shift toward seriously playful texts, which tell us much about ourselves, American and Native American.

"Friend and Brother!" the Iroquois Red Jacket greets Mr. Cram of the Boston Missionary Society in 1828; the sun is bright, our eyes and ears are open and unstopped, so for a change listen. "Brother! You say there is but one way to worship and serve the Great Spirit. If there is but one religion, why do you white people differ so much about it? Why do not all agree, as you can all read the book?" (*NAT* 70). The Iroquois, too, have faiths, Red Jacket assures the missionary, but "we never quarrel about religion." The slippage here—the split planes of reference, overtly innocent, covertly ironic—is the kind of grainy humor Huck Finn senses when Colonel Sherburn faces down the lynch mob, like eating bread "that's got sand in it." Back in Boston, Reverend Cram declines to shake Red Jacket's hand, since "there could be no fellowship between the religion of God and the works of the devil." The anthologist Peter Nabokov recounts, "The Iroquois are said to have smiled" (69).

By 1866 Cochise, a Chiricahua Apache leader, challenges General Gordon Granger at a truce talk where the Apache are pressured to surrender to the Tularosa Reservation. "The white people have looked for me long. I am here! What do they want? If I am worth so much why not mark when I set my foot and look when I spit" (*NAT* 223). God made Apaches "not as you," Cochise says, but "born like the animals, in the dry grass, not on beds like you. This is why we do as the animals." Cochise reasons: "The Apaches were once a great nation; they are now but few, and because of this they want to die and so carry their lives on their finger nails." Red is divided from white with bladelike irony. "Many have been killed in battle," Cochise goes on. "You must speak straight so that your words may go as sunlight to our hearts. *Tell me, if the Virgin Mary has walked throughout all the land, why has she never entered the wigwam of the Apache?*" (225, italics in original). The question is sharply cut. Cochise has "no father nor mother; I am alone in the world. No one cares for Cochise." He chooses to stay in his native-born mountains, rather than surrender to white incarceration on a new reservation. "The flies on those mountains eat out the eyes of the horses. The bad spirits live there. I have drunk of these waters and they have cooled me; I do not want to leave here" (225).

These speeches serve as scattered flints of heroic resistence over the five-hundred-year terrain of frontier collision. Even in translation, the bivalent shifts between text and context raise an undiscussed historical humor that characterizes Indian continuity yet today.

Terms

> An onion can make people cry, but there has never been a vegetable invented to make them laugh.
>
> WILL ROGERS

Some schematic scaffolding is useful here, given the plethora of data across the Buckskin Curtain and paucity of understanding on both sides. Interweaving Indian particularity and Anglo theory dialectically tacks between detail and concept, as Geertz proposes in *Local Knowledge,* such that we read the particular within an intercultural context and spiral toward translation in both directions. The non-Indian audience sees the parameters and partitions of its categories against the data and worldviews of native cultures. Conversely, through modes of humor so far overlooked, Indians see us trying to "see" them. When Navajos began acculturating baseball in the mid-nineteenth century, for example, they positioned the diamond at the four cardinal points and ran the bases in reverse. Each player got four strikes (the cardinal number), and each team was allowed only one out per inning. So Navajos took to baseball on their own terms, and with a good measure of Navajo humor played the game contrariwise.[11]

Arthur Koestler, in writing on comic theory, coins the term "bisociation" to describe "the simultaneous correlation of an experience to two otherwise independent operative fields." For an artistic moment, Koestler projects, these disassociated planes fuse as "dual association."[12] When incongruous parts edge each other, the superimposed slippage becomes comic—that is, playfully sensical. This "geometrical pattern of two intersecting chains" correlates in such play as "*any mental occurrence simultaneously associated with two habitually incompatible contexts*" (*IO* 25, 37, italics in original). Thus we might say that a kind of comic double logic intersects sets of "others" in gaming intercultural congruence; things coalesce playfully to "mean." "ALCO-HOLIDAYS," Freud puns in *Jokes and Their Relationship to the Unconscious* (1905). In bisociation there is a game of verbal conjunction, a form of festive palimpsest. Such (de)centering verbal and intercultural texts delight an audience in the play of non-sense through logical illusion; they overlap and double, or "bisociate," without fusing in reality. Hence an audience experiences release from the weight of meaning, an escape into ludic fantasy or art. Reality's emotional charges tag along to play against the ludic illusion. As Freud reminds us, "operation successful, patient dead" telegrams aggressive nonsense as comically diffused fear. But the experience of bisociation can shift tragically when fate closes in on a character and the slippage between operative planes shuts down. In tragedy, irreconcilables fuse agonistically, rather than playfully, and "reality" dramatically shifts into dread pattern revealed—Oedipus murderous at the crossroads, tragically incestuous, finally self-blinded. Differently slanted, as in *Don Quixote, Moll Flanders,* and *Ulysses,* the plot twists toward a comic series of falls from which characters emerge to play again. The ironic, reverse slippage between two sets of coordinates—before comedy releases the tension or tragedy locks it into place—generates the ambivalent *frisson* that tonalizes and charges both modes bisociatively. And back to classical art we witness the double-faced masks of tragic and comic muses.

Certain players animate the comic mode. In his *Anatomy of Criticism,* Northrop Frye cites the *Tractatus Coislinianus,* kin to Aristotle's *Poetics,* to establish three comic types: the *alazons,* or imposters; the *eirons,* or self-deprecators; and the *bomolochoi,* or buffoons.[13] The first two types may emerge from the origins of Greek drama, the satyr plays between the tragedies. The bisociated pairing is akin to strophic–antistrophic rhythms of characters and chorus, a binary counterpoint between *alazon* and *eiron,* which in turn generates choral voices, or "buffoons" who look on (the audience performing on stage). In *Ethics,* Aristotle adds a fourth comic type—*agroikos,* or churlish rustic—so that buffoon and churl counterplay the classic overstater and understater. From this perspective, the forms of comedy seem structurally contrapuntal, innocent to ironist, fool to philosophe.

"Comedy ranges from the most savage irony," Frye contends, "to the most dreamy wish-fulfillment romance," while remaining dramatically and generically consistent (*AC* 177). The comic plot can take six turns,

Frye argues: (1) the "hero" *transforms* a community toward some better end; (2) *escapes* an irredeemable situation; (3) *frees* the slave within a society; or (4) the wasteland *greens,* and summer wins out over winter; (5) characters *rise* above comic chaos to look down from an *ordered* view on disorder below; (6) the comic (doubling) world *deconstructs* (a decentering humor dissolves focus) as the oracles of a darker mystery take over. Interestingly enough, an epic poem such as Dante's *Commedia* or a novel like *Huckleberry Finn* will satisfy all these phyla—the ultimate Western spiritual drama or American "comedy" within a Euroamerican ethos. But Leslie Silko's *Ceremony,* an analogous American Indian fiction with "mythic" acculturations, forgoes the first four turns in plot and touches only half the fifth level, transcendent order over disorder (patterns-in-the-stars by the time of Tayo's ceremonial revelation of his destiny). The novel vaguely approaches the sixth oracular phylum (Silko's mythic "medicine" changes). Perhaps *Ceremony* spins a ritual comedy of another kind out of a tribal context in need of translation. Lagunas seem to be stuck, more or less, with the society they've had since "time immemorial," according to Grandma and the myths in the fiction; escape, linear transformation, or "freeing the slave" is a bit unrealistic in Grandmother's view. Still, the desert buds "green" (bluish-green or turquoise in *Ceremony*) while it seems a "waste" land to white ranching eyes, and the mythic journey up the mountain of the water goddess, Ts'eh, sends Tayo back down into the tribal kiva. It might be a homely return to the realistic "mess" we live in, as Frye says, here both godlike and "fallen," or comic in a regenerative cultural sense. At any rate, with this example Frye's comic emplotments seem only a partial template for native Americanist fictions.

Postmodernist theory offers some intercultural models for dialogue here. Comic deconstruction poses a seriously playful way to say that things look different from variable human perspectives, heroic to demonic to humorous. From Aristotle, Plato, and Cicero through Descartes, Hobbes, Bacon, and Bergson, Arthur Koestler finds a Western tradition of "degradation" theorized in the laughter of Hobbes's *Leviathan:* "at all times a component of malice, of debasement of the other fellow, and of aggressive–defensive self-assertion" (*IO* 56). This theory of "superiority" tallies with Bergson's ideas on the comic as social corrective or Freud's sense of *Witz* (joking wit) in the aggressive desire of the sexual drive. If such trickster aggression, indeed, surfaces in Indian comic contexts, it seems mediated toward mythic play, social harmony, and ceremonial pleasure. "One of the things that you will notice is that often in the stories there will be a movement toward a balance—the funny with the serious," Silko says of Laguna tales, "—and this goes back, this balance and this inclusion, the all-inclusive dynamic goes back to the Creation, and back to one of the basic Pueblo religious concepts."[14] The balanced "comic" world, as an Indian given, is not always so perceived in Anglo terms.

Far from being a wasteland, the Southwest from a Pueblo perspective is home in Silko's *Ceremony*. Dry and hot (sun) has its rightful lower place (desert home) in balance with wet and cool (rain) on the sacred height (blue mountain). Indian ceremony as "comic" pattern is seldom linear escape or structural transformation or social liberation, but more a celebrative acceptance of what-is, a curve back home. This longer comic sense of the given-at-home pervades tribal cultures. "At Laguna I have an uncle who's very young," Leslie Silko told Laura Coltelli; "he's only ten years older, he's just like a brother, and his wife and his sisters are very brilliant. They've traveled and gone places to school. They've all come back. They have funny ways of saying things; they like to laugh and tell horrifying stories, but the way they tell them is really funny, and you're laughing."[15] The interview continued:

Coltelli: Humor is one of the main features of modern American Indian literature, central to the real meaning of the story itself. Is there a difference between the use of humor in the old Indian stories and in the contemporary ones?
Silko: You know I haven't really thought about whether there's a difference. I'm so attuned to seeing the many similarities. Same thing, referring to the same incident, especially areas in justice, loss of land, discrimination, racism, and so on, that there's a way of saying it so people can kind of laugh or smile . . . so you can keep their interest, so you can keep talking to them. Oftentimes these things are told in a humorous way. Even punning—you know, the people at Laguna have such a delight with language. . . . So that in English they like to make puns, and they know a little Spanish, or a little Navajo, or a little anything. So their sheer delight in such things, that goes on and always has—that's an area where I can't see that there's been any big shift. (146–47)

Thus "humor" seems a more apt term for discussing Native American aesthetics than Frye's "pregeneric" comic forms. Compared with

Western linearity, Native American patterns appear more cyclical, peri-
odic, and composite—less historically progressive, less personally
transformational, less structurally end-stopped. *Ceremony* remains a
case in point. In a mythic perspective, nothing has changed by the end.
The protagonist accepts his mixed-blood or "breed" position as a transi-
tional role; the "hero" does not arrogate power individually, so much as
the "healer" takes a tribal position in relation to a common setting. And
structurally the novel does not so much end as simply suspend interest
in the action (Grandma has heard all this before). The story has talked
itself out, the joke has sputtered, while Grandmother Spider, the
creatrix, stitches away in the back of Southwest Indian perspectives.
The traditional weave on Indian looms is double, as with overlapping
patterns in fine Navajo rugs, yet contrasting designs on adjoining sides
of the rug are made of one tightly woven thread. This creates a dually
human work of art, a daily necessity when nights chill sun-baked desert
bones. Grandmother Spider's weaving brings and keeps the people
home.

Humor—cognate with "humus," or soil, and "human," or person—
implies a personality at ease and grounded in its own identity. The term
assumes a perspective on things, as it were, one that enjoys flexibility.
"Humours" in the late Middle Ages conjure up the fluids of personality—literally the flow of coloring spirits, the protean life force of
water. Humors thus suggest the fluid resilience of life itself. Humor
today might be thought of as the vision or psyche ("spirit") behind a
specific joke; it fills in the interstices and lingers after a gathering has
broken up, even laps about a room when the jokers go home.

Whereas humor indicates the psychological (personal) and cultural
(historical) tenor of a situation, a joke per se exists as a social act or
event, a specific instance of humor-in-action. So, too, wit implies an
aspect of character—a presence of mind, quickness, even quirkiness.[16]
Comedy, finally, codes a generic index for aesthetic or ideational categories—"the comic" is used here as a classificatory term. "Divine
Comedy," for example, implies a Christian context for a belief that all
things work out for the best, that "God" knows all in His heaven and
ordains earth as His province. With a Mother Earth corrective to Father
Sky, Native American ceremonies so, too, project a faith in a right
world or "good" reality. This implies belief in the order of things, an
acceptance of what-is as naturally "right"—indeed, spiritually sanctioned in this world of the living. Then, too, there is room for making

mistakes. Joking, wit, and comedy appear as socially specific, personally characteristic, and generically contextual evidences of cultural humor. They strike the human tuning fork of a tribal faith in survival and success, despite obstacles or momentary loss.

As used in feminist Indian literature, humor may even be a distant cousin to "home"; at least in the popular lexicon, humor and home strike the ear as kin. And humor has something to do, surely, with a grounded sense of home, a domestic pivot. If home is secure, or relatively certain in one's psyche, regardless of how far "away" the homeless wander, humor is not far away. In tribal Greece three millennia back, when some two thousand cultural groups were settled in the Americas, Odysseus's twenty years at war and sea, always "homing," are charted by a storytelling full of banquet goodwill, marriage proposals, and endless puns ("How odd to see you," strangers say to the homeless hero, and puns from "odd" to "ode" are played on like musical chimes). No less than Navajo origin myths or Iroquois creation cycles, Greek epics register a homing sense of humor during times of unrest, as the story summons father home. Odysseus grows too old to compete physically with the younger athletes and warriors; his game, or "odd," leg hobbles him, but adds a twist to his sense of humor, and it sets up his need to outwit the odds of physical engagement. So Odysseus tells stories, jokes, and tall tales of monsters, witches, and wild beasts. The fantastic can be comically gripping through its exaggerations, as the twentieth-century magical realists Borges and Márquez in other Americas, or Kundera and Calvino in Europe, reimagine the given.

Hence in some cases, the line from Homer to our homes may not be broken—from homecoming epic humor to the contemporary West, from tribal Greece to Native Americans today. The sailor and the farmer, Walter Benjamin says in *Illuminations* (1955), have always been our tribal narrators—storytellers coming or staying home. Certainly, the Parry–Lord thesis of oral-formulaic composition in Homeric times also applies to extended Trickster tellings, from Algonkian clans to Zuni kivas. And the improvisator, the singer of tales, slings a joke in his quiver to sidestep pointless combat. Humor may be a key to the *bricolage* of extended singing. An audience sticks around longer with laughter to ease the listening—indeed, to sharpen the spirit, to loosen the ear, and to wake up our attending. Aside from its tragic counterpart (draw blood, draw a crowd), a comic come-on seems the quickest way to attract and hold an audience, then persuade it to come back paying attention. Jim Pepper, the Kaw–Creek jazz saxophonist, tells the story of his Indian and white names in a 1988 interview:

> My great grandfather was a big man, a big tall strong cat. Big Indian. And he didn't speak English. . . . I have the same name he does, Hung-a-che-eda, which means Flying Eagle. That name could have been phonetically written out, or he could have had a translation of his name, or a name of his choice. His favorite taste was this whiskey, James Pepper whiskey. So he named himself after whiskey, which is a bittersweet story. You can still get that whiskey down in Colorado and Texas. It's a small company. I saw a bottle one time in a bar and tried to buy it, but they wouldn't sell it to me. Those were the kinds of stories my grandfather told me. He never sat there and said the Great Spirit formed this or that from an eagle turd. None of that shit.[17]

White Ideas

> Is it possible that love, hope, faith, laughter, confidence, and the will to live have therapeutic value?
>
> NORMAN COUSINS, *Anatomy of an Illness*

At the risk of further thickening the stew, we turn to twentieth-century theory, from psychoanalytic ideas at the top of the century to deconstructive intercultural projections at the bottom.

Sigmund Freud, the century's psychological pioneer, fixated on joking and humor. Indeed, when Freud's close friend and associate Wilhelm Fliess read the proofs of *The Interpretation of Dreams* in the autumn of 1899, he was disturbed by the many jokes. Piqued by his arch colleague, Freud read Theodor Lipps's *Komik und Humor* and set out to define *Witz* in its relationship to the psychoanalysis of dreams. *Witz,* James Strachey admits, hardly translates as "joking," but eighteenth-century scholars were no closer in defining it as "genteel ingenuity." Wit-at-large connotes the ability to make things up, to create on the go, to "cobble" reality. In its Viennese context, *Witz* suggests an alertness, a quick state of mind, more than gentility or the "joke" as comic relief.

Thus Freud begins *Jokes and Their Relationship to the Unconscious* (1905) with a German philosopher defining joking as "playful judgment." He ties joking mental play to finding "hidden similarities," cites Lipps on the concept of "bewilderment and illumination" in joking (deriddling, depuzzling, or decoding jokes), and sets out to track the "organic whole" of comic *disjecta membra:* "activity, relation to the content of our thoughts, the characteristic of playful judgment, the coupling of dissimilar things, contrasting ideas, 'sense in nonsense,' the succession of bewilderment and enlightenment, the bringing forward of what is hidden, and the peculiar brevity of wit."[18] It's a tall order, even for Freud.

Most theoreticians concur that joking involves some kind of insight, perception, or understanding (standing "under," Joyce reminds us), when we move from be*wild*erment to a moment of illumination, as Freud underscores. This enlightenment prisms from wild to tamed, arcs from questionable to answerable. "I think you had better put the Indians on wheels," Red Dog laconically counseled commissioners to the Sioux in 1876, the year of the Battle of Little Big Horn and the U.S. centennial. "Then you can run them about whenever you wish" (*NAT* 184). Over a hundred thousand Indians from twenty-eight eastern tribes had been "removed" west of the Mississippi River, with thirty thousand dying en route. The Winnebagos were "relocated" no fewer than five times in the mid-nineteenth century.

So how does a non-Indian reader react to Red Dog's comment? The "bewilderment" of dispossession, satirically framed, shifts toward the ironic "illumination" of an unsettling double perspective in the image of "Indians on wheels." The ironic transition from one plane of unknowing curiosity (a-*maze*-ment or decentered interest) to knowing clarity jars loose Koestler's "bisociation." The doubling association superimposes disparate levels that overlap in the joke's twin templates, still incongruously played as one. As a result we see similarities *and* differences, Freud notes as he stresses the slippage in joke perception; the joker credits himself and his audience with decoding like and, especially, unlike designs.

Joking is thus layered or bivalent understanding, an act of "ironic" perception that bisociates disparate sets of data. Things momentarily, if not ultimately, make sense. This is all a mind at play, knowing it is playing, not "really" worrying about making sense, or if judging and determining the "real," doing so in the liberating spirit of improvisation. But the *de*constructive aspect remains. The play element and the joke make sense non-sensically, so that we get it both ways—not too seriously, so as not to wreck the playful construct on the rocks of reality, and yet seriously enough to engage the mind in *un*puzzling the real. Red

Dog gives us something to reflect on: "I think you had better put the Indians on wheels."

So joking requires wit to decode reality. It seems to relieve us temporarily of the burdens of the serious, while honing our ability to "read" the world. In dreaming we do this "sub"consciously, Freud argues, and in art we create more consciously with play. Michel Foucault, in *The Order of Things,* defines the poet as one "who, beneath the named, constantly expected differences, rediscovers the *buried kinships* between things, their scattered resemblances."[19] The comic slant to such poetic kinships would italicize the *scattered* resemblances between things ("metaphor," poetry's depth charge, literally means to "bear" from one place *to* another). Jokes bear the weight of differences in bisociated coincidences, while the "comic" plane remains an artistic displacement. "Ceci n'est pas une pipe," the Belgian surrealist painter René Magritte wrote below a picture of a pipe—a doubling semiology, yes, but most critically a framed displacement with a "pipe" that is *not* a pipe (hence comic "bisociation," or having it both ways). In a joke, then, displacement in the Freudian sense becomes *framing* in Erving Goffman's sociocultural rubric: a socially framed "play" sphere apart from the "real" world, or at least playfully relieved of its strictures and burdens.

Intercultural exchange charges a "liminal" zone of bisociative play. For example, when the Jicarilla Apache discovered *tlatsizis,* or the whiteman's "buttocks bags," in the nineteenth century, they asked, "What do you put in?" "Why, you throw your buttocks in it," came the answer. So they tried hopping and leaping off cliffs into the bags, to no avail. An Apache observer noted: "Then they tied the pants around themselves, but the leg part hung down behind. Some put the pants on backward; some had the legs hanging down in front. That's the way they went around. They put the shirts on. Some wore them in the right way; some put them on backward. The hats they used for carrying water" (*NAT* 54). This buffoonery serves up pure parody of "the other," a kind of childlike delight in the strangeness of strange customs. Humor here is an a*maze*d play released in the exposed overlap and slippage between cultures. The viewer's comic insight discharges as laughter, while binary patterns stay bifurcated (though for the moment artfully bisociated). Humor remains parenthetical to the "real," yet grounded realistically in differences, and still distinct from metaphor in not pressing to "make sense." The poetry of jokes can reduplicate as a kind of sacred clowning, a mediation of play and reality, as with the Sioux *heyoka* or Pueblo *koshare*. This is holy fooling in the presence of spiritual power.

Fiction releases humor seriously through such play. In March 1886 the archaeologist Adolf Bandelier finished the first draft of *Die Koshare* (*The Delight Makers*), on Pueblo cultures and clowns. A century later, Barbara Babcock described the work as "a comic dialogue constructed of bits and pieces of cultural debris," first published in German and English in 1890, the year that U.S. soldiers massacred three hundred Sioux men, women, and children at Wounded Knee Creek. "*Die Koshare* was a seven-year imaginative effort to come to terms with that which was most alien, most other. In contrast to [Bandelier's] 'scientific' writing, fiction gave him the license to indulge in wish fulfillment, to recreate a very different cultural world that all the research in the world could not put back together or enable him to enter, and to talk about himself in relation to that Otherness."[20] Babcock traces this "monstrous jumble held together by an authorial presence" to the powers of ritual Pueblo clowns:

> Less than a month after discovering *El Rito de los Frijoles*, Bandelier first encountered Cochiti clowns, whom he referred to as Koshare or *entremeseros*—the latter a Spanish term denoting those who perform farces between the acts of a play. Among the Keres themselves, these sacred clowns associated with the Turquoise Kiva are called *Ku sha 'li*. Their equivalent appears throughout the Rio Grande Pueblos. Among the Tewa they are called *Kossa;* among the Tiwa, Black Eyes or *chifunane*. His reaction to these nearly naked black and white apparitions with corn husk horns, creating a pandemonium of disorder and delight, was one of disgust, fascination, and characteristically detailed description. ("Ritual Undress" 191)

Bandelier's scenario of comic pandemonium initiated non-Indian readers into ceremonial Pueblo play, even if the Indian sense of humor would quickly be forgotten against the tragic stereotypes in Western folklore. Early in the twentieth century, at San Ildefonso, Alfonso Roybal (Awa Tsireh) was painting clowns crawling over rainbows, chased by turkeys, riding bulls, playing leapfrog, devouring watermelons, and helping Santa Claus hoist his bag of gifts. Today, Nora Naranjo-Morse from Taos and Santa Clara sculpts ceremonial clowns from clay: "*Koshare* clowns, Pueblo women, village scenes, one-of-a-kind figurines, fetishes and animals," Stephen Trimble writes, "all with

humor, affection, and an abstracted and refined sophistication. Nora
came to clay in her twenties, in 1976, after leaving New Mexico to sell
firecrackers in South Dakota and to sort mail in Washington, D.C."[21]
And Barbara Babcock now travels and talks in performance with Helen
Cordero, Cochiti creator of "the Storyteller doll," whose ongoing tradition goes back through sacred fools.[22]

"Pueblo clowns," Babcock writes of Bandelier's "delight" makers (a
fey misnomer derived from his friend Frank Cushing), "are among the
most powerful of ritual personages, mediating between the worlds of
the spirits and the living; controlling weather and fertility; associated
both with curing and with warfare; given punitive and policing functions, particularly against witches; and in fact managing and supervising
many of the ceremonies they appear to disrupt" ("Ritual Undress"
192). There is something here in all clowns, many jokes, and much
humor that I would call a *comic double valence:* it involves "reversible"
play or reduplication with a twist. This double valence compounds the
simple and riddles the surface artfully. It may be an all-too-human,
bipedal fondness for having things more than one way—comic options,
as it were. The anthropologist Frank Cushing, case in point, cross-
costumed as a non-Indian Zuni *koshare.* The Pueblo "striped" him
black-on-white with big rings around his eyes. Now in some unifocal
sense this seems extraordinary and outrageous—a non-Zuni field re-
searcher from the Bureau of American Ethnography in the Pueblo
priesthood! Yet in another sense, bifocally comic, he is what he is: a
"white-faced" clown, striped, as Dennis Tedlock suggests, in mockery
of his incessant note taking.[23] Cushing self-parodies the white man's
penchant for writing things down, rather than remembering or doing
them. Whether through his insistence and apparent sincerity, or Zuni
curiosity and graciousness, Cushing was initiated into the sacred clown
society with full comic honors, a holy fool among men. Yet the double
valence makes him *clown* of a clown: white man in "white face,"
striped or lined for writing (word-walking) all over private Zuni culture.
He is coded strange, signed dangerous, caricatured comic: no Zuni
could miss the message. Cushing thus enters Zuni doubly marked,
comic to a second power—at once a "clown" and a white man clowning around with sacred tribal humor. This kind of italicized bisociation—having things both ways, sacred and profane—characterizes
much ceremonial Indian humor, many good jokes, and every clown
who "plays" at permitted disrespect, especially in the presence of the

gods and concerned tribal audiences. Such play appears to be a place that Indians and non-Indians can don or drop the mask and intermingle without bitterness. This type of comic ceremony offers an *il*-lusion or "in-play," as Huizinga shows in *Homo Ludens* (1944), where "others" play together at their best.

To play seriously toward a structural, dialogical paradigm (à la Claude Lévi-Strauss at one extreme and Julia Kristeva at the other) we can further plumb the pan-Indian joke about the invasion of America. "What did you call this country before the whites came?" a Mount Rushmore tourist again asks a modern-day Sioux. "Ours," quips the fine feathered friend. Deloria's jibe, recycled in Gerald Vizenor's film *Warriors of Orange,* illustrates what I would call the gaming congruence of a good joke. A simplified joking formula helps to clarify the point in terms of a dialogic equation. The algebraic formula for the hypotenuse of a right triangle ($\sqrt{a^2 + b^2} = c^2$) bears a certain symmetry, as well as transformational energy crossing from one side to another.[24] So change and balance, transformation and stability, constellate here as counterweights to dissimilarity and similarity, the bisociative polarities. The "equal to" sign indicates the active transference—the proportionate exchange between dissimilarities. We might diagram the comic equation thus: What did you call this country . . . before the whites came? = Ours. Or to abstract the algebra: primal land + invasion = predispossession common title (over half our states bear Indian names). The lead-in question naively implies the "mystery" of aboriginal tongues and minds, followed by a tacit admission of the post-Columbian present, answered curtly by a collective tribal pronoun, "ours." The joke carries the bicultural context of Anglo–Indian rifts. Mary Douglas calls its "context" the social field of comic energy, the mediative dialogue between us and them, as Koestler speaks of "bisociative" comic irony in overlapping mental planes. This all turns on the gaming congruence of a simple "American" monosyllable, "ours." From native perspectives, it serves as a footnote to what Francis Jennings has called the non-Indian "invasion" and Tzvetan Todorov the "conquest" of America.

Structurally, the dialogue joke best illustrates gaming congruence. "What does a dyslexic agnostic not believe in?" a student quizzed me on an exam. "Dog." In play, one part balances with another inversely; one mind-set transfers into a second, which results in a double perspective, a bisociative puzzle. It is a *difference,* always held in congruent tension, that divides the parts, while they reach across the transformational zone. "How is Halloween celebrated at the Bureau of Indian Affairs?" Vee Salabiye asks. "Trick or Treaty." This arcing "between" produces the joke, the either/both "bisociation" of likeness among dissimilar components. It is a slippage that implies connection.

A joke supposes something coyly or conditionally (the gaming congruence). It predicates that it is not what it might be. For example, when the Lakota healer John (Fire) Lame Deer as rodeo clown dons the red wig, "babies' bar" pillowy breasts, and calico dress of "Alice Jitterbug," he transsexually (and in the sacred clown's role of *winkte*) goes out to save men's lives. He plays but he is *not* a woman: he isn't what he might be. In Lakota the word *win-kte* is the conditional feminine, literally "woman could-be." A man *acts as* a woman in binary metaphors of gender, some of the oldest jokes in drama. John Fire's humor suggests that it's okay to stretch the human definitions, play "the other," be momentarily what a man is not, get a good laugh, and get away as "Alice Jitterbug" rescuing cowboys from brahma bulls. In fact, this may be a healthy imagining "of" the other to see oneself from another perspective. For in such play, the rules remain flexible and "disrespect" comes conditionally; that is, the game is "permitted" while everyone goes along with the anti-rite. Indeed, such playing with the boundaries—or "stretching," the Apache tell Keith Basso—bonds the people in terms of their elastic social agreements. For this joking acts out the kinetic processes of tribe and gender, bonding through space and time—never fixed, always newly assumed, tested by conditions, ready to be played out. Such flexibility remains capable of what Freud in *Jokes* terms "playful judgment." This bisociative humor tests tradition and keeps it honestly human.

A note on cultural *différence:* When Lévi-Strauss concludes in *The Savage Mind* (1962) that "all" intellects, expecially Stone Age ones, are binary, or Freud categorizes all jokes as economic mental releases from wounded feeling, Western theoreticians usurp the particulars of intercultural pluralism. What does Freud mean by "economy" in joking "expenditure," and does this obviate psychic play? Is comedy the world over fiscally conservative? Does the ego ever relax? To adapt Freud's analogy, could humor turn on a kinetic exchange of psychic currencies, more cash flow than ledger entry? "Why is semen white and urine yellow?" the irrepressible Deloria wrote to me. "So the Chippewas can tell whether they're coming or going."[25] Freud's economy is surcharged with scatology in the joke, serving a disrespect played among friendly tribal enemies; whereas the verbal formula is certainly "economical," the words tap the prodigal stirrings of an emotive psyche-in-motion. Joking seems to spark an exchange between equational complexes of feelings and thoughts—gaming congruences that temporarily play with similarity across a dissonantly charged, psychically wild field. When cultures collide, jokes mediate playfully, permitting the differences.

We all may be capable of a *sense* of humor—and joking seems as endemic to human culture as sex or song—but why do individuals laugh, or not, in given cultural settings? Some subjects—sex, death, excrement, eating, money, mothers-in-law, and the gods—appear a priori capable of comedy, though not always in proper or mixed company. Anything humanly surcharged, it seems, carries a potential for humor. If it matters or moves us, it may be funny, because it is so essential. Where certain concepts or objects seem to have *banked* human interest, Freud's "expenditure" theories make sense. Jokes give us returns on the unrepressed energies of childhood; comedy doubles our interest in given and projected assets; humor amortizes suffering. But what determines *what* we laugh at?—a specific situation, the post-Freudian ethnologist Mary Douglas holds, shaped by social context, seasoned in history, compacted with others. Without cultural setting we have no permissions (or restrictions), no disrespects (or affections) to trigger our humor. A libido needs a superego to keep the psyche honest, Freud posits. So a citizen inversely enlists a clown to ground his social seriousness, and Indian wisdom is beholden to Trickster to keep the lessons conditionally open to human revision.

What of art in this discussion? Novels grant us culture-specific contexts for such theoretical, intercultural questions: time, place, character, community, event, symbolic subtext. With such fictive data we may see how, in *Winter in the Blood,* James Welch writes for a generic, middle-aged Blackfeet man caught today between tradition and town; but certainly Welch does not speak for all males, flatters few females, and represents fewer Pueblos. Momaday's *House Made of Dawn* presents Abel's confused sense of time, culture, and place in a postwar Southwest, Jemez Pueblo to Los Angeles, but he does not give us Erdrich's mothering métis (mixed-blood) sense of Turtle Mountain in *Love Medicine* (1984). From Blackfeet barroom obscenity and street-smart wisecracks, to Tosamah's Anglo-Indian caricatures and Abel's ceremonial sunrise run, to Albertine's lyrically deadpan pun on "Patient Abuse" among Indians, the "permitted disrespects" of contemporary Indian fiction fine-tune Freud's remarks on humor, as applied to Indians, and reopen Mary Douglas's contextual insights into joking. The proofs of "science" would seem to lie in textures of evidence, telling details, careful attentions in our guessing, and the uses, finally, of questions asked: Why *do* Indians laugh? Why should we ask? There may be many particular answers, or better contexts, in which the questions resonate and reveal something about Native Americans today and yesterday— some things as yet undiscovered about survival through humor.

Metacritical Twists

How do Koestler's "bisociative" theories and Freud's "economical" analyses of joking pertain to Indian societies? From the social sciences to literature today, critical methodologies careen between the new historicisms and tricky deconstructions. A few field workers—Dennis Tedlock in dialogical anthropology, Keith Basso in sociolinguistics, William Bright in ethnolinguistics, Robert Berkhofer in psychohistory, Howard Norman in zoomorphic folklore, Jerome Rothenberg in ethnopoetics—are bridging the arts and sciences in American Indian studies. Mixing modes, the folklorist Barbara Babcock metacritically "decreates" ritual Indian clowning from Bandelier to Bakhtin. Pueblo *koshares* to Parisian dialogists, her metaphors spark with "reversible" to "deconstructive" fields of discourse play, and her audience is bounced from mirror to motley characters, looking glass to kaleidoscopic contexts. The results seem arguably enlightening, certainly decentering, as things go in academia. Some folklorists don't know what to make of Nietzschean leaps, what Babcock calls the "gay science" of intercultural play.[26]

As recently as the 1920s, the Bureau of Indian Affairs targeted Indian clowning under the "religious crimes code." Contrariwise, Babcock contends, tribal clowns mediate order and disorder. They differentiate morally between "this" and "that"—indeed, "us" and "them." So, too, clowning seems to counter the fear of nihilism by playing with chaos. Clowns parse a metacontextual text of a different kind of "nothing" that appears openly comic, rather than locked into tragic closure; for "neither ritual clowning nor irony can be dismissed as nihilism or infinitely regressive negativity," Babcock states. "Rather both are special forms of negation: what Burke calls 'aesthetic negativity'; what Derrida defines as 'deconstruction'; what Colie describes as 'paradox'; what James labeled the 'law of dissociation'; and what Arendt describes as 'thinking.' "[27] This all may take some time to sort out and let sink in. Hayden White sees such prodigal theorizing as tropes of tropes, a "metatropological" modernist game, yet a game with serious purpose.[28]

"Like clowning, *theoria*" plays with meaning, Babcock notes, citing Foucault's *The Order of Things*. She traces the wise fool from Heraclitus and Socrates, through Shakespeare, Nietzsche, and Wittgenstein, to Derrida and Barthes. Intellectually, this thicket of theory reduces to clowning *bricolage,* deconstructive criticism as "sanctioned disrespect," where Babcock leans toward Kenneth Burke's trust in improvisations. She goes on to advance that Pueblo "ritual clowning is much more than a functional steamvalve, and should be considered in terms of its aesthetics and metaphysics as well as its pragmatics." To top off the critical tank, Babcock contends "conversely, that criticism, whatever the discipline, should be considered as comedy, reminded of its playful origins, and reinvested with a comic perspective" ("Arrange" 107). Agreed, but ever mindful of nonsense, the loyal opposition asks, To what end? Not all scholars, surely few "scientists," are ready to decreate their systems these days, though the more adventurous seem to be asking seriously creative questions beyond fixed texts. Does writing devolve from comic deconstructions in the oral tradition? Can critics play creatively, as clowns fool around critically? How kinetically intercultural do social scientists dare become?

Consider, metacritically, the interplay of laughter and love through Western eyes. Julia Kristeva, in her Parisian glimpse of the modern psyche, *Tales of Love,* opens with a Greek parable of Eros's conception. Penia (need) wants and waits just outside the gates of the gods' feasting, where a favored but drunken male, Poros (satiation), falls "victim" to her wiles. Parabolically, need is feasted as the child Eros is conceived in a comic creation myth (sex and birth as standard fare). Via Kristeva the parable may suggest that love, the "creative daimon," doubles for humor. The post-Freudian Kristeva concludes: "Path of want, a want on the way, want blazing a trail for itself. But also a path wanting in devices, a path without essence. Through such an alliance of want and path, could Eros be the place where dialectic takes shape but also opens up to a daimon that overwhelms it? Love as a path that leads nowhere . . . unless it be to immediate sight, scattered totality."[29] To be sure, Kristeva is tracing Western Eros back through classical Rome and Greece, but the dawning of "immediate sight" relates to Freud's *Witz* splashing over the sides of high seriousness, as "wit" not so long ago implied another kind of improvisational "wisdom." Georges Bataille adds: "And really, laughter is a weird sort of success . . . a load of worry's off your shoulders: the frame explodes that gives order to action."[30] Freud's "economy" of dialectic in love and humor may open deconstructively to a creative "daimon." This process of retention toward release distracts the economizing psyche in a "scattered totality" called reality. There is, indeed, a world of "immediate sight," even love, outside the ego's linear limits, where we laugh at ourselves. Here Joyce's *Ulysses* correlates laughter, love, and language as the fictional arts of blooming.

In her early semiotic work of the late 1960s, Kristeva praises Bakhtin's dialogical analyses of Rabelaisian humor. Late medieval "carnivalesque" gives Rabelais a comic sense of community and fictive cultural modes free of credo. To Bakhtin, this tribal setting generates a dynamic ambivalence: radically interactive between individual and society, as in the vibrant "flash," Mallarme says, struck by pure intellect. Such a spark leads the enlightened into Socratic dialogue, the postmodernist argument goes, liberated polyphonically in "Menippean discourse." Such discourse sparks interactive talk, a dialogic beyond end-stopped structure; and critical analysis must remain process, not product. "The laughter of the carnival is not simply parodic," Kristeva insists; "it is no more comic than tragic; it is both at once, one might say that it is *serious*."[31] The authorial psyche oscillates at the kinetic interplay of "surfaces," Bakhtin posits, where the "grams" (physical phonemes, Derrida adds) of grammar are energized in a field of artistic play recalling wave–particle rhythms in physics. Thus art is set in motion: the "text" ends and "time–space" begins, in the imaginative and open cultural "context" of the text. The "word" is not so much pointillist as it is rhythmically interactive. In turn, the critic scans a polyphonic field of discourses, or "voices," from the subtexts. These might better be seen as tricksterish "inter-texts"—that is, tribal interplays of subject, object, audience, and time–space (what Bakhtin called "chronotopes," which embody or flesh out psychic–cultural "time," storied places that embed a people's collective myths). Thus, Bakhtin reasons, time historically takes on the experiential flesh of space, where culture is rooted symbolically, reified in objects and events.

And where is the comic imagination—Rabelais's humor, for example, or Trickster's wit—in all this? Reality is neither strictly comic nor tragic, Kristeva replies with analytic dispassion, but "serious," by which she underscores the given reality. The deconstructive gaps in any argument, the gaping fissures, seem at times nihilist to Kristeva, in contradistinction with Freud's final view of humor, where the psyche's decreative holes signify the possibility of humorous loops. For Freud, these loopholes in our limited constructions harbor a comic faith that things *can* work, that people *will* survive, that one *may* choose love or joy or life itself (to laugh?). As expressed by survivors of tragedy, nonvanishing Native Americans, this humor transcends the void, questions fatalism, and outlasts suffering. The break here in the tragic pattern, the loophole of a "gay science," connotes possibility, even learning by mistake or pain, rather than irreparable loss.

In Western theory, then, Kristeva's psychic circle may complete itself. If successful on any level, love generates discourses of human comedy, not without tension and potential pain, even tragic rupture from a shattered perspective (in an essay, Kristeva laments the "rainbow of pain" over twentieth-century collective Western psyches, the dark shadow of Hiroshima).[32] So in Kristeva's *Tales of Love* the uninvited, "raw" feminist guest waits famished at the garden gates, as a favored son of Metis lies drunk and asleep. The seduction seems something of a reverse rape: male leftovers of the gods' love, the human scraps and wantings, the penury of female mortal need and immortal excess. The son of wit is outwitted by the needy lady as homeless stranger at the gates. Her need, her pain, is "fleshed" in his penis, and he pens her (the Freudian scientist writing it all down): she seizes what he "wants," writes her hunger with his flesh, and, behold, love is born. Eros comes to life comically as a child of lust and inebriation, female desire and male abandon, estrangement and surfeit, pain and fulfillment—thus according to Western myth and modern semiotic psychoanalysis. It seems comic enough on the surface, and there are thousands of tribal Trickster myths to flesh out the Greek construct in American Indian terms.

Kristeva's cited passage ends on "scattered totality" as the fruit of love, the willed if unfocused reward of want, suggesting a prodigal dissonance (Hélène Cixous and Catherine Clement, in *The Newly Born Woman,* speak of crossing dangerous cultural lines, as "laughter breaks up, breaks out, splashes over").[33] In Indi'n humor "scattered totality" translates as an epiphanal sunrise, a return of light through the long night of need. At cultural ground zero, it means that Indians are still here, laughing to survive. Even Camus's absurd hero, the long-suffering Sisyphus, turns and smiles in a moment of insight—his shard of en-lightenment—as he follows the rolling stone back down the dusty mountain. "One must imagine Sisyphus happy," Camus concludes of that moment when man "knows" himself on the mount—that pause, that momentary and lucid "release," as Freud says of *Witz*.

An observer of Western history might imagine, for comparative purposes, Indian humor as an alternative to the Euroamerican vision of Armageddon. This stretches from the lamented proletarian death march along assembly lines, to the global threat of nuclear war. All in all, Western "humor," threatened by a century of war-torn angst and ennui, could take cues from Indian endurance. Tribal continuances mean survival and communal celebration to peoples who have lived *through* a holocaust. Indeed, the 97 percent mortality of aboriginal populations would indicate that surviving Indians have come through hell. Some 3 to 4 million natives in the United States alone were reduced to 250,000 by 1900. The Indian poorest of the poor today have their humor, the fact of their survival, if little else materially. This is their psychic wealth and long-term salvation.

And where does Western theory conclude? Freud ends his analysis in *Jokes* with a definition of humor—"the economy in the expenditure of effect"—anticipating further explication that comes twenty-two years later. Humor initially seemed to him, perhaps for the symmetry, the holy ghost that capped jokes and comedy in an economic trinity of *Witz:* "The pleasure in jokes has seemed to us to arise from an economy in expenditure upon inhibition, the pleasure in the comic from an economy in expenditure upon ideation (upon cathexis) and the pleasure in humour from an economy in expenditure upon feeling. In all three modes of working of our mental apparatus the pleasure is derived from an economy" (236). So ends the analysis. Thus Freud's sense of humor would be preconscious (rather than subconscious)—a mental poetry displacing pain toward pleasure, something of a psychic stock option. In this vein, Thomas Mails paints an Indian portrait of Frank Fools Crow, grandfather trickster in the Dakotas: "For all he has seen and endured in his span of years [over ninety] on the Pine Ridge Reservation, he has a surprisingly delightful, almost impish, sense of humor. It rises frequently and infectiously. . . . When he is feeling good, he loves to put people on, and as he begins to do so his glinting black eyes will engage theirs to see whether they are catching the spirit of the moment."[34] In Freud's analysis, humor is finally neither Oedipal nor Janus-faced. The "comic difference" mediates split ideational planes as congruent, and humor does not draw on infantile release from inhibition, as found in joking. Humor "completes itself," Freud says, "within a single person," rather than needing a comic butt as second party or an audience as third. Finally, humor functions as Freud's grown-up ego defending itself against suffering—self-sufficient, mentalist, indeed, dispassionately "scientific" (the blunt edge of Austrian wit is alleged to be culture-specific to Freud's time and place). Two decades later, at his intellectual peak, Freud identified humor with the superego, which "speaks such kindly words of comfort to the intimidated ego."[35] From this psychological angle, humor saves us from "emotional display" or childlike vulnerability to suffering. In effect, it serves as the psyche's Big Daddy at play. Freud summarizes: "By its repudiation of the possibility of suffering, it takes its place in the great series of methods devised by the mind of man for evading the compulsion to suffer—a series which begins with neurosis and culminates in delusions, and includes intoxication, self-induced states of abstraction and ecstasy" (*Jokes* 217). Indians in Trickster myths might not defend the case so abstractly; still consonant with tribal cultural views, Freud summarizes *Witz* as a survivalist, if not celebrative sense of humor. The analyst backed by science stops short of clown priests—the ceremonial access to benevolent spirits (more Carl Jung's province)—and he circles the communal bondings of tribal play. Perhaps these comic benefits remain endemic to tribal reciprocity and rooted in native ceremony, as the West separates enterprising "us" from reciprocating "them." Two bicultural Hopi portraits help to draw the connective and dividing lines.

"I studied clouds and paid close attention to my dreams in order to escape being trapped by storms too far from shelter," Don Talayesva says in *Sun Chief,* an "as-told-to" native life-story in intercultural dialogue, spiced with aged, insightful humor. "Mr. Voth and the Christians came to Oraibi and preached Jesus in the plaza where the *Katcinas* danced. The old people paid no attention, but we children were told to receive any gifts and clothing"[36] (the Hopi spelling for the spirit is *Katcina,* as cited in Margot Astrov's *American Indian Prose and Poetry* [1962]). Oranges and candy failed to materialize, but "when the Kat-

cinas danced in the Plaza, it often rained" (*Sun Chief* 41). Talayesva
grew up traditionally Hopi in the early twentieth century. By the age of
six, he "had learned to find my way about the mesa and to avoid graves,
shrines, and harmful plants, to size up people, and to watch out for
witches" (68). But then he was sent to a white man's school (many saw
this as being kidnapped by the government or missionaries) and discovered beds, Jesus, knives, forks, and toilets: "I had learned many
English words and could recite part of the Ten Commandments. I knew
how to sleep on a bed, pray to Jesus, comb my hair, eat with a knife and
fork, and use a toilet. I had learned that the world is round instead of
flat, that it is indecent to go naked in the presence of girls. I had also
learned that a person thinks with his head instead of his heart" (99).

The last remark, with head full stop against heart, echoes across
Indian America, Lame Deer to modern native poets such as Roberta
Whiteman. The Lakota "heart's eye," as native index to human understanding, struggles against a white "mind's eye"—intuitive wisdom
against positivist logic, tribal healer against psychic scientist. Indi'n
humor, with its emphasis on bonding and human reciprocity sides with
the heart's emotions, in some affective balance with the head's intellect.
Talayesva continues: "As I lay on my blanket I thought about my
schooldays and all that I had learned. I could talk like a gentleman,
read, write, and cipher. I could name all the states in the Union with
their capitals, repeat the names of all the books in the Bible, quote a
hundred verses of Scripture, sing more than two dozens of Christian
hymns and patriotic songs, debate, shout football yells, swing my partners in square dances, bake bread, sew well enough to make a pair of
trousers, and tell dirty Dutchman stories by the hour" (*Sun Chief* 134).
Judging from this litany, Talayesva had been "civilized" toward the all-
American Indian boy. "But my death experience had taught me that I
had a Hopi Spirit Guide whom I must follow if I wished to live. I
wanted to become a real Hopi again, to sing the good old Katcina songs,
and to feel free to make love without fear of sin or a rawhide" (134). His
wit is plain as the mesas and dry as the low-lying desert, yet richly
detailed and comically layered.

A peculiar kind of Hopi humor lies buried here, mediating cultural
collision: "I had learned a great lesson and now knew that the ceremonies handed down by our fathers mean life and security, both now
and hereafter. I regretted that I had ever joined the Y.M.C.A. and
decided to set myself against Christianity once and for all. I could see
that the old people were right when they insisted that Jesus Christ might

do for modern whites in a good climate, but that the Hopi gods had brought success to us in the desert ever since the world begun" (*Sun Chief* 178). And when Talayesva grants whites their Jesus "in a good climate," but chooses the more exacting *katsinas* essential to Hopi survival on the desert, his humor grounds pluralist comparison in a reality of differences. " 'Talayesva,' my uncles and fathers said, 'you must stay home and work hard like the rest of us. Modern ways help a little; but the whites come and go, while we Hopi stay on forever. Corn is our mother—and only the Cloud People can send rain to make it grow. . . . They come from the six directions to examine our hearts' " (224). When the missionary returns to warn the Hopi of Armageddon, "a great flood" coming to Oraibi, Don tells him, "I had prayed for rain all my life and nobody expected a flood in Oraibi" (376). This is prime Hopi humor, good-natured and graciously deadpan, high on Third Mesa looking across to the San Francisco Peaks, where the *katsinas* go to winter. It is still so.

After the first Modern Language Association conference on Native American literatures in Flagstaff, Arizona, in 1977 (seeding many professional friendships), I was invited to the Hopi Mesas by the Artist Hopid, a guild of young writers, actors, and craftspeople. Al Logan Slagle and I camped behind the Hopi Cultural Center on Second Mesa and went to sleep hearing kiva singers in the distance.

"There's a rain dance at Old Oraibi," Milland Lomakema said smiling the next morning. "Let's go."

"But—," I hesitated, "isn't the village closed to non-Indians?" A red-stenciled plyboard had quarantined Old Oraibi through the early 1970s:

NO OUTSIDE WHITE VISITORS ALLOWED. BECAUSE OF YOUR FAILURE TO OBEY THE LAWS OF OUR TRIBE AS WELL AS THE LAWS OF YOUR OWN, THIS VILLAGE IS HEREBY CLOSED.

"Some say so, yes," Mike Kabotie replied, then mused out his shop window, "but, you know, the old ones said each visitor was a cloud, and this year we need rain pretty bad."

And so we went, shared some peaches with visiting Navajos, and came under the spell of the Longhair dancers, a three-toned choral pulse that struck the horizon notes of the whole day, and many days after. At day's end we were given an ear of corn by a *katsina*. Toward evening, the land was blessed with thunder and light rain.

Over the following decade, I caught glimpses of Mike Kabotie's compact frame at an Indian arts market, a powwow, or a poetry reading here and there. He always had a twinkle in his eye, a quick joke, and a puckish way of reminding me that Americans-at-large are in so many respects guests—drifting clouds—to the Hopi high on their desert mesas. It seemed to amuse Mike. Then in the summer of 1985, I received a manuscript of poems, "Migration Tears," submitted to UCLA's Native American Series. Since I was just leaving for Santa Fe, a detour to the Hopi Mesas again seemed in line.

By late the next afternoon, I stood in the lobby of the Hopi Cultural Center phoning Mike Kabotie. "Oh, hello Ken!" he welcomed in a singsong voice. "Come on out to our trailer and watch the stars tonight. Some satellites are going over—should be quite a show." It seemed a curious setting to discuss a book of poems.

The night was moonless dark on the Arizona mesas, the stars like spindrifts of quartz across the sky. We sat on the desert in folding lawn chairs among cholla cactus and looked up, listened, and laughed— about an outhouse blowing over in the wind, about a Hopi artist who, playing Superman at the ceremonies, dived off plaza roofs, about children and family and shirttail cousins, about painting, music, politics, poverty, and poetry. All under the stars that had heard it all before. The Kabotes invited us back for breakfast.

Son of the artist Fred Kabotie, Mike (Lomawywesa) was born of the Snow/Water clan in 1942 at Shungopavi. He is well known as a painter, lithographer, serigrapher, goldsmith, and silversmith. In *Migration Tears* (1987), a first volume of poems, he re-creates Hopi traditions for modern Indians in three comic senses. First, he nurtures what is and has always been native—to grow or create (*cresare*) as a mesa farmer tends rows of squash, corn, melons, and beans—"this mud-crusted / artist from Second Mesa." His native sense of natural cycles turns on the comic (spiritually optimistic) sense of seasons, the seeding, tending, weeding, and harvesting that underlie all agrarian communities. Second, Mike thoroughly enjoys the play of his arts, the humor and humanity of his "re-creations":

My studio plaza
chaos with colors
pulsating with
      British Rocker
      Rod Stewart

And third, Mike Kabotie remains his own *recreant* wit with trickster twists, a keen originality, and an independent artistic spirit:

> Are you a real Indian? he asked
> "No," I replied, "I'm a Hopi; real
> Indians live in India."
> A whirlwind smile and
> into the tornado again

"Corn is the Mother of the Hopi" is an old mesa saying, and there is a buried mother lode, a "womb kiva" of corn blessings, in the sandstone density and porous good nature of Kabotie's verse. The opening poem in *Migration Tears*, "Hopid," is layered with the past, topped with twentieth-century adaptations:

> maize their mother.
> children of Bear, Kachina
> and Hopi clans.

Kabotie also writes with contemporary candor: "bourbon, wine an escape / their addictions." The truth lies scattered like bits of gravel in these lines. The poems may be written anywhere on the go—along the "asphalt arroyos" of the San Diego Freeway into the L.A. Basin, "gazing over alien / urban prairie" ("17th Brentwood Mesa" in the Holiday Inn), or from the home kiva with "Fathers of life / bringing blessings / gifts and messianic messages" ("Kachinum"), or "on mesa's edge," where the pain of present-tense history wedges between the traditional past and the dispossessed present, "aliens to our homeland" living under double names ("Our Land No More Forever").

This "transistor" or hip Hopi artist is never too far from the "beloved Earth Mother," even flying to powwows in wingless eagles, an uptown Indi'n soaring over traditional Pueblo lands settled long before Christ: "keresan acoma / zuni enchanted mesa / hopi painted desert." Flight 583 floats among *katsina* spirits, each of us a "bringer of rains," a visitor.

In this sense all of us, beyond tribal boundaries, take part in Native America. As the September sun sets over the Hopi "place of emergence" in the Grand Canyon, and the Kabotie family gathers at Shungopavi "inside mother's house" to eat smoking green chili, "we all

laughed / with tears in our eyes." The Hopi look out through adobe
windows onto the mesas and down into satellite screens that project a
bizarre world for all of us:

> Relaxing, we turn to watch the world
> through television windows; seeing
> bloated black children starve in
> Africa; Arabs and Jewish people
> hunting each other on barren
> deserts with devastating arsenals
> > as
> lovely young American maidens sell us
> the stunned viewer on the secrets of
> youth, as my aging mother and aunt
> chuckle and crack hopi jokes.
>
> Outside, kachina cloud-priests have
> gathered over the Hopi mesas, lighting
> the skies with bright lightning and
> crashing thunder that a deaf-mute German
> caught so well in his sonatas.

("Transistor Windows")

Kabotie's Iroquois contemporary, the painter George Longfish, put it
this way in *Contemporary Native American Art:* "Wipe your Indian
hands on your Levi jeans, get into your Toyota pick-up. Throw in a tape
of Mozart, Led Zeppelin or ceremonial Sioux songs; then throw your
head back and laugh—you are a survivor of a colonized people. Paint
what you see, sculpt what you feel, and stay amused."

God's Red Grin

> My father was one-eighth Cherokee Indian and my mother was a
> quarter-blood Cherokee. I never got far enough in arithmetic to
> figure out just how much 'Injun' that makes me, but there's noth-
> ing of which I am more proud than my Cherokee blood.
>
> WILL ROGERS

Indi'n Humor tracks the comic among tribes, toward culture, down to
character. Just as F. O. Matthiessen's thesis of an "American renais-

sance" among writers of the 1850s prefigures the Native American renaissance of the 1970s, so Constance Rourke's "study of the national character" in *American Humor* (1931) provides an analogue for our analysis of Indian humor. The obvious differences of history and culture do not obviate the useful "American" parallels, as Western theory and tribal context intersect. Indians and Euroamericans share the land here, developing concurrently if not cohesively over the past four hundred years, and today for the most part live elbow to elbow, if not always amicably. Almost two-thirds of the Indian population has moved off-reservation. Whether parties across the Buckskin Curtain like it or not, mutual humors mediate their merging fates. We all share an inter-cultural, fusional, or "breed" moment in American growth.

Rourke finds "comic resilience" in the brag and swagger of young America, a kind of homegrown humor evidenced in Abe Lincoln. This wit has come laconic and epic at once—gamecocks crowing at a wilderness of living Indians, formidable obstacles, unlimited potential growth. The country rail-splitter grew into tale spinner, cracker-barrel sage, and deadpan epic humorist. From tall talk, to rhapsody, to wonder, early Americans on the frontier laughed with Whitman's "barbaric yawp." Their humor gave evidence of inevitable fallings in immigrant cultures so young, as it bespoke the ultimate, if jejune, refusal to fail. With ludic exuberance and true grit, our forebears survived as naifs of this new land. In the Yankee, the backwoodsman, and the black of post-Revolutionary America, Rourke finds a comic sense of unity and ease characteristic of the national temper: "Their comedy, their irreverent wisdom, their sudden changes and adroit adaptations, provided emblems for a pioneer people who required resilience as a prime trait" (*AH* 86).

"Humor has been a fashioning instrument in America," Rourke summarizes, "cleaving its way through the national life, holding tenaciously to the spread elements of that life. . . . Its objective—the unconscious objective of a disunited people—has seemed to be that of creating fresh bonds, a new unity, the semblance of a society and the rounded completion of an American type" (*AH* 231–32). So, too, Native Americans anciently overcame the obstacles of environment and fate, traced the tricks of survival to mythic origins, tribally bonded through highly crafted cultural senses of humor, and sang their thanks laughing to the gods of the native new world. Their homing acculturation began tens of thousands of years ago. One day we newcomers

might develop ceremonial humors, acknowledge the Trickster among
us, and ritualize laughter for our social uses. Newcomers and natives
join here as Americans.

   Indi'n Humor seeks to negotiate the distance from native text to
national context, tribal literature to local culture. Literary artifacts may
be approached as cultural settings, Clifford Geertz says in *Local Knowledge,* and "culture" in itself offers a living "text" no less metaphoric
than a good poem to be read by the social scientist. Why Indians laugh
may be another way of asking how they are verbally skilled, in both
performative oral settings and literate inscriptions, from Iroquois false-
face masks, to Northwest totem poles, to Hopi petrogylphs, to oral
transmissions and transcriptions over thousands of years *re*transcribed
as literary texts. Indian writers today continue an ongoing tribalization
of those "words."

   Still, like the Dakota weather, Vine Deloria, Jr., says, you can depend on Indian "unpredictability." The brash, often hyperbolic humor
of Indian resistance and recent renaissance surfaced first in *Custer Died
For Your Sins,* where Deloria has a cartoonist's romp with misconcep-
tions about Indians. They are neither so "noble" nor so "savage" as
their stereotypers dreamed, when Euroamericans projected their own
seesawing sublimations over five hundred years of "enlightened" ex-
pansion. Indeed, Europeans have ethnocentrically plowed through Africa, Asia, and the Americas. And still Deloria does not come so much
to castigate whites as humorously to cleanse intercultural wounds. He
lampoons the Bureau of Indian Affairs, caricatures political history,
parodies anthropologists and missionaries, satirizes treaties and termi-
nation fiascos, and jokes about his own Lakota tribe, warriors who
fought one another when they ran out of some twenty other tribal
enemies and the endless wagon trains of migrant whites. "The Oglala
were, and perhaps still are, the meanest group of Indians ever as-
sembled. They would take after a cavalry troop just to see if their bow
strings were taut enough" (*Custer* 89).

   This is the "permitted disrespect" of family members cussing and
discussing reality. Mary Douglas identifies this illicit kinship permission as the social context for joking the world over. These comic disrespects, twists of history, and turns of fate perplex us all, but goad
Indians with whetted edges. Our wilderness was their home. After five
hundred years of dispossession—germ and conventional warfare, bounty hunting, guns, plows, telegraph poles, trains, barbed wire en-

closures, land swindles, and outright stealing—native peoples still persist on some 53 million acres of reservation land left over from the great dirt grab. It's no wonder that Deloria sees "hurt" and "humor" as particular to Indians, if not universal to humanity; clearly, humor both targets and takes some fatal sting out of history. Humor not only mediates tragedies with a sense of continuance and survival, but helps to reverse statistics that bracket Indians as the poorest of the poor, the most invisible of American minorities (while looming largest, it would seem, as mythic images of this hemisphere's original peoples). "Man is the only animal that laughs and weeps," William Hazlitt once considered; "for he is the only animal that is struck with the difference between what things are and what they might have been."[37]

Without "the reversible field" of comic play that Babcock sees in Indian ceremony, these peoples would be pinioned on the schizoid horns of savage nobility. Indian humor clarifies the splits between fantasy and fact as it tempers the strain; it strengthens the survivors to witness a difference. The arts of humor—verbal wit, focused complexity, delightful masking, comic inversion, riddling wisdom, structural symmetries—give pleasures beyond pain as they bear witness to survival. "So when you hear a story," Leslie Silko says of Laguna Pueblo, "it will often be a funny story although the occasion is sad. We have quite a number of funeral stories which are very funny" ("Language and Literature" 69).

Making humor from what hurts is an art that transcends the given. Freud dubbed it narcissicism at its highest, the ego's triumph against any threat. Humor refuses to give in to pain; it administers an aesthetic to make pain the very subject of its pleasure. "It refuses to be hurt by the arrows of reality," Freud wrote in "Humour" in 1928, "or be compelled to suffer. It insists that it is impervious to wounds dealt by the outside world, in fact, that these are merely occasions for affording it pleasure." Thus when we laugh at the "economy" of a good joke, we are celebrating the maximal "expenditure" of effective human energy— a release *through* pain, even intensified by it—in the constructive service of the ego's reward, or the much touted "pleasure principle." And perhaps the more pain, the more potential pleasure, by contrast and release, through humor. There's nothing worse than a "bad" joke, nothing better than a comic chance taken against the odds of failure, and unexpected success.

So what makes Indi'n humor, here Deloria's jibes, funny? Rather than acceding to bitterness or sorrow, perhaps we find the painful truth pleasurably released—that is, accurately and artfully channeled. Our witness is rewarded by the contagion of laughter, extended kinship, communal bond, and gratified success. When Sitting Bull defeated the U.S. Army at the Little Big Horn a week before the country's centennial celebration in Philadelphia, Americans refused to believe he was a "real" Indian. Rumors circulated that the Sioux chief had been educated among whites at the University of Missouri, at West Point, and in France. Some said that he had studied Napoleon's genius to defeat Custer! Hence in 1878 R. D. Clarke published *The Works of Sitting Bull,* a "manuscript" from French Canada (where Sitting Bull lived from 1876 until extradition in 1881) that began with a Sapphic poem in Latin addressed to Sitting Bull's "school-fellow," Chief Joseph of the Nez Perce. Stanley Vestal describes the "book," clearly a hoax:

> Following this Preface, we have a long poem of eighty-seven lines, each stanza of which is in a different language: Greek, French, Spanish, English, Italian, German, and Latin. Evidently the editor, or shall we say the author, felt that, if his French and Latin of Part I were not enough to dispel doubt, these added feats of erudition must turn the trick. The poem is addressed to the President, *"O Magna Pater,"* and is an invitation to President Hayes to come and share Sitting Bull's tipi—and his whiskey. Apparently, the editor was unaware that the Sioux chief was a teetotaler, and would not allow his young men to indulge freely in alcoholic drink.
>
> There are signs that the editor, hard as he appears to have labored at his joke, was really not without a lighter sense of humor. He makes Sitting Bull sign himself *Taurus Qui Sedet.* And there is a certain charming absurdity in addressing Chief Joseph as *Josephum, Nasorum Perferatorum Ductorem.*[38]

In fact, Sitting Bull's grasp of English extended only to spelling his English name for autograph seekers. Although a Lakota dream-singer and gifted speech-maker, among whites the visionary warrior felt "just the same as blind." He sang in Lakota, translated by Vestal ("Sitting Bull" 276):

Oyate kin, wamayankapi ye
Itancan kin henapila yelo
Miye kakes blihe miciye

Anpao kin imawani ye
Canonpa wan hi omawani ye

You tribes, behold me!
The chiefs of old are gone.
Myself, I shall take courage.

At daybreak I roam.
I seek a peace-pipe as I wander.

Sitting Bull was said to be of deep and winning humor, a leader, a true *wicasa wakan* (man-holy). His hurt and humor—the symbiotic tension in his tribal vision—are powerfully composite indices to American native lives today. In the 1880s, he addressed Indian commissioners at Standing Rock about the theft of his people's lands: "Do you not know who I am, that you speak as you do?"

I am here by the will of the Great Spirit, and by His will I am a chief. My heart is red and sweet, and I know it is sweet, because whatever passes near me puts out its tongue to me; and yet you men have come here to talk with us, and you say you do not know who I am. I want to tell you that if the Great Spirit has chosen anyone to be the chief of this country, it is myself.[39]

2

Historical Slippage

> For a people who are as poor as us, who have lost everything, who
> had to endure so much death and sadness, laughter is a precious
> gift. When we were dying like flies from the white man's diseases,
> when we were driven into the reservations, when the Government
> rations did not arrive and we were starving, at such times watching
> the pranks of a *heyoka* must have been a blessing.
> We Indians like to laugh.
>
> JOHN (FIRE) LAME DEER, *Lame Deer, Seeker of Visions*

Dark Red Humor

Freud's final words of "Humour" in 1928 lauded "a rare and precious
gift."[1] This rare gift appears toward the end of another wise book by
and about a man of *Witz,* Tahca Ushte or John (Fire) Lame Deer.
Richard Erdoes came all the way from Freud's Vienna of the late 1930s
to record the "precious gift" of a Minneconjou Sioux healer's life-story
during the 1960s and 1970s. In some comic sense, it corrects John
Neihardt's tragic portrait of the Oglala Sioux *heyoka* Nicholas Black Elk
from Pine Ridge. Indeed, Lame Deer's narrative offers rare evidence of
what Lévi-Strauss brackets as "the savage mind" at play or what
Huizinga calls *Homo ludens.*

   In 1932 John Neihardt published *Black Elk Speaks,* his translated and
edited talks with a purblind Pine Ridge medicine man who spoke no
English. The "as-told-through" story is today an Indian classic, the
most widely read text in Native American studies. Almost six decades
later comes William Lyon's updated sequel, *Black Elk,* with the taped
soliloquy of Wallace Black Elk, a sixty-eight-year-old shaman living
off-reservation outside Denver and very much in circulation as a healer,

or "Earth Man." Like the Hopi prophet Thomas Banyacya or the late Sioux trickster Lame Deer, this Black Elk has taken to the literary road with some lively tales and intercultural visions. "My way is health and help," the shaman says in his most direct and deadpan idiom. "And I'm trying to speak really simple English so any five-year-old could understand what I'm saying."[2]

"Wallace Howard" received his childhood Anglo name, ironically enough, from a Scotch–Irish cowboy who married into the South Dakota Sioux. His earliest visions of *Tunkáshila*, or "grandfather" spirits, came when he was five, so the past sixty-four years have fallen into visionary multiples of four sixteen-year cycles of teachings, travels, and healings that trail around some thirty "vision quests." There is a mix of dry wit and visionary quickness in this Black Elk—a droll, puckish, bicultural humor. The taped soliloquy probably catches Nick Black Elk's actual *heyoka* presence more realistically than Neihardt could in translation. Wallace says that his shamanic name means "welcome" and adds, "I'm just a little throw rug" (*BE* 12). A small color TV records visions in the back of his head, he says straight-faced, and his medicine pipe serves as "a little walkie-talkie" to interspecies communication with animals, stones, and trees (10, 12). Wallace spent four years making his pipe, the covenant of Lakota religion: "We don't go to K-Mart and buy a *Chanunpa* [medicine pipe], then crawl into the lodge, and the medicine comes out" (23). This "scout" for his people, who pokes around inside a white Statue of Liberty diagnosing the body politic, has the "dumbest look" on his face, a friend says, while being the "smartest man" he has ever known. Wallace keeps his audience guessing.

This is pure Indi'n humor—the "contrary" wit, the Trickster reversals, the tall tale with intercultural kickers—and none are sharper at deadpan joking than the Sioux. The question may be how far to go with his visionary tales. "It was really tough to educate those educated people," Wallace recalls of a Bureau of Indian Affairs sweat lodge in Washington, D.C. (*BE* 82). Whether at the United Nations or in Parmelee, South Dakota, Wallace Black Elk has a story to tell—from kibitzing with UFO "star people," to the spirits fixing his brother-in-law's TV, to Jesus as a collective people's healer ("I think he was a good Joe").

The tone of this (auto)biography is catchy. It adds yet another chapter in a growing canon of American Indian self-narrated life-stories, midwived by Anglo field workers. Rather than desert shamans on drugs, plains warriors on ponies, or woodland visionaries paddling into the last sunset, this contemporary healer stays frisky, down-to-earth, and very much with us. "When you run into a good thing," he advises, "like a T-bone steak, take a piece and remember your people first" (*BE* 52). The spiritual tag lines of this narrative are salted with a rare, grounded wit for "All my relatives," as the Lakota open the sacred tribal hoop to a comic humanism for everyone of good heart. *Black Elk* stretches the common definition of shamanism and lifts the Buckskin Curtain to the characters behind the great visions.

Scholars such as Brian Swann and Arnold Krupat in *Recovering the Word* have taken deconstructive shots at the Eurocentric misnomer "autobiography" in the "as-told-to" life-stories of hundreds of Indians. Silent authors such as Paul Radin and John Neihardt often "spoke for" their informants, who neither spoke nor wrote English. Nonetheless, the stories exist as intercultural dialogue. Raymond DeMallie's work with the Neihardt transcripts, *The Sixth Grandfather* (1984), indicates that little was made up by the intermediaries. Neihardt's art seems more a matter of reconstructive mosaic. The critical questions, beyond translation, field accuracy, and textual reconstruction, are ones of dialogical interpretation: What can we make of the text rearranged before us? Can we culturally interpolate the human beings behind "talk marks" on the page? Rather than discrediting texts or disparaging differences, what can we do with words translating the gaps? Will readers hear a vestige of connective humor in the dry crackle of ethnographic texts?

Lame Deer opens his story in a puberty vision pit. To understand the medicine man, he says, we must know the man's history, so Lame Deer tells of his great-grandfather's death in 1877. John's namesake, Tahca Ushte, signed a federal treaty for his people's South Dakota reserve, as General Nelson Miles with his grizzly Civil War recruits came to quell "hostiles." During a truce, the Bluecoats opened fire, and as Miles pumped the chief's hand he shouted unsuccessfully, "*Kola, kola—* friend, friend."[3] Lame Deer adds, "It sure was a strange way for friends to drop in." Considering the massacre a century ago, this great-grandson sees his namesake's death from the vision pit, not as the brunt of Bearcoat Miles's malice, or even a victim of the soldiers' savagery, but tellingly ironic.

Tahca Ushte's rifle was hung on display at the National Museum of the American Indian, the largest holding (some 4 million pieces) of Indian artifacts in the world. A gun signifies the antiquated old way, a red artifact gathered by a white museum in Harlem. At best, museum-caching "our" American Indians seems a callow kind of tourism. Indeed, in March 1986 in upper Manhattan I found such collectibles on display at the Heye Foundation as Big Foot's pipe tomahawk, Sitting Bull's war club, and Crazy Horse's medicine society bonnet perched next to a repeating rifle. Si-tanka, or Big Foot, the Minneconjou leader who died of pneumonia, was labeled "Hunkpapa chief who was massacred, along with most of his people, at Wounded Knee Creek in 1890." Downtown that afternoon, I got to the American Museum of Natural History just in time to hear a museum guide tell her covey in a strident voice that Plains Indians "died out" because they exterminated the buffalo, on which they solely depended, driving them over cliffs in "kills," as the diorama showed. She said they took only what they could carry and left the rest to rot. "Any reader of Indian novels," the docent went on to say, "knows that Plains Indians once a year gather, barbecue, dance around, and pray for a good year" at Sun Dances. Hadn't she told us they "died out" from killing off the buffalo? Adjacent halls featured exhibits on primates and prehistoric beasts.

Rather than pathos or Western angst, Lame Deer's dark humor biculturally accepts what *has* happened in hope that it will not happen again. Survival turns on acceptance of the given, humor on turning pain toward positive uses. Tahca Ushte's gun gives way to John Fire's hearing aid, and its whistling recalls the spirits' voices in his ears, the healer jokes. The Indian *listens,* learns, and looks for a better way, an Indian–white collaboration with Richard Erdoes, the silent writer, who himself listens and looks as a way to mediate the "differences." These bisociations, or connective doublings, are rendered and perceived via humor and humanist alternatives to racism and warfare—from John Fire's slouch cowboy hat and seasoned boots rather than buckskins and a war bonnet, to Erdoes's own pre–World War II childhood as dark-skinned Jewish–Catholic–Calvinist "other" in eastern Europe. Erdoes was a mixed "breed" accepted nowhere, he recalls in the epilogue of *Lame Deer,* until taken in by Lakota Indians in South Dakota. In short, the story's binary vision and intercultural teamwork turn on an irony sheared by historical tragedy, frontier Indian massacres to World War II. It is sutured by survivors' still willing humors. John's red *sense* of humor is just that, a healing and surviving native instinct, a tribal wisdom long-standing; he offers Erdoes friendship a long way from Vienna. What gives Lame Deer this ability to negotiate atrocity with comedy, to see humor along Freud's lines as "a precious gift"? The *heyoka* tradition points toward a sacred sense of comic mediation in all things worldly *and* spiritual (the two are one, Lame Deer argues from a Lakota cultural perspective, using an old iron kettle as his symbolic stewpot). And just as the *heyoka* teaches traditional Lakotas the "contrary," or "two-faced," nature of all things, so Lame Deer's bonus is a sense of Indian options: nothing is fixed, not even injustice. This bivalent fulcrum divides the tragic sense of end-stopped suffering from comic renewal; the denial of free will is reversed with alternatives, possibilities, *re*-creations. It's an argument between past and future, simplified, a historical determinism transcended by humanist futurity. Iktome, the wiley spider, represents one Lakota agent of comic change, a Trickster weaver who patches torn historical webs.

Lame Deer's red humor leaves track of a comic pattern from Freudian psychology to English social science where Mary Douglas stitches theory into social texture to argue for culture-specific joking contexts the world over.[4] Particularly among African tribes, Douglas sees joking in A. R. Radcliffe-Brown's terms of "permitted disrespect." This in Freud's purview is a subconscious kinship that plays consciously with its own human limits. When is an insult not a joke, and vice versa, Douglas asks, and why are some jokes among men not funny in the presence of women? Does gender determine humor as well as culture? Forming a human Sioux chain to pee down Teddy Roosevelt's nose, as Lame Deer recalls in the 1970s at Mount Rushmore, may strike a Santee as comic, but would probably not amuse the moral majority in non-Indian America.

Jokes depend on shared subtexts or, as Mary Douglas says, social contexts—there must be some "meeting" of minds. "What's the best thing to come out of Nebraska?" a childhood friend asked as we sat sipping margaritas on the beach in Mazatlán, Mexico. It was ten below zero on the northern plains. "I-80," he crowed. My friend could joke on this score, since we grew up together; but we wouldn't like Californians taking a swipe at our hometown. "Why does the wind blow so hard in Wyoming?" he quizzed me. "Nebraska sucks."

The point stands: our common past determines connective play.

Kinship interconnects comically—perhaps not to "others," but comedy makes them the butt, not the audience. We laugh at ourselves to "play" with common ties. We survive a shared struggle and come together to laugh about it, to joke about what-was and where-we-have-come, even if the humor hurts. It is a kind of personal tribalism that begins with two people, configurates around families, composes itself in extended kin and clan, and ends up defining a culture. And it's particularly Indian in America.

Comic bonding pivots on playful baiting, especially across tribes. "What did the Sioux say when he finished his dinner?" my Navajo librarian, Vee Salabiye, asked me one afternoon at UCLA. She waited, eyes twinkling. I stood there stoic as she drawled, "Dog gone." Without the infamous "dog-eating" Sioux *heyoka* ceremony, this joke dies on the vine. Furthermore, it helps to know something about the cultural rivalries between Lakota and Navajo. In many ways, they are more competitively alike than most other tribes—the two largest Indian nations, a history of migrations, equestrian hunters, powerful warriors, strong matriarchal figures to complement the patriarchies, vision ceremonies, and so on. In context, the strange (to "others") Sioux custom of eating dog frames the pan-Indi'n joke; but what triggers our laughter, once the social context is in place? The punch line comes curt, end-stopped, suspended in thought—indeed, "poetic." The joke carries a kind of aesthetic, or as Freud would say, "economical" micro-phonemics and minigrammar. The sound of English "Siouxed" by a Navajo, as it were, rings especially funny to Indian ears. "Dog gone" reduplicates the initial phoneme inversely, so we hear a contrary play on the syllable; its monosyllabic ring—the almost comic vowel swallowed in gutterals—plays back on itself. The chug rhyme "dog gone" might strike any ear as potentially comic, if not clever, in the way children roll words around to explore their full potentials. It's an accessible pun, brilliant in its common economy and clipped linguistic charge. Freud would find primary dream-stuff in such humor.

In the algebraic terms of gaming congruence, the play structure of a joke discussed earlier, we might equate the terms: (a) What did the Sioux say + (b) when he finished his dinner? = (c) dog × gone. The chiasmus or phonetic crossing in (dog gone) mirrors each side by the other, as the squared sign of "$a + b = c$" implies the hypertext of a "joke"—that is, play dialogue and discharge. The joke reduces, more or less, to the following core: Indian eats (primal drive) + Indian answers (play dialogue) = dog × "gone" (canine friend negated). Out West, one hears a punning curse behind the playful folk interjection: doggone → god darn → god damn! Cowboys, Indians, secretaries, truckers, even my great-aunt in her kitchen when the bread doesn't rise, are known to utter this expletive—"dawggawn." It's a pioneer idiom, an American original far from England. We could further break down the punch line, the microjoke within the joke: dog + gone = "dawg-gawn." To play the game out in the spirit of Lévi-Strauss: animal totem + negation = god darn. More emphatically, "food" (sacred) + "finished" (profane) = "famished" (parodically god damn!). So the joke on Lakota ritual told by a friendly Navajo librarian echoes secular verbal play with sacred ceremony. It is charged with the intercultural *frisson* of history and heritage in a red English dialect that reaches non-Indian ears: "I'll be doggone!" or "god darn!" or pointedly western, "Dawggawn!"

Freud's idea of "bewilderment" compounded to "illumination" makes Sioux sense here or, in my librarian's case, Navajo-*ho*: the lead-in question, innocent and common enough, though primally charged with eating, stumps the listener. There's not enough data to formulate a riposte. We wait. The charge builds. "Dog gone" lights up centuries of intertribal *agon,* as Huizinga argues in *Homo Ludens.* Man's best friend punctuates the moment in comic sacrifice to spirits of humor and hunger.

When Barbara Feezor-Stewart, one of my Lakota graduate students, heard about this Navajo joke, she asked Vee, "What's a Sioux picnic?" For a second our librarian was silenced. "A six-pack and a puppy," Barbara chuckled. Without losing a beat Vee shot back, "A beer and a six-pack of puppies?" Since then I've heard from Paula Allen that Sioux fast-food chains are serving Pup-in-a-Cup, and Navajos are eating Mutt-'n-Honey for breakfast. To twist this doggone joke one more time, the chairman of the Anthropology Department at Florida State sent me the following, courtesy of an Oklahoma Creek (still working on his thesis): "What do the Sioux use for cattle feed?" "Puppy Chow."[5]

"A joke is a play upon form," Douglas says, where two sets of thoughts scratch against each other. Often this "play" chaffs established form—that is, challenges social structure as assumed at a given moment. Douglas acknowledges Freud's research into *Witz* as freeing play (shifting comic planes, joking infantile regression, freedom from emotional stress in humor), while she grounds abstract theories of "economic" release in joking cultural particulars. Comic "form consists of a victorious tilting of uncontrol against control," Douglas notes, "an image of the levelling of hierarchy, the triumph of intimacy over formality, of unofficial values over official ones" ("Social Control" 366). To be perceived *and* permitted, a joke "offers a symbolic pattern of a social pattern"—that is, a gaming congruence between accepted and playfully competing forms, with a sense of generative slippage between. The action here, the energy of the joke, lies in *inter*action: congruence and incongruence, norm and variant, the real and the fictive. Jokes, then, become "anti-rites," Douglas posits: a cultural "rite imposes order and harmony, while the joke disorganizes" (369). Yet it could be that jokes *dis*organize the monostructures of society in order to *re*organize a static and suspect order into polymorphous, kinetic "play." Here we could spin any number of Indian wheels, computing the comic root of Custer's feckless "Take no prisoners!" or Powhatan's dour "There goes the neighborhood" or Sun Chief's laconic "I regretted that I had ever joined the Y.M.C.A."

Yet the people, not the computation, count here. The Cree performing artist Buffy Sainte-Marie wanted to show viewers of the children's television show "Sesame Street" "that Indian people are here, that we exist, that we're not dead and stuffed in museums; that we're not stiff, up-tight, hard, as portrayed over recent television."[6] Indian people have lives full of beauty and "fun," Buffy countered: "it's not all heavy. There's a kind of lightness that Indian people have. It's down home, it's funky. . . ." And with a parting shot, she added, "When I walk into any place in the world, knowing I can give people a touch of Indian culture, I feel like Santa Claus."

In the deconstructive parlance of our day, a joke decenters the certainties of "structure." It sets free the creative impulses that organize structure *as* play in the first place. This is probably what Edmund Husserl in Germany, Mikhail Bakhtin in Russia, and Jacques Derrida in France, among others, intimated before the engines of academia co-opted the slippage—perhaps, at least, there is more play in their deconstruction than systematizers allow. More recently, Geoffrey Hartman qualifies the Americanization of French deconstruction: "Its play with the words of a text, at the same time, which is often—in Derrida—as consistent and extravagant as that of the midrashic rabbis, sets up an impasse in which an ancient interpretive skill is recovered yet cannot be grounded by either faith or theory. Like clowns or jongleurs, deconstructionist critics repeat the same act with language, obliging us to think of its negative, dismantling, as well as promissory, aspects."[7] The social sciences at the participant or phenomenological fringe of so-called hard science seem less fixated, if less playful, than their deconstructive counterparts in literary criticism. However one discredits the Carlos Castaneda series on the Yaqui *brujo* (sorcerer or medicine man), "Don Juan"—a fictive, comic character steeped in fact—*the* fact remains that this recreant native writer from South and North America (Lima to Los Angeles) deconstructed anthropology in a healthy, playful way. Humor keys the Socratic wisdom here, the trickster correctives to academic systems that overload the field with throw-away theory and soggy statistics. Among southwestern anthropologists, Alfonso Ortiz, Dennis Tedlock, Barbara Babcock, and Keith Basso, in particular, have come to redefine their sciences by studying ritual clowns, reexamining black-and-white striped (parodied) predecessors like Frank Cushing pondering the "reversible" Pueblo field of sacred play, and analyzing the jokes Apaches tell about whites.

So far, so good. When Mary Douglas claims, however, that the joker should be classed universally as a kind of "minor mystic"—only "a humble, poor brother of the true mystic" ("Social Control" 373)—the litmus of social context slips. What about Lakota *heyokas,* Pueblo *koshares,* Navajo Ma'ii, Iroquois false-face gods, Swampy Cree Wichikapache, or Blackfeet Na'pi, the Sun Father ("Old Man" himself)? Na'pi may be a fool, but he's all-powerful, a god as surreal jester, in complementarity with his wedded partner, Kipi'taki, Old Woman or the moon. "Needless to say," Douglas concludes from African tribal folklore, the joker "is always a subordinate deity in a complex pantheon" (373). There may be some truth in liminal mediations of tricksters tribe to tribe, but ethnocentric generalization to check the clown seems comparable to chaining Freud's simian libido in the psyche's cellar.

At the penultimate moment, Douglas slips on a Euroamerican bias (perhaps a Western slant against the comic, a fear of the repressed libido?). The scientist here, no less than Freud, seems a bit hamstrung by her own social context; her theory proves culturally bounded, as she warns others of warping contexts. It appears to be a question of seeing ourselves as others see us, and seeing beyond ourselves through them. Western cultural "sets" resist the jester–trickster as anything more than a "subordinate deity," a lowly clown to relieve serious pressure.

There are different ways of seeing. Joseph Epes Brown, editor of *The Sacred Pipe* (1971), insists that his friend Nick Black Elk was an inventive *heyoka,* not a narrowly tragic visionary, as the West might see the "major mystic" in Neihardt's recorded life-story. "Well, he was always doing funny things," Brown recounts. "That is why it was always good to live with him, because you never knew what to expect."[8] The old healer's purblindness came from proclaiming that he was going to make the earth rise; he placed gunpowder just under the ground's surface, and it blew up in his face.

> Well, just as a *Heyhoka,* a sometimes clown figure, he liked to make people laugh; he felt happy when people were laughing. When there were any little children around he would always be doing funny things with them or telling them funny stories, to make them laugh. I think he understood that there is no access to a deeper spiritual reality if there is not the opening force of laughter present there. It tends to open the heart for receiving greater values than those of this world. That is why it was always a happy experience to be with him, in spite of the fact that in many moments of his life he was a very sad, tragic figure, because of his feeling that he had never been able to bring to reality the task that had been imposed on him through his visions. . . . So he was sad; and on the other hand (and this is typical of the dual nature of the *Heyhoka*) he loved to laugh and to make other people laugh. ("Wisdom" 63)

In the Neihardt transcript, Black Elk's thunder vision, the mark of a *heyoka* from birth, is filled with dancing and transforming animals, men, and gods. The grandfathers appear "older than men can ever be—old like hills, like stars." The great vision begins with the western sky's cup of water and bow (ludic powers "to make live and to destroy") and ends with a "sacred hoop" embracing a divinely comic vision "wide as daylight and as starlight." And finally, the spirits process, "a good nation walking in a sacred manner in a good land."[9] "All these were rejoicing, and thunder was like happy laughter," Black Elk remembers over half a century later.

Our perceptual shift from joking to "humor" redefines verbal wit toward comic humanism. Just so, Freud revised his theories from *Jokes* for over twenty years to the 1928 essay "Humour." Social and symbolic contours tonalize the contexts when Indians laugh. Around non-Indians, the deadpan humor can be more "cigar-store Indian," for it is built into the bisociative slippage of intercultural exchange, often a silent witness to cultural fissures. The best jokes remain unspoken. Lame Deer's fa-

ther from Standing Rock, Silas Fire to whites and Let-Them-Have-
Enough to Indians, was "a kind, smiling man," his son recalls, yet
whether teasing, loving, or disciplining John, "for weeks he did not say
one goddamn word to me" (*LD* 22). So how do we analyze silence or
detect humor in reticence? For starters, watch any mime or good
clown—Charlie Chaplin or Harpo Marx or Hopi Mudheads pantomim-
ing whites or Lakota *heyokas* hunting rattlesnakes.

The pitfalls, perhaps, of such elusive comedy and its Indian contexts
are many: whereas Freud glosses all psyches abstractly (the curse of
white thinking, Deloria says), Douglas unintentionally imposes an ethnocentric bias on all joking contexts. Both scientists generate systems
that must be stretched to explain Indi'n humor. Each seems to gener-
alize to a fault, psyche to society, when placed against culture-specific
tribal humor. Hopefully, they help us to see our own margins of error
and cultural warp.

Comic Indi'n Outcast

> I was born a full-blood Indian in a twelve-by-twelve log cabin
> between Pine Ridge and Rosebud. *Maka tanhan wicasa wan*—I
> am a man of the earth, as we say. Our people don't call themselves
> Sioux or Dakota. That's white man's talk. We call ourselves *Ikce
> Wicasa*—the natural humans, the free, wild, common people. I
> am pleased to be called that.
>
>   JOHN (FIRE) LAME DEER, *Lame Deer, Seeker of Visions*

Two folkloric myths, almost global clichés, circle such "between"
births as John Fire's: the castaway and the changeling. The first myth
casts a tragic shadow over the orphan, breech-born, forever lost between cultures. It portrays the child as historical outcast, homeless
victim of circumstances. The second can be comic, if strange: nature's
wild child blessed as *different* by the spirits and animals, potentially a
culture hero. This child is charmed from birth to wander, misbehave,
and discover the fortunes of "other" humans-at-large, their variant
cultures, tongues, and climates. Such a pluralist perspective blesses the
wandering hero, the sacred clown, the heroic beggar—from Odysseus
at sea, to Socratic seeker of honest men, to Jewish schlemiel across
Europe, to Shakespearean wise fool, to American hobo. John (Fire)
Lame Deer comes in good intercultural company, if not exactly mainstream peerage.

Indians "at the forest's edge" of white negotiations, where treaties were broken as they were made, have long hung "between" pillar and post, and have long been pitied. Yet in Lame Deer's story there is little self-pity, some "good anger," lots of probing humor. Mostly he kneads a mix-and-match ethnic set of opportunities bagged from his peregrinations as "a find-out." Lame Deer's life is liminal, to use Victor Turner's term in *The Forest of Symbols,* and he looks in many directions at once as he crosses several thresholds. John travels intertribal boundaries, Oglala to Minneconjou bands and back to his father's Standing Rock Hunkpapa, all Lakota or Teton Sioux tribes. He journeys nation to nation in a pan-Indian revival of hundreds of disparate peoples (some like the Crow or Chippewa are old Sioux enemies). He translates Indian to white, or non-Indian, in the cases of other ethnicities, ages, and genders emerging as "nationalisms" in the 1960s (Black Power, Women's Power, People Power, Gray Power).

Richard Erdoes wrote to my graduate student Geoff Sanborn in response to an article that Sanborn had published on *Lame Deer:*[10]

I met Lame Deer in 1967 when he came with a group of Rosebud Sioux to New York to join Martin Luther King's peace march. They all wound up in my place where my wife, Jean, managed to feed the whole crowd. We had a very large, sprawling, high-ceilinged rent-controlled apartment on the upper-Westside. Lame Deer was pounding the drum in my studio. Old Henry Crow Dog doing the same in the living room. John reappeared a few weeks later, Indian-style—unannounced and uninvited, ringing our doorbell, standing there with a cardboard box containing his worldly possessions, saying with a broad grin: "I liked you. I think I'll stay for a while." He stayed about two months that time. He enjoyed New York hugely. He was a good artist himself, spending many hours in my studio, sitting at one drawing table while I worked on another, grabbing my brushes and colors, producing drawings which somehow resembled his verbal story-tellings. We became close friends, visiting back and forth endlessly. This went on for about two years. Then he began pestering me: "You are going to do my book." I protested: "John, I'm an artist, not a writer." "My medicine tells me you're going to do my book." "John, not only am I not a writer, English is my second language." "My medicine tells me . . ."

. . .

So began the strangest of collaborations between an essentially sophisticated European and an old Sioux Medicine Man who seemed to me to come from another century. What made it work was that we both had a sense of humor, his at the same time savage and pixie-like. He was often like a child, pouted like a brat when a woman refused him her bed (this didn't happen often.) He also got occasionally *lila itomni,* that is uproariously drunk. Another bond between us was our love for storytelling, painting, and drawing. Our art was, of course, different, but somehow related. I learned to speak the most god-awful Sioux uttered by any two-legged, however had the advantage of speaking German, which meant that I could pronounce the sound in the Lakota language which American anthropologists render: *h·* or *x·*, which is absolutely identical with the German *"ch"* as in *"Nacht"* or *"ich."* In the process I became more and more Indian and he more and more Viennese, if you can imagine such a thing.[11]

For the 1972 meetings of the American Anthropological Association, Barbara Babcock conducted a "Forms of Symbolic Inversion Symposium" and in 1978 published collated papers in *The Reversible World.* She wrote in the symposium abstract, " 'Symbolic inversion' may be broadly defined as any act of expressive behavior which inverts, contradicts, abrogates, or in some fashion presents an alternative to commonly held cultural codes, values, and norms be they linguistic, literary or artistic, religious, or social and political."[12] Lame Deer's life sets a daily text for these concepts. He plays out Turner's "ritual paradox," where inversions of the ordinary world produce richly metaphoric, comic reversals of expectation.[13]

Tahca Ushte, literally translated "Deer Lame," should no more connote lameness in the Anglicized slippage (indeed, a lameness distinguished, as with Odysseus or Oedipus) than Young-Man-Afraid-of-His-Horses should connote "his" fear (*others* feared his horses). But then there's *John,* the everyman's appellation in the West, Don Juan to boot, which seems culturally parodic, given our Christianized "Saint John," the baptist who served as precursor to Christ. The Gospel of John the Evangelist scripts peyote sacraments in the Native American Church (John Fire as joking prophet to an Indian generation in rebirth?). Momaday plays relentlessly on this name throughout *House Made of Dawn:* Angela Grace St. John, the white seductress; Juan Reyes, the albino Indian; the peyote text from the Gospel of John; John "Big Bluff" Tosamah, the pan-Indian priest. And there's *Fire,* the old joke John tells of his grandfather's new name: Anglos needing a ready handle for an illiterate native, when a "Fire!" broke out nearby. This surname seems aptly comic, given John Fire's energy, unpredictability, and wit. Everything cobbles about a sacred Sioux clown.

From the beginning he mediates contraries—a "full-blood," or "real," red Indian born in an American log cabin worthy of Kentucky's Honest Abe. Such humble origins project mythic antecedents, American "man of the earth" Lakota-style, as he says, *"Maka tanhan wicasa wan."* Lame Deer insists on the cultural specificity of his Indianness, his separate tongue, his opposition to "white man's talk": "Because there is a difference, and there will always be a difference, as long as one Indian is left alive. Our beliefs are rooted deep in our earth." Yet this bisociative Indian "between" tribal grounds at one point is pursued back and forth along reservation lines by shooting tribal police: "The find-out, it has lasted my whole life. In a way I was always hopping back and forth across the boundary line of the mind" (*LD* 65). And here at the liminal or adjoining edge of things the *wicasa wakan,* or "man medicine," mediates the known and unknown fringes of culture as bisociative healer.

Lame Deer seems, indeed, an Indian with a vision, but a red comic one—a man of boundless "bullshipping" humor, he says, a generic medicine man at large. John serves as hybrid healer rather than traditionalist. Around Winner, South Dakota, he was more a joking *heyoka* than a traditional Thunder dreamer, or medicine man, something of a sportive priest who loved women and wine, a quick street teacher. John did not hold still and cared little about propriety; as a matter of fact he drew gossip like fleas to a hound. From national talk shows to Dakota sweat lodges, he went everywhere, did everything, said anything: "an outlaw and a lawman, a prisoner and a roamer, a sheepherder and a bootlegger, a rodeo rider and a medicine man" (*LD* 40). Lame Deer learned to read and write and sign-paint in prison, the army, and saloons. In a sense, this "sign-painting" holy man became a cultural semiologist who spent his life splashing buckets of humor all over red–white fences (as well as the Winner city ballpark's outfield fence). He learned to "read" the world "symbolically," he says, from *cante ista,* or the "heart's eye." Again, his "vision" implies an instinctual wisdom at the comically integrated center of things—affective, sensual, natural wit.

Chthonic man around the globe has a primal bone to pick with "civilization." Part wink, part warning, Lame Deer tells his non-Indian collaborator: "We have a saying that the white man sees so little, he must see with only one eye. . . . We Indians live in a world of symbols and images where the spiritual and the commonplace are one. To you symbols are just words, spoken or written in a book. To us they are part of nature, part of ourselves . . ." (*LD* 109). Intriguingly, the phrase "part of nature, part of us" is the title of Helen Vendler's 1980 book of essays on modern American poets, her rubric lifted from Wallace Stevens half a century back: "As part of nature he is part of us." But whereas Stevens embodies and projects the imagination interacting between nature and culture, object and subject, thing and spirit—a kind of poetic continuum whose Mason jar "would" bridge émigré and Tennessee wilderness—the literary critic delimits "nature" from "us" with a comma. That small syntactic signifier suggests a binary opposition, or at best *apposition,* between the natural world and man. Yet to Lame Deer "nature" spells "ourselves," over the white cultural comma splice: "the earth, the sun, the wind and the rain, stones, trees, animals, even little insects like ants and grasshoppers. We try to understand them not with the head but with the heart" (*LD* 109). Lame Deer voices a common or native vision of the sacred everyday. Victor Turner sees this vision tribally in "ritual paradox," where dichotomies fuse in an extraordinary ordinary. To Lame Deer, "What to you seems commonplace to us appears wondrous through symbolism. This is funny, because we don't even have a word for symbolism, yet we are all wrapped up in it. You have the word, but that is all" (109). There is always an exception to such generalizations (conversely, "artists" are the "Indians" of Euroamerica, John told his friend Richard—recreant, liminal visionaries who refuse to conform, scorn material boundaries, and outlive their poverty). As a nontraditionalist in a very American tradition of original thought, Lame Deer talked back, refused convention (red or white), and personified Freud's freed childhood libido. He was no cultural purist on either side of the Buckskin Curtain. John traded on an uninhibited and naturally quick wit, and he viewed America through a unified sensibility in the face of historical fissures. "We call ourselves *Ikce Wicasa,*" he insists, "—the natural humans, the free, wild, common people." The Lakota *call ourselves*—"*we* the people," Iroquois meant (as scores of tribes referred to themselves in terms of "the people," according to Deloria's *God Is Red*). It is an old American myth, accompanied by outrageous brag, tall talk, and wild humor, perhaps at base the "native" genius and naiveté of this continent.

John (Fire) Lame Deer, liminal Indi'n, thus figures as *both* holy and humorous. The *heyoka* tilt of his vision gives him access to peripheral and primal life in the secular–sacred world (*Takuskanskan,* or, literally, the "power" that "moves" what "moves"). The native clown here is kin with the shaman, the mystic with the common man, as John's humor mediates the edges of understanding. Laughter as charged discharge, in Freud's sense, calls under, through, and beyond controlled consciousness. Here among the Lakota is another kind of prayer, not so much an invocation or lament for visionary help as a resourceful celebration of vulnerability in expectation of the gods' blessings. Comic outcast is holy seer.

Up to his death in 1976, John loved to talk and sport with words and people. He chuckled and spoke in a wry, singsong monosyllabism. His was a sort of grainy lyricism with comic undertones, and he played a charismatic character about Winner, as locals joked and gossiped about him. Erdoes reports that Lame Deer dubbed a bald sheepherder "Barefoot Head"; the greenback, "a green frogskin." John loved similes: a startled horse bolted "like a greased fart on a lightning rod." He had a street knack for kennings: a bucking rodeo bronco was a real "fartknocker"; himself, "an old wood-tick now." A "man-thing" hidden in a cowboy's saddle horn or the "moist spot" of many women did not escape his eye, and he had a weakness for moonshine, "pure grizzly milk and rattlesnake piss." A white Nebraska farmer's family gave him a warrior's send-off to "kill white men" for the government, and he went off to war in 1941 "drunk as a boiled owl."

This seems pure verbal bisociation—the binary mind at play with coined comic couplings. The boundary-hopping, *prepositional* man "between" possibilities is as well the word coupler, the metaphorist, the visionary clown by nature. His language, behavior, and vision coalesce all of a humorous piece—inventive, basic, grounded in sexual, scatological, and barnyard witticisms, hardly beholden to Puritan repressions. For a social scientist wanting straight answers, John was seldom the conforming informant. He told a nosy anthropologist that love in a tipi should be conducted "like the porcupine—very carefully."

Finally, one would argue, his wit was integrative. The dissociative splits between Indian and white, Indian and Indian, Indian and individual tragically have left too many dysfunctional, schizoid, and undeniably dead natives between "two worlds." So, too, the photojournalism of men like Edward S. Curtis as a humorless kind of salvage ethnography, however kindly intended, has bequeathed unsmiling visual stereotypes of Indians "vanishing" between two worlds. Note, by contrast, the "-emic" snap of "Kiowa George" Poolaw photographing his friends and family in turn-of-the-century Oklahoma, or Stan Zuni

(M.A. student at UCLA) catching R. C. Gorman at home in his Arizona hot tub in the early 1980s, or Lee Marmon these days finding an elder smoking a cigar and wearing "white man's moccasins" (Converse tennis shoes) by the Laguna road. John Fire bridges such fissures:

> You can't be so stuck up, so inhuman that you want to be pure, your soul wrapped up in a plastic bag, all the time. You have to be God and the devil, both of them. Being a good medicine man means being right in the midst of the turmoil, not shielding yourself from it. It means experiencing life in all its phases. It means not being afraid of cutting up and playing the fool now and then. That's sacred too. Nature, the Great Spirit—they are not perfect. The world couldn't stand that perfection. The spirit has a good side and a bad side. Sometimes the bad side gives me more knowledge than the good side. (*LD* 79)

> We Sioux are not a simple people; we are very complicated. We are forever looking at things from different angles. For us there is pain in joy and joy in pain, just as to us a clown is a funny man and a tragic figure at one and the same time. It is all part of the same thing—nature, which is neither sad nor glad; it just is. (201)

It's as basic as sitting down in nature's "outhouse" and taking full stock of things. "Sometimes I think that even our pitiful tar-paper shacks are better than your luxury homes. Walking a hundred feet to the outhouse on a clear wintry night, through mud or snow, that's one small link with nature" (*LD* 121). As in days of old, Lame Deer lights the sacred medicine pipe with a buffalo chip, and he would use "the bitterness of gall for flavoring" to digest buffalo guts against the winter's cold. His is a necessary, life-giving exposure to what-is, more often than not comic in deracinated America. John sees us driving to "super"markets with Saran-wrapped souls. "Soon you'll breed people without body openings."

For the Lakota, all this recreant red humor comes into focus traditionally in the *heyoka*. A healer significantly named Wachpanne, or Poor, taught Black Elk the riches of his thunder vision, the "laughing and weeping" faces of bisociated reality. As "fellow clown" with another initiate, One Side, in the late 1870s, Black Elk had the right half of his head shaved. "This looked very funny, but it had a meaning; for when we looked toward where you are always facing (the south) the bare sides of our heads were toward the west, which showed that we were humble before the thunder beings who had given us power. Each of us carried a very long bow, so long that nobody could use it, and it was very crooked too. The arrows that we carried were very long and very crooked, so that it looked crazy to have them" (*BES* 161). The crooked and crazy clowns of this world—liminal halves of Babcock's "reversible" worlds—may channel the powers "to make live and destroy," the thunder gifts of the western grandfather, for a society of hunters whose courage was of necessity often "contrary." The twisted conditioning of sacred clowns served as a warrior's test toward higher wisdom. And the sacrifice of a dog—the oldest domesticated animal in the Americas—completes the *heyoka* ceremony with ceremonial recognition of the hurt in sacred humor.

There is a sophisticated, yet childlike humor in this wisdom of the "poor" (Wachpanne). "When the ceremony was over, everybody felt a great deal better, for it had been a day of fun. They were better able now to see the greenness of the world, the wideness of the sacred day, the colors of the earth, and to set these in their minds" (*BES* 163). As with psychotherapy, this humble "wit" suggests Freud's ideal trust of the world as a sacred space: "Every little thing is sent for something, and in that thing there should be happiness and the power to make happy. Like the grasses showing tender faces to each other, thus we should do, for this was the wish of the Grandfathers of the World" (163).

Street-smart and worldly, Lame Deer updates the traditional "contrary-wise" *heyoka* as "an honest two-faced" who works "backwards openly": "To us a clown is somebody sacred, funny, powerful, ridiculous, holy, shameful, visionary. He is all this and then some more. Fooling around, a clown is really performing a spiritual ceremony. He has a power. It comes from the thunder-beings, not the animals or the earth. In our Indian belief a clown has more power than the atom bomb" (*LD* 236). As Joseph Epes Brown has commented on Black Elk as *heyoka,* a sacred clown shatters "the structure of the rite in order to get at the essence of the rite" ("Wisdom" 56). The *heyoka*'s thunder power is depicted "as a zigzag line with a forked end," Lame Deer says. The bisociated contrary fuses loose ends in lightning's "link from the sky to the earth, like the stem and the smoke of our sacred pipe. That light gave the people their first fire. And the thunder, that was the first sound, the first word maybe" (*LD* 240). From kennings, to hopping "between" tribal boundaries, to bicultural and bilingual couplings, to "contrary" behavior and stand-up comic humor, John (Fire) Lame Deer lived Indi'n humor, at work healing the fissures of American history.

Heyoka thunder power.

Black Elk traditionally seems to have been the more ceremonial *heyoka*, as compared with Lame Deer's free-wheeling clowning; but the two medicine men acted out comic complementaries central to the Lakota this century. When the ethnographer Frances Densmore asked about sacred clowns eighty years ago, her informants at Standing Rock and Pine Ridge replied that the "enacting of the part of a fool in connection with a thunderbird dream was an example of the antithesis by which Indians sometimes disguise their meaning. In this it might be said to resemble the 'sacred language'."[14] So by comic inversion the *heyo'ka ka'ga,* or "fool impersonator," tapped the powers of Thunder (echoed in laughter?) to teach and heal the people: "A man who has dreamed of the thunderbirds; a person who does things contrary to the natural way of doing them; and, in some instances, a joker" (*TSM* 158). Densmore cites Stephen Riggs as backup to her field work: "The nature of the *Ha yo'ka* is the very opposite of nature. He expresses joy by sighs and groans . . . and sorrow and pain by the opposite sounds and looks. Heat causes his flesh to shiver . . . while cold makes him perspire" (159). The psychic nexus here lies in the *heyoka*'s contrary strength of ego, trained in the wisdom of inversions. "They feel perfect confidence when beset with dangers, and quake with fear when safe" (159).

Thus when Indians like the late Grandpa or "Buffalo Bill" Monroe in my extended family turn the white world upside-down in cultural collision—refusing the Puritan work ethic, disdaining private property, questioning the patriarchal monotheism of a religious vision forking between heaven and hell, suspecting material "progress," even becoming tragically addicted to sugars, fats, and alcohols never before in their diets as buffalo hunters and grain gatherers, fighting back against encroachment on their lands, and finally resisting acculturation with a stubborn and sometimes self-defeating red pride—their *heyoka* traditions may be at the heart of a contrary ethnicity. And a certain humor of inversion, a mirroring slippage from white ways, seems Lame Deer's enduring legacy. Iktome, or Spider Man, serves as his spiritual muse in a web of jokes that catch and rarify reality. These tricks trap and bind the natural twists in things to give Lame Deer a sense of subtle designs in Indian–white interactions. Coyote totemizes his animal go-between. The garbage man of the plains is a scavenger who can live on the fringes of power, even eat offal to survive. And the *heyoka*'s sacred play or holy laughter cleanses wounds, reinforces social norms, and relaxes rules so the people can live with them. All this fooling around tests the temper of the *wakan,* or natural "power," in things. The Sun Dance, finally, is where ritual "play"—dance, chant, pageantry, sacrifice, prayer, communion—draws the people "comically" together in serious ceremony, renewed annually at the summer solstice. From vision quest, to Sun Dance, to ceremonial sing or *olowan,* to battle cry and death chant, the Sioux are wrapped in ritual behaivor—it is "the sacred way," Black Elk says, that tilts toward Lame Deer's Indi'n humor. The core of the way is one of contrasts and contraries. Its "play" is what Huizinga defines as the *sapiens* of *Homo ludens.*

Neoprimitives

"Animals play just like me," Johan Huizinga opens *Homo Ludens.* Dogs invite contests, wrestle, chase, snarl, pretend to bite, "get mad," and permit aggression (to modify social science for the moment). Such contest does not demand conquest. It seeks to engage, play *with,* and maintain touch, literally and symbolically, in a social grouping. Cats game, chimps chuckle, gorillas gambol, dolphins frolic, and horses romp. Plato in the *Laws* sees this to be life's intrinsic play or the "leaping" of the young, as in water and wind, fish and birds (the earliest linguistic contexts for "play" as leaping or frolicking).

As a bridge here with Indi'n humor, the Dakota word for "joke" is *WO-e-ha-ha-WO-h'dah-'kah,* according to Paul War Cloud's *Sioux Indian Dictionary* (1971). My Rosebud Sioux graduate student Barbara Feezor-Stewart says that the Siouian *ha-ha,* the sound water makes "moving," clearly means "stream" or "running" water (as in *mni-ha-ha,* or "water-running-sound"). The initial *WO* indicates a "man speaking," while *e* is "it," and *h'dah-'kah* signifies more or less "BIG goings-on." Thus in the Dakota word for "joke" we have something roughly like "Man-speaking-it-as-running-water-sounds-as-man-speak-ing-BIG-doings." That seems funny in itself. There is linguistic delight in motion here for a seminomadic people "moving" west over a millen-nium. As mentioned, their Prime Mover is Takuskanskan, loosely "What-Moves-moves," literally the "power" of the "sky" to a re-duplicative multiple. The sound of moving or fresh water on the arid northern plains of the "Great American Desert" has always been a source of joy. In the Siouian word for joke, *WO-e-ha-ha-WO-h'dah-'kah,* also surfaces the old Greek *alazon,* or overstater, as well as the chiastic "man speaking" and the delightfully onomatopoeic *ha-ha* for the sound of running water as laughter. The commotion here, the "BIG doings," or *h'dah'kah,* is also comically chiastic on a phonetic level, *ha-ha* and *h-dah-'kah.* In summary, the linguistic core of the Dakota word for "joke," *ha-ha,* illustrates the stream-ing idea of "play" as primeval *laughter* in oral etymology.

Huizinga would have appreciated Indian evidence of his thesis, where play and joke form a confluence in Dakota *ha-ha.* The Anglo-Saxon *plega, pleagan* means the "play" of rapid movement, hand grasping or clapping, music, and bodily movement in general. Thus to play may be among the oldest human, indeed animal, pleasures (along with eating and making love?) as primal forms of tribalizing. Huizinga catalogues play's characteristics: "a voluntary activity or occupation executed within certain fixed limits of time and place, according to rules freely accepted but absolutely binding, having its aim in itself and accom-panied by a feeling of tension, joy and the consciousness that it is 'different' from 'ordinary life.' "[15] Graphing these criteria brings us closer to defining humor's kinships, as Freud and Douglas would frame culture's joking and play instincts:

free   **we choose to play**
      pretended   **we "act" out the game**
            detached   **we don't care *too* much**
                  acted apart   **we play in a separate "magic circle"**
                  orderly ("form")   **we accept or modify the rules of the game**
            agonistic (tension/solution)   **we resolve or abide by the odds**
      "apart together" (social grouping)   **we bond momentarily**

This voluntary suspension of the "real," re-created in a play sphere, depends on an *illusion,* literally meaning "in play," Huizinga underlines. That is, we suspend the weight of the real to play at reality a distance from it—a kind of *sur*real game that doubles back in sports, the arts, free markets, fast cars, and warfare on too *"real"* human concerns, which we never truly give up. There is always an *agon,* something at stake, in terms of Freudian vulnerability, the martyr's agony, and the idea of an "other," the an*tagon*ist who games with/against us. Every game or struggle necessitates an-other (as with "words," Bakhtin argues for dialogue). Thus price, prize, and praise constellate an etymological ethnography of agonistic stakes for Huizinga. But play always means a serious nonseriousness. If things are being "played for real," they both matter and (we pretend) don't. "For the appearance and names of these gods," Socrates says in Plato's *Cratylus,* "there is a humorous as well as a serious explanation, for the gods are fond of a joke" (*HL* 150). This doubling extends the bisociative planing of comedy, diagonally inclusive rather than exclusive. The "serious" seeks to exclude play, but not the reverse, Huizinga notes—play seems a higher index to the flexible ego, the nonthreatened psyche. From chess to cursing to pro football, play may be for keeps, but still "played" for fun. And mostly it's the playings, not the played components or even players, that please us—not the marbles, the Dutch say, but the gaming.[16]

According to one of Huizinga's sources, the "play" of highly serious play or liturgy comes "zwecklos aber doch sinnvoll"—that is, "pointless but significant" ("directionless though sensical," Romano Buardini translates the German in *The Spirit of the Liturgy* [1922]). The "aber doch" tips off a doubling characteristic of comic play—"no, but yes" or "isn't, still is." This torqued connective implies the play of the whole beyond negations or ruled exclusions—comic possibilities, open forms, freedom from static restrictions. Thus the context is one of bisociative humor and play: "The true poet, says Socrates in Plato's *Symposium,* must be tragic and comic at once, and the whole of human life must be felt as a blend of tragedy and comedy" (*HL* 145). Socrates via Huizinga here sounds much like Black Elk discussing the *heyoka* ceremony: "You have noticed that the truth comes into this world with two faces. One is sad with suffering, and the other laughs; but it is the same face, laughing or weeping" (*BES* 159).

The arts, as Huizinga argues, strike a taproot into the vital past of humankind. Poetry, the play of language, lies "on that more primitive and original level where the child, the animal, the savage and the seer belong, in the region of dream, enchantment, ecstasy, laughter" (*HL* 119). This touches the pure play of humor. *Homo Ludens* was published in 1938, translated during the war, and reissued by the Swiss in German by 1944; it was prepared in English by the author for later publication. To a Leyden philosopher of cultural forms in the 1930s, when Hitler and the high serious thugs of political ideology rose to power, "dream, enchantment, ecstacy, laughter" were in peril of being lost forever. Hence to Huizinga, the "play" of the primitive personal childhood, animal other, aboriginal New World native, or holy visionary seemed precious indeed. They still are.

Huizinga's nostalgia for the ludic (the older Latin word for "school" as "entertainment") appears to be Euroamerica's longing for more idyllic times, more ideal "play," more gaming congruence in jokes, the comic, and humor. Civilization is "played," Huizinga argues, and play predates culture: "it arises *in* and *as* play, and never leaves it" (*HL* 173). To "play" at play is Huizinga's ideal intellection here. Behind free play lurk fascist shadows where the false, rigged game is deadly, the rules are made by others, the cost is tragic (spoil-sport "puerilism," Huizinga feared, "that blend of adolescence and barbarity" with brownshirts "goose-stepping into helotry" and bluff façades on public buildings [205]). And so Huizinga returns philosophically to the classics and American Indians, where Blackfeet, Inuit, and early Greek and Chinese examples spice his neoprimitive theories of cultural play at its best. A positive "sophist" such as Lame Deer or Socrates emerges as "the central figure in archaic cultural life who appeared before us successively as the prophet, medicine-man, seer, thaumaturge and poet and whose best designation is *vates* [Latin, prophet]" (146).

It may be that postindustrial society, in its distance from "the savage mind," has long been longing for what it feels to have lost "back there" in the beginnings. By the eighteenth century, Huizinga says, the wig was discarded and "all Europe donned the boiler-suit" (*HL* 192). Grown-up games of nuclear war and economic Armageddon, from the Christian Second Coming to Julia Kristeva's nuclear dread, seem all too "serious" today, and they should be. For over a century, the West has driven itself to the point of global destruction, concomitantly looking back to *fons et origo* (while mass-murdering its indigenes). Back or down "there" lie the font and origin of culture before modern triumph and folly: we mythologize Darwin with the species, Lyell on geology, Spencer in social science, the Grimms in folk culture, Marx in political economy, Mendel in botany, Frazer in cultural anthropology, Nietzsche in philosophy, Freud in psychology, and Einstein in physics. And behind Huizinga stand such neoprimitive philosophers of cultural and symbolic forms as Frobenius, Vico, Schiller, Frazer, and budding anthropologists like Frank Boas and his student Edward Sapir. Durkheim, Lévi-Strauss, and the British functionalists follow. So the myth and ritual of primitive society—"the primaeval soil of play," Huizinga says—provide the endpapers for modern society (5). And neoprimitive arts seem premodernist: "In this sphere of sacred play the child and the poet are at home with the savage" (26). This is where Freud, in a rare moment of "scientific" nostalgia, condenses his theories of *Witz* into a simple conclusion: "the euphoria which we endeavour to reach by these means [jokes, the comic, humor] is nothing other than the mood of a period of life in which we were accustomed to deal with our psychical work in general with a small expenditure of energy—the mood of our childhood, when we were ignorant of the comic, when we were incapable of jokes and when we had no need of humour to make us feel happy in our life."[17]

So what does play have to do with humor, we ask, and where do we draw the line discussing American Indians? Play would seem to be the social expression of a vitalist energy that charges humor, as Henri Bergson argues in "Rire" (1899); both play and humor "express" human pleasure, but play derives from the noncognitive (the young animal "leaping"), while humor as its conscious extension is triggered by a mature moment of bisociative "in/sight." That is, humor (with its doubling comic mode and discharging jokes) turns on *under*standing, whereas play often libidinously pits one vector against another (ant*ag*-*oni*sts) and games toward a resolution, cognitive or not.

Laughter discharges what seems to be the psychic moment of gaming congruence: we "see" into the play sphere and know its illusion ("in play"), often illuminating a more *real* arena of concerns. Pure play need not be bisociative, but is held as "true" illusion, at least in the moment of playing. In play or game alone, we struggle to beat the odds, to master the radicals, to "perfect" the art, and to win, rather than connecting the cognitive dots of a comic analogy with reality and its attendant burdens. Play may finally *be* humorous—that is, an antiritualist "rite" that strikes us as both apt and illusory, real and surreal; and most certainly humor is *played out* in jokes and comic contexts. Humor implies the human search for understanding (often frustrated, but not stifled); play seeks absorption in voluntary pleasure, however high the stakes. Both entertain, occasionally enlighten, and trace back archaically and profoundly in human history.

Buckskin Cartoons

My Lakota brother keeps a plaque above his desk in the American Indian Center of Alliance, Nebraska: "The Indian scalps his enemies. The White Man skins his friends." While waiting to board a plane one day, I found the "Tumbleweeds" cartoon in the *Los Angeles Times*. Why is there, in the first place, a cartoon strip joking about Stone Age Indians, and none caricaturing blacks, Chicanos, Asians, or Armenian-Americans, for that matter? Why are there comic books in every language on Indian "warriors" of the plains? It seems an inverse compliment: America cannot forget its "first" peoples, as the globe cannot ignore the "New" World. We "play" native images, from competitive sports, to cars, to cigars and Red Man chewing tobacco (hemp was "native," Raleigh found, and Americans still smoke under the label of his surname). In Mazatlán, Mexico, site of an Aztec seaport and silver mine conquered by Cortez, I happened upon a tag-team professional wrestling match between Los Apaches and Los Mohicanos. So Indians get singled out for special treatment, even among Mexicans, like "exceptional" children with learning disorders compensated by primitive mythic powers (animal mystiques, sexual prowess, warrior energies). "Children, the insane, and primitive peoples all still have—or have rediscovered—," Paul Klee told Lother Schreyer early in this century, "—the power to see."[18]

Cartoons may pay a fixative tribute to "our" Indians, but the terms

Tom K. Ryan, "Tumbleweeds."
(By permission of North America Syndicate, Inc.)

are crude and the humor is non-Indian, if anything. The Stone Age "brave" brings back a box of old scalps, and the chief in feathered headdress complains of Anglo ingratitude: "We try to be charitable!" A bad joke? Willem Kieft, governor of New Netherland in the early seventeenth century, seems to get folkloric credit for inventing scalping, and white bounty generated a brisk trade for three centuries. The few scalps I have seen were in Euroamerican museums on white-curated "battlefields." So once again, the Indian carries a comic onus for the "savage" stereotype, non-Indian originated, perpetrated, and blamed on the aborigine. "Indian giver," Cotton Mather might say. Stereotyping inverts the truth, as a way of protecting the scalper from his own infamy and history. And the Indian comes off as stupid (the buck-toothed brave), savage (scalpers), and wry (stoic cigar-store warrior, with bow, arrow, and lone feather).

This last note, the wry humor, serves as inverse saving grace for some Indians who like "Tumbleweeds" (others find the comic strip offensive). If Americans attribute a sense of humor to Indians, they may come to see natives as more human, less treacherous, quicker-witted (as the caricature masks white betrayal). Yet a smile moves toward mediation: to "return" war trophies is a gesture toward righting things. Expiation, or purgation—certainly Freud's sense of "release"—shifts comically from the negative to a positive intercultural exchange between old foes.

How does the "Tumbleweeds" joke work? We enjoy "seeing" and then "knowing" the cartoon's humor. The time delay charges the joke—initial "bewilderment," Freud says, breaks open in "illumination." This "scattering" light, to borrow Kristeva's adjective, depends on our assumed understanding of the context, as Mary Douglas would interject—Indians scalping whites and trying to return the hairlocks in a modern-day gesture of "burying" the ethnic hatchet (*glasnost* with Russia). This came during the late 1980s, when the Great White Father was once more sharpening his strap on the stock market as he shaved poorly supported programs for the needy. ("Trickle down," the Republicans said, and the stock market quadrupled in five years, while Reaganites and inside traders pissed all over the poor. Meanwhile, according to *Forbes,* the number of billionaires in America doubled in 1987.)

But the cartoon's pleasure is ours, if the present pain of America also registers. Our ego feels rewarded by "knowing" what visual slippage is all "about" here. Humor gives us access to truth while it protects us from reality's shock. So viewers enjoy cartoon solutions to old guilt, as though scalping were a slip of the pen, or caricatures of Indians simply innocent gaffes. It is a cartoon, after all, a play-world, some say, and "real" Indians died at Wounded Knee or with the buffalo (the Geronimo or Ira Hayes late warrior syndrome). The cartoon is tensed with history. Hurt pressurizes the humor toward affective catharsis, what Freud calls the "economy" in *de*-pressurizing such tension. The payoff comes in letting go of pain. So our relief (the laugh) releases us from reality, concomitant with our recognizing the complex context and symbolic undertow of "Indian" humor, on both sides of the Buckskin Curtain.

Would Indians find this cartoon funny? Perhaps not—too many dead relatives and scattered museum scalps, too few reparations and little land returned. And, basically, what passes for "charity" today would make a miser weep. "The people with real dependency on [social] programs are deprived of what they need," President Ronald Reagan said on February 5, 1982, "because available resources are going not to the needy but to the greedy." Given political double-speak, what's funny about folk distortion? The aesthetics of cartoons (pissing the king's face in the snow, or down Teddy Roosevelt's nose at Mount Rushmore) reduce reality to clean, telling, playful lines. Such antics are both a version "of" the truth, simplified, and a distortion, clearly drawn, where we can play with things at a cartoon remove from mimetic reality. In the case of this "Tumbleweeds" comic strip, the buck tooth, headdress, braid, blanket, buckskin breechcloth, and stone face are not smudged with any other data. The stereotypical errata foreground our "signs" of Indians. This seems to project immediate, uncomplicated visual signaling, as the dialogue "plays" with a somewhat more complicated twist on old frontier reparations.

Here from a native viewpoint lies dark red humor with a bite, to be sure, yet its satire is preferable to the Indian Wars, continued bitterness, more murder. A comic cut helps to negotiate our Euroamerican history of genocide, removal, inattention, or dismissal. Potentially, at least, Americans see themselves seeing Indians in "Tumbleweeds," when they care to think about Indian–Anglo relations. If we laugh, Lame Deer showed, we can think.

culture to Culture

In March 1986 the Center for Great Plains Studies convened an international gathering of scholars and tribal leaders at the University of Nebraska. The focus was Indians. The first Native American had graduated from the Lincoln land-grant school only a decade earlier, and in 1986 some forty Indians intermixed with the 26,000 Cornhuskers on campus. For thirteen years, Lionel Bordeaux had been president of Sinte Gleska College, chartered in 1971 by the Rosebud Sioux along the South Dakota border, Lame Deer's country. Bordeaux spoke about one of two four-year accredited and tribally controlled Indian colleges in America (Navajo Community College is the other). Sinte Gleska ("Spotted Tail") enrolled some five hundred students a semester and so far had produced one thousand G.E.D. graduates where the average reservation education was less than ten years. "From a cup of coffee to a diploma," Odel Good Shield said, "that's a long road."

Once there was a late-migrating winter bird, Lionel Bordeaux began, that procrastinated and finally flew all alone and fell exhausted into a Nebraska barnyard, only to be crapped on by a cow. It was revived under the warm cowshit, so the bird woke up singing. It thought that spring had returned early to Nebraska. A cat heard the chirping, dug the lone bird out of the dung, and ate it. The moral is succinct: everyone who dumps on you is not your enemy; everyone who digs you out of the dung is not your friend; when happy in a warm pile of shit, keep your mouth shut. To abbreviate pan-tribally—bless the cowshit, fool the cat, and stay quiet until you know what you're crowing about.

Now this, to my mind, is a "real" Indian joke, bio- and geo-specific to the northern plains. It seems culture-specific to the Sioux, and comically "ludotopic" to Indians today, where time takes on the wild flesh of ludic space (improvising from Bakhtin's lexicon in *The Dialogic Imagination* and Huizinga's *Homo Ludens*). When to move, where to migrate: these issues preoccupied plains tribes for good reasons. The Lakota, by choice or circumstance, had been seminomadic for over a millennium; they relocated up the eastern seaboard, across the Great Lakes when encroached on from the East, and out onto the plains by the late seventeenth century. There they traveled north and south seasonally with the buffalo herds. The Sioux, as French trappers renamed them ("snake" people via the Ojibwa slur) spread as far south as Kansas, and as far north as Canada—a formidable presence from the Missouri River to Montana. When the horse or "holy dog" (*sunka wakan*), showed up on the plains magically at the end of the eighteenth century, the Sioux along with the southern plains Kiowa rode for a century as plains centaurs, Scott Momaday imagines. In any respect, they moved around, wintered in the Black Hills, and saw themselves as brothers to the buffalo, kinsmen of the eagle, and psychic companions of the horse. Spider, or Iktome, tricked the Lakota, two-faced them, teased them, all to help them quick-wittedly survive reality's doublings and illusions. Coyote showed them how to survive on next to nothing. So animals taught, directed, and guided Sioux tribes, fed them, carried them across the endless shortgrass prairies, and took them into their natural world in which Indians felt "animal-person."

Bordeaux's little brown bird is a kinsman, then, a tribal totem, the word meaning "my fellow clansman," from the Ojibwa (Freud discussed totemic kinships in *Totem and Taboo* [1913], and Lévi-Strauss followed more than fifty years later with *Totemism* [1962], which deals with a subject that has interested anthropologists since Frazer's *The Golden Bough* in 1890). The bird's misfortune prefigures our fortune, future, and heuristic comic feast, as in the Christian conception of the "fortunate fall," or *felix culpa*. This nondescript, late-to-learn, misguided little migrator, a sorry pilgrim and generic fool, falls into our laps as a lesson. It obviously has to do with survival, in an area where the weather changes about as quickly as men's minds, and the environment remains as relentless as animal hunger. The comic payoff comes through what we, a "native" audience, hear and learn in The Fall— what we can laugh about by way of learning things useful and perhaps pleasing.

The reversals in the story are characteristic of countless animal stories in the bestiaries of Native America, which Ovid would itch to write down. The weather changes; animals move; some delay. One young naif tarries too long; it falls into the dark soup; the "gods" defecate on it. The innocent wakes up, opens its mouth at the wrong time, and another hungry wayfarer, somewhat cleverer and luckier, satisfies the claws of hunger in late winter. The complexity of the plot, along with its narrative simplicity and down-to-earth basics, flows rich with reversals, surprises, and grim yet funny conclusions. Late fall becomes winter, the bird learns too late, and out of exhaustion and desire fantasizes false spring. A lyric birdsong out of season brings disaster—it's still winter (poor timing), and a hungry cat gets fed. We lose our bird and gain a moral: don't go it alone, or attend to the changes, if you must. Know what's going on, but don't think you know it all. Tribe transcends the terminal *first* person, the existential "hero" as clown in communal terms at best. The comic mistake is a valuable teaching. Every Trickster tale in North America turns on this point. It is endemic to what Richard

Preston among the eastern Canadian Algonkian in *Cree Narrative* (1975) sees as a "conditional" sense of reality—nothing is fixed, except the folly in people's minds, the illusions inversely sparked by reality, and the inexorable laws of mortality. There is always hurt in humor, and vice versa, because that is the way things are. It's the way one learns about truth, the hope for survival, and the joy of having survived to the moment. So keep your mouth shut and pay attention.

Hopi child clown. (Photograph by Owen Seumptewa, Hopi)

Hence, that infamously clipped plains plain style, verging on absolute reticence ("yep," "nope," at best "mebbe"), and the mask of the silent warrior, the cigar-store Sioux laughing up his buckskin all the way to the meat cache that gets him through a hard winter.

Surely there's some aggression or stricture here, what Huizinga calls the *agon* of all play: things hang critically at stake, and talk runs secondary to experience. Just as surely, humor comes into play, peppering the pain, even transcending it; for Bordeaux's bird is just wordplay, an artistic tale elegantly and still modestly structured, concise, witty. We are *not* little birds. We need not perish in the cowshit. We need only know that we can mistake circumstances, must evade predators, should identify our friends, and want to know the right time to open our mouths. Our lives depend on it.

Lionel Bordeaux *told* this story. It was an "oral" text, a contemporary performance before an audience, tribal in origin, Indian as pumpkins, buffalo, and beans. He spoke as one of "the people," unpretentiously street-smart, scatologically basic, critically sharp to things-as-they-are. As I listened, it seemed that Bordeaux was speaking to me, an alleged specialist in American Indian studies. Both of us no doubt felt ourselves as the bird at stake; both of us wanted to survive educational winters, academic cats, departmental barnyard politics. Secretly we were hoping to elude or snatch the cat (if cats had wings, the Chinese say, there would be no birds). We were there to talk across the red-and-white fence, and he told me something interesting: listen, think about it, apply it, and appreciate the art of survival, a critical skill.

Postscript: don't forget the joke. It was a lesson in coding and decoding texts. Rather than the fashion of jamming the reception and littering the texts, here one might argue the ludic reconstruction of a kinetic message and moral. Quicken your wit, temper your ego, work with a contrary world-as-it-is, and hope for better.

3

Playing Indian

Old men should be explorers?
I'd be an Indian.
Oglala?
Iroquois.

THEODORE ROETHKE, "The Longing"

Comic Interface

While Freud and Huizinga collate the constants of joking and play,
closer to home Lame Deer and Vine Deloria detail the "precious gift"
and pan-tribal "cement" of Indian humor. The contemporary writings
of Native Americans take shape as we deduce, define, and refine the
particulars and parameters of tribal humor: culture-specific in time and
place, textually detailed, contextually grounded. Where non-Indian the-
orems break down or blur, tribal paradigms rethread a doubly woven
translation that interfaces cultures. Lionel Bordeaux's fable about the
late-migrating bird tells us much about the straight-on, seminomadic
Sioux, while "Tumbleweeds" says something about non-Indians looking at Indians as totemic natives ignobly cartooned. It is informative to
look at Indians watching non-Indians watch Indians. The comic lens
warps both ways, as we see ourselves framed in seeing "others."
    In January 1988, John Trudell and I were interviewed on the televi-
sion program "Mid-Morning Los Angeles." A former AIM leader,
Trudell spearheaded the 1969 Alcatraz occupation. He led the 1972
sacking of the Bureau of Indian Affairs (BIA), and a few hours later his
entire family was murdered by an arsonist in Utah. John dropped out of
sight for a decade, then returned to public life as a rock lyricist and poet

with Grafitti Band [*sic*], accompanied by the Kiowa guitarist Jesse Ed Davis.

As the interviewer warmed to the idea of Indians among us, the fact surfaced that over five hundred *different* tribes remain extant in the United States alone (two thousand distinct peoples in the Western Hemisphere).

"How do Native Americans feel," the interviewer asked, "when we lump them all together as Indians?"

"Well, not so bad," John replied, "we lump all whites together." The interviewer did a double-take, and John added off the cuff that whites seem "almost genetically" predisposed to media control by the greedy, an observation left untouched.

"Don't you resent the term 'reservation'?" the interviewer asked.

"No, not really," John replied, "because I think all of America is a reservation today." This country, rich off native lands and resources, should rightly "give back" 10 percent of the GNP to its indigenous peoples, John thought, to be shared equally by the needy. That lit up the phone board.

Heyoka-style, this Santee activist-turned-rock-lyricist played "contrary" on public television. He consistently reversed the interviewer's questions with the straightest face possible, and warped the projections back on white consciousness. This deflecting trick mirrors the "other," while reversing any advance with comic shields. John Trudell stayed cigar-store stoic: carefully considering each question and dropping ethnic depth charges all along the way. Such a scenario has been repeated for five centuries now across Indian America, from treaty councils in Philadelphia "at the forest's edge," to Sitting Bull's speeches in the 1880s, to "field work" with anthropologists in Arizona in the late twentieth century, to UCLA classes in American Indian studies. Cultural awareness comes by way of self-caricature, as America invents the Indian "other."

Rayna Green, Cherokee Smithsonian folklorist, thinks that whites have been playing Indians, and deadpan Indians "playing" whites, since the beginnings of cultural contact.[1] The historian Robert Berkhofer says much the same in *The White Man's Indian* (1978). From Henri II and his entourage at Rouen in 1550 (dressed as Tupi Indians for a Brazilian weekend in the French "village"), to colonial white women "captives," to the Boston Tea Party, to Sam Houston and frontier "squaw men," to the nineteenth-century "Improved Order of Red

Men" (a club along the lines of the Elks or Kiwanis), to Boy Scouts at
Camp "Runamucka" and YWCA fathers and daughters adopting "Indian" names, to the Washington Redskins in the 1988 Superbowl, whites
have, in effect, issued themselves a catchall license to play ethnic native
outside the mainstream. It is the native radical in our Western obsession
with free men and women, the imagined wilderness, the lost woods, the
recaptured natural world.

At Las Vegas and Reno, a tourist can rent an Indian village. Back
East in 1988, rumors surfaced that Nancy Reagan and Joan Mondale,
wife of the former vice president, may be "distantly related" to
Pocahontas (cf. "Lady Rebecca" of the English court in 1614). By the
1960s, Carlos "Castanets" (Castaneda) added hallucinogins to the
equation, Rayna Green notes, and the flower generation blossomed
playing Indian. "Indianness becomes the key, then," Green surmises,
"to being American." A native seems to need an Indian root to legitimize and give license to American behavior.[2] And Indians are not
above playing Indians, from "Ms. Mazola" advertising corn oil on TV,
to Iron Eyes Cody in plains regalia lamenting pollution, to the Lord's
Prayer in sign language (Professor Green's favorite dumb show).
"Spear an Indian, Save a Fish," Wisconsin protestors of native fishing
rights chant, and the picture is complete in xenophobic caricature. Playing Indian is not only hilarious from both sides of the sideshow, but
endemic, if not generic, to the American character in a brave new
world. And in a larger sense, playing Indian is a Euroamerican mono-
myth popular from the time of Vespucci and Columbus, whose quincentennial we are celebrating.[3]

"All Men, All Kinds"

> Whatever the period, Native Americans have always reviewed the
> white man's national and personal characteristics and dramatized
> his actions, follies, and motives through art, performance, stories,
> and jokes. They have caricatured the fire and brimstone of the
> missionaries, the financial gouging of the traders, the hypocrisy of
> the great white chiefs, and the credulity of the anthropologists.
> DEIRDRE EVANS-PRITCHARD, "How 'They' See 'Us'"

In 1984 on a Fulbright lectureship, I researched European images of
Indians in Tuscany, Italy, where Amerigo Vespucci was financed by the

Medici five hundred years ago. In Heathrow Airport that summer, heading home, I spied Keith Basso's *Portraits of "The Whiteman": Linguistic Play and Cultural Symbols Among the Western Apache* (1979), published by Cambridge University Press. *The Tempest* seemed not so distant.

An impatient American matron, standing in line to declare her four value added tax rebates, sniped: "Are there any more of these 'foreigners' around?" She paused for emphasis. "We should keep 'em out, the Indians, the blacks."

"We're all foreigners, lady, to someone," I volunteered in a mutter.

"Well, yes, but . . . twenty years ago it wasn't like this—now the working jobs are too low for the blacks. It's whites doing the cleaning. . . . See where this has got us?"

On the plane I sat next to a kindly British bluestocking, a seventy-nine-year-old widow flying to visit American friends in Orange County, California. She had met them at the "Tom Mix or something ranch" and was drawn to "this tall dark man with a little bunny. I thought it was a pussy. You know I can't resist animals." She was a small woman in a plain blue suit with a pink blouse. Her cataracted eyes blinked as she engaged me in conversation: "I think they may be Indian."

"From India?" I puzzled.

"No . . ."

"American Ind. . . ?"

"Red Indian . . . by the name *Sky* Cloud." Her turquoise earrings, necklace, and Red Cross pin sparkled. "I have no fear. I simply *know* people, do you know what I mean?" She added that she admired the way Buddhists lived and hoped her visit wouldn't go wrong.

I still don't know exactly what she meant. That plane trip home nags me as though I'd just glimpsed the world to be round.

As I read Basso's Apache jokes about "the whiteman" high over Eric the Red's ocean passage to the New World, I thought of my antiethnic compatriot in line at the airport, a bona fide Ugly American, and my bluestocking flight mate. The American was intolerant of any "other," the Briton curious about Indians in southern California. I wondered how Indians would cartoon this exchange.

Why *do* Euroamericans play Indian? There would be no need to study something we already know: hence the anthropological "other" as Native American. Film and fictional "Indians" get even more exotic. Scholars have varying intentions, from personal to professional ambition, from tribal friends to tenure, but all Euroamericans seem to enjoy what Freud calls regressive "release" in playing out childhood libidos as "free" natives. This nativist impulse engages the intercultural play of choosing the "other" side in Cowboys and (American) Indians. We indulge a permitted "disrespect" of sorts in our native libidos, as well as knowing that we are *not* Indians. This ethnic othering results in a culturally comic bisociation, fundamentally ironic, steeped in historical slippage. Finally, with undaunted humor we freely play the challenge of the national frontier, and we go native in some aboriginal play-sense. The antiethnic American tourist at Heathrow, shopping bags in hand, stands on one humorless side of this paradigm, refusing the "other's" otherness; and the visiting Englishwoman sits next to me on the curious opposite, wanting to know more about the dark man with the furry bundle, *Sky* Cloud. Offstage audience to this split would be today's Indian. I take notes in Basso's margins, reading of Cibecue Apaches in their kitchens joking about whites:

J: Hello, my friend! How you doing? How you feeling, L? You feeling good?

[J now turns in the direction of K and addresses her.]

J: Look who here, everybody! Look who just come in. Sure, it's my Indian friend, L. Pretty good all right!

[J slaps L on the shoulder and, looking him directly in the eyes, seizes his hand and pumps it wildly up and down.]

J: Come right in, my friend! Don't stay outside in the rain. Better you come in right now.

[J now drapes his arm around L's shoulder and moves him in the direction of a chair.]

J: Sit down! Sit right down! Take your loads off you ass. You hungry? You want some beer? Maybe you want some wine? You want crackers? Bread? You want some sandwich? How 'bout it? You hungry? I don't know. Maybe you get sick. Maybe you don't eat again long time.

[K has stopped washing dishes and is looking on with amusement. L has seated himself and has a look of bemused resignation on his face.]

J: You sure looking good to me, L. You looking pretty fat! Pretty good all right! You got new boots? Where you buy them? Sure pretty good boots! I glad. . .

[At this point, J breaks into laughter. K joins in. L shakes his head and smiles. The joke is over.]

K: *indaa? dogoyą́ą́da!* ("Whitemen are stupid!")[4]

An Apache breaking into English at home "frames" himself as a stand-up comic in whiteface. Such fatuous italicizing collapses when it points a finger, thus comically plays nonsensical surface against more serious Indian values. The mask of dialect gives J a persona to play out dangerous intrusions which sets up a displacement in the "other" tongue not to be taken too seriously, but certainly never to be forgotten. For the moment, both cultures are game for gambol, Apache norms suspended, Anglo offenses bracketed.

J doubly encodes cultures by calling undue attention to what everyone sees and knows. Welcome needs no fanfare among friends in Apache camps, where talk is relaxed and economical. Feelings can be quietly shared, not paraded: "my friend!" is not going to appreciate prying directives. "Maybe you sick, need to eat aspirins!" Basso notes a reservation sarcasm. The caricature "permits" playing out differences between Apaches and whites at the latter's expense. It mediates underlying "disrespect" by bringing offense to the surface, a joke played back on the intruder. "I know all what make you sick, *everything!*" the Apache joke. "So just you don't *forget* it!" The dramatic context is as old as a Greek actor playing *alazon,* or an Athabascan storyteller donning Coyote's mask.

Apache jokes work like stretching stiff new deerhides into soft buckskins, the Cibecue tell the anthropologist. This tanning metaphor, or civilizing trope, is not just another instance of the poetic Indian mind at play, but a cultural interface between Indians at home and imposing "round-eyes" in transit (missionaries, politicians, medical "experts," former VISTA workers, aging hippies, social scientists, tourists, teachers). "Don't," "bad," and "not" head the list of unholy white negatives—generating counter-Apache jokes in English, where the natives code-switch to "play" whites. "Lots of Whitemen, you can tell right away they looking down at you. They look too much, talk right away, shake your hand, like that. Some make lots of questions right away. No good. They just doing it for theyselves. So we try to get away fast" (*Portraits* 107). Thus Basso argues, the jokes show us not only ourselves once removed, "out"-landish and nay-saying boors caricatured among Indians, but Apache values in microcosmic inversion. "Some never learn to wait" (107). It's another contrary lesson, via Indi'n humor.

Less than an individual, "Whiteman" is a genre made up of cultural symbols and social categories (akin to "Euroamerican" or "western-

er"). Whitemen shake imperative fingers at "Indians" all the time—
"they" represent what the Indi'n is *not,* or so the Cibecue mime visitors. The coercive non-Indian is here anti-Indi'n. Indirection, nonasser-
tion, and name avoidance constitute Apache norms, while whitemen
misuse names and call Indians "frens" like "it was nothing, like air,"
Apaches complain. Whitemen touch one another "like dogs," say
natives whose modesty limits direct physical, visual, and cultural contact. Anglos "run over" others with their talk. "It's like shooting rabbits with a .30-.30" (*Portraits* 52). The Apache as a people remain
(ideally) reserved, self-contained, explicitly coded in their behavior. So
the "privileged license" of playing whites sets Indians free to test their
own values by mocking their opposites. "Whitemen" and "Indians,"
John Trudell said deadpan on TV, gunnysack each "other" ideationally.
These images fantasize others in regard to what we are not. Jokes
function in this instance like bubble mirrors that fisheye the tribal terrain
conversely at dangerous intersections.

"Whitemen" invert the Apache "good," *nzhoo* (ideally, at least,
attentive, quiet, considerate, reserved, humble, understated) by being in
caricature inattentive, garrulous, rash, petulant, arrogant, pretentious.
"Whitemen make lots of noise. With some who talk like that—loud
like that and tight—it sounds too much like they mad at you. With
some, you just can't be sure about it, so you just got to be careful with
them all the time" (*Portraits* 55). Still, consider Silas John Edwards's
1904 logo—"all men, all kinds"—that serves as a section divider and
unifier in the Basso book. The ideogram functions as a comic signpost
presenting understated visual evidence that Apache humor is not simply
anti-white. The icon poses a more playful, if barbed, engagement with
the dangerous joke of an "other" among Apache kin. The cultural threat
of Euroamerica outside, and delicate tribal balances inside, charge intercultural joking with the "danger" of stretching deerhide into buckskin.

"All men, all kinds." (Icon by Silas John Edwards, Apache holy man)

Too much pressure, too little care, not enough know-how, more fuss than necessary, can damage the social play of red–white humor here. Silas Edwards was an Apache holy man who recently died at ninety-six. His ideogram suggests translateral balances, a torqued pattern that crosses in what Huizinga might see as a comic *agon*. The arms and shoulders stand open, yet supportive and supplicative of power above. They greet the gods and all "others," as do so many southwestern petroglyphs of hands open to the rising sun. They seem, too, to be lifting earthly burdens and the body itself. Above the proportionately small head (the mind's limits?) float four lines of winds, possibly "minds" or spirits. These lines rise upward as cultural persuasions— "all men, all kinds"—not just Apache or "white." The figure appears to wink (if not entreat) that it takes *all* kinds, all senses, all peoples to make harmony in this world. The image implies a pluralist humor, a many-minded recognition of peoples the world over. It is essentially a comic perspective, an open gesture of good will, a balanced vision of things.

This doesn't mean that Apaches feel no hostility toward the "whiteman." They play *through* their hurt, finding some measure of humor in intercultural friction. As Basso observes, "jokers use jokes to make sense of Whitemen" (*Portraits* 18). These jokes sharpen the portrait and clarify the problem. They humanize the difference, stylize the confusion, and finally lighten the burden of reality. As in Vincent Craig's Indian cartoons (which first appeared in the *Fort Apache Scout, the Navajo Times,* and the *Yakima National Review* in the 1970s), the caricatures refocus an otherwise too serious *otherness* in Indian affairs. Immediate visual evidence, a cartoon can turn threat back on itself in *Portraits of "The Whiteman."*

These cartoons tell us much about Indi'n humor. Born a full-blood on the Navajo reservation in 1951, Craig is an ex-marine, Navajo tribal policeman, musician, and law student who wrote the comic pop song "Rita," a top-ten Arizona Indian tune, in "Joe Babe" Navajo-English. Deadpan Navajo, the song is about an Indian who goes to prison for stealing a "crazy candybar" for his girlfriend. With zany precision, Craig's humor copes with the suffering he sees as a cop: "Indians can relate humor to anything. They get a laugh out of any type of situation. Whether it is hardships, poverty, adverse conditions, happy conditions, whatever, Indians can find something to laugh about."[5]

Originally, the cartoonist created Joe Frybread, a "rez" traditional,

and Billy Beans, an uptown Indi'n, to play off old- and new-style natives fencing with the "whiteman." They serve as a kind of Don Quixote and Sancho Panza, *alazon* and *eiron* in comic nomenclature. Mutton Man, a superhero, is a more recent invention who parodies white and red cultural myths as *bromolocho,* or buffoon. Craig's cartoons generally caricature the "whiteman" or a bespectacled native parody—a noisy, Anglicized Indian undercut by a tribal straight man. These "portraits speak for themselves," as Dell Hymes opens his foreword to Basso's study. Craig's strokes are bold, but not nasty; the visual cutouts often tell more than a shoebox of social statistics. Although the "whiteman" speaks English, and the Indian thinks in a related if abbreviated tongue, these two voices never interact in dialogue. One makes noise; the other thinks ironically to himself. "He thinks you looking him over," Basso's informant complains, "—like he's some cattle in a corral." There is a binary planing or shearing, hence the "comic" bisociation across cultural slippage. "My idea of success," Craig says, "is to have a law degree hanging over my desk, and be making my

"IN ESSENCE... COMMUNICATION IS AN IRREVOCABLE ESSENTIALITY!"

living as a cartoonist" ("Navajo Laughs" 18). He has since become a tribal judge.

Robert Freeman, a California Indian cartoonist, makes a living at intercultural caricature. Through Indian eyes Fort Knox appears as the white man's "sacred ground," and a desert skeleton is "the best White man I've ever seen." Tonto rides up to a seedy, squat Lone Ranger on a pony: "Guess Who?" A potbellied Indian man in Bermuda shorts wa-

ters his lawn outside a tipi: "That's a half-breed for you." Mounted braves peer into the distance toward smoke signals: "Can't make it out, but I think his tipi's on fire." And one of two men in a war party gestures toward a distant wagon train: "You go first, I went last time." A lone buffalo stampedes through an Indian village with grafitti on its side: "Chief Big Bear Is an Airhead." And "Custer's Last View" frames six grimly grinning braves staring down. These are the most Indian-sparked intercultural cartoons since those depicting Will Rogers,

I didn't get a shave, figuring I might pass as a native.

the Cherokee cowboy wit, who visited the Soviet Union in 1926 and wrote *There's Not a Bathing Suit in Russia* (1927).

Lame Deer recalls that at the age of five, he looked around his grandmother's skirt at his first "whiteman," who was bearded like a mattress come to life, bald where hair counted, and chewing something brown that tasted so bad he had to spit it out constantly. He sat heavily on his horse with a leather saddle hiding his "man-thing" in the horn. The comic discharge, the "play" of dissimilar cultural planes, connects this five-year-old Lakota's sketch to contemporary Indian cartoons. From tribal eyes, Anglos can look about as incomprehensible as the cigar-store Indian or "dog-eating" Sioux seem to whites. And Deloria's anthropologist "on the great summer adventure"—hula hoop, thick glasses, flying jacket, Australian bush hat, Bermuda shorts, and tennis shoes—sets out with a blonde "sexy wife with stringy hair" to make "OBSERVATIONS" of native life, as caricatured in *Everything You've Ever Wanted to Ask About Indians: But Were Afraid to Find Out!*

These cartoons' tone insults toward cultural negotiation. We can laugh at ourselves, as Basso does, laughing with natives laughing at us. This generates an intercultural sense of humor. After all, through native eyes we are the guests, the historical intruders. The not-too-serious play here rounds off our differences. The message, as such, seems more inviting than threatening—a bid, a bet, sporting across killing fields. Both sides double back reflexively to work toward bicultural acceptances of differences.

Cartoon by Carl Gawboy. (Courtesy of Carl Gawboy)

"AS AN EXPRESSION OF SELF-DETERMINATION, INDIAN
CENTERS HAVE SPRUNG UP IN COUNTLESS URBAN AREAS."

Cartoon by Carl Gawboy. (Courtesy of Carl Gawboy)

Brecht called this bisociation the "double-take" of comedy (*Portraits* xv). As Clyde Kluckhohn lectured on Hopi ritual clowns miming Navajos and non-Hopis, "For Hopis, making fun is a way of making sense" (96). The clown, the cartoon, the joke hangs between cultures. For a moment we "permit" some show of disrespect, leaving us "free" to laugh at our own shortcomings. Humor strengthens clarity beyond ethnocentric blinders, resilience under old scars, or healing beneath present wounds. Our intercultural laughter suggests a better future.

The elder Apache Nick Thompson taught Basso Cibecue place names and "stalking with stories" through the tribal persona of a "Slim Coyote." Names and narratives carry tribal norms by way of the permitted disrespects of humor. "This is what we know about our stories. They go to work on your mind and make you think about your life."[6] The Arizona landscape is the Apache locus for such moral narratives, which not only entertain and instruct, but anchor the people tribally. "I know that place," says a young woman cured of wearing curlers by her grandmother's story. "It stalks me every day" ("Stalking" 40). From Trickster tales to tribal gossip, the people's daily narratives embed chronotopic "maps" in Apache minds. "Storytellers are hunters for the Western Apache," Basso summarizes, "—and stories, arrows; and mountains, grandmothers—by virtue of shared beliefs about the world" (50).

All this metaphoric cultural thinking is mixed up with a lot of clowning around, including sexual jokes about Basso's sunburned nose as evidence of advanced venereal disease. With his blue Nike sneakers trimmed incandescent orange and his "Disneyland" T-shirt, Nick taught this linguistic anthropologist how namings put the Apache back into the *right* "places": "That story is changing you now, making you want to live right. That story is making you want to replace yourself" ("Stalking" 42). Stories put people back into the right physical place; that is, "place" determines right behavior, and tribal placement determines Apache identity. What others might dismiss as just talk or simply a river or only a hill keeps the people "*spatially anchored* in the Arizona desert," Basso writes, keeps them morally in line, culturally Apache. Humor bedrocks these stories. "These are all good places," Nick tells Basso of his Cibecue home. "Goodness is all around. I'm happy you know that now." The anthropologist recalls that they then began "to laugh . . . and laugh and laugh," and wearing a blue and white "Ford Racing Team" cap, Nick, crippled from childhood, sped off in his new wheelchair (47).

"Serious thinker and salacious joker alike," Nick loved to tease this white anthropologist with "farewell" jokes: "He says I look lonely. He urges me to have prolonged and abundant sex with very old women. He says it prevents nosebleeds. He says that someday I can write a book about it. Flustered and at a loss for words, I smile weakly and shake my head. Delighted with this reaction, Nick laughs heartily and reaches for his coffee and a chocolate-covered doughnut" ("Stalking" 24–25).

For some thirty years Keith Basso has frequented Cibecue, speaking an Apache dialect, soaking up the place, and thinking about Indians. His classroom with Slim Coyote is often under an old cottonwood. Basso's Apache jokes mirror Indians and whites intermixing, resistant to merging, idiosyncratic in regional dialects and cultural slants. This academic crossed the Great American Desert and lived in one southwestern place long enough to be talked with, joked about, and trusted— indeed, to catch the finer nuances and long-term contexts of modern Indi'n humor from the "other" side looking back. He has learned "their" language and mapped a sociolinguistics of everyday work and play, from stringing fences to singing 49s (powwow social songs). In lieu of Indian exotica, Basso contextualizes discourse from kitchen caricature to campfire kitsch, trading post to beer party—the extemporaneous humor of tribal culture in the making.

Another linguist-cum-poet, not so formally trained, lived with the Pit River Indians in north central California fifty years back. Jaime de Angulo, the "Buckaroo Doctor," served as a linguistic field worker for Boas, Kroeber, Radin, Lowie, and Sapir at the University of California, Berkeley, in anthropology's formative days. De Angulo had a brilliant ear for languages, a coyote flair for the unconventional, and a wanderlust to live on the margins. Born Parisian Basque in 1888, he came to Wyoming as a dislocated sixteen-year-old cowboy; by twenty-four, he had a medical degree from Johns Hopkins. De Angulo then ran a Monterey cattle ranch and during the 1920s taught at Berkeley, while mastering seventeen Indian languages and translating for Carl Jung. After a tragic accident and second divorce, he lived in 1940 as a hermit in Big Sur, seen only with Robinson Jeffers, the musician Harry Patch, or Henry Miller. Jack Kerouac sketched him in *Desolation Angels*, Marianne Moore corresponded with him, and Kenneth Rexroth became his compatriot. Ezra Pound, William Carlos Williams, Robert Duncan, and Allen Ginsberg befriended de Angulo during this hard time, when he found Indian company preferable to white society. Jaime began to wander, go "wild," and lost his shadow, as Pit Rivers say. Pound called him "the American Ovid," and Williams considered de Angulo "one of the most outstanding writers" he had ever met. "Those are Coyote's bones, grandchild," de Angulo wrote, "the lightning never strikes over them." Blessed and cursed, Jaime de Angulo came as close to Coyote, the western Indian sacred clown, as a white man can.

De Angulo died in 1950, the year before Black Elk passed away. In his last years, he wrote *Indians in Overalls*, championed by Ezra Pound, who was then incarcerated in St. Elizabeth's mental hospital after being indicted for treason. Robert Duncan typed the manuscript at home and recalled "two brilliant old cranks, the one living in a cage, the other dying of cancer, contemplating the irony, and the absurdity, and the humor in their respective fates."[7]

De Angulo's portraits show his Indian friends as logical and compassionate people, "real Stone Age men" and women, gifted with an inventive if bedraggled humor: Jack Folsom, the mountainous Lena, Sukmit the hunchback Indian doctor and bosom friend ("how many ditches have we shared for a bed with a bottle of firewater?!"), Blind Hall the medicine man, Robert Spring, Old Mary, Old Kate the medicine woman, the cowboy Wild Bill (who told him much about Coyote Old Man). "I never saw such a goddam lot of improbable people," de Angulo writes in amazement and consternated love.[8]

The California Pit River Indians are still a troubled people when seen from the outside—land disputes, factions, political feuds, government betrayals, water and fishing complaints, and a decades-long battle with Pacific Gas and Electric Company. They hire, fire, and burn out *pro bono* lawyers faster than madrone dries on the hillsides. "I went to sleep with my head full of old-time stories, tin lizzies, *damaagomes* [medicinal powers] mixed up with engines, coyotes and sagebrush," de Angulo says (*Indians* 223). It is the sleep of the lost found elsewhere.

The Pit Rivers called whites "wanderers" or tramps (*enellaaduwi*), since they seemed homeless in the Gold Rush—"smart, but they don't know anything," Wild Bill said (*Indians* 241). Joking was often all the Indians in Ishi country had left from the land-grabbing, scalp-taking, and bounty-hunting. But de Angulo was taken in by these native Californians a decade after Ishi, the last Yana Indian, surrendered in Oroville. They slept in ditches and traveled where they liked and lived off the land, mostly on rabbits. De Angulo learned their tongue, *achumawi*, and relayed his notes to Berkeley academics, who did not always admire his life-style. "Decent anthropologists don't associate with drunkards who go rolling in ditches with shamans," de Angulo noted when the academy balked at financing his field work (225). For a "damn fool white man," as his medicine friend Sukmit teased, de Angulo made a pretty good Indian, an "Indian white man," Old Mary said. They credited him with an appreciation of their humor, their deeper culture and lives. He joined them to "sing together" waking up the *damaagomes*.

Is, kaakaadzi, the people greeted him, "Person, you are living." He lived his linguistics, not in catalogued grammars, but in the syntax of the everyday. He mastered the singsong Pit River speech (bitonal), gambled in the "hand-game" (marked bones for wagers) with Paiutes and Modocs up north, and soaked up their rhythms of movement—dancing, even dreaming and breathing, their songs, stories, creation myths, coyote tales, speeches, and quarrels. There was always a comic argument. De Angulo sparred with Sukmit: " 'What do you know about electricity?! Electricity doesn't work that way!' 'Hell, what do you know about *damaagomes?* You are nothing but a white man, a goddam tramp.' 'No, I am not a white man!' 'Yes, you are a white man, you are a white man forever!!' "

"Old Mary chuckled from over the campfire, 'You two always quarreling like two old men. You Indian, you white man, ha-ha-ha! You both crazy!' " (*Indians* 226). Wild Bill told him all about Coyote Old

Man, whom some tribes say thought up this contrary world (see Angulo's *Indian Tales*). Another gamer with bones credited the creator
Jesus as "the best gambler in the whole United States!" (216). But
Indians could never understand monotheism: "What is this thing that
the white people call God?" Wild Bill wanted to know. "They are
always talking about it. It's goddam this and goddam that, and in the
name of the god, and the god made the world. Who is that god, Doc?
They say that Coyote is the Indian God, but if I say to them that God is
Coyote, they get mad at me. Why?" (237). All Indians in America
know something of Coyote Old Man or his cousins Raven, Rabbit,
Deer, Loon, Spider, Crow, and Bluejay. These are the Trickster spirits
of old, still stirring things up. It's a certain comic vision embedded in
old myths. Laughter carries a powerful medicine when ignorance and
fear threaten, as so often among peoples. "All men, all kinds" must
come together, Slim Coyote said. And thus the Pit River people share a
rare and precious humor, recorded gently and deftly by Jaime de Angulo:

> So I sent them back on the train. Funny-looking pair they made at the station,
> bewildered, he with his long hair and his black sombrero, his long arms and
> his hump; she clutching a bundle; and her gray hair under a bright silk
> handkerchief we had just bought for her.
>   I spoke a word to the conductor for them. He smiled broadly; "Sure I'll
> take care of them. I know Indians. I was raised in Oklahoma." As the train
> pulled out, old Mary gave me the Pit River goodby: "*Is tus' i taakaadzee,*
> Man, live well! *Ittu toolol hakaadzi-gudzuma,* We also will live." (228)

Caliban, Again

> You taught me language, and my profit on't
> Is, I know how to curse. The red plague rid you
> For learning me your language!
>
> CALIBAN, in *The Tempest*

From a Basque hobo, to a Santee AIMster turned rock lyricist, to a
Harvard linguist and a Navajo cop this century, Indi'n humor convexly
mirrors red–white intercultural exchanges. The Buckskin Curtain filters
comic warps all the way across the Big Water. Since the Renaissance,
Europeans have fixated on the American Indian as new/old "free"

people of the Western world. D. H. Lawrence relocated to New Mexico among Pueblo Indians in New Mexico in the 1920s, and was culturally emblematic of Euroamerican migrations for some three centuries past. Raleigh's emigrant godson went back to Italy, the Old World motherland, published *Mornings in Mexico* (1927), and died of tuberculosis before he could return and write more of "native" Americans. "Lorenzo's" ashes lie beside his wife, Frieda, on the western slope of the Taos mountains, where his self-designed shrine intimates phoenix rebirth.

Ezra Pound, William Carlos Williams, H.D., and other Imagists rediscovered American Indian visual and verbal arts through the wild delights of Jaime de Angulo and insistences of Mary Austin, midwife of modern primitivism. Their contemporary nativism capped four centuries of Western organic thinking (as documented in Jerome and Diane Rothenberg's *Symposium of the Whole* [1983]). This neoprimitivism, supercharged with Indians, was registered simultaneously among the Fauvists in France, the short-lived Vorticist movement in England, Picasso's prodigious wonder over native African masks, the widespread interest in cave paintings eighteen thousand or more years old in southern France, and T. S. Eliot's "Waste Land" uses of modern ethnology.[9] In short, the "primitive" or "native" or "ethnopoetic" concerns of twentieth-century Euroamerican thinking, particularly in the arts, can be focused in play fascinations with the American Indian, long a symbol of native nobility and concomitant "savagery." This line runs from Montaigne writing on misconceived "cannibals," to Shakespeare's Prospero as the artist's shamanic surrogate, to Rousseau's noble savage, to *Chief Joseph of the Nez Perce* (1983), the epic poem by Robert Penn Warren, who became the United States' first poet laureate in 1986.

Non-Indians inventing "Indians" have long costumed and choreographed a comic pageant. Rousseau's "noble savage" sparked European romantics to idealize our lost brothers in the forest: Schiller, Schlegel, and Coleridge in the nineteenth century godfathered American "native" romantics in America, from Thoreau, through Whitman, to Hemingway, Snyder, Creeley, Berry, and Bly, among many others. Certainly, some of their works—Thoreau's *A Week on the Concord and Merrimack Rivers* (1849) or Snyder's *The Old Ways* (1977)—caught glimpses of Indi'n humor. Yet the divine rhymer Indian prevails, heroic tribal mascot or tragic capitalist victim. In the Lévi-Strauss syndrome, American primitivists claim European kin from Gauguin, to Pirandello,

to Stravinsky and Gaudier-Brzeska (who sculpted, Pound said, like a
"Red Indian" under a London railway bridge). Originally, Stravinsky's
ballet score *Le Sacre du printemps* (1913) was costumed and choreographed as something of a Pueblo folk dance with Russian sacrificial
overtones. Kafka fired up the "wish to become a Red Indian" in his
unfinished *Amerika* (1927): "If one were only an Indian, instantly alert,
and on a racing horse, leaning against the wind, kept on quivering
briefly over the quivering ground." Puccini even wrote an opera, *La
Fanciulla del West* (*The Golden Girl of the West* [1910]), with an Indian
female chorus. "Know then," Johann Herder wrote to a friend at the
end of the eighteenth century, "the more alive and freedom-loving a
people is . . . the more savage, that is, alive, free, sensuous, lyrically
active, its songs must be."[10]

Why? Other than opera buffa, what does this primitivist pulse signify
in Euroamerican thought and culture? What is the Western world culturally playing out in images of Indians? Why are we missing Indi'n
humor? Why this fascination with "wild" men who told the newcomers
that their native home was not a wilderness until the Euroamerican
invasion? Who are the Indians today, and what are they doing and
saying? When they laugh, do we listen?

"Chi sête?" wonders Cesare Pascarella's Christopher Columbus,
"Who are you?" as he "discovers" New World natives in *La Scoperta
dell'America* (*The Discovery of America* [1894]). "So'un servaggio,"
growls the "native" American parody in thick Roman dialect, "I'm a
savage."

Five centuries ago, the misnamed "red" Indian (from Iroquois face
paint, less than ruddy skin) was grafted on European thinking as a
stereotype plucked from medieval imagery of the "wild man" and in
turn transformed into a New World Caliban. The tag names mutated, as
Tzvetan Todorov sees in *The Conquest of America: Cariba*—Columbus
may have heard *Caniba,* or "dog"-headed cannibals under the Chinese
"khan"—cannibal, Caribbean, Caliban. Our wild stereotype derives
partly from tin ears and loose tongues. "There is nothing in that nation," Montaigne wrote with self-reflective irony, "that is either barba-
rous or savage, unless men call that barbarism which is not common to
them" (*Of the Cannibals,* a 1603 translation available to Shakespeare
while he was writing *The Tempest*). At the same historical moment in
the English Renaissance, a person crossing London Bridge could see
several dozen decapitated heads on pikes. Pilgrims released from the
Thames Clink Prison nearby had any number of reasons to emigrate.

   "Barbarian," from the original Greek usage, meant simply they
"stutter" (bleating *bar-bar* like sheep); loosely, they do not speak our
language. It seems ironically xenophobic to have misnamed "Indians,"
faulted them for not speaking "our" English, and five hundred years
later to have discovered a literary renaissance in red English. According
to the first popular visual images culled from explorers' wild accounts (a
1505 German woodcut in Augsburg or Nuremburg), the "Indian" foraged about naked, promiscuous, bestial, befeathered, warring, lawless,
godless, and cannibal. "Tumbleweeds" is tame stuff next to this savage
stereotyping. "They also fight with each other," Amerigo Vespucci
added: "They also eat each other even those who are slain, and hang the
flesh of them in smoke. They live one hundred and fifty years. And
have no government" (*Mundus Novus* 1503). Emerson years later ob-
jected to the Italian's tall tales: "Strange that broad America must wear
the name of a thief! Amerigo Vespucci, the pickle-dealer at Seville, who
went out in 1499 . . . in an expedition that never sailed, managed in
this lying world to supplant Columbus, and baptize half the earth with
his own dishonest name!" (*English Traits* 1856). Today, 87 of the 230
Brazilian tribes of Amerigo's day are extinct.
   With a "fascination of the abomination" reemerging four centuries
later in Conrad's *Heart of Darkness* (1899), Euroamericans inversely

The People of the Islands Recently Discovered (German woodcut, ca. 1505).

projected themselves onto their subjugated "native" and adopted a dark surrogate son (or daughter, as with Conrad's Cassandra, the Congolese mistress in the jungle who counters Kurtz's white "Intended" waiting for her romantic "hero" back home). So was born the barbaric wild child "Ca–Caliban"—stuttering Caribbean bastard of the Renaissance, *Tempest* offspring of a black African witch and an unknown paternal beast. It seems a twentieth-century twist on Kristeva's parable—Eros conceived as Penia seduces a satiated Poros at heaven's gates. "This thing of darkness," Prospero concludes, burying the book and reclaiming Caliban, "I acknowledge mine" (V.i.275–76).

The strange humor of intercultural and interspecies history stretches dangerously thin here. Hayden White argues that we have "despatialized" the wilderness by domesticating desert, forest, jungle, and mountain: "So that, instead of the relatively comforting thought that the Wild Man may exist *out there* and can be contained by some kind of physical action, it is now thought . . . that the Wild Man is lurking within every man."[11] Perhaps this precarious interiorization can also be seen in the caging and cataloguing of wild animals in zoos, a European public institution of the nineteenth century. Animals and Indians have long represented America's wild "others." "On the other side considering so good a Countrey, so bad a people," Samuel Purchas wrote in 1625 in *Hakluytus Posthumus or Purchas His Pilgrims:* "having little of humanitie but shape, ignorant of Civilitie, of Arts, of Religion; more brutish than the beasts they hunt, more wild and unmanly than that unmanned wild countrey, which they range rather then inhabite; captivated also to Satans tyranny in foolish pieties, mad impieties, wicked idlenesse, busie and bloudy wickednesse." Noble to ignoble spins on the xenophobic fear of our "savage" natives serve as the West's libidinous litmus test.

"Skins Red"

'Ban, 'Ban, Ca–Caliban
Has a new master. Get a new man!
Freedom, high day! High day, freedom!

CALIBAN, in *The Tempest*

In 1984 driving east of Trento along Lago di Caldonazza, I was intrigued by a campsite road sign, "Punto Indiani." There stood the international logo for camping—silhouette of a tipi, two crossed sticks covered with animal skin. This geodesic cone may have been the first "home" outside the cave. Living outdoors on vacation from "reality" allows us to fantasize the martyred Indian "wild" life of the West, where the "natural" way is now recreationally commercialized. The postindustrial nuclear family, an older *sacra familia* under urban stress, moves back to nature childlike on weekends, where natives cartoon our playing Indian: Dad at the campfire, Mom in the tent, Junior on the grass with the family dog. This desacralized trinity plays Indian outdoors as a skeletal tribe tracking glimpses of endangered wildlife, too often slaughtered road kill.

Dylan Thomas, the boy-poet and *enfant sauvage* of Wales, found his own Gaelic wilderness in "the Gorsehill jungle" of *Portrait of the Artist as a Young Dog:*

> On my haunches, eager and alone, casting an ebony shadow, with the Gorsehill jungle swarming, the violent, impossible birds and fishes leaping, hidden under four-stemmed flowers the height of horses, in the early evening in a dingle near Carmarthen, my friend Jack Williams invisibly near me, I felt all my young body like an excited animal surrounding me, the torn knees bent, the bumping heart, the long heat and depth between the legs, the sweat prickling in the hands, the tunnels down to the eardrums, the little balls of dirt between the toes, the eyes in the sockets, the tucked-up voice, the blood racing, the memory around and within flying, jumping, swimming, and waiting to pounce. *There, playing Indians in the evening, I was aware of me myself in the exact middle of a living story, and my body was my adventure and my name.*[12]

The Welsh poet's imagination equates sensuous childhood on all fours, dark nature, leaping animals, and riotous Indians at the existential center of a storied universe.

Wars, mechanization, taxation, racism, and nationalism have devastated Europe many times over. Yet the land still holds promise of daily bread and beauty (Mother Earth holds on), the animals decline to die off en masse, and the greening world is reminiscent of ancient tribal ways idealized in ceremonies, architectures, spirits, and arts (D. H. Lawrence, to Frank Lloyd Wright, to Carl Jung discovering *Black Elk Speaks* and Jackson Pollock spilling paint creatively à la Navajo sand painters). The world is potentially still a "house made of dawn," or so Scott Momaday reminds us by borrowing his Pulitzer novel's title from the Night Chant, a Navajo healing ceremony. It is an imaginary house at the moment, once dreamed real and redreamed as natural in Gary Snyder's *Earth House Hold* (1969), with open forest walls, a floor of Mother Earth, a roof of Father Sky. This is an old myth, gone fictive and *re*mythicized, as Hayden White argues of the wild man. The people's "house" would ideally be inhabited by two-leggeds, four-leggeds, wingeds, and roots all living together naturally. Native Americans refer to this "walk in balance" or "beauty" variously as alignment, harmony, reciprocity—*hozhó*, the Navajo say. It provides a mythic base for a sense of humor and well-being, a naturalistic vision of this earth and all its living things.

The traditional Indian world, in such mythic *re*-creation, points back to a natural world that Euroamericans fear they have lost, but then rediscovered in the act of losing. The death of Sam Fathers in Faulkner's *The Bear* signals The Fall of Caliban once more. This cultural myth elegizes the "vanishing" Indian–black American of the true wilderness before our Civil War, our Adamic self-expulsion from the sylvan Garden: "He lay there—the copper-brown, almost hairless body, the old man's body, the old man, the wild man not even one generation from the woods, childless, kinless, peopleless—motionless, his eyes open but no longer looking at any of them. . . ." The fictive death (and mythic resurrection?) of our American Indian godfathers triggers an elegy for our "greening" world—unpolluted, unaxed, unfenced, and unplowed. Here humanity would live in harmony with "wild" animal and vegetal life (the so-called wilds became so as we left or lost them). Under this house made of dawn, however, there would be less distance between tipi and *casa*, no walls between "in" and "out"doors, and literature could be drawn from dance, song, and ancient storytelling. The word would signify human presence, everybody together, speaking harmoniously. So we dream, given our fears, dislocations, and losses. Indian humor (through revisionist eyes, seeing ourselves see "them" in the warp of illusory play) may take us comically closer to Native America by understanding our distances and played kinships.

The popular mind, we know, invents Indians wildly the world over. Not long ago in Italy, the *Indiani metropolitani* dressed up like "savages" in skins and war paint to run through northern city streets, acting out anarchy as European "reds" in some 1979 Tuscan leftist version of the Boston Tea Party. Simultaneously, the Italian neoconservative wing adopted the noble Indian warrior as *its* totem: they thought that the stereotype conveniently linked ideas from Norse myths, *The Hobbit,* the

Ayatollah Ruhollah Khomeini's Islamic fundamentalist crusade, all ritually "wild" in a right-wing perspective. Indians get around. In effect, the Caliban myth went 'round the European political circle. Truckers pasted Indian decals on *autostrada* trailers. "Navajo American Marine," one double semi was marked south of Rome during Easter weekend in 1984. *Bisonette della Strada,* or "Buffalo of the Road," was written over the hood. "RIBELLIAMOCI CONTRO!" a poster proclaimed in downtown Florence, "LET'S ALL REBEL!" The poster's antimilitary, antiestablishment, antipenal campaign was illustrated by a mounted plains warrior with a war bonnet, buffalo horns, and carbine. Poster-size blowups of Edward Curtis's photograph of Geronimo, kneeling with a Sharp's rifle, were being sold on the Ponte Vecchio, the old butcher's bridge in early Medici days. It was here that American troops waded across the Arno and liberated Florence at the end of World War II.

Back home in northern California, Gary Snyder wiped his son's bottom and rhymed in *Ax Handles* (1983): "No trouble, friend, / you, and me, and Geronimo / are men." Add to this Uffizi wall graffiti, which featured warriors with rifles and tipis and squaws, near the statues of the solar heretic Galileo and the bastard genius Leonardo. "Go to a mountain-top and cry for a vision," an Italian with crayon had translated an American modernization of a Lakota vision song in Jerome Rothenberg's *Shaking the Pumpkin* (1972). Spray paint emblazoned "Ⓐnarchy" on the wall in its now international logo. All these street images superimposed a confusion of noble calls to the wild freedoms of the West on our lost Indians.

Fifty issues of Tex Willer comic books, cowboy-and-Indian thrillers with half-breed heroes, flooded my local newsstand in suburban Florence (one jungle and five Jedi comic books completed the rack). There seems no end to savagist curiosity. *Newlook,* a French soft-porn magazine, in January 1984 featured a forlorn "Wa Hu Wa Pa" of the southern Cheyenne, a sadly undressed Indian maiden in scanty feathers and furs. She was truly one of the *Pellerosse,* or "skins [feminine] red," a photographic "puma," the ad promised, on sale across from the Florentine Baptistry: "C'est la femme la plus dangereuse de l'Ouest," or "the most dangerous woman of the West." Meanwhile, back home around Thanksgiving 1984, Brooke Shields embraced a red-necked turkey on the cover of the revived *Vanity Fair* and posed Indianlike for a naked savage prince and four busty nymphs in "Running Bare," a fall fashion article. The sexy call of the wild hearkens back to Vespucci's naked

Tupinamba, Cortez's captive Aztec concubine La Malinche, Caliban's lust for Miranda, and repressed Euroamerican dreams of female animal libidos.

I discovered the ubiquitous war bonnet on a package of rosemary while seasoning Tuscan spring lamb. "Super Sioux" read the red, white, and green Bolognese label. The spaghetti Western is still with us, friends, spicing the wild discovery of America, over and again. "So' un servaggio."

Descendants of Columbus

> You laugh at my enthusiasm for savages as Voltaire laughed at
> Rousseau for wanting to walk on all fours.
>
> JOHANN HERDER, "From a Correspondence on Ossian
> and the Songs of Ancient Peoples"

Intercultural jokes pose certain kinds of comic treaties between differing peoples. "Heaven," a German-American friend told me, "would be organized by the Swiss. The French would cook and the English police the place. Italians would be the lovers and Germans the mechanics." Social context frames comic heavenly psyches. "And hell?" he grinned: "Organized by the Italians with the French as mechanics, the English cooks, the Swiss lovers, and the Germans the police." I suspect everybody would play Indians in both places.

Italians are not alone in savage fancies. The Germans dress up like Indians and return to nature in "Cowboy Clubs" (better old-time Kiowas than many of his kinfolk, Hanay Geiogamah once joked of Berliner "cowboy–Indians"). The English sport "Red Man" societies. The Dutch have NANAI—Nederlandse Aktiegroep Noord-Amerikaanse Indianen—plugged into the pan-Indian *Akwesasne Notes* from Upstate New York Iroquois, with a German periodical counterpart, *Amedian: Berichte aus dem Indianischen Amerika.* The Russians fancy a freshly translated anthology of American Indian literature, *I Stand in Good Relation to the Earth,* through the Gorky Institute of World Literature in Moscow. Until her recent death the Polish had a kindly old woman known as Indian Grandma, *Indianska Babcia,* who wrote to Indian political prisoners, slept with a handful of Wounded Knee dirt under her cot, and organized the Polish Movement of Friends of the

American Indians (PRPI). The French have Lévi-Strauss, a self-labeled "savage mind."

"What would I not give / To bring back the rare and orchid-like / Evil-yclept Etruscan?" D. H. Lawrence pined sixty years ago in Tuscany.

> Evil, what is evil?
> There is only one evil, to deny life
> As Rome denied Etruria
> And mechanical America Montezuma still.

> ("Cypresses")

Our American natives back home remain the "new" men and women of the old garden, Adamic Calibans and dusky Eves. We must ask honestly: Have Euroamericans merely relayered an exotic archaeology of wild man images? Why should these peoples so permeate our Western nostalgias, romantic fancies, and wild desires? Can a long-muted Indi'n humor correct these longings, or at least update and place them in more realistic, if not healthier, contexts?

During the summer of 1984 in Munich, a hospitable dealer in native arts took me to the opening of a South American Indian ethnographic exhibit, presented by a friend of his, a "free-style" German ethnologist—in the central Platz of Dachau in the brand-new Dresdener Bank. Looking through a teller's window to the open floor exhibit, I jotted some notes:

> South American Indian arts and cultures, photos of native people, here in Dachau, in the Dresdener Bank, with a smiling Schwabish president, champagne, snacks, and eventually steins of beer—with the cries of dying Jews in the air, over the pink stuccoed Bayern homes, the roofs pitched against heavy snowfall, all smacking of German affluence and shrewdness and good will, quaint in a storybook way, like Disneyland, and still the horrible palimpsest of gas chambers, wooden bars of soap, waterless showers, files of Jews dividing in two, the workers and the dispensables, and right there in color photographs, "Indianer," acculturating like good civilized tribes, a transistor radio on one man's arm, and the head-hunting Jivaro, with priceless saffron feathers, poisoned spears, hallucinogens: "Die *letzten* Indianer" it says, the last. And the poster asks, "Wer ist ein Indianer?"

Who, indeed, *is* an Indian, according to whose *wild* definition? William Carlos Williams believed "the average American to be an

Indian"—that is, "an Indian robbed of his world" (*In the American Grain*). In order to check ethnic slumming, how much of "the horror" need be remembered? American Indian humor mixes compassion and judgment even in the darkest of Trickster histories—incest, murder, violence of all sorts, compulsive recreant behavior—while it plays with encoding variable tribal rules. It is one of the few true voices left of survival. Still, hurt is hurt, and however palliative the humor, the dark reality remains a part of history defined by definitive Indian losses.

In the West with Indians, clearly we regret and regress where we decimate. Euroamericans have been tracking Caliban in print, as he has been dispossessed in person. Such tunnel-vision pity leaks from Pope's "Lo! the poor Indian" of "untutored mind" and "simple Nature" and "faithful dog" in his *Essay on Man* (1733), to Elias Canettis' 1976 Munich address elegizing the "incomparable creations by people who, hunted, cheated, and robbed by us, have perished in misery and bitterness."[13] Perished? Who are these 2 million survivors in the United States? What about some 30 to 40 million Native Americans present today in the Americas? According to this Nobel Prize *Dichter,* the "writer's profession" now is to preserve and resurrect the "inexhaustible spiritual legacy" of Indian cultures. All good intentions notwithstanding, how and for whom? Is Frye's comic spring under the ground of Indian humor? Could not Indians speak, write, and joke for themselves?

Removal, reeducation, and relocation have devastated but not vanquished Native Americans. Without indulging defeat or cultural sado-masochism, we *must* remember a measure of what happened, if only to keep it from happening continually. Indi'n humor is a way of recalling and going beyond tragedy, of working through the hurt of personal history, of healing old wounds and hearing the truth of what's happening among Native Americans. It is the most vocal and effective voice among Indians today, if not yesterday.

To Euroamerican leftists in the romantic backwash of the past century, Indians would symbolize the failures of New World capitalism and underscore the needs for social redefinition. They argue for a more communal contract between individual and state, especially in light of so many of our tribes dispossessed of pastoral communalism (count the number of small American farms going under these days). Marx saw British labor dispossessions in his father's factory over a century ago and went to the British Museum to write his way through the causes.

"Was anybody more Indian," asked a pamphlet at the European American Studies Conference in Rome in 1984, "than Karl Marx?" Somehow the British Museum, colonial archive of the West, seemed the fitting place for Marx to pen *Das Kapital* (in 1867, the year preceding the Red Cloud Treaty, which is still contested in the courts).

Up through three floors of the British Museum today towers a cedar Haida totem pole. At the top of this Indian stairwell in 1984 stood an exhibit on Jamestown colony, "Raleigh and Roanoke," since come to America. The new "virgin land," or Virginia, by the end of the sixteenth century offered an ideal military outpost, the notes said, from which to attack Spanish fleets sailing with stolen gold and silver up the Gulf current from Central America. "God for gold" was native trade among Westerners, Todorov reminds us. This first "lost colony" of Roanoke, however, disappeared Indian-style into the Algonkian woods, leaving only one word, the cryptic message "CROATOAN" carved on a post. So from the initial English contact with "salvages" we retain only John White's original drawings, etched by Theodore de Bry in the London-published *America* (1590, when Shakespeare was beginning his theatrical career). These are tattooed, naked, animal-skinned, feath-

After Jacques Le Moyne, *The Youth of Florida* (1591).

ered, hunting, warring, dancing, playing, fornicating heathens, not so distant kin, the intruders thought, to South American "cannibals."

Caliban, again. What Raleigh noted then as "cockes combes" in Huron hairstyles resurfaces today—dyed turquoise, orange, or blue—in the London punk street scene. The "savage" still lives as the West's "other" child.

In another part of London in 1984 was mounted a New England native exhibit, "Thunderbird and Lightning," headlining the Museum of Mankind. This museum, near fashionable Sackville Street, houses the ethnological treasures of the British Museum. In the heart of the archive, radial center for Britain's borrowed artifacts of the world— ghostly Polynesian and African statues, Maori masks, and Inuit carvings—sits a crystal Aztec skull. It grins from a glass case and is about the size of a grapefruit. This crystal cranium, likely stolen by Cortez from the Aztecs, sums up stereotypes of the Euroamerican Caliban, yesterday to today. Its chiseled teeth grimace through time. As I stood staring at the afternoon light blur through this memento mori, a guard brought in a brown felt cloth to cover the case at closing time.

Why?

No one knew. I went from attendant to director to research librarian, and all shook their heads. I pressed a guard, who finally offered that the "colored" who cleaned in the morning was afraid of this grinning crystal skull from the New World, a native *risus sardonicus*. So they agreed to put it to sleep under a brown cloth. I left the Museum of Mankind hearing Marlow mutter of the Intended in *Heart of Darkness:* "I could not tell her. It would have been too dark—too dark altogether. . . ."

The Indian *is* America to the Euroamerican, on both sides of the Big Water. The image is an intercultural invention with its own ghostly and ironic reinventions. Indian America reflects at once our shame, our promise, and our native origin. Indian humor could be our salvation, a new way to look at what we have made of our world and what can still be done. The Native American figures as national icon of our original ecologist, our "wild" man, our fertile woman, our warrior, our noble savage, our skilled craftsman, our communalist, our "free" outdoorsman, our hunter, our fisher, not so often our planter in folklore (though 90 to 95 percent of native diets were from horticulture), finally our prophet of the future. And as the world struggles to tribalize against self-annihilation, that future brightens comically against collective darkness.

"O brave new world," Miranda delights in *The Tempest,* "That has such people in't!"

A drunken Stephano defers to Caliban, "O brave monster! Lead the way."

4

Old Tricks, New Twists

I

Some say that Coyote first appeared on a raft
That Coyote created the world
That Coyote is very old   the first one
That Coyote put the stars in the universe
That Coyote fucked up the planets
That Coyote is the giver and taker of life
That Coyote stole fire for the people
That Coyote can change the seasons

II

Some say that Coyote dances in a feathered cape trimmed with
    flicker quills
That Coyote plays a flute and is the best dancer around
That Coyote has more clamshell and magnestie beads than you
    can imagine
That Coyote can make redbud burst into bloom by staring at it
That Coyote wanted to be a falling leaf and tried it
That Coyote was looking for figs and followed a male
That Coyote is a poet
That Coyote is a fool

III

Some say that Coyote is on the streets and in the alleys
That Coyote lives in L.A. and San Francisco and eats out of
    garbage cans
That Coyote talks to his asshole and usually takes its advice
That Coyote howls at the moon because it never stays the same
That Coyote doesn't like change
That Coyote is change

IV

Some say Coyote wears a black leather jacket and hightop
    tennis shoes
That Coyote thinks Rose is a good singer

That Coyote eats frybread peanut butter and jelly
That Coyote will use you if you don't watch out
That Coyote will teach you if you let him
That Coyote is very young   the new one
That Coyote is a survivor

Some say Coyote is a myth
Some say Coyote is real

I say Coyote is
I say Coyote
I say Coyote

HARRY FONSECA, "Coyote"

Red Renaissance

For Europeans, no less than Americans, Caliban reemerged a chthonic shaman shrouded in vines of rhetoric, recently Don Juan of the desert courtesy of Carlos Castaneda. "By the shores of Gitchie Gumee," Longfellow metered Schoolcraft's Algonkian narratives to Finnish Kalevala rhythms, as he silted Iroquois heroic myths into Ojibwa trickster cycles. Mary Austin, with "Amerindian" insights in *The American Rhythm* (1923), argued for a primal American earthbeat that pulsed with mystic savagery in twentieth-century art. In reference to the new *vers librists* and Imagists, Austin prefaced George Cronyn's *The Path on the Rainbow* (1918), among the earliest anthologies of Indian song-poems: "the discovery that the first free movement of poetic originality in America finds us just about where the last Medicine Man left off." Americans instinctively reached "for a deeper footing in their native soil," Austin thought, and Indian song-poems struck bedrock. Natives held an Edenic balance with nature that Western man longed to recapture, if indeed paradise ever was his province.

About this time, Lawrence was coming down West, from England via Germany to New Mexico, to chant "the insurgent naked throb of the instant moment" in his American *New Poems* (1919). Again, for Europeans of the past five centuries, America was radically new, Indians mythically old and exotically remote. They extended a natural way of life that every culture looks back to—a native green garden before the

Fall. It has been a biblical myth institutionalized in the West for two thousand years, bracketed at the other end by an Apocalypse awaited with strange Fundamentalist faith.[1]

The American Indian, to recapitulate, seems mythically our fresh origin in the New World: a romantic paradox that images ancient beginnings mythopoeically new, Adam and the fallen angel superimposed on Caliban. Americans mythologize the Indian Adam, from Hiawatha to the late actor Will Sampson, from Longfellow through Austin to Peter Matthiessen's native manifesto, *Indian Country* (1984). This is "America as Lost Paradise and the Indian as its Dispossessed Spirit," Peter Nabokov snipes.[2]

So these days, from Tzvetan Todorov, to Umberto Eco, to Claude Lévi-Strauss, the Old World is rediscovering the discovery of Caliban. In the Bologna train station, I found *La Riscoperta dell'America* (1984) by the Italian literati Umberto Eco, Gian Paolo Cesarani, and Benjamino Placido. "La conquista del West?" Placido asks: "Un massacro." Essayists of the primitive backtrack the "native" American through a wild new populace of Old World expatriates and New Natives radically American—restless, nomadic, volatile, godless, cultureless, and ahistorical. "So' un servaggio." So goes the stereotype. To Europeans, rightly or wrongly, America seems naturally wild at heart, and at the heart of this heathen nobility lurks the red man, *pellerossa* or *servaggio* in Vespucci's homeland, the buried archetype of the "wild" man.

Of course this is stereotyping at its worst, not for the first time freezing the dynamics of two thousand living Indian cultures in a two-faced cliché of American rebellion, noble and savage. The historian Robert Berkhofer prefaces *The White Man's Indian* (1978): "In the end, to understand the White image of the Indian is to understand White societies and intellectual premises over time more than the diversity of Native Americans." Fewer cardboard ideologies, indeed, more authentic talk and real information would serve to correct President Reagan's faux pas at the spring 1988 Soviet–American summit meeting, when asked by Russian students why an Indian delegation followed him to Moscow requesting a meeting denied hundreds of times in the United States:

> They from the beginning announced that they wanted to maintain their way of life. . . . And we set up these reservations so they could, and have a Bureau of Indian Affairs to help take care of them.

Maybe we made a mistake. Maybe we should not have humored them in that wanting to stay in that kind of primitive life style. Maybe we should have said, "No, come join us. Be citizens along with the rest of us."

I'm very pleased to meet with them, talk with them at any time, and see what their grievances are or what they feel they might be. And you'd be surprised, some of them became very wealthy because some of those reservations were overlaying great pools of oil. And you can get very rich pumping oil. And so I don't know what their complaint might be.[3]

This ethnocentric whitewash pervades America from top to bottom. The Bureau of Indian Affairs was started in 1824 as a branch of the War Department, and three decades later the government declared war against plains Indians. Reservations (President Reagan first called them "preservations") were established through military alliances, sale, trade, or dispossession of other lands. By 1889 "reserve" lands remained wasteland tokens for outright theft and betrayal. At the turn of the century, more than half the initial reservation land was stolen back. Today, tribal natives are statistically the most destitute in the world's richest country, and unemployment ranges from 50 to 90 percent on their reservations. Their diverse life-styles are not "primitive," but culturally different from the American mainstream. "They" *are* U.S. citizens as of 1924. Clearly not interested in Indian "grievances," Reagan never agreed to meet with any of their delegations. To fall back on red herrings of "oil-rich" Indians insults the common intelligence. "Most Indian people cannot get jobs pumping gas, let alone rich pumping oil," snapped Suzan Shown Harjo, executive director of the National Congress of American Indians.[4] It was a moment ripe for red humor. So Conrad's (June 1988) lampoon of the president dreaming about a "rich Indian" in a Cadillac, being driven past "polluting trees" to the welfare office for food stamps papered the country, a week after Reagan met with Gorbachev for the first Soviet–American Moscow summit since Richard Nixon's reign.

Reductionist red thinking glosses some 30 to 40 million American natives today in the Western Hemisphere. They considered their heritages and homelands everything but wild, until the arrival of European hordes. From Peru to the Bering Strait, most would simply like to be left alone, to live out their own lives as they choose: "a cultural leave-us-alone agreement," Deloria says in *Custer Died For Your Sins,* separatism with tribal humor.

Several hundred excellent Indian writers are alive today, among them recipients of Pulitzer, MacArthur, Before Columbus, Nelson Algren,

Los Angeles Times, and National Book Critics Circle awards: to name but a few, N. Scott Momaday (Kiowa–Cherokee), Leslie Silko (Laguna Pueblo), Louise Erdrich (Chippewa), James Welch (Blackfeet–Gros Ventre), Linda Hogan (Chickasaw), Lucy Tapahonso (Navajo), Wendy Rose (Hopi–Miwok), Roberta Hill Whiteman (Oneida), Mary Tall-Mountain (Athabaskan), Simon Ortiz (Acoma Pueblo), and Paula Gunn Allen (Laguna Pueblo–Lakota). These are interculturally collaborative Indians in societies where mixed-blood success among whites has not been long in favor. "They are certainly an improvement on the pale face, but not on the red man," Simon Pokagon, an educated Potawatomie and first major Indian novelist, reported tribes saying of "Half-breeds" ("The Future of the Red Man" [1897]). Once a negative racial slur, neither white nor Indian, the unifying concept of "breed" may indeed be a working definition of the American democratic experiment at its fullest. This is a new bicultural model of fusional diversity and complementary difference. Demographic immigrations and native migrations have pooled what is by now an international genetic bank, at its base mixed "native" American. Ray Young Bear is perhaps the exception in print, a "blood," or full-blood, writer who claims to first compose in his native Mesquaki, and then translate the poetry into English. Regardless of variants to prove the rule, "red" English comprises a common Indian tongue, the printed word presents a pan-Indian medium, and Western literary forms stand open to Indian experiences and experimentations. This remains acculturatively so, even as oral cultures—ceremonies, songs, and stories—revitalize the pre-Columbian origins of a reemerging Indian literature.[5]

The wilds call through old "blood" stereotypes that spellbound Lawrence among Southwest natives, so many Calibans, so nobly savage and contrary to white culture. "How deep the men are in the mystery they are practising," Lawrence intoned over Hopi snake dancing, "how sunk deep below our world, to the world of snakes, and dark ways in the earth, where are the roots of corn, and where the little rivers of unchannelled, uncreated life-passion run like dark, trickling lightning, to the roots of the corn and to the feet and loins of men, from the earth's innermost dark sun" (*Mornings in Mexico*). In "Hasty Pudding" (1792), written soon after the republic's founding, Joel Barlow husked the American ear more humbly: "all my bones are made of Indian corn" (indeed, cultivated corn is some twelve thousand years' native to the Americas).

Do not take this wrong. Deeply naturalistic mysteries ground hundreds of tribal ceremonial complexes today—from Iroquois Strawberry Festivals to Lakota Sun Dances, to Navajo Night Chants, to Pueblo Green Corn ceremonies. In some respects to be an American is to coexist with, if not to inherit, Indian tools and traditions, the fruits of ancient evolution in this hemisphere. Just as surely, Indian rituals involve sacred and secular play, fine charges of ritual humor. The several thousand Western Indian cultures differ significantly from one another and especially from other hemispheric cultures, though they may be closer to old China than England, to tribal Africa than post-Roman Europe.

Many "academic" Indians are now writing tribal literature in Western forms—adapting origin myths, trickster gods, healing ceremonies, or winter count histories to novels, plays, essays, and poems about being alive today. They know only too well, through their own pain, the psychopathology of Indian history and the need for alternatives. The Montana Blackfeet–Gros Ventre poet and novelist James Welch writes of surviving winters in the blood:

> That night the moon slipped a notch, hung
> black for just a second, just long enough
> for wet black things to sneak away our cache
> of meat. To stay alive this way, it's hard.
>
> ("Surviving")

From Montana to Maine, shadowy scavengers prowl Indian history. Welch wants options; he knows his people's losses well enough not to be trapped in them, even as he writes a trail through them.

"Any people at any time," writes D'Arcy McNickle, the Flathead historian, novelist, and Oxford scholar, "is a survival of fragments out of the past" (*Native American Tribalism*). This survival requires redefinition, as "being Indi'n" continues to evolve; witness the intertribal play of cultural recipes in Luci Tapahonso's "REALLY HOT CHILI!"

> Myself, I don't eat it straight.
> It's better mixed with beans or the kids' stew,
> which is plain without chili.
> They tease me about it but it's okay.
>
> Navajo fry bread and mutton are my specialty.
> Like my brother said I get along on sheep thrills.
>
> Some Pueblos just don't understand.
>
> ("Feast Days and Sheep Thrills")

More than 60 percent of the present 2 million Indians in the United States today, from superpower Navajo and Sioux nations to pockets of Quawpaw, Papago, Kwakiutl, and Penobscot, live *off* the reservation. California, whose tribes were decimated during the nineteenth century, is home to the second highest state population, 242,164 in the 1990 census. Los Angeles houses close to 120,000 Native Americans from all over. To the east, Oklahoma (literally Choctaw "red earth-people" land and Indian Territory during the 1830s Jacksonian Removal period) has some 60 tribes *without* reservations and 252,420 Indians. More than half the population of these 500 surviving tribes is mixed-blooded, or "breed," and the majority of 2 million live in urban wildernesses of the poor or in frontier ghettos south of the tracks.

Still, close to forty thousand native peoples are in American higher education, and some fifty-five American Indian studies college programs were in place by 1984. Twenty-four tribal colleges (sixteen accredited) were operating by 1991. This progressive biculturalism tends to upset Euroamerican stereotypes. Roberta Hill Whiteman speaks to her son from *Star Quilt* (1984), written while teaching in Oneida and on the Rosebud Reservation (she is on leave from the University of Wisconsin–Eau Claire, finishing a doctorate at the University of Minnesota in comparative literature):

We're caught in some old story,
I'm the woman winter loved
and you, the son of winter, ask
where did he go and why?
This poem gets cut to just one sentence:
You grow old enough and I get wise.
Yes, the days ride stallions
and leave us in the dust,
yet the details of these days
must imply a different ending.

This Indian mother would go beyond Caliban's curse. She would be educated in what-is, what Czeslaw Milosz sees as the "witness" of poetry and truth. Traditional Indian wisdom, a mother's nurturing, and poetic schooling coalesce in Whiteman's poetry, from the elders' teachings, to biosphere, to blank verse.

Indians need "wise" husbands, wives, doctors, lawyers, teachers, businesspeople, engineers, politicians, scientists, comedians—and writers—to speak to essential issues, to express Indian views, to offer male and female models of articulate success in both Indian and white America. The shamanic warrior, shadowed by Castaneda's fictional Don Juan, is not enough, if alluringly "nonordinary" in his trickster pasture. Native peoples cannot eat dust, they cannot farm lies, and they cannot survive on pastoral savagery or shamanic riddles. They will laugh intelligently to survive. Lady Coyote in Nia Francisco's " 'Snake Juice' Talk" (*Blue Horses for Navajo Women* [1988]) vows to run for Navajo public office:

> "Navajo women from
>   Low Mountain and Chinle Valley
>   will rally and rally
> for my campaign
> just about every day
>   at the new court house,"
> that's what she said
>
> "The Hopis took our land!
> We will take back our Navajo men!
>   and also take their Hopi men!"
> that's what she said
>   to her cousin
>
> (Sigh)
> It's only "snake juice" talk
>   and eatin' too much
>   "Big Mac" sandwiches for soo long!!

A humorless ethnocentrism holds Indian peoples at a disadvantage on both sides of rez lines. A bicultural or comically bisociative model might help to correct a "savage"-based separatism. Things change, and tribes reconstitute. Peoples define and redefine themselves culturally over time. "Nothing is that simple," Silko's mixed-blood medicine man says in *Ceremony,* "you don't write off all the white people, just like you don't trust all the Indians." As Dawson No Horse, a Lakota holy man, sang out with laughter during a night-long healing ceremony a few years ago in South Dakota, "We're gonna make it as we go along, addin' on an' addin' on, generation to generation."

Many cultures are "addin' on" these days, for mutual survival. Some European scholars—Äke Hulkrantz in Sweden, Christian Feest in Austria, Berndt Peyer in Germany, Gordon Brotherston in England, Jacqueline Fear in France, among many others—want to update Indian images to counter the Old World stereotypes of Caliban. In Italy, Gaetano Prampolini (University of Florence) and Laura Coltelli (University of Pisa) have initiated a Native American Series through La Salamandra Press in Milan to translate new Indian prose works.

The point stands, here and abroad: today's Indians are capable of contemporary literature, visual art, music, economic decisions, and political actions. This encompasses a broad spectrum, from the Mohawk poet Peter Blue Cloud writing Coyote poems, to the Navajo painter R. C. Gorman embossing pillowcases so we can "all sleep with" him. It stretches from the rock band Redbone (for "mixed-blood") singing "Crazy Cajun Cakewalk Band," to John Trudell and the late Jesse Ed Davis caricaturing Pat Boone with Grafitti Band lyrics.

> You take Pat in his white bucks
> Singing "Love Letters in the Sand,"
> Hell man, what's real here?
> I mean, Pat at the beach in his white bucks,
> His ears getting sunburned,
> Told us something about old-wave delusion.[6]

This new Indian coalition includes the on-and-off Navajo tribal chairman and Coyote business magnate Peter McDonald (pan-tribally "McDollar") replaced by a grass-roots Peterson Zah. It stretches from the Hollywood comedian Charlie Hill to the Chippewa AIM leader Dennis Banks trapping Pine Ridge prairie dogs to improve pasturage. Five hundred tribal voices in the United States emerge from diverse histories and aesthetics of Native America. Euroamericans deserve access to the full range of emerging cultures, with a sense of multiple perspectives, as free as possible from wild stereotypes, jargon, humorless diatribe, and anti-intellectual backlash.

Silko's medicine man says in a much-quoted passage from *Ceremony,* "long ago when the people were given these ceremonies, the changing began, if only in the aging of the yellow gourd rattle or the shrinking of the skin around the eagle's claw, if only in the different voices from generation to generation, singing the chants. . . . Things which don't shift and grow are dead things." Indian literature today records the humors of growing and changing peoples. Momaday ends

The Way to Rainy Mountain (1969) with a hundred-year-old woman singing of the Sun Dance:

> We have brought the earth.
> Now it is time to play;
> As old as I am, I still have the feeling of play.

A-hó!

"My Fellow Clansman"

James Wright wrote to Leslie Silko in the late summer of 1978, "I trust you don't mind hearing from a stranger." Both were poets, not entirely strangers. Wright had heard Silko read in Michigan three summers back, and now wanted to say "how much the book [*Ceremony*] means to me. In some strange way it seems inadequate to call it a great book, though it is surely that, or a perfect work of art, though it is one." He thought to call it "one of the four or five best books I have ever read about America," but that was not quite the point. "I think I am trying to say," Wright concluded, hesitant of misstatement, "that my very life means more to me than it would have meant if you hadn't written *Ceremony.*" It is strong praise, indeed, from such a candid man, so precise a craftsman. "I am very happy that you are alive and writing books," he closes this first letter from his last year's correspondence.[7] (James Wright died in 1980.)

Silko sent Wright long letters about the Arizona desert, her struggles to write, the black rooster that lorded over her yard, her horses and chickens, and her torments in being a mother separated from her children. The letters reveal daily privacies of her mixed-Indian humanity. James Wright reminded Silko of her Ohio grandfather, whose father, Robert Marmon, came west to marry her Laguna great-grandmother. She praised Wright's "directness and leanness" before everything else: "when I heard you I thought well maybe academic background only runs so far, and then finally it is simple guts and heart" (*Delicacy* 4). Just a year later, September 12, 1979, she was writing from Tucson: "I don't think anyone—no American—has ever written like you do, has ever written this American language like you do. You are fearless of the language America speaks and you love it. . . . You bring such grace and delicacy from it, coax out the astonishing range of dissonances and harmonies it allows us, that with your poems behind me I can speak confidently now about a beauty which is purely from the American heart." Wright's midwestern style touched Silko's idiomatic sense of American speech, echoed in the iconic cogency of red English. "When I say 'American' language I mean it in the widest sense—with the expansiveness of spirit which the great land and many peoples allow. No need ever to have limited it to so few sensibilities, so few visions of what there might be in this world" (83).

The English Institute had crabbed Silko's sense of style and vision, imposing a "standard" on American speech, as opposed to "the gully and railroad track, the sumac and coal smoke" in Wright's Ohio poetry. The home-grown complaint seems an issue of local poetic speech, regional tongue and heart, personal survival and humor. James Wright wrote to Silko from Paris on August 8, 1979:

> But no one could live with such passionate imagination, and write as beautifully as you write, without bearing some scars also, and it was these that I wanted to tell you I recognize and—in my own way—bless. We all seem doomed to a freedom to choose between indifference and sadness. I can't— or won't—be indifferent to life, and yet when I turn my face toward it, how sorrowful it seems. Referring obliquely to the beautiful works of art that perished when the Romans destroyed ancient Carthage, Virgil wrote, *sunt lacrimae rerum*—"These are the tears of things." The phrase has stayed in my mind since I was a boy, likely a troubled boy, long ago, in Ohio. (*Delicacy* 73)

This troubled Ohio poet and the mixed-blood Pueblo collaborated with a candor to die writing and courageous humor to go on living. When Wright told of his throat cancer, Silko responded with a long trickster tale about an almost unkillable, irrepressible New Mexican. "I like the story because there's this humor in it right along," she told her afflicted friend,

> and it intrigues me that there is this man who is known almost solely for the simple fact that he is alive. When I think I'm getting more than my fair share of trouble I always remember Hugh Crooks stories or Harry Marmon stories (Harry got out of the physical ones unscathed, but there were always jail and police and lawyers and fines, and still Harry is a free man). Maybe if a person can manage way more than his or her fair share of trouble, then another sort

of perspective or dimension is involved, I don't know. At Laguna they say it just makes you tougher. (*Delicacy* 101–2)

The coyote in her will not break down and speaks her last word before Wright's death. "*The best days are the first to go. The best of men has gone too,*" Anne Wright wrote to Leslie Silko on March 25, 1980.

Death hangs over the young American psyche like a fiery post-Edenic sword. And so, perhaps to relieve the pressure, or to regress natively, or simply to fantasize against pain, we turn to the animal in us and zoomorphize America in male *totems*. Americans cartoon "other-than-human animals," as the Cree say—coyote, eagle, bear, or horse—as we kill off our "wild" animals or put them in zoos. Sequoia National Park, where I write for the moment, "is recognized as part of the International Network of Biosphere Reserves," said Amadou-Mahtar M'Bow, director general of UNESCO, on October 26, 1976. "This network of protected samples of the world's major ecosystem types is devoted to conservation of nature and scientific research on the service of man. It provides a standard against which the effect of man's impact on his environment can be measured." UNESCO's "Program on Man and the Biosphere" encompasses an area of surviving redwoods named by the Austrian botanist Stephan Endlicher after Sequoyah, the Oklahoma Cherokee "writer" who invented the first Indian alphabet. Endlicher "thought of Sequoyah as a giant among men, and the tree, a giant among trees," says the National Park Service brochure. The park is rich in shards of Mono or Monachi California Indian life—metates and firepits, pictographs and burial sites, arrowheads and burden baskets—but there are no Indians in sight.

The Monachi lived here from the fourteenth to the nineteenth century; their predecessors inhabited the area a millennium before Christ, when now-standing sequoias were saplings. The Potwisha led Hale Tharp to the redwoods in 1858, and there he built a cabin in Crescent Meadow, which John Muir thought to be the most beautiful in the Sierras. But a display in the Lodgepole Visitor Center tells us: "Following a series of gold strikes in the Sierra foothills north of Sequoia, men came into the mountains, dredging and damming the streams, killing Indians and each other." In a glass case, two delicately woven Monachi tule baskets lie next to steel wolf traps, a pick, axe heads, a logger's saw, three large-bore rifles, horseshoes, and iron nails. Men such as Jedediah Smith, Kit Carson, "The Great Pathfinder" John G. Frémont, and "Peg-leg

Smith" (who amputated his own leg after an Indian "skirmish") hunted wolves, bighorn sheep, cougars, grizzlies, and Indians to near extinction in the area. "Shoot anything that moves, chop down anything that grows" went their rule of thumb, according to the visitor center display. Sequoias were converted into bowling alleys, dance floors, and even a tree house at the 1893 Chicago World's Fair, a quadricentennial Columbiad to celebrate the "discovery" of the New World. Finally, to protect the giant trees from loggers, Congress established Sequoia National Park in 1890, the year of the Wounded Knee massacre.

Today, Smokey Bear protects our forests from fire and litter, and the golden eagle emblemizes our express mail service. The UCLA Bruins battle the UCB Bears, Washington State Cougars, Oregon Ducks, and Stanford Cardinals (formerly Indians) in a state whose logo is the "golden bear." Yogi Bear luffs through Jellystone National Park on Saturday-morning television, flanked by Mickey Mouse, Tweety Bird, and the Road Runner. For "grown-ups," Fritz the Cat romps softly pornographic. Satan has long been the Snake in the Garden. We speak an adjectival bestiary: hawkish, hennish, bullish, foxy, wolfish, bearish, antsy, dogged, feline, mousy, squirrelly, snaky, mulish, goosey, moleish. We coin kennings from animal behavior: snake-eyed, owl-eyed, lynx-eyed, bug-eyed, bird-brained, pigeon-toed, sow-bellied, chicken-hearted. We can crow, rave, duck, bully, and weasel; grovel like a dog, growl like a bear, soar like an eagle, sing like a bird, drink like a fish, or run like a bat out of hell. We get drunker than a skunk (for Lame Deer, a "boiled owl") or find ourselves poor as church mice (for Bessie Fay in the 1930s, "poor as Job's turkey"). Why this fabled bestiary the world over? Why so male-bragged in America? And why wedded fatally to vanishing Americans?

Cousin Coyote

Almost every Indian writer at one time or another says something about Old Man Coyote. Biologically, he's survived the holocaust, as have Indians, and both laugh, indeed sing a lot, especially by night. Geologically, coyotes (and natives) long ago settled across this continent from Upstate New York to southern California— "from British Columbia to Guatemala," William Bright says, "and from the Pacific Ocean to the Great Plains."[8] Gary Snyder frames the Indian–coyote correlation in *The Old Ways:* "the greatest density of North American Indian population north of Mexico was Napa County and Sonoma County California just north of San Francisco Bay. The image of California Indians as shiftless, and as having no interesting material culture persists although they had elaborate dance, basketry, feather-working, ritual systems. The irony, then, is that these people who were the least regarded, have left modern poetry with a very powerful heritage—Coyote."9

Whether he is "first-born" Ma'ii among the Navajo, or Siouan garbageman of the plains, or California bungler who brought mixed blessings of acorns and death, or the first Northwest coastal fisherman, or just another stray survivor on the Mojave Desert, Coyote appears ubiquitous in Indian and American thinking, as he remains wild and free. "Let me just say / once and for all / just to be done," Peter Blue Cloud concludes. "Coyote / he belongs to none."10 That is to say, coyote barks for all from the edges of urbanity. And the ethnolinguist Dell Hymes drops science momentarily to have phonetic fun with his "5-Fold Fanfare for Coyote":

befuddled, besmirched, beleaguered, belittled begetter—
profane, prophylactic, prolix, procrustean precursor—

> WANDERER
> MISCREANT
> FORNICATOR
> BUNGLER
> PRONOUNCER—11

Coyote is scruffy, spunky, satiric, sneaky, sharp-eyed (adaptive night and day eyesight), and he loves to laugh at the moon and man. Biologists named him *Canis latrans,* or "barking dog," more descriptively perhaps "singing" or "laughing" dog, given his ululating laugh-song. Some argue that he is marking ground as he sings; others, that he is calling his mate or family; others, that he is counting territorial heads. His daily name, coyote—either two or three spoken syllables—comes from the Nahuatl *coyotl.* The Aztecs even named a spirit for him, Huehuecoyotl, or Old Man Coyote, god of the dance.

Paleontological coyotes evolved into their present form and features thirty thousand years ago, when saber-toothed tigers were stalking southern California. Probably there were two million coyotes when

Columbus "discovered" the Americas, and as many stalk four-footed and scruffy today. Coyotes continue to adapt, even to evolve, by cross-breeding with dogs or wolves (coydogs or coywolves). Now hunted for pelts that yield $3,000 fur coats, coyotes have extended their range across the United States to Maine, well beyond territory they roamed and homed ten thousand years ago. On the southern boundary of America, the word "coyote" means "breed" or *mestizo,* and it tags labor brokers who ferry illegal immigrants across the border. Like Indians, coyotes get around.

Among the Navajo, a mythic Coyote appears as "symbol of that chaotic Everything within which man's rituals have created an order for survival," Barre Toelken concludes.[12] Coyote's mess, then, calls for ceremonies to correct disorder, just as the Navajo clown "does not play the part of a comic reliever [W. W. Hill's surmise] but acts as a test, a challenge to order, a living representative of that full world of good *and* evil which exists around us" ("Poetic Retranslation" 89). In short, Coyote bears the Navajo onus of what-is, the burdens of reality, while corrective ritual clarifies and idealizes what-ought-to-be. No chaos, no ceremonial clairvoyance; no Coyote, no ritual order; no clown, no cure.

Coyote seems principally a comic quadruped who mocks human rules. He is known as scavenger, thief, and deviant who violates his own rules and reasons by any human standards. Whatever man does, Coyote plays contrariwise; he survives, ironically, on the fringes of a "civilization" that he mocks and contradicts. Coyote acts as our animal anti-image, our complementary inversion, thus a perfect figure for the fool-clown (*Homo canis?*). For Coyote is contraheroic, an animal personification of the comic will to survive—Nietzsche with pointed ears, Sitting Bull of the bushy tail, Schopenhauer of the garbage can, Geronimo of the backroads, Hegel of the alleys. He survives as a powerful thinker, yellow-eyed schemer (with man's eyes, the Navajo say). He is predator and omnivore (as humans), trickster extraordinaire. He dodged the extermination of the wolf, shadowed the demise of the grizzly, stalked the shrinking elk, and stared at the dying eagle. Indians say that when a feather falls, the eagle sees it, the deer hears it, the bear smells it; the coyote does all three at once.[13]

Coyote's compassion, as it were, rings through his laughter, neither pitying nor pitiable, but realistically cognizant of what does happen. He represents our trickster "other," a joke on ourselves, our howling lunar half who cons humanity, steals its refuse, survives on and parodies civilization, and dies along winding roads as evidence of how far clever-ness will carry us. Coyote plays our worldly fool, clown teacher, canine brother, and neglected sister. His is a realist blues riff on the devastation of human, plant, and animal—our symbiotic food chain—in a fragile ecosystem. He chants the concomitant will to survive with humor. He mirrors our social behavior, mocks our intelligence, and lives off our castoffs. Indeed, coyotes eat rubber hoses, leather belts, or paper trash bags when times are bad. Perhaps because his intelligence is most matched to that of man, coyote will outlast the devastation, outwit the stupidity, and laugh-sing his freedom home, all the while we stand listening behind the locked doors and screened windows and flush toi-lets of "civilization." If we survive, so will he; if we don't, he might anyway. He pantomimes our punk poet, our holy derider, our conscien-tious objector and comic savior (if we will listen). For he plays with, indeed survives off, all that we hold sacred and trash. Coyote is a contrary without equal.

The comic zoo-epistemology here suggests that coyote is enough "like" us to ape or "coyote" us. But, then again, as an animal he is distinctly, scruffily *not* us, so that we repress the likeness, while we play up the *un*likeness in comic scapegoating. He hangs around us, whether we like it or not. We could call this a comic kind of interspecies bisocia-tion with "brother" coyote. It can take place with "br'er" rabbit, raven, spider, skunk, bluejay, deer, or any animal deemed worthy to be our joking enantiomorph, or "other-than-human-person."

William Bright has written what might be the last word on *Canis latrans*, or "barking dog," from zoological, mythic, and "neopoetic" perspectives in "The Natural History of Old Man Coyote." Paul Radin, Mac Ricketts, Jarold Ramsey, and Dell Hymes explore the translative linguistics of Indian myths about coyote, and Hope Ryden, J. Frank Dobie, and Don Gill detail the animal's naturalistic behavior. Indian and non-Indian poets even get into the act with anthologies such as *Coyote's Journal,* Gary Snyder's "The Incredible Survival of Coyote" in *The Old Ways,* Peter Blue Cloud's *Elderberry Flute Songs,* and Harry Fonseca's Coyote and Rose series of dance paintings (Maidu ceremonies and creation myths, *Swan Lake,* and now *The Four Seasons,* all comically cartooned). Only the bear and eagle have been iconographed as often in America. And coyote is distinctly postmodern. "Crapulous old man," Snyder christens his scruffy cousin in an early beat poem, "A Berry Feast." Coyote seems the ideogram for America's Dharma bum, the original hobo, the frontier wanderer who opened the continent for "settlement." So Indians joke about Columbus, the First Euroamerican, a lost explorer who stumbled on a hemisphere and mistook one side of the world for the other.

If coyote prowls as the most ubiquitous animal trickster in America, antitotemic to the eagle, he emerges as the most slippery, strangest to track, and worst scapegoated. The Karok call him *pihneefich,* Bright says ("Natural History" 349), "Shitty Old Man," for his alleged coprophagy (eating excrement). The male roams from his den up to a hundred miles with no fatigue, and the female forages over two hundred miles.[14] But here's the human rub: coyotes court, as do humans, and remain monogamous for at least a year or more after the female births pups. Some pairs remain bonded for life. Their young are raised neotenous—that is, dependent on the parents for a relatively long period. During this time, they *learn* survival strategies, rather than relying only on instinct or inherited behavior—in this learning, again, they are most like humans. Males gather food for nursing females, adoptive adults baby-sit the pups, and the extended community forms a loose family or tribe. They "play" together, learning the social codes and tricks of survival. And yet humans mythologize their wanderlust, savagery, scandalous behavior, thievery, trickery, duplicity, and general immorality and untrustworthiness, just as they overlook coyote monogamy, their quickness and speed, and their sense of play. Not only do coyotes howl in good humor at the moon, but they dig up and urinate and defecate on cyanide traps! As Euroamericans misread *Canis latrans,* so do they negatively stereotype Indian variance from mainstream norms: family cohesions, tribal loyalties, sharings, enduring traditions, the "civilized" ground on which natives have been cultured and humored, like coyotes, for millennia. How like *Homo ludens!*

Anxious to become "native" again, Euroamericans play animal or Indian—in this case, male coyote with a vengeance. Perhaps totemic coyote projections, apart from the Cherokee princess syndrome, remain mostly male simply for reasons of sociological power: the myth-makers of America have been mostly Anglo males who relive the lawless frontier when they can get away with it. No real friend to strangers, the generic American male has warred against the animals of the land, as he has decimated the natives and indentured the émigrés. At best, "natural" animals, Indians, and other ethnic minorities have been "reserved" for posterity as species vanishing in the homogenous melting pot. And

Indians roam the heart of America's bestiary: witness the names for new cars and professional sports teams (Comanche, Winnebago, Thunderbird, and Cherokee to Braves, Warriors, Redskins, and Blackhawks). "Geronimo" Pratt, the California Black Panther in the late 1960s, or Charles Thompson, the black Oklahoma quarterback wearing a "Hanta Yo" neckband in the 1988 Orange Bowl, present interethnic curves on this cultural paradigm of men playing Indian.

Almost seventy years ago, D. H. Lawrence saw a generation of Indians swallowed by "the great white swamp." In *Studies in Classic American Literature* (1923), he prophesied that the demise of our red "Daimon of America" would precipitate a psychic crisis in this country. Coyote-like, America's natives didn't vanish, notwithstanding Edward Curtis's doctored photographs (air-brushing out alarm clocks in tipis and screening a file of Navajo riders so they would seem to disappear into the darkness). The delayed crisis came in the 1960s as a countercultural "yippee!" A decade earlier, Allen Ginsberg, Jewish hipster, struck a beat blue note: "That no good. Ugh. Him make Indians learn read. Him need big black niggers. Hah" ("America"). Gerald Vizenor has parodied these days in the video *Harold of Orange,* in which Charlie Hill leads a pan-tribal Minnesota coalition to raise miniature citrus trees on the rez and scam white liberal sentiment for "our Indians." In the 1960s, "Wannabe" Indians convened urban powwows and disappeared back into the suburbs, milked of guilt; Leslie Fiedler recorded their exit in *The Return of the Vanishing American* (1969) ("with thanks to the Blackfoot tribe who adopted me," the dedication reads). Fiedler fingered a recurring myth: the American male, gone west, found himself historically homeless, unwived, without progeny, and alienated from the "virgin land" he had raped. The solution: be an Indian, or, barring native adoption, "Come back to the raft agin, Huck honey," as Fiedler mugged the male drag between whites and blacks in the 1960s. It's radically funny, if not wholly convincing. The supposition gets us thinking. Fiedler's joke on his own gender is a sad story, a bad street gag about homeless American manhood.

Among Indians by the 1960s something was stirring—the National Indian Youth Council, the National Congress of American Indians, and the 1968 Alcatraz occupation by the American Indian Movement in the year Fiedler foresaw the "return" of the "vanishing" American. The next year, Deloria published *Custer Died For Your Sins,* and Momaday won the Pulitzer Prize for *House Made of Dawn.* As for Old Man

Coyote, "he's always on the edge of disaster," Harry Fonseca says, "and so are we."[15]

Fonseca's Critter

Harry Fonseca mixes things up creatively and comically. Born in 1946 of Maidu, Portuguese, and Hawaiian descent, he grew up around Sacramento as a postwar child of the California beat generation and the flower rebellion. When Harry was a teenager, his uncle Henry Ke'a'a'la Azbill, a Konkow Maidu elder, took him into the Sierra foothills—the

Harry Fonseca (Maidu), *Coyote Dancer #2* (1982).
(Courtesy of Harry Fonseca)

American and Feather River drainages—for a traditional Indian education. "We were watching the dances," Fonseca told Margaret Archuleta. "It was late, maybe two in the morning, the dances were very
serious, very sacred. When into the round-house comes this dancer who
makes fun of the other dancers. I didn't know what was going on. I was
told it was Coyote."[16]

The Maidu Oleil, or Coyote, plays ceremonially up and down California Indian country. At Grindstone, near Chico, Craig Bates first met
young Harry Fonseca with his uncle:

Henry had invited me to attend the *Hesi*. He was taking his nephew, this tall
skinny guy with bushy hair. Harry was excited because he wanted to do some
sketching. We were sitting in the round-house. Harry was busily drawing the
dancers, when the dancers approached Harry to see what he was doing.
When they saw the drawings, they took Harry's drawings away from him.
Harry was upset and disappointed. After the dances were over, on the way
home Henry told Harry, "They must have taken your drawings, but they
can't take away what's in your mind. Now go home and do this."[17]

So the mixed-blood artist acculturates both red and white through
Coyote, a liminal trickster who comes and goes comically for Indians
and non-Indians alike. Fonseca artistically recorded the "sacred
dances" and traditional Maidu culture in the early 1970s. "My work is
of the old transformed into a contemporary vision," he said in 1976 for
an American Indian Arts and Crafts Board publication: "hopefully my
work will aid in the reawakening of the Native California Indian
culture."[18]

Fonseca taped his uncle Henry telling the Maidu creation story, told
early in the century by Henry's grandmother Sokanneh. She had heard it
from her Concon grandmother, who married into the Mechoopda village
near Chico. Frank La Pena, Wintun artist teaching at California State
University, Sacramento, assigned the taping for a class. In 1976 Fonseca received a Special Projects Grant from the California Arts Council
to record the myth visually. *Creation Story* (1977) became his first
major work, a centrifugal spiral from Maidu Big Man, or Helinmaiden,
on the original raft with Turtle, through the creation of this world,
animals and humans, fire, seasons, sex, war, burials, roundhouses,
ceremonies, and storytellings. A rainbow, symbolizing futurity, arches
over the upper-left-hand corner. Two upside-down Coyotes play flutes

as naked humans discover one another nearby. The two-dimensional figures, mythic detail, and green-tinted chiaroscuro mix "primitive naive" or American Fauvism with native California improvisation. Across America, Coyote had made something of a grand reentry by 1977. Linguistic anthropologists such as Boas, Sapir, Gatschet, Kroeber, Powers, Burns, and Dixon earlier scoured California archaeological digs for coyote's scat (Kroeber transcribed the smutty parts in Latin). A new generation—Jacobs, Hymes, Bright, Tedlock—worked and reworked this loam. Paul Radin struck folkloric paydirt with Winnebago Wakdjunkaga in *The Trickster* (1956), sixteen years later issued in paperback, fattened with afterwords by Karl Kerenyi and Carl Jung and an introduction by Stanley Diamond (1972). "And so he became and remained," Radin summarized, "everything to every man—god, animal, human being, hero, buffoon, he who was before good and evil, denier, affirmer, destroyer and creator. If we laugh at him, he grins at us. What happens to him happens to us."[19] Kerenyi traced him to the Greeks, and Jung added that Trickster was probably the oldest archetype known to humans. Diamond contrasted him with Job. So by 1977, Gary Snyder revived "Old Man Coyote" in *The Old Ways,* having just won a poetry Pulitzer for *Turtle Island.* James Koller edited *Coyote's Journal* (still kicking in 1987), and Jarold Ramsey "reclaimed" classic Northwest texts in *Coyote Was Going There* (1977).

Could whites co-opt Coyote? "A sad thing in recording these animal stories is the loss of spirit—" Ramsey quoted Archie Phinney, Nez Perce translator trained by Franz Boas, "the fascination furnished by the peculiar Indian vocal tradition for humor. Indians are better story-tellers than whites. When I read my story mechanically I find only the cold corpse."[20] That same year, Barry Lopez retold in his own prose sixty-eight Coyote tales from forty-two tribes in *Giving Birth to Thunder, Sleeping with His Daughter,* now supported by Barre Toelken's paperback foreword: "The trick consists in finding equivalents rather than direct translations of connotative words or rhetorical strategies. In effect, Lopez has done these tales over in such equivalent terms, giving us the story, the style, and Old Man Coyote himself, without betraying the magic."[21]

Harry Fonseca rediscovered the Maidu Coyote through his uncle Henry and dances at Grindstone, but he also heard the barkings across America. One day in the mid-1970s, Fonseca was watching the television correspondent Bill Moyers interview Joseph Campbell on animal totems, and Coyote popped out of the TV to reinforce his painting (he said as we talked in December 1985 about organizing his ten-year retrospective at the Los Angeles County Museum of Natural History). "I was doing Coyote long before I saw or heard Joseph Campbell," Fonseca later wrote me. "However, after listening to Campbell I knew I was plugged into something—couldn't see the forest (Coyote) for the trees (I was in it!)."[22] By 1979 his "Coyote" seriagraph recorded winter roundhouse ceremonies, along with "Bear" in the spring renewal dances and Acorn Dance designs in *A Gift from California* (1980). The ink drawings *Coyote I* and *Coyote II* came in 1981; the watercolor *Coyote Flute Player*, a year later. This launched a modernist series still going strong today, "The Artist as a Young Coyote," having come through *Swan Lake* into *The Four Seasons*. James Joyce (*Portrait of the Artist as a Young Man*, a joke title coined by French modernists exasperated by questions "about" their paintings), Dylan Thomas (*Portrait of the Artist as a Young Dog*), and Euroamerican fabulists (artists as fox, rat, cockroach, crow) were close on the literary horizon.

By the spring of 1979, as Fritz Scholder mounted a Heard Museum photographic exhibit of Indian Americana, "Indian kitsch" was in fashion. "And it continues," Scholder noted in the accompanying booklet, which I found some years later in the Mayflower Gift Shop in San Francisco's Chinatown: "The military currency used in Viet Nam shows a proud Plains warrior. The Arizona Bank's logo is a kachina. Navajo is a truck line. The Super Chief is still going down the line. Life-size Indians sit or stand in curios stores, usually with caveats of DO NOT TOUCH. Rows of kewpie dolls, pressed from plastic in Japan, Korea or Taiwan, can be found along Route 66. From belt buckles to billboards, the Indian is in."[23] Indian–white interactions have generated a genre of buckskin artistic comics, from Awa Tsireh's Pueblo *koshares* chased by turkeys and Fred Kabotie's Hopi clowns in the 1920s, through Delmar Boni's *Great Native American Dream #1* of sunglassed Apaches fantasizing a collective ice cream, and T. C. Cannon's coyote Caddo dancer in *His Hair Flows Like a River* (1973). Contemporary parodies have become popular art: Woody Crumbo's *Land of Enchantment*, with caricatured white tourists gawking at a roadside Navajo weaving; Alfred Young Man's *The Vacation*, with Devils Tower, Cadillac, and patriotic Native American with flag; and Richard Glazer Danay's *Indians Are My Favorite Hobby*, a spoof of a third-grade notebook essay.[24] Fonseca's *Snapshot or Wish You Were Here, Coyote* (1979) caps the caricatured series with a bushy-tailed, toothy trickster in Hawaiian vacation attire posing before adobe pueblos.

Why the craze and concomitant Indi'n humor? Raymond Stedman tracks four hundred years of caricaturing stereotypes in *Shadows of the Indian* (1982). Perhaps laughter encodes the first and final defense against a wandering tourism. The Kandinsky–Klee plains modernist Jaune Quick-to-See Smith prefaced a catalogue to a 1985 National Endowment for the Arts traveling exhibit, *Women of Sweetgrass, Cedar and Sage:*

> Humor has an important role through the Indian world in general. It is a tie that binds tribe to tribe to tribe. Humor has been a panacea for what ails. The women tend to express their humor in a more subtle way than the men (who are often more blatant and slapstick). Imogene Goodshot's beaded sneakers and baseball cap are a commentary on modern Indian life and acculturation. Mary Adams' "Pope's Basket" begets 164 little baskets on its surface. Indian humor is known to be sardonic, sometimes sinister and it always appears in unlikely places. Little Turtle's photographs always juxtapose funny and bizarre objects with reality. Humor is considered to have a role along side the art forms, the landscape, storytelling and religion. Humor is a mainstay of Indian life.

All this is to say that non-native tourists and cigar-store Indians pose fair trickster game. Coyote is very much afoot here.

Barbara Babcock collates Trickster scholarship in " 'A Tolerated Margin of Mess': The Trickster and His Tales Reconsidered."[25] Borrowing from Mary Douglas in *Natural Symbols* (1970) and *Purity and Danger* (1966), Babcock sees the Trickster archetype as an old antinomian clown flourishing in "dirty" impurity on the margins of tidy village clearings. Trickster embodies, inversely, the "positive dimension of living marginally," stretching civilized norms toward their natural origins, thus tempering the xenophobic impulse to read the "other" as not-me. Trickster acts out taboos as the *via negativa*. He becomes, as antistructural antihero, "the negation offering possibility"—the comic *dis*arranger who dissolves boundaries, unsettles certainties, shakes up fixed ideas, and twists the stiff tail of long-faced moralists. He "confounds classifications" in this deconstructive role and plays out the shaman's marginality without the attendant mystery. His lessons come comically obvious, though deeper complexities and contraries bubble beneath the surface of his antics.

So, too, Jarold Ramsey portrays the Trickster-Transformer as a mythic, binary *bricoleur* at the crossroads of cultures-in-process: mediatively vital, bisociatively multiplex, liminally alert, comically ubiquitous, normatively and often inversely funny. "Indeed, the saturnalian spirit of these stories offers yet another literary illustration, I think, of Freud's theory of wit and the comic, whereby it is supposed that the psychic energy we customarily employ in maintaining repressions can, under certain circumstances, be released and redirected to the cause of celebration" (*Reading the Fire* 32). Trickster's wit plays out our dreams ("in-play," as Huizinga decodes the word "illusion" in *Homo Ludens*). Frank La Pena, Fonseca's teacher, recalls: "Harry says laughing at ourselves is important. Traditional people talk about the importance of laughter and joy because when one is happy," he adds, "it is easier to accept and learn new things." Thus Trickster allows tribal peoples to adapt, to grow, to survive, to celebrate continuance. Perhaps reality from an Indian perspective is blessed with comic benevolence beside all the erratic luck. "His salvation is his irreverence for circumstance and his extreme good luck in bad situations," La Pena reviews Fonseca's retrospective, "Coyote: A Myth in the Making," which traveled from Los Angeles to half a dozen major American galleries, Oakland to Omaha to the Smithsonian, from June 1987 through March 1989.[26] This visibility seems no minor stroke of good fortune for a contemporary artist. Isabel Foreman surveys Fonseca's canon:

> Coyote in myth can be creator of the universe or the butt of jokes; Coyote in art is Fonseca's Coyote. Exuberant, vivid, joyous—Fonseca says his Coyote isn't just having a good time, he's having a *great* time. He's in a leather jacket, standing in front of a pinball machine with his arm around Rose, who as Coyote's squeeze has a wonderful style of her own. He's dancing under the stars in high tops and suspenders. He's in a tux, conducting his own version of "Swan Lake." He's a vaudeville Uncle Sam. He's Old Man Coyote, in a Salvation Army coat, holding a brown paper bag wrapped around a flask of white port he's already high on, Old Man Coyote dancing under the amused and forgiving stars.
>
> "He can be anything," Navajo poet Lucy Tapahonso says of Coyote in general and Fonseca's Coyote in particular. "He can be anybody. He can be an educator, a BIA official, a millionaire, a clown. He's likable. People understand him. He's funny. He's always taking the risk we don't want to take. He doesn't have a safe life." ("Coyote, Coyote" 6)

Fonseca's Maidu paintings of the late 1970s take a distinctly kinetic and comic turn when Coyote enters. *Coyote #1* (1979) features an

Harry Fonseca (Maidu), *Coyote #1* (1979). (Courtesy of Harry Fonseca)

acrylic dancer portrayed two-dimensionally, wearing the traditional feathered cloak, appearing somewhat bearlike and topped with a coyote headdress. Distinctive to this portrait are the crossed dance sticks. The coyote head, small for the bearlike body, seems to be listening for a distant howl. Pebbles and coyote tracks, headed in contrary directions, are scattered on the ground below. Three years later, in *Coyote Leaves the Res, New York, New York,* a bushy-tailed Coyote with Picasso's hieroglyphic eyes leans in black leather jacket against a bluesy urban wall. He's spangled with silver metallic zippers and sports high-top tennis shoes, shuffling off to the side ("Woww, graffiti," a towhead crooned next to me at the 1986 Los Angeles exhibit, as his friend mumbled, "Funny pictures"). "The leather jacket, Levis and high-top tennis shoes," Fonseca said of this painting, chosen as a poster to speak for his traveling retrospective, "are the contemporary expression of traditional trappings." The oil spatula blacks, aqua blues, and grays play against the glitter in Coyote's punk zippers, offsetting the black–white contrast of his T-shirt and Converse high-tops. It's a frontalist "lineup": a wily character about to angle off stage left, a street-smart hipster not about to stand still long. There's no way to disguise his phallic, bushy tail. "God's dog" here surely "digs" whatever's around—a sportively untamed, omnivorous symbol of the trickster majority of Indians now living in America's urban wilds.

Rose enters the scenario as "personification" of the liberated woman, "larger than life," Fonseca says, "partner-in-crime and companion" to Coyote.[27] In *Pow Wow Club* (1980) she wears a rose-red dress with glitter-on-acrylic spangled camellias. Silver stars sparkle on a violet background. One leg is lifted in her dance, high heels and painted fingernails glistening crimson. Coyote levitates by her side in a pink-and-black checked suit, red-glitter camellia (matching her dress) in his lapel, with a pink-and-green striped tie against a pale blue shirt. It's dizzying. The tile dance floor is checked black and white, the painting framed in lavender. Both of Coyote's high-heeled, gray-and-black dancing shoes rise off the floor. They soar with his gray bushy tail, reaching for the dancers' arched necks, Rose's raised arms, and the two camellias under her left ear. The couple's razor-toothed grins tell all: Coyote play transcends predatory hunger. His phallic tail adds a touch of Freud to the picture. And the pair's high-heeled dancing shoes say something about travel and tricks in the West.

Sportive shoes are key to Fonseca's bicultural Coyote vision. One of

Harry Fonseca (Maidu), *Coyote Leaves the Res, NY, NY* (1982).
(Courtesy of Harry Fonseca)

Harry Fonseca (Maidu), *Pas de Deux #2* (1984) and *Tennis Shoe*.
(Courtesy of Harry Fonseca)

147

his showpieces is a left-footed Converse All-Star painted pink, speckled red and green with slices of watermelon (cf. Lee Marmon's "White Man's Mocassins"). This old hipster travels and finds pleasure any-where, as fashionable as the original wild red rose in *Homa ludens*'s hair, or the stony metallic flash that first caught a neolithic hunter's eye, or *Homo viator*'s delight stepping into the first decorated pair of animal-skin footwear. "Coyote likes anything that shines," Fonseca says.[28] Dress is his "thing"—au courant streetwear costume, radical chic, where country and city, poor and rich, lean and well-heeled mix. Coyote would be "with it" in his striped tank top, New York City loft to Shingle Springs reservation, his mythically old and modernly macho leathers, the metallic flare of his zippers. He does not discriminate. He's daring, comically *over*done, garishly modish in checks and stripes, tails, punk insolence, or ballet tights. Coyote mediates the "old ways" and new fads. He improvises the next step in the embattled dance of native life; he acculturates Indian resistance to and the necessity of accommodating with a Euroamerican "invasion" over tribal soils, so-cial ways, cultural mores, and fragile ecosystems. He banquets on caviar or trash, salmon or tripe. Ramsey contends that Coyote is a bisociative comic figure, a conjunctive pluralist. As a figure of two-dimensional cartoon or California funk, he's one of a kind.

Coyote, Star Dancer comes on "break-dance" style with a Maidu flute and dance sticks, while *Rose and the Rez Sisters* play a Supremes Indi'n soft-shoe. In *Shuffle Off to Buffalo,* Uncle Sam Coyote slides footloose across the vaudeville stage, furry ears sticking through a tri-colored top hat of stars and stripes. "I make him do all kinds of things I wouldn't have him do if my face were up there," Fonseca said in 1981 (notes to "Coyote" exhibition). Fluffy, sheeplike buffalo border the painting. In *Coyote's Ark* (1985), a grinning trickster clutches two hapless sheep on board with striped zebras, spotted giraffes, speckled leopards, and a comic-trunked elephant sailing a ferny sea of green. Overhead, a pastel rainbow and pink, fluffy clouds tie a border of white doves to the succulent sheep tucked under Coyote's arms. His orange-striped tank top and blue beanie glitter dead center in the ark.

Clearly Coyote is having fun wherever he appears. And Fonseca finds him funny, not to mention successful. *Coyote in Front of Studio* features a soapboxed plains war bonnet, a pipe bag, and a handful of cigars before Fonseca's Quail Studio in Shingle Springs. The red T-shirt, zippered black leather, baggy jeans, and high-tops are still there, along with Coyote's shifty, doubly frontal eyes (the flat surfaces expose his

Harry Fonseca (Maidu), *Coyote in Front of Studio.*
(Courtesy of Harry Fonseca)

binary comic vision as pop cubist). In *Coyote and Rose Doin' It at
Indian Market with a Little Help from Gail, Yazzie and Jody* (1982), the
Indian tourist pair sells *koshare* striped *katsinas*, Pueblo pottery, and
Navajo silver belts.

The rainbowed sky of *Coyote's Ark* bespeaks success (the painting

Harry Fonseca (Maidu), *Coyote and Rose Doin' It at Indian Market with a
Little Help from Gail, Yazzie and Jody* (1982). (Courtesy of Harry Fonseca)

won an award at the Southwest American Indian Arts Festival in Santa
Fe). Influenced by Matisse and by Picasso's circus period, Fonseca
painted striped Coyote *koshares* eating watermelon and pink cotton
candy in *Albuquerque Impressions,* all five clowns wearing red, blue,
and green high-tops.

By 1984, after a year of study at the Alvin Ailey American Dance
Center in New York, Fonseca completed his "Swan Lake" series. These
several dozen paintings and sketchbooks merged the myths of two
hemispheres, he said, in bedtime stories for his daughter. A sleek, black
cutout of Coyote as maestro in "tails" (his own gray bush for once
hidden) opens the series of "pas de paw" art, baton on high against a
damask curtain and Art Nouveau footlamps. *Pas de Deux #1* mixes
media in a collage of acrylic, glued velvet curtains, glitter, and spray
paint. Rose *en point* dances her daintiest in tutu, tights, and tiara, while
Coyote shadows her classical form in punk leather and street high-tops.
Grace, balance, and delicacy appear in their strength, matched against

Harry Fonseca (Maidu), *Pas de Deus #1* (1984).
(Courtesy of Harry Fonseca)

the airborne appearance of Roxie and Killer, who are wild and threatening against a black-and-white tiled floor. The Black Swan shows up in
white tights. Finally, Coyote and Rose are rescued by a heroic white
swan, who wings them onto fluffy clouds under a pastel rainbow and
winking pink stars. "I don't know how Rose and Coyote got on the
swan's back," Fonseca confessed. "That's not important. The thing is
they didn't kill themselves and they weren't overcome by evil. They
didn't let outside forces take advantage of them" (notes for "Coyote"
exhibition). It's Native America's understatement for half a millennium,
a survivalist vision charged with Indi'n humor.

"Humor is a mainstay of Indian life," Jaune Quick-to-See Smith
concludes in *Women of Sweetgrass, Cedar and Sage*. Trickster seems
the impresario, and Coyote his Western archetype. All that glitters is up
for grabs and throwaway gold with this comic vision. Scavengers may
be heroes, survivors culture bearers, *bricoleurs* artists. Lawrence Beck,

Yup'ik sculptor, describes the making of *Punk Nanuk Inua* (1987) from
scrap mirrors, spatulas, feathers, and spare car parts:

> Several years ago I was in a junkyard in Skagit Valley north of Seattle looking
> for some parts for my dog sled (my Toyota). The first mask that I had cast in
> aluminum was a traditional oval shape. I saw a similar one on the side of a
> car. I was far enough away and the sun hit the side mirror on a 1968 or '69
> Oldsmobile Cutlass. I saw this mask there, an Eskimo mask on the side of
> this car. I got this idea I would use the materials that are in my environment
> as found objects. To me it just made sense. So this experience in the Skagit
> Valley junkyard led me to a whole new direction in my art. In my studio I had
> some dental mirrors, feathers and a box of auto parts. I assembled this stuff
> together remembering and using as inspiration the Yup'ik mask forms I'd
> seen in a museum.[29]

Trickster Slippage

> Archetypes, like taxes, seem doomed to be with us always, and so
> with literature, one hopes; but between the two there must needs
> be the living human being in a specific texture of time, place and
> circumstance; who must respond, make choices, achieve elo-
> quence and create specific works of art. . . .
>   [Stanley Edgar] Hyman's favorite archetypical figure is the
> trickster, but I see a danger here. From a proper distance all arche-
> types would appear to be tricksters and confidence men; part-God,
> part-man, no one seems to know he-she-its true name, because he-
> she-it is protean with changes of pace, location and identity. Fur-
> ther, the trickster is everywhere and anywhere at one and the same
> time, and, like the parts of some dismembered god, is likely to be
> found on stony as well as on fertile ground.
>   RALPH ELLISON, "Change the Joke and Slip the Yoke"

Ellison's uneasiness with Trickster scavenging on rocky terrain in *Invisible Man* leads him to suspect "a critical game that ignores the specificity of literary works." He feels that Hyman's "fascination with folk
tradition" blurs the "distinction between various archetypes and different currents of American folklore" and causes the critic "to over-
simplify the American tradition." That is to say, Trickster can be mis-
perceived, mixed up, and misused by critic or artist. And within tribal
boundaries, skill, if not integrity, is necessary to invoke Trickster, as

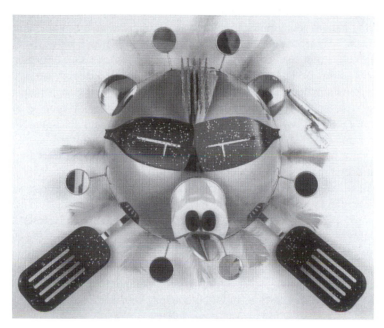

Lawrence Beck (Yup'ik), *Punk Nanuk Inua* (1987).
(Courtesy of Lawrence Beck)

with scholars looking across cultures. Critical norms come into play here.

Coyote facing disaster, as Fonseca says, may prove an opaque totemic mask removed from tribal contexts. One danger in cavalierly appropriating Trickster lies in slurring "other" cultures, indulging the hurt of history fictively, milking the massacres, playing ethnic. There are issues of cultural taste, even among Coyotes. Indians observe an almost sacred witness of their past, particularly their suffering. Here a sense of permitted boundaries and tribal respects comes into serious play, as Coyote's inverse behavior turns on tribal encodings. In this regard, who grants Trickster permissions of disrespect? Are there artistic standards of trickery? Does anything go?

Tribal values would seem to condition a play with limits—Navajo Ma'ii, or Cree Wichikapachi, or Blackfeet Na'pi, or Lakota Iktome—as opposed to generic "trickster" appropriations (for example, Road Runner cartoons on TV). The danger here, especially among urban, mixed-blood Indians (not granted tribal license by blood alone), is that "camp" offenses can trash suffering. Pan-Indian slurs may turn tribally specific particulars into tasteless parodies. Granted, this raises issues of personal bias—more or less how any reader views the redeeming humor in Trickster's pranks. Discussing African folklore, Robert Pelton cautions that "the knotty logic of the trickster is best unraveled by keeping him firmly situated within the cultural context."[30] As a liminal figure who decenters institutional inertia and yet mediates chaos toward narrative chronos in Ashanti tribal society, "Ananse rejects truth in favor of lying, but only for the sake of speech; temperance in favor of gluttony for the sake of eating; chastity in favor of lasciviousness for the sake of sex; honesty in favor of trickiness for the sake of human interchange" (*Trickster* 51). This contrary logic, where the fool antiheroically tests the claims of heroism, where the trickster mocks the shaman and riddles the king, turns out to be logic nevertheless—the double lens of patterned (narrated) ambiguity. Trickster serves less as archetype, Pelton reasons, than as "entelechy"—that is, the vitalist potential of "interplay" between nature and nurture, raw and cooked, wild and civilized:

> Thus the Ashanti tell the meaning of their lives in stories and name those stories *anansesem* [spider stories] . . . conveying to their children, and reminding themselves, that life itself is a twisted story, a process in which the human mind and human words are always drawing forth from the rawness of the earth and body a surprising pattern, which, however partial and dimly known, is charged with permanent value and meaning. They are saying that Ananse, whose actions are so outrageous and nonimitable, nevertheless reveals, especially when this pattern seems most darkened and dead, both the rawness and the order hidden in all of Ashanti life. His stories are a passage enabling structure to enfold chaos and become again *communitas*. (70)

"The bear is in me now," Gerald Vizenor opens *Darkness in Saint Louis Bearheart*, "Listen ha ha ha haaaa."[31] Vizenor's fictive, postmodernist comics are told through a fourth-grade prisoner of the Indian Wars who has been handcuffed in a closet by the reservation superintendant. This native victim hibernates and reemerges as shamanic bear among "*the warriors of freedom*": Proude Cedarfair, tribal hero as isolato and inheritor of Chippewa resistance to white "*Shitwords.*" The novel swells with revolutionary jive, "Neo-HooDoo Manifesto," as Ishmael Reed put it some twenty years ago (American blacks call it "signifyin' " and "doin' the dozens" on the streets to draw an audience).

Rather than amoral or nihilist, the traditional Trickster cycles inversely educate and amuse Indian people in tribal norms. A Navajo or Cree audience sees how not to be, entertains deviance, and bonds through Trickster's infamous disconnections. This all requires craft, intricacy, a sense of audience response, and a true humorist's tact. Few situations are less funny than wit that doesn't work. In the self-adopted mode of "word warriors," Vizenor's novel opens with tongue-twisty sibilance: "Four Proude Cedarfairs have celebrated the sacred cedartrees" (*Darkness* 3). With a creaky pilgrim plot in self-reflexive prose, the drama stays two-dimensional, the dialogue tilts descriptively flat: "spume from his hostile words gathered on his bulbous purple lips" (18). Expectedly enough, "Whitemen possessed trees and women and words" (4), and the inevitable red–white atrocities (trees axed, women raped, words warped, warriors slain) savage the land until one clown-warrior rises from the carnage. With the mystic aid of "clown crows" and mythic bears, Proude Cedarfair frees "the people" to escape civilization westward. Semen and cedar spatter their path into the sunset; all of contaminated America soon follows suit.

This fiction fattens in rap. The characters traipse west as manikins in a plot spiced with stale metaphors, crude sex, occult crows, evil whites, and desperately clever Indians called "circus pilgrims," carried over from Tom Wolfe's "merry pranksters." It's America-on-the-road, Columbus through Kerouac—here Cheyenne Autumn, the Long March, Wounded Knee, and Road Runner all rolled into one gory exodus at America's hapless end. The author shares his fantasy of a frontier holocaust somewhere in the near future, where stock-in-trade violence and kinky sex color the "vision": "When the end of gasoline came, the violent filiation used knives and forks and spoons in their ritual assassinations. The dark eyes of tribal victims were popped with spoons and heel tendons were severed. While the victims struggled to escape, crawling on hands and knees with images swirling from each dangling eyeball, the whites stabbed at the victims with sharp forks. Before death came to most of the tribal victims their ears and lips and genitals were removed" (*Darkness* 50). One of our heroines is a legendary "boxer-fucker" (dogs, that is); another is fond of paragraphs of fellatio with Proude's spousal penis, "president jackson."[32] On that score, here is *Bearheart*'s grand finale, Trickster's pornographic license in extremis:

Forcing her [Rosina] to turn and kneel in front of him he [Double Saint] thrust his penis against her soft warm mouth. The huge purple head butted against her closed lips. Then he squeezed the muscles on her chin and when her mouth opened he pushed hard against her lips until the bulbous head slipped past her teeth. He held her head against him with her braids. His penis throbbed in her mouth. With the tip of her tongue she touched the opening on the head. Circling his penis with her tongue, her muscles relaxed until president jackson was against the back of her mouth. He moaned when she touched his testicles and then his penis throbbed and spurted and flooded her mouth with warm sperm. (*Darkness* 236)

A mass exodus of cripples join our red pioneers as they move west—a nightmare "vision" of deformed America on the lam. The thirteen red disciples falter, some fall by the wayside, yet the four directions somehow hold, and evil is defeated. This fiction of a sadomasochist America, then, serves up dissonant Trickster jokes—cheap puns, degrading sex, random violence, and a clichéd journey to uncertain ends.

All this carnage, cocksucking, and throwaway dirty talk takes Vizenor's pilgrims into the "fourth world" (one behind the Pueblos) outside Santa Fe. Proude and one fellow pilgrim, the two surviving word warriors, leave their women in a world behind and turn into mythic bears at the Anasazi winter solstice. "In seconds, faster than birds could soar, the bears roared from the four directions ha ha ha haaaa" (*Darkness* 241). Such a finale purports to be the mythic resolution of fictional mayhem. The reader is teased with a billboard logic of opposites in this brave old world, where walking backward plays Trickster's trump—"you fall on your ass and not on your face" (192).

Vizenor's second novel, *Griever: An American Monkey King in China* (runner-up in the 1987 American Book Awards sponsored by Berkeley's Before Columbus Foundation, dedicated to recognizing "cultural diversity"), pushes Trickster farther over the line. Griever De Hocus travels as an English teacher to Tianjin, China, near Beijing. Instantly, this hocus-pocus huckster (with reputed scholarship from Arthur Waley's *Monkey* and Anthony Yu's translation of *The Journey of the West*) metamorphoses into a modern "monkey king," based on the legendary monk who brought Sanskrit scrolls from India to the Greater Goose (Dayan) Pagoda outside Xi'an, thus carrying Buddhism across the border and trickster into the Middle Kingdom (see Maxine Hong Kingston's *Tripmaster Monkey: His Fake Book* [1989]). Vizenor defines his comic hero infratextually: "Griever is a mixedblood tribal trickster, a close relative to the old mind monkeys; he holds cold reason on a lunge line while he imagines the world. With colored pens he thinks backward, stops time like a shaman, and reverses intersections, interior landscapes."[33]

The novelist writes a disjointed dream narrative through the mixed-blood mask of Griever, slippery antagonist, victim of red–white American racism, friend of caged chickens and dead frogs at home and abroad. This sarcastic "native" as the Orient's Ugly American doesn't so much take the reader to China as drag the audience down through a dark authorial sardonicism. The cartoon characters—all jumbled, no-dimensional, kvetching about China—carry on with talk that goes nowhere.

> "Eating with you is like, is like," sputtered Sugar Dee, "is like going to the dump for lunch, or, or flushing a toilet in the middle of a meal."
> "Would you like to hear about where the vegetables grow?" the trickster teased. "How about some wheat and rice dried on the side of the asphalt roads, winnowed under the wheels of tourist buses."
> "Never."
> "How about the water?"
> "Never mind."
> "Salmonella ice cream on used sticks?"
> "Listen, my mind is closed now for dinner." (*G* 101–2)

These conversations pool in trash-can diatribes at dinner, peevish criticisms of Chinese communism, and parodic pornography (an isolated genre?):

> Griever lowered her panties and thrust his tongue into her wet vagina. She bounded on the rail and his nose brushed her clitoris; he burrowed and inhaled the wild humors. She danced on a broad amber beam with the peach emperor, a wild ichor burst from her sheath. He stood between her thighs and she touched his ripe testicles; his stout penis bounced on her wrist. The trickster beat her hard black nipples with his penis; lower, he pushed harder, once, twice, sperm burned the hollows, and then he hauled her down from the rail, bucked and bewailed the curtain.
> "The wild moon," he whispered under her hair. (105–6)

Griever's miscegenated romp results in a pregnancy, potentially an international scandal. The author solves this dilemma with scar-faced

Hester dunked dead by her Chinese father among the bones of drowned, unwanted babies in a blue pond. So Griever "de Lindbergh" escapes from China in a self-fabricated aeronautical "ultralight" with another mixed-blood girlfriend (blonde this time), his liberated cock ("Matteo Ricci"), and an archaic recipe for blue chicken. "Everything is a play over here," Griever writes to China Browne back home, "so we must be the new scene" (234).

A hackneyed theme of freedom proffers the novel's raison d'être, raising a question asked these days: Free to what? To exploit Indian issues? To rip off Trickster? To trip through intercultural insult? From one perspective, the novel mistakes trickster "lessons" for license in bad taste, showing no understanding of "them" as "other," little sense of Sinology today or yesterday, less tact in dealing with the gap between the novelist's own Western consciousness and that of over a billion people who compose a quarter of the world's population. Could a Chinese trickster so foul Native American air and go unscathed? "Nothing but dust" in China, Colin Gloome grouses (G 189). "Griever pinched his ear and spat near the cages. Frustrated, his humor turned sour; he demanded, in his loudest voice, the liberation of all the chickens" (40).

From a Native American perspective, the Trickster genre isn't nihilist or even tasteless; it plays with boundaries, surely, releases libidinous energies in sexual, scatological, or otherwise violent escapades. Trickster narratives delight in contraries, and they reversely imply social norms by telling stories well. The tales break rules to bring principles of behavior into a field of play. The tribal issue is one of audience response within a cultural context. Trickster does not occupy an amoral corner of tribal thought; his escapades are neither contextually unfocused nor easily tossed off. Just so, a writer cannot easily arrogate the license to cartoon Trickster in the name of tribal fiction.

So why all this funny talk, fellatio, cryptic comedy, and mindless violence? Why dip into these alleged "Trickster" fictions? Paul Radin argues that the Winnebago Wakdjunkaga shows us playfully how not to behave. Trickster's reverse norm turns on a sense of normative context, as Barre Toelken has discussed Navajo coyote tales in performance. With a cultural screen as backdrop, characters act out coded implications, their actions resonate with cultural overtones, and they dramatize the absence of order to call tribal judgment into play.[34] Yet there is no sense of implied tribal values in Vizenor's fiction. The "permission" for "disrespect," advanced by Mary Douglas, is neither earned nor conditionally granted. Freud's joking "economy" runs in the red. A nihilist shadow darkens *Homo ludens* here, critically postmodernist for theory's sake, questionably at "play" in Huizinga's terms. If the appeal is to picaresque, a "novel" journey from epic odyssey through *Don Quixote, Pickwick Papers,* or even *Lolita* in a western literary tradition, neither straight man nor comic fool nor dreamer livens the interplay. Besides the publisher's hype and author's co-option, there's little sense of how these fictions claim tribal origins.

This opinion does not cancel the urban comic edge to Vizenor's Trickster video in *Warriors of Orange* (1984), where a band of politicized warriors led by Charlie Hill upstages and cons white liberals into funding a miniature orange farm and "pinch bean" coffee houses on the reservation. The humor here is incisive, country dry, by any measure ironically Indi'n, as in the rare commercial film *Powwow Highway* (1989). From the opening shot of a dusty country road, Buffy Sainte-Marie lays the musical track with "Trickster" and "Fast Bucks," while Floyd Westerman lampoons the Bureau of Indian Affairs on the local rez jukebox, and the trickster male collective bangs a Ponca 49 song on the side of their orange bus. "White men got white from many neckties," Harold Sincere (a.k.a. Charlie Hill) kids his Men of Orange, who set out for the city to squeeze liberal sentiment one more time in the "old foundation game." The bottom line: "We get a little money, they get a good name."

When Harold's jilted non-Indian girlfriend of a decade back appears for the fund raising, the jokes quicken. "Call me Fanny, Felty," she says straight-faced, and Harold teases her, "Remember the oral tradition." A certain spirited play and sense of improvisation animate these funky scenes. When red and white sides cross-dress in T-shirts for softball (red "Anglos" and white "Indians" in opposite colors), the trickster reversals take on a Marx Brothers romp. These "wild word hunters," or, as Vizenor borrows from himself elsewhere, "social acupuncturists," pop a bouquet of cultural balloons about Indians as stoic warriors, nubile people of peace, or vanishing primitives. They are decidedly quick to pounce on liberal guilt, and no less tricky than contraries of old. "You're a rotten Trickster, Harold Sincere," Fanny thanks her bad debtor for a ten-year-old loan repaid (he's ripped off a white philanthropist with the bromidal grandmother's burial story). The urban Indian punchline comes along a Minneapolis freeway: "Nothing as cruel as civilization and loneliness." This is not a new war cry, but the comic twists in this thirty-minute film give it a contemporary off-reservation spin.

To be sure, Vizenor's narrative histories of the White Earth Reservation (*The People Named the Chippewa* [1984]) ground his tricks among real people and historical ballast. His retellings of Ojibwe lyrics and stories, in *Summer in the Spring,* authenticate a versatile translative voice:

> when my midewiwin drum
>   sounds for me
>   the sky
>   clears
>   the sky is blue
>   he hi hi hi
> when my midewiwin drum
>   sounds for me
>   the waters are smooth
>   ho ho ho ho[35]

Vizenor's talent may best focus in Imagist poems—for example, in the *Harper's Anthology of 20th Century Native American Poetry* (1988), edited by Duane Niatum to update *Carriers of the Dream Wheel* (1975):

> the whole moon
> burns behind jamestown
>
> seven wings of geese
> light the thin ice
>
> asian sun
> bleeds on the interstate
>
> pressed flowers
> tremble in the prairie stubble
>
> paced on the mirror
> my fingerprints blot the past
>
>   ("March in North Dakota")

No postmodernist flap hyperbolizes these understated lines. Yet in the hastily published *Trickster of Liberty,* outtakes resurface from *Bearheart, Griever* and UC Berkeley's dirty laundry (stolen computers, personal gossip, academic smut), all in slapdash, cartooned big words:

"The Woodland trickster is a comic trope; a universal language game. The trickster narrative arises in agonistic imagination; a wild venture in communal discourse, an uncertain humor that denies aestheticism, translation, and imposed representations. The most active readers become obverse tricksters, the waver of a coin in a tribal striptease."[36] The author leaves his own byline in the epilogue: "The tribal trickster liberates the mind in a comic discourse that reveals new signs, identities, and uncertain humor" (*TL* 156). And in the spring of 1990, the University of Minnesota Press announced four "new" books by Gerald Vizenor: *Griever: An American Monkey King in China* (reprinted), *Bearheart: The Heirship Chronicles* (reprinted under a different title), *Crossbloods: Bone Courts, Bingo, and Other Reports* (reprinted magazine stories, book reviews, and miscellaneous bylines), and *Interior Landscapes: Autobiographical Myths and Metaphors* (journalist memoirs).

Alan Velie crowns Gerald Vizenor "the Isaac Bashevis Singer of the Chippewa" in the promotional blurb for *Interior Landscapes*. His Trickster fictions have a following, to be sure, and some think he's funny. His violence may pay back a frontier lawlessness, as others hold, and expose the bankruptcy of myths gone sour. And as a brash caricaturist, a self-parodying and quick-trick stylist, he is certainly one of a kind. Recycled tricks or no, there's no undisputed way around Gerald Vizenor's contemporary presence in American Indian letters.

Caveat emptor: Trickster raises the radical in us, crimps the wild card in the literary deck, and so is not to be overly formalized or critically fixed. Paul Radin sees him as the inchoate archetype (a tantalizing oxymoron) behind all types. Dogmatizing trickster tastes, then, can be tantamount to spitting into the wind: better not to protest too much. Surely, taste is a measure of personal bias, each perceiver's long road home—and there's no accounting for one's own ruse nipping another's rose. So to chisel the rules in rock might work against the genre's sheer prodigality, its contagious excess, its liminal permutations.

Still, style goes a considerable way toward gracing fallen angels, and literary tact here with Indian humor involves matters of cultural strategy. There is an art to such matters, if it is to be literature, oral or otherwise. The simple questions may be most valid: Why write and read such stuff? What are the author's intentions (to be so bold)? And how do the literary effects register on an audience, tricksters all, but for the grace of bad example?

Vizenor's fiction strikes me as clearly and questionably postmodernist, yet in that mode self-referential to a fault (a rhetoric to dazzle, or
simply to fog story and character for reasons beyond my understanding). In this sense, the hyper-reflexive texture of the writing—the self-
involvement—obscures tribal codings or cultural groundings. Point of
view isolates itself in rap talk that rules out character development,
dramatic structure, and thematic plotting, not to mention contrary
lessons in tribal opposites. The fictions seem to suck back into their own
infectious verbalizing; as such, they lack the inverse implications and
antipoetic gaiety of Trickster cycles both in oral traditions (see Barre
Toelken's Navajo Yellowman stories or Howard Norman's Cree
Nibènegenesábe narratives) and in more recent literary echoings
(Erdrich, Allen, Welch, Silko, Momaday, and Ortiz, among many).
Robert Gish complains that *The Trickster of Liberty* victimizes the
reader with "the novelist's own indulgent word-way trickery" and simply is "not funny" ("less condiment and more meat," he caps his
review).[37] At least for this reader, the effect of *Griever* or *Bearheart* or
Trickster is not to draw me toward a tribal dialogue or into ancient
questionings, pluralist probings, and comic forgivings, but to estrange
one in the West's existential loneliness—dispossessed, disdainful, libidinous without communal focus.

Indi'ns Playing Indians

> "If I had twenty dollars, I'd buy me a . . . a . . . a living bra!
> Aaee."
>
> FINA, in Hanay Geiogamah, *Body Indian*

The American Indian Theater Ensemble first performed Hanay
Geiogamah's *Body Indian* at La Mama Experimental Theater Club in
New York in 1972. Political street theater salts this Kiowa playwright's
work, along with Bertolt Brecht's sense of carnival, the Marquis de
Sade's surreal theater, and the grim historical humor of Arthur Kopit's
late 1960s play, *Indians*. Yet *Body Indian* seems distinctive unto itself—
a pan-Indian play, dangerously humorous, something tribally akin to
dark comic theater of conscience. The Indian capacity for humor has
been historically a "blessing," Geiogamah told me. It's "one of the
fundamental miracles of our lives . . . part of religion."[38] Indian jokes

are embedded deeply in the cultures, he agreed, and they serve as secular prayers to ground and revitalize tribal people.

Body Indian dramatizes off-reservation Indians on the Oklahoma skids, drinking away meager lease payments, mooching *al-hong-ya* (money), scamming, laughing, singing "49" songs, and stealing from one another to stay alive. Jeffrey Huntsman, in his introduction, calls this Indian drama "funny and fierce."[39] For a native dramatist to portray Indians so sardonically, so realistically on the joking "down" side of tribal visions, seems the absurdist test of "permitted disrespect." Such comic "license" elicits the candid respect of Indians challenging the negatives in tribal life today.

The play opens in red English dialect: "Well, I'lll beee! B———obbye Leee! Come in, hites, come in! Long time no see." *Hites,* or "close friends," jive and roll their own kin to "keep the party going," as the stage directions say for the fifth and last scene of this clipped one-act. Passed out on a railroad track, Bobby Lee has lost his leg. He drinks more now to kill the pain, but wants to enter "a AA deal for alcoholics" in Norman and pay with his lease check. Bobby has some pride left. "Bobby Lee, hites, come on, guy, share your drink with us," begs Eulahlah. "Geee. We always help you out when you need it. Help us out. Share with us." To "help out" is the pan-Indian idiom for ceremonial support, an ironic echo of the tribal "giveaways" that passed property communally among the people. The cheap wine is running low, and each time Bobby passes out the others fleece him to buy more. Then, when all is gone, almost all is lost, the others steal his artificial leg for "bootleg" wine (the terrible pun). "He tol' me he saw in his deetees a row of lillel' chickens sittin' on those jail bars singin' Indian songs," Howard defends the hock of Bobby's leg:

> He said he felt like he was fallin' through the whole jailhouse floor into the sewer lines.

> He said his hair was long as an old lady's, and his fingers were all shrunk up, like he was a-dead.

So they hustle off for refills, and Bobby's "sardonic smile" freeze-frames the end of the play. He turns to face an oncoming nightmare train projected on the back wall—a primal mixture of horror and grim humor, the *risus sardonicus* of victims in extreme agony. It is the body's spitting grimace in the face of the executioner. Bobby Lee addresses

himself from the opening lines of the play: "Welll, h———ell———o,
Bobby Lee. How are you, hites? Lo———ng time no . . . seee."
The comedy is bleak; the impoverished situation all too Indian.
"Where's his money, Grampa? Grampa, hey, does he have any money?
We need some bad, man." The desperate bonding among bros and
sisters, "uncles" and "aunts"—*Pah-bes* and *Pah-be-mas* in the drama's
regional Kiowa dialect—seems that of starving scavengers. They stick
together to die tribally. Their misery mixes the gravel and glue of a
liminal "good time." Indians have one another, for better and worse,
old bonds, new burdens. "Yeah, yeah, ya'll are kin," Bobby's "uncle"
says—a qualified tribalism, where "kin" means ideally communal,
born poor, dispossessed, and desperate. This "kind of" irony is known
particularly among tribal natives derailed by the mainstream. And
Geiogamah does not spare words or the truth to show the low comic
survival of losers' humor, a homeopathic psychic medicine, along with
the dehumanizing cruelty in homeless Indian contexts. The dramatic
intent draws on honesty, witness, revelation, cathartic change—an
artistic–social commitment to acting out the truth, hoping for a better
life. It's engaging trickster theater, a breed of mythic humor and psychological realism to wake the people up to themselves.

What's funny here? Nothing easy, surely, though the throwaway singing and laughing and dancing add Brecht's surreal touch to the suffering. Geiogamah and his Indian troupe thought they were enacting a
tragedy until the opening-night New York audience laughed through all
five scenes and reset the drama as "tragicomedy" (see Appendix C).
The stage jokes tell us something about intertribal connections in the
backwashes of colonial tragedy. "Are you going to war dance for us,
Howard?" one of the women teases an out-of-work, aging warrior. The
women rattle the chains of cultural despair and sociological bondage
among peoples whose yearly income may be a few thousand dollars.
Their material index of despair seems the highest in America:

ALICE
(slowly) I wish I had some meat now. My kids been eatin' only com-
modity meat for 'bout two months now. Junior's unemployment ran out a
month ago. There ain't no jobs nowhere.

. . .

BETTY
(slowly) All those white people think Indians have it good because they
think the government takes care of us. They don't even know. It's rougher

than they know. I'd like to trade my house for a white lady's house on Mission. I'd like for a white lady to have my roaches.

. . .

ALICE
    I wish I had a check from anywhere. (The bottle is moving around.)

EULAHLAH
    So do I.

ETHEL
    So do I. I'd get my son out of county jail if I did.

Relief from these depressions comes through more bad jokes, worse wine, and a "49" song and dance, "One-Eyed Ford." People use what they have, grimacing to tough it out.

The interplay, the scrapping, the banter, the common losses all come on the edges of Indian survival, as the white man's train passes through and ends each of five scenes. Victims of the machine in a New World garden, still alive (if lame, beaten down, or even lifelessly drunk), such Indians prove a certain tribal truth that Geiogamah catches on stage. Not "vanished" Americans, but "real" portraits, these characters play out the ironies of postwar Indian survival. They are the "good-time" veterans of addictions surviving on poverty's rags and crumbs in suburban slums, the struggling remnants of native civilizations trying to find a way out, a road home. "Good times," however desperate, are better than no times at all.

For Geiogamah, to show the play of pain—the endurance of the walking wounded—strikes some grim measure of comic triumph. "Some of those schools ain't so bad," Eulahlah says of "GI" or government school kidnapping, "but some of them sure no good." (Officials rounded up rez children like calves and shipped them to boarding schools hundreds of miles from their homes.) Here is dramatic courage to face the truth, as Bobby's "sardonic smile" meets the oncoming train. The railroad historically ran over the backs of Bobby's people, and he turns to bare his teeth (the Greek meaning of "sardonic"), indeed to deny defeat, as Freud argues of humorous defiance as the ego's final will over circumstances. Bobby holds out for better, even at the bottom. He knows what has happened: his artificial leg has been stolen by "relatives" to buy cheap wine, a tribal painkiller. But he *knows*—and in so knowing, he does not give in to victimization, nor is the audience relieved of his agony, the struggle in "play." This is where Viktor

Frankl says that suffering, given a certain self-distance, translates into dark comic "sacrifice" (*Man's Search for Meaning*). We grant pain significance and seek better. "It's like a jack-in-the-box smile," Geiogamah explains, "his smile just pops up, like a clown's painted-on smile. You know it's painted on." Bobby is "taking responsibility" for himself, addressing himself. He's "cleaned out" and "cleansed," the dramatist feels, to say "hello" to himself and start again from the bottom. The survivalist humor of this perspective saves a prisoner from death-camp despair, steers a neurotic from the shoals of self-torment, sears a romantic view of Indians with reality, and shows Indians where they start rebuilding. Such dark red comedy survives tragedy; it alchemizes suffering toward ironic perception and comic possibility. "Pervasive and yet evasive," Geiogamah says of tribal humor, it cuts through the "hypocrisy" of Indians fooling and fleecing themselves. Bawdy art is trickster's ground zero for Indi'n humor.

Foghorn premiered in West Berlin when Geiogamah's troupe toured Europe in 1973. It is an ensemble piece, a tribal "play" in old ways modernized—a series of mock improvisations, trickster-style, on Indi'n–white caricatures and clichés, designed to entertain and teach as concise theatrical satire. "Almost all the characters in this play are stereotypes pushed to the point of absurdity," the dramatist notes. "The satire proceeds by playful mockery rather than bitter denunciation. A production should aim at a light, almost frivolous effect (the basic seriousness of the play will emerge all the more effectively if the heavy hand is avoided)." While performing *Foghorn* in West Berlin, Geiogamah's troupe was invited to visit the Berliner Ensemble at Brecht's old theater in East Berlin. Certainly, the Germans recognized overlapping patterns, Geiogamah recalls. He had been distantly familiar with Brechtian theater of alienation, social realism, surrealism, and the many tricks of European drama since working the previous year with Wilford Leach, artistic director at La Mama, as well as reading Martin Esslin's *Brecht, The Man and His Work* (1960).

Geiogamah's staging and music set the tribal context to *Foghorn*, since the play turns more on group improvisation and audience interplay than sculpted "lines." The fabled oral tradition, dramatically speaking, has long relied on improvisational creativity. By using taped electronic music for a pilgrimage, a Zuni sunrise chant, Pocahontas's Indian Love Call, the William Tell Overture (theme of the Lone Ranger radio and television show), the song "Pass that Peace Pipe (and Bury that Hatchet)," and the concluding AIM unity song about Wounded Knee, life in *Foghorn* musically mimes Indian life in the streets. The actors relished "playing" these parts, Geiogamah recalls, vicariously finding rich humor in impersonating Lady Bird Johnson or the Lone Ranger, "just such a compendium of silly little stereotypes." This added to the play's "buoyancy."

"It is not important if the audience can see offstage into the wings," the playwright adds, "or if other elements of the production are exposed." This is "real" life *played* with "slapstick" props, projected images of Alcatraz, Wounded Knee, and national monuments, much clowning, more cartooning, and an overall sense of festive carnival that Bakhtin, in *Rabelais and His World,* locates in the comic tribal matrix of Europe's Middle Ages. The "play" of such double-play, Koestler would argue, "bisociates" the real and the surreal, cultural history and Indian American art.

Foghorn opens with Columbus's lookout spying "¡Los indios!" and exclaiming "¡Estos hombres, cho-co-la-tes!" Quickly history fades to white "settlers" branding Indians bad and barking: "Don't talk back"—"Vermin! Varmits!"—"Filthy savages"—"I say let's force 'em off the land!" A senator "generously" sets aside wasteland reservations, and a century later, all in quick succession, Indians "reclaim" Alcatraz Island and plan to rescue whites and educate non-Indians natively to "save" them from themselves.[40]

"My blessed savages," a nun addresses her brood of Indians, and a "clownish" schoolteacher terrorizes "bucks and squaws" learning English, "the one true language, OUR language!" Thrashing an American flag, one child stutters the "first word of the American way": "Hell-O. Hell-O." It means "bright" in German, inversely "Oh hell," and the ironic point is not lost on Indians on a German stage. Pocahontas sings her legendary Love Call (as John Barth caricatured licentiously in *The Sotweed Factor*) and tells the "true" tale of the "big, big captain's" detumescent, hairy, "pink" failure to take her virginity, an old comic gag. Tonto, tired of shining the Lone Ranger's boots and suffering his egoism, slits the masked man's throat.

Foghorn reaches a carnival pitch with a chorus-line number, "Pass that Peace Pipe," written by Indians in 1943. "Everything was just wild," Geiogamah says, "absolutely wild, and it got wilder and wilder." The playwright gives carefully choreographed directions: "Between each of the stanzas of the song, delivered as a wild production number, an actor wearing a bull's head is spotlighted with a pretty girl in pigtails, who reads from a giant roll of toilet tissue. The bull also holds a roll, and unwinds enough tissue to wipe his behind each time a treaty is called out." And with "magnificent visuals" the cast carried on, the playwright recalls, "improvisations, animation, buoyancy." His actors had great subliminal fun playing meanies abusing Indians over the years:

IF YOUR TEMPER'S GETTIN' THE TOP HAND
ALL YOU GOTTA DO IS JUST STOP AND
PASS THAT PEACE PIPE AND BURY THAT HATCHET
LIKE THE CHOCTAWS, CHICKASAWS, CHATTAHOOCHIES,
CHIPPEWAS DO!

The play winds down with a rough-and-tumble "Wild West" show to the 1973 AIM occupation of Wounded Knee (earlier that year) and subsequent trial. The frolic ends on a sober pan-Indian note: "NOT GUILTY!"

These vignettes play out the anger and pain of being Indian for five hundred years under Euroamerican occupation. *Foghorn* was originally performed as the lobotomy of a magnified head, the foghorns harassing Indians just off Alcatraz in 1969. The play opens the floodgates of Indian caricatures behind the cigar-store mask. Its joking taps a deep historical resentment and cauterizes a contemporary wound festering in social ills. And the humor lies in recognition, in release, in "playing" out the hurt, as the play celebrates what it means to be alive today in Indian America.

The third of three Geiogamah plays in the University of Oklahoma paperback *New Native American Drama* (1980) is *49*, a work that affirms all Indians coming together in powwow (Algonkian for "making medicine") to celebrate their tribal identities. "More than anything else," Geiogamah said, "I wanted the young people [in the cast] to be affirmative in the face of despair and unreasoning force." With a musical assist from Jim Pepper and an orchestra of native instruments— "bells, rattles, ratchets, bull-roarers, Apache violins, flutes, whistles, various sizes of drums, piano, and guitars"—tribal bodies move in concert, singing and dancing on an 1885 Oklahoma ceremonial ground, the arbor circle at the center. This ideally round, formally "comic" circle centers the people against a century of assault on their native good humor. The circle's harmony and balance—core simplicity and sense of completion—provide a formally comic "control line," Geiogamah feels, among the Kiowa. The balladeer sings through their trouble, and they answer:

> I GOT A DRUM
> LET'S MAKE A SONG
> I'LL SING TO YOU, HONEY
> ALL NIGHT LONG.
>
> TAKE YOU DOWN TO ANADARKO WITH ME, HONEY
> TAKE YOU OUT TO TAHLEQUAH
> UP TO THE OSAGE COUNTRY FOR THE POWWOWS
> HONEY COME ON BLAZE WITH ME
> HONEY COME ON BLAZE WITH ME
>
> COME ON DANCE 49, HONEY
> COME ON SING WITH ME
> COME ON DANCE 49, HONEY
> COME ON, BE WITH ME.

The life forces of grounded belonging, loving senses, social singing, communal stimulants, and bonding against adversity tie the people to their past and with one another. The dancers stand together against the police, defy disruption, and reassert their rights to being Indian in "native" America. It is a drama of resistance and tribal assertion through social union—an upbeat play that pulls the drumbeat and bull-roarer and cedar flute notes from past into present. This follows an "umbilical control line," Geiogamah told me, attached to the tribal past, threaded through an ongoing humor:

> I see the Indi'n capacity for humor as a blessing. And I see it as one of the fundamental miracles of our lives. It's a miraculous thing that's pulled us through so much. It's a force that's part of religion. I don't see religion so much as just being our bundles or our prayers. It's everything from the past that we've brought forward with us, our memories, ancestors, especially that, all of these things are religion to me—singing, dancing, stories, suffering, all of that. And respect and caring for each other. So in that sense humor is definitely a part of religion. I truly believe that the older Indi'ns laughed, and laughed, and laughed. (Appendix C)

This seems reason to go on going on, trickster-style, whatever the odds, for survival is the bottom line, and tribal continuity sets the essential terms. Everything goes onward from there.

"So to me," Hanay Geiogamah concluded his interview, "it's like a small miracle if you can bring laughter into somewhere, it's a blessing." *A-hó.*

Jaune Quick-to-See Smith, *Charlo Series* (1985).
(Courtesy of Jaune Quick-to-See Smith)

Dan Namingha, *Polaccaca* (1985). (Courtesy of Dan Namingha)

Dan Namingha, *Action-Reversed Role* (1989). (Courtesy of Dan Namingha)

Roxanne Swentzell, *The Emergence of the Clowns* (1988).

Steve LaRance, *Water Recreation Spirit* (1988).

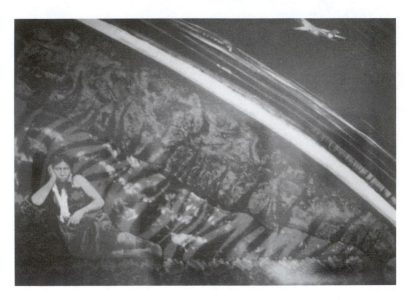

Jean LaMarr (Paiute–Pitt River), *Cover Girl Series.*

Larry McNeil (Tlingit–Nishka), *Real Indians* (1980).

Rick Glazer-Danay (Mohawk), *Buffalo Gal Wearing Blue Jeans* (1986).

Alfonso Roybal (San Ildefonso Pueblo), *Clown on Rainbow over 3 Cactus.*
(Courtesy of the School of American Research)

J. D. Roybal (San Ildefonso Pueblo), *Two Koshare on Burro* (1985).
(Courtesy of the School of American Research)

Lomoyeswa [Louis Lomay] (Hopi, Old Oraibi), *Mudhead Dancer* (1989).
(Courtesy of the School of American Research)

Oscar Howe, *Buffalo Dancer.* (Courtesy of Oscar Howe)

Oscar Howe, *Candi Ompapi*. (Courtesy of Oscar Howe)

T. C. Cannon (Caddo–Kiowa), *Collector #5*.

T. C. Cannon (Caddo–Kiowa), *Grandmother Gestating Father and the Washita River Runs Ribbon Like*.

Harry Fonseca (Maidu), *Coyote Clowns*. (Courtesy of Harry Fonseca)

5

Feminist Indi'ns

> . . . revisionist work, so much the work of women, is not adven-
> titious, and should remind us that in the search for the primitive,
> which to a considerable extent is a search for the feminine, women
> should not be left out of the account.
>
> SHERMAN PAUL, "Ethnopoetics"

Doubly Othered

> Pocahontas' body, lovely as a poplar,
> Sweet as a red haw in November, or a paw-paw in May.
>
> CARL SANDBURG, "Cool Tombs"

Revising history means looking back (re-vision) at what we were, and
thus are now. Whatever "the primitive" connotes, on a credit side the
primal origin or on a debit side the "other," women were incontestably
there from the beginning. They are standing up to be counted today.
Monica Sjöö and Barbara Mor strop the male phallus on a feminist
whetstone in *The Great Cosmic Mother: Rediscovering the Religion of
the Earth* (1987), suggesting that female chromosomes determine life
from the start, that mother precedes father, that socializing women
invented speech, and that culture began feminist. Radical Euroamerican
feminism may be exploring a primitivist separatism that Indians have
long experienced and may not exactly relish.

"God made *Pocahontas* the Kings Daughter the meanes to deliuer
me," John Smith puffed in *New England Trials* (1622), "& there-by
taught me to know their treacheries to preserve the rest." Whether
fourteen years earlier, the twelve-year-old "princess" Pocahontas saved
Smith's head with her own or no, she was in fact lured aboard an

171

English ship in 1613 and held prisoner, just about the time *The Tempest*
played in London. John Rolfe, too, fell under the spell of the dusky
maiden, whose "naked" bottom cartwheeled with the boys, according
to William Strachey, "all the fort over" and aroused Rolfe's "unbridled
desire of carnal affection: but for the good of this plantation, for the
honour of our countrie, for the glory of God, for my owne salvation,
and for the converting to the true knowledge of God and Jesus Christ an
unbeleeving creature, namely Pokahuntas." So Rolfe wrote an English
friend in a letter on display under glass, in October 1971, at Oxford's
Bodleian Library. "In the utmost of many extremities," Captain Smith
alleged in *The Generall Historie of Virginia, New England & the Summer Isles* (1624), "the blessed Pokahontas, the great Kings daughter of
Virginia, oft saved my life." She has entranced men in the wings of
American patriarchy for four centuries and become, Paula Gunn Allen
says, a dusky sub-metaphor for white women.[1]

From the beginning, native women were sensually forbidden doubles
to pale, Puritan, sexless "virgins" languishing in the repressed wake of
Eve. To Old World gentlemen, "primitive" meant unbridled, naked
sensualism, Lilith reincarnate, as civilization denatured their own idealized women. In 1613, Pocahontas, as an amber Miranda "saved"
from Caliban's rude island, was abducted to an English ship and per-
suaded to marry Master John Rolfe (did she have a choice?). The Indian
princess forswore her father's heathen ways, accepted Christian baptism, learned English, bore a mixed-blood child, and emerged "Lady
Rebecca" in the English court. About to return to Virginia to see her
father in 1617, she died at Gravesend, where Marlow's "Nellie" waits
anchor in Conrad's *Heart of Darkness*.

Such is the stuff of legend and fiction, historically salted. In Mary V.
Dearborn's *Pocahontas's Daughters: Gender and Ethnicity in American
Culture* (1986), the story proves a cultural paradigm for ethnicity with
psychofeminist frills. The mainstream feminist critic reads our melting-
pot recipe in a more intimate female chamber—as an ambivalent broth-
el-cum-marriage-bed for ethnic American women. According to Dearborn, women of color seem "twice" outsiders to the dominant American patriarchy. On the eve of Pocahontas's colonial naturalization in her
own country, the dark "she" figures doubly as "the other" who Ameri-
canizes through mixed marriage. Barring intermarriage and begging the
arts, the Dark Woman publishes through the fatherly midwiving of
white males (Dearborn notes, for example, Anzia Yezierska and John

Dewey, Zora Hurston and Franz Boas, Mourning Dove and Lucullus McWhorter, Mary Antin and William Dean Howells, Gertrude Stein and Carl Van Vechten). The ambivalent bridging that results from such psychic miscegenation, Dearborn argues, both redefines and disrupts the Big House of patriarchal nativist codes—that is, American male authority in some genteel purity of lineage. These male-dominant patterns begin with the "founding fathers" and their westering sons.[2] In Dearborn's estimation, the illegitimate ethnic daughter, descendant of Pocahontas, searches for and rejects the father; she bridges with and separates from mediating men in power; she wedges into some old American split of patricide and filiopietism, truly an American "house divided." A wanting Penia seduces the satiated male Poros at heaven's gates, Kristeva retells Eros's seeding, as miscegenated gender tales mythologize the New World.

This all sounds fetching. In the Pocahontas phylum, though, it ignores Luther Standing Bear and Charles Eastman leaning on their white wives to write and help publish books. It also may overlook the fact that George Custer's wife had a lot to do with writing his "autobiography." More recently, N. Scott Momaday tutored under Yvor Winters; James Welch and Roberta Whiteman studied with Richard Hugo; Wendy Rose, Joy Harjo, and Simon Ortiz all attended the Iowa Writers Workshop. As discussed, Leslie Silko and James Wright corresponded with poetic intimacy in the last year of his life. Today Louise Erdrich and Michael Dorris write as husband and wife with "three-eighths" Indian bloodlines (why do we fractionalize Indians, split under rubrics of pedigree or peerage?). Their books benefit from both native backgrounds and eastern education at Yale, Johns Hopkins, and Dartmouth. Biculturalism would not seem such a bad thing, with Indian context and Anglo text meeting across a creative middle ground. Mates, good friends, editors, lovers, or mentors remain just that—partners, peers, colleagues, or models whose cross-cultural creative processes bridge ethnic, gender, and class barriers. The old native pureblood or monocultural stereotypes give us only one simplified story, out of fashion now even among anthropologists, who tend to stress ontology over biology in cultural development.

More than a quarter century after Betty Friedan's *The Feminine Mystique* in 1963, where are we? The United Nations declared 1975 to 1985 the Decade for Women. But despite Sandra Day O'Connor's appointment to the Supreme Court in 1981, Sally Ride in space in 1983,

Geraldine Ferraro nominated by the Democrats for the vice presidency
in 1984, and Wilma Mankiller elected principal chief of the Oklahoma
Cherokees in the 1980s, America is struggling with equal rights for
women. What about Coyote Old *Woman*? She has been slighted, if not
slurred, in the myth making of America, and now she snaps back as a
bushy-tailed, nonconformist, trickster Indian feminist. (The Mohawk
writer Beth Brant fictionalizes her cross-dressing in comically seducing
a vixen: "Mmmmm yeah, this Fox is pretty clever with all that stuff she
knows. This is the best trick I ever heard of. Why didn't I think of it?"[3])
This independent woman may be marginalized or estranged, eccentric
or straight, artistic or studious, lesbian or otherwise liminal to Ms.
Moral Majority. Yet she nips at the high heels of the Nancy-Jane-and-
Erica syndrome of Anglo mainstream America, from the Daughters of
the American Revolution, to exercise salons, to trash novels.

At the other end of the historical spectrum from Pocahontas, a
woman such as Mary Crow Dog, a Rosebud Brule Sioux *iyeska,* or
"mixed blood" with a white father, takes her stand with her men at
Wounded Knee in 1973. Mary washes dishes and sews sleeping bags
from rags, while Annie Mae Aquash (a Micmac later assassinated)
cooks and keeps spirits high. Some women hold bunkers and "man"
guns. They hold out for seventy-one late-winter days along Wounded
Knee Creek in South Dakota, where three hundred Minneconjou Sioux
were butchered in 1890.

A volunteer white nurse berates the Indian women on "feminist"
grounds, but Mary answers that the war at hand must be fought, and
then the warriors' machismo can be deconditioned—for the moment
every effort counts, and the pecking order is irrelevant. "We told her
that her kind of women's lib was a white, middle-class thing, and that at
this critical stage we had other priorities. Once our men had gotten their
rights and their balls back, we might start arguing with them about who
should do the dishes."[4] The old gender loyalties bond her with the tribe
as a whole, beyond new social redefinitions, and she is renamed *Ohitika
Win,* or Brave Woman, after the siege. "Again I come back to the old
Cheyenne saying: 'A nation is not lost as long as the hearts of its women
are not on the ground' " (*LW* 137).

Below the knoll where half the butchered women, children, and old
men were dumped in a mass grave in 1890 like so many beef carcasses,
Mary bears a child in battle, named after her friend Pedro Bissonette
(later killed). A Roman Catholic chapel with AIM militants in the

basement looks down on America's Auschwitz. "In that ravine, at Cankpe Opi, we gathered up the broken pieces of the sacred hoop and put them together again" (*LW* 155). Rebirth in the face of death points symbolically and realistically toward the sunrise. And still these Indians laugh to survive: "Wounded Knee was a place one got scared in occasionally, a place in which people made love, got married Indian style, gave birth, and died. The oldest occupants were over eighty, the youngest under eight. It was a heyoka place, a place of sacred clowns who laughed while they wept. A young warrior standing up in the middle of a firefight to pose for the press; Russell Means telling the photographers, 'Be sure to get my good side' " (131). Teasing keeps the tribal holdouts together: "[Pedro] would come up and ask whether I wanted to play basketball. That always got a big laugh because I was so huge. We actually laughed and kidded each other a lot. It helped us to last as long as we did" (133).

Mary hardly began as a princess. Her white father walked away from "all that baby shit" to a bottle in Omaha, she says, and her mother found work a hundred miles away and then remarried a wino "who started us kids drinking when I was barely ten years old" (*LW* 15). On the prairie near He Dog in a homemade shack without electricity, heating, or plumbing, Grandma Brave Bird and Grandpa Noble Moore "raised us on rabbits, deer meat, ground squirrels, even porcupines" (19). Then Mary was taken away to Catholic boarding school at St. Francis.

In her own words a "loner" from the start, Mary was stealing vestry wine and could "drink a quart of the hard stuff and not show it" at twelve. This is some distance from Powhatan's aboriginal court and John Smith saved by a dusky royal maiden, later Lady Rebecca at the court of James I. "In South Dakota white kids learn to be racists almost before they learn to walk" (*LW* 22). Mary was raped at fourteen. She rebelled against the nuns' terrorism at Catholic boarding school (sexual harassment, physical beatings, beratings), and was kicked out of St. Francis for knocking down an abusive sister and publishing an underground newspaper, *Red Panther*. The American Indian Movement gave her a sense of dissident power and pan-tribal unity to talk back. "My aimlessness ended when I encountered AIM" (72). "Some people loved AIM," she says with a laconic Sioux sense of humor, "some hated it, but nobody ignored it" (74). Here twenty years ago were the renascent stirrings of "all-nations" red pride. "They had a new look about them, not that hangdog reservation look I was used to. They moved in a different way, too, confident and swaggering, the girls as well as the boys" (75).

This young red revolutionary married a "medicine man" after "the Knee," Leonard Crow Dog of the iconoclast Crow Dog clan, or *tiospaye*. These self-exiled Lakotas were full-blood renegades, even among their own people, following old Crow Dog's grudge murder of Spotted Tail three generations back. The crow and coyote, pan-tribal tricksters of old, figured as their namesake guardians. Leonard spent two years in the federal penitentiary, he claimed, for healing the wounded and leading Indian people in spiritual ceremonies at Wounded Knee (as a *wicasa wakan,* or "man holy," he could not fight). The family homestead was burned down by arsonists, friends died mysteriously by "exposure" or in strange car wrecks, and the FBI and South Dakota troopers terrorized Leonard's extended family. Mary gave birth to three more children and learned to love her people in the aftermath of "Pedro's baptism of fire." She made strong Indian coffee, "the kind that the Sioux like which will float a silver dollar" (*LW* 174). She figured out how to deal with stubborn Sioux men, "the worst gossips in the world," including her husband: "our men were magnificent and mean at the same time. You had to admire them. They had to fight their own men's lib battles" (69). She began to speak out against the violence among her own people, the substance abuse and wife beatings. In turn, she learned to accept, to forgive, and to help the men. "Facing death or jail they had been supermen, but facing life many of them were weak" (244).

Remarried in her late thirties, Mary carries on, committed to her people, both men and women, most of all the children who shape the future. "A nation is not lost," she repeats often, "as long as the hearts of its women are not on the ground" (*LW* 137). Certainly, Pocahontas, sadly interred at Gravesend, understood this womanist hymn on her own terms, four hundred years before Mary Crow Dog told her own story.

The collaboration between mainstream men and native women can transcend ethnic gender quarrels. Just before James Wright died of throat cancer, he repeated in a letter to Leslie Silko: "I want to share the worst of this news with a very few people whom I admire and value the most . . . who strike me as embodying in their own lives and work something—some value, some spirit—that I absolutely care about and believe in. . . . I will find my way through this difficulty somehow, and one of the best things I have is my knowledge that you exist and that you are going on living and working."[5]

Many of us are saying something of this to several hundred Native American writers today, particularly the women. We would not be writing were it not for them. Theirs is a feminist rebirth of native cultural values and oral voices by way of the printed word; indeed, it is a renewal of oral tribal continuities some forty thousand years old. And this renaissance has flowered since the 1977 publication of *Ceremony* and the initial emergence of the refounding four: Momaday, Silko, Welch, and Ortiz. Among the countless tribes of writers here, they speak for 2 million Native Americans.

One could list hundreds of fine books, and still more talented authors. It might simply be noted that artists and scholars of Native America, Indian and non-Indian, have collaborated to give American literature a rebirth. With these writings, James Wright adds for all of us, "my very life means more to me." In *And That's What She Said* (1984), Rayna Green anthologized feminist Indian authors, while Brian Swann and Arnold Krupat gathered autobiographical essays by American Indian writers for *I Tell You Now* (1987). Second generation to *Smoothing the Ground* (1983), more seminal scholarly essays in *Recovering the Word* (1987) have been edited by these two red engines of the East Coast. Duane Niatum has updated *Carriers of the Dream Wheel* (1975) with the *Harper's Anthology of 20th Century Native American Poetry* (1985). Paula Gunn Allen has capped her myriad arts of verse, prose, and scholarship with an editing coup, *Studies in Native American Literature* (1983), the deeply thoughtful feminist work, *The Sacred Hoop* (1986), and the collection *Spider Woman's Granddaughters: Short Stories by American Indian Women* (1989). And more since then.

Native women are nurturing a double renaissance, to be sure. From Italy, Laura Coltelli in 1990 published *Winged Words: American Indian Writers Speak,* interviews with nine leading Indian authors (the tapings, synchronized on a Fulbright travel grant in 1985, were published by the University of Nebraska Press, the buffalo pony of Indian publishing). Joseph Bruchac III, in addition to spearheading *The Greenfield Review* for over a decade, has edited interviews with twenty-one leading Indian poets, *Survival This Way* (1987). And from Gordon Brotherston's *Images of the New World* (1979), a British scholar's study, through Jarold Ramsey's *Reading the Fire* (1983) and Dennis Tedlock's translated *Popul Vuh* (1985) and "field work" thinking in *The Spoken Word and*

the Work of Interpretation (1983), studies of oral "texts" and performing contexts help us rediscover the rich traditions of some two
thousand original native cultures in the Americas.

The artists themselves remain prolific today, especially the women. It
is difficult to keep pace. Roberta Whiteman's blank verse in *Star Quilt*
(1984) is deftly sensitive, as is the loping free verse of Joy Harjo,
certainly all the lucid work of Linda Hogan, most recently the poems in
Seeing Through the Sun (1985) and the novel *Mean Spirit* (1990). Luci
Tapahonso brightens the horizon with a third collection of poems, *A
Breeze Swept Through* (1987), illustrated in Klee fashion by Jaune
Quick-to-See Smith. James Welch won the *Los Angeles Times* Novel of
the Year award in 1987 for *Fools Crow,* and in 1989 Doubleday released
N. Scott Momaday's *The Ancient Child,* a novel about a mixed-blood
painter who returns to Oklahoma and his Kiowa origins. Additionally,
Ray Young Bear has just published *Eagle Heart Child* (1992) and Louis
Owens, his novel *Wolfsong* (1992). The Native American renaissance
seems to be entering its second generation.

Coyotess

A Coyote slipped across the road
before we knew. Night, the first skin around him.
He was coming from the river
where laughter calls out fish. Quietly a heavy wind
breaks against cedar. He doubled back,
curious, to meet the humming moons we rode
in this gully, without grass or stars.

. . .

Crazed, I can't get close enough
to this tumble wild and tangled miracle.
Night is the first skin around me.
                    ROBERTA HILL WHITEMAN, "The Recognition"

Certainly the majority of tribal Indian women would not be compli-
mented by the Romanized epithet "coyotess," as many live out traditional women's roles through home, marriage, children, extended family, clan heritage, and cultural history in a settled, indeed peaceful,
context. The "coyote" arts of exploration, exploitation, braggadocio, or

battle may seem male sports. Yet Indian women, by virtue of being "Indi'n," stand de facto as cultural contrary to Anglo virtues. Urban feminists to tribal traditionalists, by chance or choice they figure as sociological coyotes marginalized in America. As Indian women in the still male-dominant West, they shoulder the role of double contrary, twice "the other." Here in the "high-tech Indi'n" sense, as Paula Allen quips, stands a humorous Supermom with a deconstructionist *différence*.

With two-thirds of the native population now *off* the reservation, the Indian mother has struggled to keep family, clan, home, and land together through five centuries of war on native cultures. She has suffered the devastation of her brothers and sisters, "warriors" dying in battles, dependence, self-pride, and terror facing insurmountable technological odds. She has stood constant as a match to her mate, despite personal losses or particular betrayals. In contradistinction to Anglo feminists, she was never without gender power, essential tribal work, self-definition, an equal vote (though this varied from tribe to tribe). She generally held the physical and cultural respect of the other sex (with some variable exceptions). "So there's this tradition of humor," Allen explains to Laura Coltelli, "of an awful lot of funniness, and then there's this history of death. And when the two combine, you get a power in the work; that is, it moves into another dimension. It makes it transformational. It creates a metamorphosis in the reader, if the reader can understand what's being said and what's not being said." And so Indian humor circles around to take a feminist stand on critical issues: "It makes for wit, for incredible wit, but under the wit there is a bite. It's not defensive so much as it's bitter. It also makes for utterly brilliant, tragic writing as well. Because it's so close to the bone. . . . And so when you laugh you know perfectly well that you're laughing at death."[6]

The coyotess comes in many tribal pelts, heterogeneous and culturally diverse. By far the majority (perhaps 90 percent) of some five hundred U.S.–based tribes historically functioned as matrilocal, matrilineal, and "mother-right" cultures. So Indian women retained power from Iroquois matriarchal polygamy, to northern plains serial and later multiple monogamy (the men were being killed off in the Indian Wars), to southern plains ownership of women (though here women earned positions of power), to Pueblo mother-right power complexes in the Southwest. *She* has been a wild card in the cultural deck we call "native" America. And her province is "home," a sense of nurturing, with a subtlety in negotiation, a strength in maintaining cultural history.

In a new study of feminist poetics, Alicia Suskin Ostriker strikes a dissonant chord about American "feminine confinement and constraint."[7] She argues that American feminism seeks to roll back "the condition of marginality: nonexistence, invisibility, muteness, blurredness, deformity" in the "divided self" of our women (*SL* 10–11). Ostriker draws a meta-critique of "ghettoized" women, a separatist complaint and call to arms against the primitivizing of women. She dips into R. D. Laing on schizophrenia to analogize "a normal woman's dilemma" as self divided against itself (84). She quotes Erica Jong on fucking, Simone de Beauvoir on biology, and Sylvia Plath on patricide—wildly sassy texts, to be sure. The literary feminist serves here as psychoculturalist. "Identified with the Nature which men have sought to conquer, woman has remained trapped, forced by her body to serve as the eternal Other, an emblem perhaps of sacred mysteries, but a physical, social, and political inferior. Biologically a victim of the species, she becomes by extension a victim of culture" (94). De Beauvoir's *The Second Sex* (1949), "the great-godmother of all feminist texts," tolls the tocsin for women imprisoned in their flesh. "If anatomy is destiny," Ostriker adds, "we all want to escape it" (92).

Western misogyny, from Saint Paul to J. Alfred Prufrock, has planted a thorn in woman's crown; moreover, patriarchal America, with its stern fathers and lawless frontiersmen, would manacle women to the hearth. Aside from biology, perhaps, the Euroamerican problem of "Nature" and the feminine "other" lies embedded culturally in Christian history: "Let the woman learn in silence, with all subjection," 1 Timothy says. "But I suffer not a woman to teach, nor to usurp authority over the man, but to be in silence. For Adam was first formed, then Eve" (2:11–13).

Indian women feel differently, as Mary Crow Dog is quick to say: "To me, women's lib was mainly a white, upper-middle class affair of little use to a reservation Indian woman. . . . I had an urge to procreate, as if driven by a feeling that I, personally, had to make up for the genocide suffered by our people in the past" (*LW* 244). Such a native motherhood charts a separate history and heritage from that of mainstream feminism. Indian women derive from a matrilocal base and cross-gender cooperation (tribal reciprocities, clan balancings, mother-right powers). Among their own people, the women were not disempowered or repressed or disfranchised until recently—this coming by and large with the white "man." The Great White Father refused to recognize matrilocal power and insisted on Indian men signing treaties, voting in councils, and making deals, when such as the Iroquois, Cherokee, and Pueblo nations were politically and religiously constellated around matrilineal clans.

So among tribal peoples we have feminism with a difference: a reassertion of traditional tribal values, a redefinition of clan roles, and an adaptation of old cultures to new conditions. "Hearth" and "home" are not loaded words to these Indian women, even if some define themselves outside conventional native patterns (as with Lulu in Erdrich's *Love Medicine*). Coyotess complaints seem not so much male-directed as intercultural, less personally motivated than historically sensitive. Ostriker, Kristeva, or Jong may consider tribal women overly domestic from a Euroamerican slant, or burdened with child rearing, but, then again, American feminists do not notice Indians much anyway. Dearborn and Ostriker have read every feminist American poet and critic but the Indian ones. Considering the distance between "stealing" the language back and the sacred-to-secular tribal faith in "the word," perhaps it is just as well not to look the "other" way. There is almost an irreconcilable difference between Western heroics and native balances, plots of empowerment and narratives of reciprocal exchange, as Allen suggests in *The Sacred Hoop*. Pocahontas would have lived much longer as an Algonkian mother than as a Renaissance lady in King James's court.

Sylvia Plath driving a stake into Daddy's "fat black heart" or Diane Wakoski dancing on the grave of a motorcycle son of a bitch may draw a crowd to a reading (or a critic to an analyst), but it is hardly a cultural paradigm worth emulating. At best, this is exorcism, a cry for help; at worst, Western millennial distress. "This is a doomed country, it seems to me," Susan Sontag bemoaned in 1966; "I only pray that, when America founders, it doesn't drag the rest of the planet down too."[8] There are alternatives. If Emily Dickinson is (coyly) "Nobody," Paula Allen is (brashly) some/body. "When a piano or couch or refrigerator needs moving, we move it," she says of Laguna women back home. And here Ostriker's ideals, integratively, dovetail into Indian tribal coordinates: "Mutuality, continuity, connection, identification, touch: this motif constitutes the imperative of intimacy in women's writing, and in this motif we find the elements of a gynocentric erotics, metaphysics, and poetics, constituting a radical challenge to some of our most cherished cultural and psychic assumptions" (*SL* 165–66). It is what Lipsha in Louise Erdrich's *Love Medicine* (1984) identifies as "belonging" in a home-based family.

Paula Allen's *The Sacred Hoop* gathers seventeen of her broadly ranging essays on "tribal-feminism" (perhaps a redundant term) into a "patchwork quilt" of interdisciplinary thought on women, Indians, and Western "patriarchal colonialism."[9] Allen seems less defensive than Ostriker, though no less determined: "The new song our ghosts push from their hearts is a song of bitterness and grief, to be sure; but it is also a song of sanity, balance, and humor."

"Humor is widely used by Indians to deal with life. Indian gatherings are marked by laughter and jokes, many directed at the horrors of history, at the continuing impact of colonization, and at the biting knowledge that living as an exile in one's own land necessitates" (*SH* 158). Allen draws traditionally on gynocratic histories of Native America for definitions of cultural home, "anciently based on a belief in balance, relationship, and the centrality of women, particularly older women" (223). She thanks her feminist friends (all color of 'skins) for sharing their "discoveries, uncoveries, recoveries, the hair-raising adventures of childrearing, career building, and super-womanhood" (x).[10]

It is instructive to place Allen next to Ostriker (Beacon Press did when it released both *The Sacred Hoop* and *Stealing the Language* in 1986). The former seems cross-cultural and mediative; the latter, infratextual and steeled for controversy. Perhaps the slants reflect their respective cultures, one interculturally tribal, the other ideologically academic. For all the hurt in her history, Allen is not bitter—outrageous at times, yes—but never castigating or nasty. From "dying savage" through "earth-loving guru," she argues, the "Progressive Fallacy" casts the Indian as "cosmic victim" (*SH* 77–78), and she has had enough of that. "When Western assumptions are applied to tribal narratives, they become mildly confusing and moderately annoying" (237). Her own Keres people are culturally "conflict-phobic," seeking resolutions or coalitions, while "Euro-American culture is conflict-centered" (238). Indians seek to balance the odds; Euroamericans, to win—one accommodates; the other struggles. And Indians regard time as cyclical and space as spherical, while Anglos see time as linear and space as sequential. "Indians never think like Whites," Allen sweeps saucily across this schism (243), which gives pause for thought.

If Indians remain radically and inversely "other" to Euroamerican mind-sets, and if red feminists invert their sisters' mainstream counter-complaints, have we doubled back to a human (indeed, integratively humorous) perspective that was there all along? Have we reversed the separatist reversal when Indian women invert WASP feminists who invert WASP patriarchies? Does the negated negation, or double negative, give us back our gender-collaborative tolerance of the "other" through Native American feminism? Allen offered this thought in an interview at the 1982 Modern Language Association convention:

> [W]e were complaining ten years ago that nobody ever paid any attention to us . . . of course American writers borrow from Indians and have since the beginnings of American literature. That's an issue that ought to be addressed by American literature professors. . . .—I don't care where you look—you're going to find Indians in there somewhere—as characters, as symbols, as rhythms—. . . .
>
> So, exploit us! And do it out front now. There is no America without the death of an Indian. And there can *be* no America without acknowledgement of one of its major sources. Every time you flush the toilet, some Navajo goes without water. You understand that. Staying in this hotel in LA means that those folks out on the res are in trouble because we have all these goodies. And that's true across the board, for every aspect of American life. There is no America that is not deeply wedded to the Indian.[11]

We are either closer to home here with Indian feminist humor or twice removed from cultural reintegration. When she was a student at UCLA's law school, Indian attorney Rebecca Tsosie reacted to Joy Harjo's "The Woman Hanging from the Thirteenth Floor Window":

> [T]his woman could be any number of women, or even ourselves. Her poem speaks to those of us who have felt the dull throb of pain at 4 a.m. when the cold glare of neon signs holds no comfort against the lonely grey drizzle of early city mornings. City nights are as hard and unyielding as the oily asphalt of city streets. Companionship in after-hours clubs is limited to pimps in purple-feathered hats and diamond-studded rings, to Black or Mexican proprietors that keep pistols in their belts and whiskey in their hands, and to other Indians who are as lost and lonely as you are. I think of a young Hopi girl in Oakland. She is not more than sixteen and she is dancing with a Black man dressed in a flashy white suit. They are dancing to a passionate "Brown Sugar" that thunders from the jukebox and drowns out the city-sounds—the screaming sirens and the low moan of the trucks rolling on out of town. She is dancing sedately, her face a quiet mask, and the Arizona mesas and low

thunder clouds appear for a moment in the smoky haze, and then are gone, gone far, far away so that not even a memory remains. Sometimes you feel that you can never go home again. Sometimes you feel that you have forgotten how to speak, that your eyes are hollow, burning sockets that are unable to cry. Pain releases itself in low, animal cries, in the chatter of teeth at the terrible cold of a city night, and in the desire to escape somewhere, anywhere, even out of a 13th story window.

At the root of the pain is fear—fear of the cold, anonymous city, fear of going back to the poverty of the reservation, fear of racists and rapists and of what the schools will "teach" the children, fear of what vision the next drink will bring, and fear of what will happen if there *is* no drink. ("Changing Women" [manuscript])

These are "the facts" personalized, Corn Tassel might say. So do we feel culturally embittered, or tempered by tribal humor?

Allen gets seriously funny about bicultural adaptation: "while we change as Indian women, as Indian women we endure" (*SH* 12). She has a coyotess wit to dart across bullet-pocked hardpan, snatch her prey or count coup on the opposition, and meld back into the sagebrush. It's a scavenger's nip and tuck, carried on with high humor, quick intelligence, and real stakes. Her gynocratic perspectives come from "the cutting edge of tribal resistance and cultural persistence" in a pan-Indian renaissance, her own life from "the Keres Pueblos of the American Southwest, who are among the last surviving Mother-Right peoples on the planet" (11). Ritual gynocracy defines her Indian feminism, the pan-tribal concepts of a creatrix—Laguna Thought Woman, to Cochiti Spider Woman, to Hopi Hard Beings Woman, to Iroquois Sky Woman, to Lakota White Buffalo Calf Woman—who spiritually minds and bears all, including the male and material world. "Woman bears, that is true. She also destroys. That is true. She also wars and hexes and mends and breaks. She creates the power of the seeds, and she plants them" (14). This creatrix, then, is "mother of us all," the mother–father in everyone.

Silly, weak, bitchy, or biologically burdened "ladies" do not figure, at least ideally, in Allen's Laguna upbringing. She was raised around powerful women of "practicality, strength, reasonableness, intelligence, wit, and competence" (*SH* 44). There are divorces and brutalities and disappointments, to be sure. "Most of all I remember the women who laugh and scold and sit uncomplaining in the long sun on feast days and who cook wonderful food on wood stoves, in beehive mud ovens, and over open fires outdoors" (45). And this need not be viewed as matrilocal regionalism. Those chuckling and clucking old women have been around gossiping, cooking, joking, birthing, scolding, working, and casting spells for quite a long time. They are our common cultural matrix, the ancient anima.

Allen writes of both Indian men and women. They can figure as gods, spirits, healers, leaders, poets, and novelists. She is not gender-exclusive, nor is hers a holy war for women's rights. The pain in her position remains undeniable, as with the alienated "breed" or "an Indian who is not an Indian" (*SH* 129). Such a person can disassociate tragically, "unable to be Indian, unable *not* to be Indian" (134), resorting to anodynes of drugs, alcohol, madness, violence, and voicelessness. The catatonic "mute" may be dispossessed of voice and self. It is high time to turn from Pocahontas's Gravesend death to more positive Indian lives today, Mary Crow Dog and Paula Allen and Louise Erdrich. This means finding alternatives to alienation, homes for the dispossessed, lifework for the directionless, a renewed sense of ceremony and balance for men and women together in America.

Move Over, Buddy

> Coyote is a tricky personage—half creator, half fool; he (or she in some versions) is renowned for greediness and salaciousness. Coyote tales abound all over native America, and he has been taken up by contemporary American Indian poets as a metaphor for all the foolishness and the anger that have characterized American Indian life in the centuries since invasion. He is also a metaphor for continuance, for Coyote survives and a large part of his bag of survival tricks is his irreverence. Because of this irreverence for everything—sex, family bonding, sacred things, even life itself—Coyote survives. He survives partly out of luck, partly out of cunning, and partly because he has, beneath a scabby coat, such great creative prowess that many tribes have characterized him as the creator of this particular phase of existence, this "fifth world." Certainly the time frame we presently inhabit has much that is shabby and tricky to offer; and much that needs to be treated with laughter and ironic humor; it is this spirit of the trickster–creator that keeps Indians alive and vital in the face of horror.
>
> PAULA GUNN ALLEN, *The Sacred Hoop*

It is tempting to talk about Simon Ortiz as wanderer or Barney Bush as coyote, since the trickster seems so male in twentieth-century America. In Ortiz, the antiheroic coyote stands in for the poet. And Bush chants in *My Horse and a Jukebox* (1979):

> Moccasined feet stepping down steadily
> to each drum beat
>   The wind keeps singing
> "I been out drinking
>   all night long, way-ya hey-he"
> Unlike that night, this night is for sleep.

This gangly Shawnee–Cayuga can laugh all night with the best of Indi'n jokers and storytellers. His Acoma cultural cousin, Simon Ortiz, surely knows coyote from the bottom up. But what, then, of coyotess? There's outrageous humor in Paula Allen's one-liners, an Indian feminist who cartoons herself with "a cannon between my knees." Wendy Rose throws rocks at Anglo anthros, and Janet Campbell Hale swears that Custer lives in Humboldt County. Mary TallMountain recalls the "good grease" of her lost Inuit childhood. These coyotesses are coming home, and readers collect the scraps of their feminine poetics in eddies such as *Blue Cloud Quarterly* (now defunct), Malki Museum Press, UCLA's Native American Series, Strawberry Press, *Greenfield Review* (also out of print), "A" Press, *Contact II*, Thorp Springs, *La Confluencia*, Turtle Island, Many Smokes, West End Press, *Wassaja, Wambli Ho, Akwesasne Notes*, and any number of liminal journals. Until feminism became an academic industry, a reader had to know where the stream pooled to find these voices; still they lie undiscussed, despite studies by Dearborn and Ostriker.

"Who is Coyote? Trickster, Helper, Teacher or Fool?" asks the back cover of the Berkeley anthology *Coyote's Journal*. The first catch comes in the linking verb "is," which implies a uniplex worldview or a simple answer to the universal riddle of zoomorphism (reverse anthropomorphism). The second slip comes in the binary conjunction "or," implying a choice between categories. For mythic Coyote may be all these and more, since s(he) personifies unlimited liminality or an "inchoate" first principle, both male and female. S(he) is a marginal figure who scavenges the leftovers, and here s(he) somehow assembles the edges toward the tribal center. Indeed, at times Trickster serves as the Comic Hero or Culture Bearer, bringing fire or foodstuffs or survival skills, or simply and universally making the whole thing up (Blackfeet Na'pi and Kipi'taki). Still, tricksters function from the outer limits of the civilized center as something of piecemeal collators for all the rag-ends and rejects of the world *recycled*—the radical figure cohorts with raven, crow, bluejay, loon, wolverine, spider, rabbit, shark, and other fringe figures. Thus Coyote represents the fouler, fornicator, devourer, and deviant in our human–animal world, a fallen god from the spirit world. Yet s(he) overcomes these follies and resurrects; that is, once down or dead, s(he) comes back to life, back for more, back to gamble again, lose, win, or draw. S(he)'s a player, not a defeatist, a trickster in the best and worst sense. S(he)'ll fool an opponent in a no-holds-barred game, but humor and intrigue a gambler back. S(he)'s all too human: animal at his or her best, godlike in dreams. Coyote seems then a comic redeemer of the real, hero of folly, eliciting these necessary questions:

> Should anyone expect to be "redeemed" in a world where our own wits must stay sharp to survive?
> What does heroism add up to against the biggest of all odds, death? Can you trust Trickster (to keep you on your toes . . .)?

What of scattered women's voices in a popular anthology such as *Coyote's Journal*? Joy Harjo seeks a variant of hearth and home in some form of mate, companion, friend, or community where sexual gender is not so much an issue. She opts for self-chosen roles from her cultural parameters, as well as her own lifework. Home for the coyotess involves *placing* herself in collaboration with her origins, especially in rapprochement toward fathers, understanding with mothers, and attention to elders. The issue is coming together, not tearing apart. Her quest is literally back to a native land from which Indians have been so often dispossessed. "Indian at the banjo," Diane Glancy writes, "with a spatula they lifted us from the land" ("They Gave Us the Umbrella"). There is a kind of comic archaeology in questions of origins, as the Indian coyotess plays anthropologist looking back at Anglo migrations:

> & how swatting flies
> the ancestors must have wondered
> what land bridge the white man
> crossed, what mammoth he followed
> from the other way
>
> ("How")

In spite of removals, whether Oklahoma Cherokee or Arizona Navajo,
Glancy says as coyotess at home,

> I sweep the hogan and talk with
> Gramma Bolivar. We make fry bread.
> Her pickle-jars are water-glasses
> and the kitchen smells like clove and
> the grease of our cooking.

The kitchen is where one kind of woman's work goes on (recipes remain
the most stable texts of human culture).[12] Here the stories, songs,
gossip, rumor, and all-around talk pass daily and generate certain
folkloric texts for Indian women. Hearth and home still seem honest,
fulfilling work to tribal women (and men), however idiosyncratically
they go about it. This may be more a mother's purview than a daughter's
separatism.

The humor of love, a coyotess caring, goes to work here. Relationships, however strained, will hold and go on. So the coyotess nurtures her home in old and new ways. "La-la-la-la-la-la," Sioux mothers
sing lullabies to their sleeping children, softly imitating the distant
coyote's song in descending plains triads. A mother's humor is forgiving, whenever possible, and, short of that, sometimes snappish, but
always bonding, even in anger. The point is not to forget. It's a far cry
from Coyote's amorality, brag, and license on the other side of the
gender shadow. Glancy ends her title poem, "One Age in a Dream":

> One after another
> the guilts will let go—
> Bump against them
> drawn up tightly as a string
> at the mouth of a gunny sack.

Guilt can be transcended with love, punishment with nurturance. There
will be a "reconciling," Allen writes, of "laughter and rage" (*SH* 163).

Even as Diane Burns sasses tradition in *Riding the One-Eyed Ford*
(1981), "Our People" embrace to

> rub
>   the wounds
>   together.

Indian women hold out for love as home's most lasting humor, an affection beyond common pain. This is not to be dismissed as sentiment. *"It may be the frontier no matter where we live,"* Glancy says in "Token," beginning *One Age in a Dream. "Character through hardship / The encouragement of pain. Yep. That's it."* So, twitching, wagging, or flapping that long bushy tail, the coyotess comes home. S(he) gathers her past and present family, nurtures and cooks up continuations, new professions, and professings, as if to say, "I'm home, honey, you better believe it, and I've got some things to say."

Paula Gunn (Francis) Allen was born in 1939, the year Hitler smashed into Poland. Her Southwest blood mixes genes from everywhere—Lebanese cowboy father, matrilineal Laguna mother, Lakota and Scottish-American grandparents, and a few German shirttail cousins scattered across the desert. She grew up speaking English, a little Spanish, some Keres, smatterings of Arabic and German, plus the "liberal arts" languages of Catholic boarding school. Of the many Native American talents these days (cross- and intersections to make your head swim), her work stands out as that of a reigning coyotess: half a dozen books of poetry, a novel, an edited curriculum anthology, a volume of feminist essays, a collection of Indian women's short fiction, another of native feminist healings, plus hundreds of smaller pieces and more coming (including another book of stories). Her early chapbook, *Coyote's Daylight Trip* (1978), set the quadrupedal terms. In the city among uptown Indi'ns, berated by an old racist crone shrieking "GO HOME" in the laundromat, this coyotess washes her soiled clothes and wonders how to get home:

> *I would go home, crazy old woman,*
> if I knew where that might be,
> or how.

("The Last Fantasy")

Homecoming proves to be an American obsession five hundred years in the making. Everywhere American Indians used to be, we are; where we didn't want to be ("waste" lands), there Indians are today. For home is not where it used to be, or it is radically changed where it was. Most of us, including the deranged ones in the public laundromats, feel some measure of homeless kinship. Sauntering by, the "bewitched princesses in beards" suggest to Mrs. Paula Allen (estranged mother of three dependent children) that home comes in many wraps, not all of them heterosexually male-dominant. Cross-gender ambivalence raises the sensitive issue of transsexual tolerances among tribal peoples, from Lakota *winktes,* or bisexuals, to the Pueblo admonition to act the warrior, "Be as a woman!" There certainly seems a bisociative play, even celebration of sexual variance, among Indian ceremonial traditions and societal workings, as illustrated in *Living the Spirit: A Gay American Indian Anthology* (1988) and documented in Walter Williams's *The Spirit and the Flesh: Sexual Diversity in American Indian Culture* (1986). Perhaps tribal tolerance comes in part among limited numbers of interdependent peoples where everyone matters; each is "family," and all compose the tribe, hence "belong."

Paula Allen is native to a Spanish–Laguna cowtown, Cubero, New Mexico. She once tried to hitchhike home from San Francisco across the Mojave with a speed-freak homosexual who manically drove into the sun and "just kept racing out of range at the pass" ("The Long Ride Home from Where You Live"). It's a John Wayne parody of the American tourist "couple," Anglo and Indian transsexuals disappearing over the eastern pass. And so, first of all, Allen says that the title poem, "Coyote's Daylight Trip,"

means:

Bringing Home the Fact.

And "consider the facts," as Corn Tassel challenged two centuries ago. Allen's Lakota grandfather, Old Coyote, is mute. "Coyote and this night be still. / I wonder how a man can cling to life," she asks in "Lament for my Father, Lakota" (*A Cannon Between My Knees* [1981]). This coyotess sings raucous, sad blues, like some free-verse Janis Joplin of Native American letters, expressing a comically mournful longing to come back home.

Free-lance men in the wake of Western history—estranged frontiersmen and weaponless warriors—leave a woman little choice but to fend for herself. "I love you honey, but the bar's closed," a man says wastelanding in Allen's *The Blind Lion* (1974). So in *"Coyote's Daylight Trip,"* after *"Bringing Home the Fact,"* comes the poet's second step, *"History Happens."* Coyote cops lesson number 2: this is the way it is. And number 3: *"I See Myself As Death."* It's Kierkegaard with a feminist canine twist. In the initial ritual, coyotess elegizes her losses: "I bury my dead. I mourn / for four full days." As she says thirteen years later in *Wyrds:* "My hands do all the crying." The image is one of disturbing tension in weird, bewitching words.

So there is real grief here, even bitterness to be purged. "The Turning Point" (written in Nova Scotia, where Eric the Red first came west a thousand years ago) features personal reversal as a woman who knows herself aphasic, lesbian, Zen, meta/physical, ideational, and anti-historical:

> The language of my mind slips daily out of phase
> unlocking secrets I have no word, no image for. I
> write words backwards, leave the familiar shore,
> exchange the alien known for the estranged familiar:

America's "hopeless" images "have broken my heart," the poet grieves, "alien country / superimposed over my home" (*CDT* 34). So "Coyote Sings the City Blues" and learns from "old comrade windsong" the fickle, intangible currents of true "return," a recurring cycle of events. It's not so much a place as a placement—re-placing oneself in time and space, wind-ing home. Turn and re-turn mean double twists in coyotess's tail, or tale—a comic shift, as it were, from loss, through the loss of loss, to the gain of the given "reality." She shifts in perception, spinning on coyote's comic-sighted wit.

Viktor Frankl survived the grimmest coyote pens of all at Auschwitz and Dachau, the fascist threat to a people's will to live. In the dark of the death camp in 1944, he quoted the metaphysical fool, Nieztsche, to a Jewish typhus ward: "Was mich nicht unbringt, macht mich starker" (What does not kill [literally, "un-come" or unmake] me makes me stronger). Jews and Indians share more than a few tribal bonds in this respect, as the Nazi prisons were initially called relocation camps. Frankl, who lost his wife, mother, father, and brother in the camps, taught himself and his fellow prisoners a humor of survival—to laugh at the executioner's shadow with "a grim sense of humor."[13] Without his strength of humor, Frankl would have been lost. Gordon Allport prefaces Frankl's account of a three-year descent through hell: "to live is to suffer, to survive is to find meaning in the suffering" (*MSM* xiii).

So here in the darkness of Indian America, the poet in Paula Allen asks Socratic questions, Southwest-style, that pose the conditional or future possibility. Rather than one paw in the past, one mangled by the

jaws of American despair over where to find home, she asks, Lone
Ranger–fashion, "Quien sabe? Which way did the truth go?" ("Hanging Out In America" [*CDT* 48]). The old spidery teachers still weave
their tales in the closets, corners, and crannies of American deserts.
Coyote's Daylight Trip ends with "Grandmother" and the ancient trust
in spinning patterns, telling stories, stitching verses, making things up
again, as Mary Crow Dog finds the pattern in telling her life-story. This
is a way of humoring the hurt—that is, going on going on, coyote-
fashion, mending the tears:

> After her I sit on my laddered rain-bearing rug
> and mend the tear with string.

Hers is neither triumph nor defeat—more a place to start. Stringing
back the pattern gives her something positive to do, an art that could
prove useful, as for the old ones. Coyotess mends things, cobbles
reality. It's the beginning of a life-journey in verse toward what Julia
Kristeva in *Tales of Love* defines as the decentered ends of love, "immediate sight, scattered totality."

From *Shadow Country* (1982) through *Wyrds* (1987), Paula Allen's
bewitching scope, poetic strength, and undulating insight have been
steadily deepening. As in "Never Cry Uncle," for her mother's gay
brother, Ook (named Laguna-fashion when he cried " 'ook! 'ook!" for
all to see), she refuses like a tenacious coyotess to give up or give in to
grief. With her Uncle Ook, who drove her to her first powwow in a
yellow convertible, Allen even resorts to "dumb" Indi'n jokes. She
grins down the pain and binds wounds with memories of "hardtimes
friends":

> beat senseless he was,
> and left for dead. but he didn't die.
> just got locked up again. now he listens
> to the hum forever buzzing in his head.
> he only makes dumb indian jokes.
> he only remembers his hardtime friends.

For the lost, dispossessed, or "deviant" (coyote's kids) comes an im-
provised Lakota protector, "Koshkalaka, Ceremonial Dyke." This re-
calcitrant "woman-who-won't-marry" moves with shadowy strengths,
spirits in corners, gods forgotten, mothers in closets:

they say that some
there are who are not
except by means of grace,

She (we?) may be "strange droppings" of such spirits, "maybe god-spoor," but after all "wilderness is wild." The poet claims the right, indeed the delight, to go home and be who she is:

heyoka time.
                      koshkalaka.
ceremonial dyke. another way of making.
re making. initiated means re made.
are the days of *heyoka* coyote? *koshkalaka?*
                      (spider the changer)
                      (spider coyote)
when the earth turns to mush,
before it becomes ripe, is it
transformational time?
did you hear a flute
in some other distance?
did you feel the passing
of butterfly wings?

So things and people and coyotess can be "re made"—that is, reified again as real "things," spirit-infused. Coyote and spider, mixed Laguna–Lakota guardians, comic and all-powerful, transform the poet by way of "meta/phor," or "bearer" of things one place to another. Cross-gendering, "wyrd" uncles watch over all this:

one of my uncles is ook. one is oak. another is
indian scout. the last is unnamed.
they all play guide to my perversity,
trickster to my straight.
believe me, I know coyote
                      when I see one.
even when he's got another name.

                                                      ("Koshkalaka")

The "funny" female ones, coyotesses in some respects, are all called home by the gods to accept and forgive. Paula Allen recalls in the dedication to *Wyrds,* as Uncle Ook would say, "going home after a visit with us, 'See you in the funny papers.' "

Howling Down the Moon

Coyote limns a visionary cartoon of our "other" world. S(he) howl-
sings the dreamer's humor.

> Molten Moon
> drips down into the pine needles.
> Coyote tracks embers
> all along the embankment.
> "Yipyip-Eeeeooowww!"

("Night Songs")

As a displaced Apache–Comanche in New York City, Judith Volborth's
childhood dreams were punctuated with coyote's animal wit, "a wet-
nosed Coyote / about to sneeze," as she says in *Thunder-Root* (1978).
Coyote gave her a persona to sing her native dream place, matching wits
with the fates, fabling her bestial self through extended animal kin in
such characters as Lone Hare, Dancing Bear, Night Otter, even Black-
Coat, the pestilent missionary.

Volborth charms the traditional coyote trickster, inspired clown and
bestial god, into a lyric singer whose howl, rightly heard, is the music
of wild, gentle things. The poet finds patterned release in Coyote's
antics, melody in his yelp, design in his running, whirling, and spinning. Attuned with the moon, this lyrical Coyote is not simply a fool of
license and comic exaggeration—but a singer and a player, clever and
sensical in his or her own terms, ludicrous often, yet appealing as a
(native) American kin with all creatures, including city Indians. Still
brother to the poet in her often shy retreat, Coyote tells Turtle Medicine,
"I've waited this long already" for the world to quiet down so he can
get some sleep, for the lice to go away, for Black-Coat to shut up. And
yet he waits, as does the coyotess. S(he) can be patient chanting shadows while the molten moon drips into pine needles; the goal is a mind of
liquid illumination, a poet's incandescent clarity of vision.

Wendy Rose talks back to Indian-curious tourists as the archaeologist's harpy. She strikes a broken key boldly in *What Happened
When the Hopi Hit New York* (1982). Here is a bitter child "specimen"
of aboriginal America who buried arrowheads in California

> for archeologists to find,
> rubberbands and cardinal feathers
> on willow twigs—call them prayer sticks

and sell them fifty cents apiece.
Hey mister
wanna buy a kachina doll?

("Stopover in Denver")

Rose sometimes trades on stony inarticulations or the mute refusal to speak, a kind of ironic catatonia that ducks behind the cigar-store Indian's impassive mask. "By the silence of petroglyphs, / stiff birds and stick women, / I am answered," she retreats behind obdurate things in "Searching for Indians in New Orleans." Her hard syllables and poetic cherts and shards bang against the Americanization of the Indian, "syllables that harden / as they touch the new snow," in "Indian in Iowa City."

Younger Indians like Diane Burns punk their verse with sassy humor, as four-footed friends skulk in city rags. Bright tribal dress gives Trickster away in "Houston and Bowery, 1981":

Inside the ribbon shirts
coyote laughs / wolf waits
The village criers hang out on the corner.

The social 49 dance that goes on all hours at powwows gives Burns an "up-town Indi'n" context and verse line in *Riding the One-Eyed Ford* (1981):

Forward
. . . I've heard that the songs are to honor the war dead: 50 warriors left and only 49 came back and so the 49 sang honor songs for the one who didn't come back. Or 50 left and only one came back. I've also heard the term originated with the 1849 Gold Rush. . . . The "one-eyed" Ford is eyeless because we never had money to fix it and there was no truth to the rumor that it is related to Gerald. This book is a true story.

War story, Gold Rush gore, pioneer whores: Indians sing out of and beyond pain. Broken-down Fords or family in-jokes place Diane Burns in tribal contexts where she belongs. There's good (if a bit scandalous) fun in these lines:

I don't care if you're married I still love you
I don't care if you're married

After the party's over
I will take you home in my One-Eyed Ford
Way yah hi yo, Way yah hi yo!

  Modene!
  the roller derby queen!
  She's Anishinabe,
  that means Human Being!
That's H for hungry!
and B for frijoles!
      frybread!
      Tortillas!
      Watermelon!
      Pomona!

              . . .

  Hey!
I'm no nun!
'49 in the hills above
    Ventura
Them Okies gotta drum

                                            ("Big Fun")

Chicana cuisine, Chippewa origins, California relocation, the Depression poor of America—these mixed Indian contexts keep a young woman up singing all night.

Nila northSun takes this howl even farther afield in *Diet Pepsi and Nacho Cheese* (1977). Her Irish "white grandpa" struck silver on the Nevada reservation, "gramma" said:

  he fed all the indians
  he was a good man
  but then
  he marry white woman
  & we go back to reservation

                                            ("gramma")

This is red English bringing "the facts" home, the plain-style truth told by candid women. Pocahontas's granddaughter falls ironically into America's old game of playing Indian, as she looks at herself and laughs:

        i can see an eagle
            almost extinct
            on slurpee plastic cups
        i can travel to pow wows
            in campers & winnebagos
        i can eat buffalo meat
            at the tourist burger stand
        i can dance to indian music
            rock-n-roll hey-a-hey-o
        i can
            & unfortunately
                I do
                                        ("moving camp too far")

The "good times" come to a grinding halt in an end-stopped song of
questionable medicine, America on the powwow highway:

        he's a rootin tootin indian
        that doesn't do shit when
        the pow wow circuit has come
        to an end for the summer
                                        ("indian dancer")

With all the plosive power of American idioms and an up-front candor,
postmodernist Indi'n humor checks the ready romance of the noble
savage and dusky princess, Pocahontas or Mary Crow Dog. The
coyotess here talks back to her scavaging friends of all color hides.
    What Moon Drove Me to This? (1979) Joy Harjo, the Creek poet,
asks: "But she is dancing / at Pine Ridge / inside his wild horse eyes,"
Harjo pines with no small self-parody in "San Juan Pueblo And South
Dakota Are 800 Miles Away On A Map." Up there, John (Fire) Lame
Deer strikes a familiar full-moon note under the snowy Dakota night:

        he must be coyote
            ma'ii
        seeker of visions
        old man
        thousands of years old
        it must have been you
        i saw
        sometimes ago

outside of that
south dakota bar
in the middle of winter
making tracks
like coyote
    wine stains
    in the snow
just barely made it home
that time
    didn't you?

Coyotes prowl Indi'n America from Tahlequah to Tacoma to Tallahassee. "Yeah. It must be that Kansas City coyote again. / That's what she said," Harjo says in the Powwow Club ("Old Lines Which Sometimes Work, And Sometimes Don't"). Her honest contrary humor tempers the candor here. Because "It's The Same At Four A.M.":

He's half Creek, half plains.
I'm part Creek and white.
"Which part do you want tonight?"
    I ask him.

The forty-nine singers are drumming
Creek stomp dance songs on the hood
of someones car.
I pull his arm
"Come on, let's dance."

But he wants the other half.

So for the coyotess, romance may be a bit sour with hung-over warriors (Harjo), and gender a sore issue (Allen), and punk a countercultural raspberry that makes young sense (Burns), and anthropological mystique an insult (Rose), and coyote's sneeze a release (Volborth), if not an answer to the lyric pressure in a young Indian urban psyche. By the 1980s, the coyotess was coming home strong in poetry and prose. Joy Harjo's *She Had Some Horses* (1983) opens contrariwise, reversing field in a kind of anti-imagination, through a purgative of fear, counterlove, and incantation:

There is this edge where shadows
and bones of some of us walk
      backwards.

Talk backwards. There is this edge
call it an ocean of fear of the dark. Or
name it with other songs. Under our ribs
our hearts are bloody stars. Shine on
shine on, and horses in their galloping flight
strike the curve of ribs.

                                                                    ("Call It Fear")

The thunder and energy of galloping horses give Harjo icons of transformation, chanted rhythms of motion, animal accumulations of power.
Certainly, there is hurt in her gently enduring humor, but her wit comes
cut, incisive, and penetrating, her courage lasting. Home always hangs
a horizon way, as it does for her former husband and children's father,
Simon Ortiz; but she braves the contrary-doubled "long return" coming
back home. Bars, booze, midnight highways and Kansas City moons,
lovers leaving and returning, turn her against conventional romance,
"straight" stories of husbands and fireside wives. This coyotess, like
Paula Allen, is not necessarily a nester, a domestic, or a "nice" lady,
but instead a powerful woman, horse-sister, and coyote-cousin in search
of her own voice and power, her own radical Indi'n style, her own
chosen dreams. This includes her own humor, hearth, and home.

Nearly everyone had left that bar in the middle of winter except the hard core.
It was the coldest night of the year, every place shut down, but not us. Of
course we noticed when she came in. We were Indian ruins. She was the end
of beauty. No one knew her, the stranger whose tribe we recognized, the
family related to deer, if that's who she was, a people accustomed to hearing
songs in pine trees, and making them hearts.

                                                . . .

The next dance none of us predicted. She borrowed a chair for the stairway to
heaven and stood on a table of names. And danced in the room of children
without shoes.

You picked a fine time to leave me Lucille.
With four hungry children and a crop in the field.

And then she took off her clothes. She shook loose memory, waltzed with the
empty lover we'd all become.

She was the myth slipped down through dreamtime. The promise of feast we
all knew was coming. The deer who crossed through knots of a curse to find
us. She was no slouch, and neither were we, watching.

The music ended. And so does the story, I wasn't there. But I imagined her
like this, not a stained red dress with tape on her heels but the deer who
entered our dream in white dawn, breathed mist into pine trees, her fawn a
blessing of meat, the ancestors who never left.

("Deer Dancer")

Her Name Means "Home"

Chickasaw Linda Hogan (whose Irish name in Navajo means "home") is
bringing the feminist news back. As a mixed-blood mother and Chickasaw coyotess, her traditional role as homemaker is not subverted by
lifework as an artist. Estranged Western *artistes* are called back to the
cultural center in Native American homes. On the road or back home in
Oklahoma or Colorado, Hogan has survived her aesthetic *Eclipse*
(1983) and is writing the moon back full. Indian women today, Paula
Allen observes, write from "a sense of familiarity with what is strange,
a willingness to face, to articulate what is beyond belief, to make it
seem frightening and natural at the same time."[14] Hogan chooses to
return home, in peace, to raise her adopted Lakota daughters in a
promising future informed by the native past, taking her stands against
misuses of the motherland and her peoples.

If homelessness in some painful way sums up our common modern
condition, then going home is—for Indians—even more acute, more
essential. Their belief in child raising, tribal sense of community, and
historical regard for ancestral land provide a deep-rooted base for Indian
feminism. These values are not to be dismissed by marketplace
cynicisms. A woman's traditional care for extended kin, plants, and
animals; remembered cultural history; and ceremonial belief in the spirit
of place have been challenged, dismissed, uprooted, warred against,
relocated, and re-relocated. This is old news.

The good news is homecoming: home is knowing who you are where
your people have roots, an ancestral sense of time and place—specific
to relatives, animals, plants, earth, sky, the dead, and the gods. "How
are you peopled?" the Pueblos ask in a traditional form of greeting.

"Although I was born in Denver, Oklahoma is my tribal homeland,
after the Trail of Tears," Linda Hogan wrote to me in 1981,

and the place where most of my family remains: my grandparents were born
and died in Indian Territory and were very clear that it was the territory and

not the state. It is the place of my blood and heart. The strongest energies of my growing up years are from Oklahoma soil, creatures, and people, from listening at night through the sound of frogs and insects, to the stories and lives of Chickasaw family and friends. Now, however, I am firmly rooted in the mountain lands of Colorado, the Red Rocks area. Transplant has taken. I have sent down a long tap root and want to stay here and probably die here. I've become familiar with the edible plants, with the seasons, the migrations of owls and geese, the deer herd, the position of stars and planets, when things grow, when the hills thaw and fall with rockslides, what goes on with the lives of the people.

Hogan's quest to come home voices a modern and native consciousness in this country, after the long diaspora of American and American Indian history. This homing can be bisociated humorously. Such adaptive fusion appears appropriate to a mixed-blood woman, rebuilder, collaborator, teacher, and adoptive mother. In an earlier volume, *Calling Myself Home* (1978), Hogan asks "Blessing" along the backroads of America, listening in the shadows of cultural eclipse:

Chickasaw
chikkih asachi,
they left as a tribe not a very great while ago.
They are always leaving, those people.

Blessed
are those who listen
when no one is left to speak.

And blessing voices still rise out of her father's Oklahoma bottomlands—magpies and mosquitoes, spiders and salamanders, crayfish and catfish. In the older sense of a language of the earth's people, speech is never lost for those who listen to the simplest things.

The problems here have been compounded by history, economics, genetics, and gender. False domination seems a key crime against our common humanity. In a poem in *Eclipse,*

Men smile like they know everything
but walking in slant heel boots
their butts show they are tense.

. . .

We're full of bread and gas,
getting fat on the outside
while inside we grow thin.

            . . .

The earth is wounded
and will not heal

            . . .

Night comes down like a blackbird
with blue flame that never sleeps
and spreads its wings around us.

                                                        ("Oil")

Blackbird is a close cousin in the Trickster clan, and Hogan's "Saint
Coyote" slips out of the night a "Luminous savior" to save us from
blaming the "other" for our suffering:

That saint,
always gambling,
crossing dark streets
walking among skin and shadow,
always lying
about who created death and light.

The women, especially elders and daughters at either end of the spectrum, summon coyotess humor to survive "stories of loss." These are
not so much laughing matters as deeper wisdoms articulated as humors
of survival. They are registered in smiling kinships. This would seem an
ancient lesson in the comedy beyond tragedy, the staying power of a
bonding tribal sense, the belief in comic futurity. Somewhere within
suffering, people find the humor to endure and go on. The coyote track
ends across a field of snow, and over this sign fly birds of visionary
renewal:

In her eyes
the small reflection of us
beginning to exist
to stretch across the round horizon,
the soft cloud of animals rising,
rising dialogues of dust and air

where all things fuse and burn
inhabiting earth,
inhabiting skin and hair
like silence around itself.

("Who Will Speak")

Seeing Through the Sun (1985) leads into Linda Hogan's Oklahoma
novel, *Mean Spirit* (1990). In "The Truth Is," she riddles with resolutions, comic bisociations, mixed-blood contrary humors.

In my left pocket a Chickasaw hand
rests on the bone of the pelvis.
In my right pocket
a white hand.

. . .

Girl, I say,
it is dangerous to be woman of two countries.
You've got your hands in the dark
of two empty pockets.

. . .

Relax, there are other things to think about.
Shoes for instance.
Now those are the true masks of the soul.
The left shoe
and the right one with its white foot.

Still, behind the humor resides the hurt, the terror in wild imaginings,
metaphors of fear in "November":

My hair burns down my shoulders.
I walk. I will not think we are blood sacrifices.
No, I will not watch the ring-necked pheasant
running into the field of skeletal corn.

Feminist tragedies, from a fictive Tess Durbeyfield through a fatal Sylvia Plath, threaten the sunrise with everlasting dark. It's best not to be
fooled: strike an edge to one's voice, a cut to candor, a truth to humor,
and keep on.

I will walk into the sun.
Her red mesas are burning
in the distance.
I will enter them. I will walk into that stone,

walk into the sun
away from night rising up the other side of earth.
There are sounds in the cornfield,
Shh. Shh.

("November")

6

"Bring Her Home":
Louise Erdrich

> . . . the interesting thing about the use of humor in American
> Indian poetry is its integrating effect: it makes tolerable what is
> otherwise unthinkable; it allows a sort of breathing space in which
> an entire race can take stock of itself and its future.
>
> PAULA GUNN ALLEN, *The Sacred Hoop*

Modes

Indi'n humor breathes life into a native legacy of dispossession that
would mute survival. "Humor is a primary means of reconciling the
tradition of continuance, bonding, and celebration with the stark facts of
racial destruction," Paula Allen sees in *The Sacred Hoop*. Intertribal
jokes bond clans against outsiders, as they humanize cross-cultural lines
of defense. Comedy opens exchange with "others"; it softens battle
lines toward some measure of tolerance, if not intercultural trade.
Laughter in these charged circumstances spills across cultural boundaries, opens ethnic blockages, and reconfirms tribal pride to counter
xenophobic fear. A people's humor can both focus and release tension—a way of "economizing" the psyche's suffering, Freud contends,
and relieving the ego's defensive need to control. Hence Indi'n humor
draws the people together tribally, drives out an ethnocentric aggressor,
and redirects expectations toward a more collaborative future.

Through Northrop Frye's mythic cycle of integration, purgation, and
renewal, comic futurity hails the "victory of summer over winter" (*The
Anatomy of Criticism*). If life begins in the east as comic renewal,
matures ritually in the warm romantic south, suffers the tragic western

nightfall, and ironically endures the northern dark, only to begin again with sunrise, a traditional cycle of continuity would seem to bend linear time toward a curve of human renewal. Coexistent generations season their reciprocal lives tribally through one another, codeterminant and codependent. Thus an inclusive sense of humanity, young to old, tempers the existential panic that one moment engulfs all. Death does not take everyone at once. Each human moment (represented in a time of day, direction, season, and cultural aesthetic) holds relative significance; all passages balance across an ancient, ongoing "sacred hoop" that bears, fulfills, harvests, and cleanses the human condition.

In Frye's paradigm irony, a wintry survival mode, opens to comic rebirth in early spring, as the sun returns to greening young things. Such balanced configurations give the implicit sense of a natural design, even a "comic" order to the cosmos. A literary renaissance is one historical index to this resurgence. "The most important theme in Native American novels," Allen claims in *The Sacred Hoop*, "is not conflict and devastation but transformation and continuance." Frye's model seems distinctly "native" American, a four-winds "sacred hoop" in color-

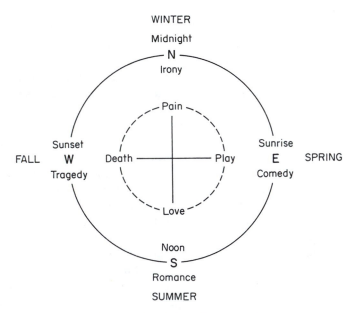

Northrup Frye's four literary modes.

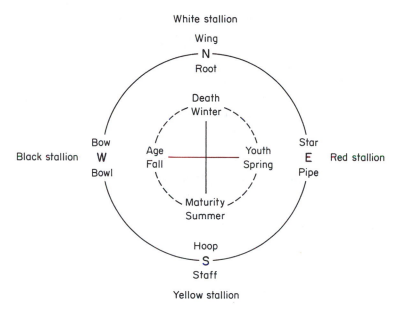

Black Elk's "Great Vision."

coded Lakota vision, Cheyenne prayer wheel, Mayan cardinal points, or Pueblo icon for the sun: ⚹ (New Mexico's logo for its state license plate). The generic paradigm overlaps with Black Elk's "Great Vision" among the Oglala Lakota.

Western literature may carry analogous modes. In Shakespeare's canon, to draw one example, tragedy in *King Lear* gives way to irony in *The Winter's Tale,* which is balanced by comedy in *A Midsummer Night's Dream* and romance in *The Tempest.* And Dante's "great visions" are no great distance from Black Elk's. In the *Inferno,* the pre-Renaissance visionary sees Satan head-down in hell's circle of ice. As Dante and Virgil descend farther over the monstrous devil's thigh, dropping from tufts of shaggy anal hair, they *reverse* direction and strangely start upward again—emerging from the devil's anus to look up and see the stars. Here is a coyote vision of divine scatology, "from ass-hole to laugh-hole," Peter Blue Cloud jokes in *Elderberry Flute Song* (1982). Down gives way to up, evil to good, fated loss to transcendental faith. Nothing is lost or wasted in our gods' green garden, not even the fallen, which fertilize the earth as comic grist. From this perspective, Satan stands on his head, upside down as God's paradisaic excretion, a "fortunate fall" for all. This comic reversal of tragedy seems anciently mythic, humanly sensible, and modernly necessary, from *The Divine Comedy* to *Paradise Lost* to *Love Medicine*.

The next three chapters detail Frye's comic terms in American Indian fiction. Louise Erdrich's *Love Medicine* integrates marginal mixed-bloods with a forgiving feminist humor; James Welch's *Winter in the Blood* purges Montana winter warriors with dark comic blues; N. Scott Momaday's *House Made of Dawn* and Howard Norman's *The Northern Lights* envision collaborative renewals across tribes, Indian–Anglo reciprocities from Los Angeles to Toronto. Indian humor registers here in intertribal dialects from New England to Montana to New Mexico, along the Canadian-American plains, to the Mojave Desert and Pacific Coast. The fictions contour the Algonkian language swath from the Abnaki spoken by Pocahontas, through the lake regions of Cree speakers (Eastern, Central, Swampy, Plains), out to the intermountain Blackfeet, and down into the Southwest, where Athabathscan Navajo and Apache filtered into Pueblo lands.

Through translation and idiomatic adaptation, "Indi'n" English now constitutes a working pan-tribal tongue for contemporary Native American writers. Transhemispheric tribal dialects—biospherically interconnected, culturally overlapping tribe to tribe—network Chippewa métis of Turtle Mountain; Blackfeet–Gros Ventre buffalo hunters in the Rocky Mountain shortgrass plains; Cree, Scandinavian, French, and Russian miscegenations of Canadian-Americans and "now day Indi'ns" on the plains; and southwestern desert mixtures with southern California's ethnic stewpot. The jokes remain culture-specific and intertribally complex, the comedies not unmixed with conflict, and the humor regional. In the fiction and art of today's Indians we find clear responses, even comic answers, to past calamities.

Homing

MOYERS: Many of your characters have this wonderful, wry look at the world, this ability to see the world with a raised eyebrow in a sense that's quite charming. And is that in real life as well? That's not invented?

ERDRICH: It may be the one universal thing about Native Americans from tribe to tribe, is the survival humor.

MOYERS: What do you mean? The humor that enables you to?

ERDRICH: To live with what you have to live with. You have to have a world view, you can just laugh at some of the—there's a dark side to humor. And you have to be able to poke fun at people who are dominating your life and your family, and—

DORRIS: And to poke fun at yourself in being dominated, I mean, it's both—

ERDRICH: Yes, yes. We're a mixture of Chippewa and Modoc and German American and French and Irish. I mean, all of these different backgrounds have an aspect that is part of us. And if we took ourselves too seriously in any way, I feel that we would be overwhelmed. . . . And almost the most serious things have to be jokes, I think. It's the way we deal with the most difficult events in our lives. I mean, we're both members of our tribes and have tribal backgrounds. Once you're a citizen of both nations, it gives you a look at the world that is—it's different. And there is that edge of irony.

Interview, "Bill Moyers' World of Ideas"

Louise Erdrich has lyricized a renewed native canon with three novels, *Love Medicine* (1984), *The Beet Queen* (1986), and *Tracks* (1988), as well as two books of poems, *Jacklight* (1984) and *Baptism of Desire* (1989). She has collaborated with her Modoc husband, Michael Dorris, on a quincentennial novel, *The Crown of Columbus* (1991). Her motif, shared across America, is coming home to the motherland, literally to the kitchen hearth. Where do we "belong," the fictions ask, and how do we fit together as "native" Americans? *Love Medicine* initiates a tetralogy covering our century. The novel garnered more literary awards, according to *Publishers Weekly,* than any other book in printing history (1984 National Critics Circle Book Award, American Academy of Arts and Letters Prize, *Los Angeles Times* Novel of the Year, among many others). It's an extraordinary tale of mixed-bloods "homing" on the Canadian-American border.

The exact geographical center of North America does not lie somewhere shoulder-high in an Iowa cornfield. It is directly south of the Turtle Mountain Reservation in North Dakota, forty-three miles from the Canadian border. Here some thirty years ago, Louise Erdrich, a

Chippewa mixed-blood from the off-reservation hamlet of Wahpetan, found her way home tribally with her mother's relatives. Their "kitchen" stories and road sagas promise to be among this century's most compelling American fictions.

Erdrich's patronymic also takes her back to German ancestry, via her father, Ralph Erdrich, and his mother, Mary Erdrich Korll, as acknowledged in *The Beet Queen*. Her mother's Chippewa lineage, tracing through Turtle Mountain today, informs *Love Medicine*. Thus a polysemous mixture of native Euroamerica—German, Scots, French, Cree, Chippewa, and Polish Slavic—spices Erdrich's fictions. This mix is quintessentially American, a multicultural mélange, with webs of lineages from everywhere. We Americans truly constitute cultures-in-process, on the go, relocating, digging down, making it work where we can—but never "pure," or uniform, or easily cohesive, or simple to analyze or to understand. We come as orphans and adventurers, the novels say, dislocated natives and émigrés; we stay on as drifters and discoverers, soldiers of fortune and women of courage, whose children and grandchildren still settle America, trying to come "home" on the range. Out west of the big river, it is home-on-the-go, the pinch-hit comeback to "home plate." This is the playing end of all stories that would end well, as far back as *The Odyssey*. For some, home is still around the corner, from Homer to Linda Hogan "calling myself home."

Erdrich's art, then, sifts a polyphonic ethnography, speaking through many mixed voices of the past. There is no native regression, no playing heroic Indian or antiwhite, and the novels resist a litany of historical grudges. Erdrich seems a true humorist who sees that things *are* as they are, very mixed American; and here's how they look and work according to multiple points of view, her stories say, trading on local detail, turning on participant narrators. The young woman Albertine, for example, comes home early on in *Love Medicine* and muses next to her cousin Lipsha from a greening winter wheat field:

> I tipped the bottle, looked up at the sky, and nearly fell over, in amazement and too much beer, at the drenching beauty.
>   Northern lights. Something in the cold, wet atmosphere brought them out. . . . At times the whole sky was ringed in shooting points and puckers of light gathering and falling, pulsing, fading, rhythmical as breathing. All of a piece. As if the sky were a pattern of nerves and our thoughts and memories traveled across it. As if the sky were one gigantic memory for us all.[1]

The artist here, inside her character, seems blessed by crystalline perception—to see into things through alterity. To perceive an "other" pattern in these natural northern lights, our native arts of North America, both strange and everyday, draws an American reader from region to continent, locale to nationality, across estranging skies. There is light in the darkness, pattern to the pieces, resurgent memory beyond loss. And so Erdrich's lyric irony seems an integrating codex to contemporary (native) America. Sheared perceptual planes in her work register a vision that bisociates native and immigrant Americans—the novels ironically witness division and call for bridging. Her stories grace daily beauty under a sky "for us all." This is where a woman's nurturing, forgiving humor calls us home.

There are many Indian angles on this America of thousands of native and immigrant cultures. In the larger intercultural complex, what does it mean to be Montana-born, as Welch writes, with "winter in the blood"? What are the minimalist poetics in "a certain Slant of light" to Emily Dickinson's Amherst eye "Winter Afternoons"? Climatically and culturally, Dickinson to Erdrich to Welch, we are dealing with a continental region, Atlantic to Pacific oceans, that for hundreds of generations framed an Algonkian corridor across North America (see the initial linguistic fieldwork of Boas, Sapir, and Bloomfield early this century). And here Indians and whites first cross-acculturated.

In the Canadian North, natives of many races speak from deep-freeze meteorologies that determine ground-zero epistemologies. The cold edges everything. And the "opposite-thinking" Cree equate figure–ground physics with complementary aesthetics, not to say metaphysics. How does this crystalline northern mind work *inter*culturally in America? "Quite Opposite—How Complicate / The Discipline of Man—" Emily Dickinson riddles American contraries (no. 910). A "mind of winter," contrary indeed, is neither sentimental nor cynical, Wallace Stevens muses, but simply *is* in the North. "Good-by and keep cold," Robert Frost blesses his bedded orchard roots. A thaw at the wrong time ruins everything, any fool knows, or should. Timing is all, realistically seasoned. This is a land of *tipikochiyetim,* the Swampy Cree say, where summer–winter contrary things are interdependent and delicately balanced in the fleshed spaces of time.

For every hill comes an American hollow. "At the end of the big farms and the blowing fields was the reservation," remembers Albertine, driving home to open *Love Medicine.* "I always knew it was coming a long way off. Even in the distance you sense hills from their opposites—pits, dried sloughs, ditches of cattails, potholes. And then the water. There would be water in the hills when there wasn't any on the plains, because the hollows saved it, collected runoff from the low slopes, and the dense trees held it, too. I thought of water in the roots of trees, brown and bark smelling, cold" (*LM* 10). This "opposite-think-ing" land of inverted hills and water-filled hollows breeds bisociative peoples. Their languages work by concision, by vast implication of scant data, by hunger and humor. They live the exacting play of rever-sals, dark to light, across variously patterned waters and twilights. Here is where the homeless, through complementary contraries, find a home. Here they learn to laugh across differences, to come together within a common context.

So, too, Erdrich's integrative homing seems natively Euroamerican. "Here I am, where I ought to be," Isak Dinesen wrote in *Out of Africa* (1937), some sixty-five years after her Danish father had lived with "les sauvages" in Wisconsin. Whether at home, coming home, or going to a home, "A writer must have a place where he or she feels this," says Erdrich quoting Dinesen, on the other side of the globe in North Dako-ta. As both Native and American, Erdrich speaks to a historical, homing sense of locus, "*a place to love and be irritated with*. One must experi-ence the local blights, hear the proverbs, endure the radio commercials. Through the close study of a place, its people and character, its crops, products, paranoias, dialects and failures, we come closer to our own reality. But truly knowing a place provides the link between details and meaning. Location, whether it is to abandon it or draw it sharply, is where we start."[2] Humans come from and back to such lovingly irrita-ble homes.

At birth, we "no longer live beneath our mother's heart," this mother of six (three adopted) remarks. So what "land" do we land in, belong to, or return to as "home"? How do we think and feel about all this? How do we account for our diverse humors? What are the regional, historical, even racial or cultural definitions and differences? What bonds and separates us? Our quest in the Western world, registered as far back as the Homeric odes, appears to be one of the *nostos*, or "homecoming," as Joyce re-created the myth on modern Irish terms in *Ulysses*. Where we were born, both "native" and in what "nature," shapes the kind of "animal–person" we are, as the Cree say. All of us long for "being" home, and *be*longing defines us, as Lipsha discovers in *Love Medicine*.

What exactly is *native*, then, to America, and where is *home*? For many in America these are troubling questions. "A Dungeon but a Kinsman is," Dickinson laments, "Incarceration—Home" (no. 1334). The dispossessed are doubly estranged. "Coming home was not easy anymore," Welch's nameless Blackfeet narrator admits to begin *Winter in the Blood*. "It was never a cinch, but it had become a torture." Is this "native" America, Erdrich's "*place to love and be irritated with*"? Can any one man analogize for "others" across a continent of humanity, or any one woman welcome all? What naturalized terms connect or disconnect men and women? Where do we hear a native humor, as Constance Rourke asked six decades back in *American Humor*? Indians may offer an alternative cultural paradigm to five hundred years of westering dislocation. Despite disillusions and comic refusals, "You *can* go home again," Mary TallMountain tells us in *I Tell You Now*.

The Orphans' Picnic

> ERDRICH: Yes, I'm enrolled as a Turtle Mountain Chippewa, and from time to time, our family would spend time visiting there, or I'd go by myself and visit grandparents, aunts, uncles. I never lived on the reservation for any stretch of time, so all I know is from visiting there, and loving the place and the people.
>
> "Interview with Louise Erdrich"

A three generation, fifty-year saga, Erdrich's *Love Medicine* records a raconteur's world, peopled in amazed pity and humor and deep sad joy, all in witness of simply, albeit complexly, being alive. Hers are not the expected stereotypes of Indians—Sioux warriors, Hopi maidens, Yaqui shamans, Pueblo potters, or Navajo sheepherders—but miscegenated métis who marry "full-blood" dirty-blond Norwegian teenagers like Lynette from Rolla, North Dakota. Chippewa girls sing "Delta Dawn" at the high-school talent show or dance French jigs at a powwow. Their family names are often Gallicized, like Dacoteaux, Bordeaux, or Lazarre. Still, they're "crazy Indians," as Henry Junior says, infected with the past and the lost and the still-to-come promise of a native rebirth, holding out for the comic vision—Christ in the gunmetal sky, fresh-baked pie at the Kashpaw family reunion, moonshine in the woods at Uncle Gordie's.

There is little, if any, old-style ethnography in Erdrich's fictions: no Chippewa chants, no ceremonies to the Great Spirit, no wizened old medicine people. Instead, her stories detail pickups and bars and nuns and crazed uncles and fierce aunts and small issues of how "Indi'n" kin are, or aren't by intermarriage. Bloodlines and traditions and the "old ways" do not seem the overriding concerns of these people, as daily survival precedes cultural purism. What does not come with the terrain and times must tend to itself.

"Indi'n" is an idea of oneself, possibly, and "being Indi'n" goes on despite the idea. It reckons the way things are today, people living who they are in the presence of their history and culture—not the fiction that Indian buffs fantasize or anthropologists conjecture. Today's Indians speak "locally real" talk of tradition, as Clifford Geertz argues with cultural common sense in *Local Knowledge.* With a certain comic realism, each dialect cocks a different ear, each lip curves distinctively, and tribes turn on differences. The "Michif," "Mitchief," or "métis" today remain mixtures, just as the narratives in *Love Medicine* bisociatively portray a complex mix of terror, humor, and pity. This near tragedy is textured with comic pathos, a wild or tender humor, the indomitable spirit of a regional community. "It really is beautiful around there," Erdrich says, "and the Chippewas have the best sense of humor of any group of people I've ever known."[3] As the post–Civil War South continued, fallen, enduring, still heroic in resistence to Yankee intrusions, idiosyncratic to itself and its history, so Native America in the northernmost Dakota survives the wars of removal and racism and neglect and cultural genocide. Indians have endured the last hundred years here of reservation displacement, poverty, wasteland economy, clan feuds, and desperate confusion over white–red schisms and fusions—all with a knife-edged, surviving sense of comic continuity.

How do we approach the integrative humor of an off-reservation mixed-blood who attended Dartmouth and Johns Hopkins, then published novels reviewed in *Life, Time, Newsweek,* the *New York Review of Books,* and the *New York Times Book Review,* and went on to win a record number of literary awards? Start with kinship, the family. Continuing collective identity, a clan concept, holds out against the modern decimation or fraying of what is left of the cultural past. This family sense begins with Indian mothers caring for children *in* that identity, genetic or adoptive, "blood" or "took in." And these cultural determinants involve the passions between men and women, including angers and strong differences of opinion, with all the human complexities and the attendant comedies of conjoining. Erdrich's fiction is layered with such disparately humorous tissue.

Second, Indians identify with their land and landscape, the extended living environment, even in a supposedly desolate, flat place like North Dakota, where beet and wheat farmers, along with merchants, trappers, and explorers for several hundred years' running, have encroached on native land and intermarried with Indians. These mixtures flood the fictions. Indeed, they pool our history of the Americas.

Third, self-identity and lifework—that is, implicit belief systems and what people do with them—seem central to being Indian. Each Native American harbors private concerns over these communal issues: Who and where are "the Indians," and where does the individual fit in and believe as such? With the majority off-reservation today, Indians are redefining themselves. To ask the question Who is an Indian? begins clarifying Indianness, since bringing culture to consciousness, especially in times of change, reinforces one's hold on a heritage. These questions encompass myths of a cultural "self": how and why we *think* we are who we are, how we project the "idea" of being Indian, as Momaday says in *The Names* (1976). "Belonging was a matter of deciding to," Lipsha concludes in *Love Medicine* (*LM* 225). Surely these are questions of national inclusion and racial exclusion—the old wounds, scars, cultural collisions, debts to be reckoned and lived with, perhaps, as with the still-disputed 1868 Red Cloud Treaty, or the Big Mountain coal controversy, or limiting tribal enrollments to quarter-bloods, or the enormous issue of southwestern water flowing through reservations to Los Angeles today. With mixed motives, many people look to being Indian. There are always old and new mixes, métis, with multicultural identities in the making.

Spiritual concerns? For Indians these involve the everyday to the eternal, but with special recognition, often ceremonial, of a long "American" heritage—indeed, a rootedness here like no other peoples. Traditional ecology cannot be scorned as green-thumb mysticism. And, to be sure, there remain vast mixtures of differences among Indians: old grudges, traditional enemies, long-standing regional disputes, alliances, betrayals, and new bondings, as with the Lumbees or the Lakota–Chippewa pressing for tribal recognition.

So are Indians, then, "like us," cultural mixtures from a receding past in a land of an overwhelming present, strugglers for identity, transplants, redefining men and women and their hybrid offspring? Perhaps so, indeed more so than at any time before; but still American Indians, with their alternative senses of family, kinship, communal property, lineage, language, history, geography, even space–time conceptions, live with significant ethnic and tribal differences from mix-and-match mainstream Americans. Here we consider the perceptions of "native" Americans as a kind of contingent guardianship and pride in the continuities of American history, in its oldest cultural and geological sense going back tens of thousands of years. This sense of land tenure goes along with new cultural interfusions, not to say blood mixtures, that are breeding and bonding us all. Balance and resolution, the comic mode at best, pattern our communal ideals here.

With *Love Medicine* and *The Beet Queen,* we have the first two Erdrich novels of contemporary North Dakota, expertly chiseled: one of mixed Indian bloods, one of "plain" folks with mixed and relocated origins, all essentially American from the northern rural heartland. Fictively, *The Beet Queen* portrays Depression orphans Karl and Mary Adare, who live on next to nothing, surviving a runaway mother and no father; but they own their own determination, as Indians have always known survival, just as Erdrich's German-American father and Chippewa mother persisted through the 1930s. The struggle to survive and the native humor of such carry no ethnic restrictions. All the Depression characters in *The Beet Queen* seem orphaned in some way or another. Jude Miller, Adelaide Adare's abandoned infant, was fathered by the all-too-married visitor Mr. Opler, who drowns under a grain spill. The hapless Jude is a county-fair foundling "named for the patron saint of lost causes, lost hopes, and last-ditch resorts" by Catherine Miller, since her own three-day-old son has died.[4] The resurrected orphan grows up to be a priest and will come back as shadow hero in the final novel of the tetralogy, *American Horse.*

Each of these new characters in North Dakota is a transplant, a graft, a foundling or "took in," as with Lipsha in *Love Medicine,* or Tayo in Silko's *Ceremony,* or Abel in Momaday's *House Made of Dawn,* or Welch's two narrators: "No Name" in *Winter in the Blood* and Jim

Loney in *The Death of Jim Loney*. Karl and Mary Adare and their unnamed baby brother are abandoned on the carnival grounds as their mother flies over the horizon, redhead in a flaming dress, with Omar the biplane stunt pilot. Mary cries away all her sentiment, and then with a "brain of ice" clutches to life as tenaciously as a prairie boulder hunkered in the shortgrass. Her rootedness is complemented, better contrasted, by Karl's wanderlust, his wildly inventive, bisexual imagination. Thus the novel is made up of real things and wondrous imaginings, the ordinary *ex*traordinary, humors beyond loss. Native, in this sense, pertains to what vitally survives.

The imported sugar beet is Erdrich's comic symbol common to North Dakota: a homely root (the seed as tubrous taproot?) from which we refine sweet relief, if not poison in overuse. "Small trees were planted in the yards of a few of these houses," the novel opens, "and one tree, weak, a scratch of light against the gray of everything else, tossed in a film of blossoms. Mary trudged solidly forward, hardly glancing at it, but Karl stopped. The tree drew him with its delicate perfume. His cheeks went pink, he stretched his arms out like a sleepwalker, and in one long transfixed motion he floated to the tree and buried his face in the white petals." In this ironic 1930s North Dakota Eden, motherless children wander as innocents of old, until a housewife turns her dog loose on Karl, and he tears away a blossoming branch (a northern "golden bough"):

> It was a such a large branch, from such a small tree, that blight would attack the scar where it was pulled off. The leaves would fall away later on that summer and the sap would sink into the roots. The next spring, when Mary passed it on some errand, she saw that it bore no blossoms and remembered how, when the dog jumped for Karl, he struck out with the branch and the petals dropped around the dog's fierce outstretched body in a sudden snow. Then he yelled, "Run!" and Mary ran east, toward Aunt Fritzie. But Karl ran back to the boxcar and the train. (*BQ* 2)

The Beet Queen seems less fictively expansive than *Love Medicine*— fewer characters, more restrained points of view, and tightened chronology—yet somehow just as daring. If not so "native" American, there is still a tough, comic lyricism here to match that of Eudora Welty. Erdrich sketches no-nonsensical, efficient scenes with a clipped prose style, restricted tricks, and fewer offbeat wrinkles. By comparison with *Love Medicine,* the epiphanic endings to sections are underplayed, though played they are: "There was the branch, still faintly good to smell" in the railroad boxcar with Saint Ambrose (his name is "no joke," he says, then adds that his first name is Giles). After their tenderly strange brush with sex, Karl "stood in the blackness. He didn't want to vomit or scream. He didn't want to cry on the lap of anyone again. So he stood frowning keenly at nothing as the train rolled on, and then, light and quick as a deer, he leaped forward and ran straight out the door of the moving boxcar" (*BQ* 26). Karl's leap ends the first chapter and sets the novel's offbeat tone.

The Beet Queen, then, is Erdrich's non-Indian novel dedicated to her father's German-American branch of the family. The story seems distinctly North Dakotan, with all the action under the surface—flat, horizontally imagined, spare. Wallace Pfef's closet homosexuality wildly illustrates a northern plains deviance from mainstream norms; Mary Adare's lyric toughness another, Karl's multisexual flair yet another, all parodically American. None is expressly Indian; all are surreally Dakotan and marvelously the creations of a trickster's imagination. The writing is consciously flattened, compared with *Love Medicine,* out of respect for a certain "plains" style and perhaps in response to critics of her first novel's lyric flights. Erdrich's complexities of character, flashbacks, and metaphoric richnesses web the first novel. This second fiction strikes one as tough, somewhat grainy, and controlled in Aristotelian time–space, while still possessed of what Studs Terkel called a "wild, crazy, unexpected humor." [5]

"I think it's there," Erdrich responded, "that's why the book is the way it is." This iconoclastic humor has its source in *Love Medicine.*

Going Back

> In Native American novels, coming home, staying put, contracting, even what we call "regressing" to a place, a past where one has been before, is not only the primary story, it is a primary mode of knowledge and a primary good.
>
> WILLIAM BEVIS, "Native American Novels"

From the beginning of *Love Medicine* to the end, characters are leaving and going home. June represents a lost surrogate mother, a wandering aunt among all kinds of other mothers. Sister Leopolda, the churchly superior mother, stalks a young girl in feline virginal rage. The adoptively maternal Marie mothers her clan in compassionate grace; a casually sensual Lulu shines in comic salvation. June, a feminist Mary Magdalene, dies at the beginning to trigger all the stories as martyred savior. "The *snow* fell *deep*er that *East*er than it *had* in *for*ty *years,* / but *June walked ov*er *it* like *wa*ter and *came home.*" This sentence sets up the long-legged iambic hexameter of a sprung walking rhythm. A ceremonial cadence, it pricks up the reader's ears. Iambs and anapests churn toward spondees in a slant-rhyming, inverse couplet of "snow" to "home." The sentence poetically cadences a three-in-one heroine walking beyond her death: the crucifixion (Easter), temptation in the wilderness (her forty years), and prophesied resurrection ("came home") of Our-Mother-of-the-Earth. She is as locally specific to Turtle Mountain as juneberry pies and June bugs in the sloughs. All this figures in one woman, transculturally named for the distant Roman goddess Juno, wife of the god-of-gods. She was the protectress of marriage and childbirth, a derivative of the Greek Hera, designating springtime. "June" dies in late "March," a martyr of winter, in Frye's terms a spiritually comic herald of spring rebirth.

So this martyred-and-mythically-reborn June, an adoptive "mother" to Albertine and known as Aunt June to all the Kashpaw kids, walks as Christ "like water" over the spring Dakota blizzard. Hers is a liquidly feminized land—pockets and rivulets of natural springs—a terrain named for the turtled humps of hills called "mountains" along the truly flat land of the Canadian border. In short, the goddess, the feminine who births all men, the earthen "mother-of-us-all" (as the Pueblos say) "came home" across the water to be buried and resurrected in her surviving kin, her native clan. "So there was nothing to do," her son ends the novel, "but cross the water, and bring her home." June's surviving ghost is the adoptive nurse, the feminist humor of the story.

At the close of *Love Medicine,* June's son Lipsha (known last to himself as anyone's son) drives his just-recognized father, Gerry Nanapush, to the border river and hopefully "home free." This takes place after Lipsha deals himself "a perfect family," or royal flush, in a hand of poker for his mother's Firebird (from the Fertile Crescent "phoenix" and the Aztec Quetzalcoatl, or "feathered serpent" of the resurrected sun). June's less affable son, King, bought the Firebird as an ironic phoenix from her life-insurance settlement (what better icon of America than a car mythically named for rebirth?).

A bisociated sense of kinship underlies the imagining of all the characters—positive and negative siblings, pairs, or even twins—from Lulu and Marie as lovers bonded in vying for one man, to Nector and Eli as twin brothers, to cross-generational pairings. In myth and comic romance, such twinning lies at the beginnings of creation. "I still had Grandma's hankie in my pocket," Lipsha says at the novel's end. "The sun flared. I'd heard that this river was the last of an ancient ocean, miles deep, that once had covered the Dakotas and solved all our problems. It was easy to still imagine us beneath them vast unreasonable waves, but the truth is we live on dry land. I got inside. The morning was clear. A good road led on. So there was nothing to do but cross the water, and bring her home" (*LM* 272).

Crossing the water suggests an ancient real and imagined passage to another world. Mediterranean sailors followed the sun west, out of the gates of Hercules, to the rediscovery of a "new" world and its western frontier. The road to, the voyage across, the flight out, the journey beyond—frontier-style, all these imply "the way," to and from what we could call home. Home designates beginning and ending; as such, it implies continuum and *re*union. For Momaday, it is a "way" to Rainy Mountain in *Oklahoma,* or "red earth," where his ancestors lie buried. Such is the ongoing odyssey in Western literature, a comic venture through travel, trouble, and talk–song of the "way home." And Lipsha's idiomatically inclusive phrase, "bring her home," is, I believe, distinctly American, even "native" American. It conjures up a history of leaving home "east" and pioneering "west" across an uncharted sea of prairies. The explorers left city, family, dogs, and cats behind. Many of their women stayed back home (Sacajawea led Lewis and Clark west, as Tekakwitha's ghost questionably blessed them). Only recently has a homing "mom" caught up with a wandering "dad." And revisionist historical thought, Sherman Paul has observed, tracks a native or primal "search for the primitive, which to a considerable extent is a search for the feminine."[6] Such nativist refeminizing of role models comes in this century through Frances Densmore's *Teton Sioux Music* (1918), Mary Austin's *The American Rhythm* (1923), Constance Rourke's *American Humor* (1931), or Louise Erdrich's current fiction, among many others. In some measure we live in a time of trying to include the excluded, the "natives" among us.

Turtle Mountain—Erdrich's Kashpaw homestead—stands out as the most densely populated of 315 Indian reservations in the country—six by twelve miles of 10,000 mixed-blood hill people straddling the Canadian border near the exact geographical center of the continent. Albertine recalls on "the rutted dirt road home" in *Love Medicine:* "the yard of stunted oaks, marigold beds, the rusted car that had been his [her grandfather's] children's playhouse and mine, the few hills of potatoes and stalks of rhubarb that Aurelia still grew. . . . The hollyhocks were choked with pigweed, and the stones that lined the driveway, always painted white or blue, were flaking back to gray" (*LM* 17). The flowers, trees, cars, tubers, seeds, and stalks natively code reservation country life. Marie Lazarre says that only "tough wild rhubarb flourishes here" among mixed natives: "the end of the world to some. Where the maps stopped. Where God had only half a hand in the creation. Where the Dark One had put in thick bush, liquor, wild dogs, and Indians" (42). Down the road a piece and through the forest, Lulu Nanapush roots her homegrown determinations: "And so we stuck together on that strip of land that was once sun beat and bare of trees. Wives and children, in-laws, cousins, all collected there in trailers and more old car hulks. Box elder trees and oak scrub were planted and grew up. We even had a gooseberry patch" (228). Anyone who has lived on or passed through a northern plains reservation would recognize this native place. By the novel's end, the grafted dandelion rises up as a native boutonniere.

Three Kashpaw and Nanapush generations live out modern twists of an American epic at Turtle Mountain. In the beginning there is a girl, Marie, in deadly psychic battle with a cloistered nun who scalds her back for Jesus and rams a fork through her hand, raising the maiden to stigmatic glory and lifelong combat, only to be forgiven forty years later on the nun's fetid deathbed. We see a reverse beatification when Marie takes her own daughter, Zelda Kashpaw, to the nun's bedside, the darkness illuminated by a "beam of light" on the old woman's white hair "straight and thin from her skull like the floss of dandelions" (*LM* 166, a portent of the novel's closing). "At least you have not forgot me," Marie says, knowing that hatred is remembering love in pain:

"I felt sorry for you," I said.
But this only made her laugh, a dry crackle like leaves crushed underfoot.
"I feel sorry for you too, now that I see." (117)

Confronting the "mother" ironically, this is grandma "saint" Marie, the French-Chippewa matriarch ironically named for the virgin–mother.

She has countless children and more adopted "took-ins" like Lipsha.
Marie learns by fourteen that she will "suffer for my smile" as a mousy
satan in Sister Leopolda's schoolroom closet (*LM* 44). A trickster devil
becomes her dark ally against the proselytizing harpy of Christ. A
sadomasochistic "sister" with a "strange" grin and "twisted jokes"
about saving little girls from passion tells Marie: "You have two
choices. One, you can marry a no-good Indian, bear his brats, die like a
dog. Or two, you can give yourself to God." Marie thinks to herself,
"sometimes I wanted her heart in love and admiration. Sometimes. And
sometimes I wanted her heart to roast on a black stick" (45).

The two women face off for life, grinning like canines across religious, cultural, and temperamental differences. Locked in archetypal
agon over a spoon at the nun's death, Marie recalls, "When I smiled
into her face she smiled back. It was the huge bleached grin of a skull"
(*LM* 121). Forty years earlier in the convent (with a mixture of Gretel
and the Witch at the oven, spiced with old-time slapstick), the child is
branded "Saint Marie of the Burnt Back and Scalded Butt! I broke out
and laughed" (54). There will be salt in her laugh thereafter, "Saint
Marie of the Shining Sea":

> She [Leopolda] bent forward with her fork held out. I kicked her with all
> my might. She flew in. But the outstretched poker hit the back wall first, so
> she rebounded. The oven was not so deep as I had thought. . . .
> "Bitch of Jesus Christ!" I shouted. "Kneel and beg! Lick the floor!"
> That was when she stabbed me through the hand with the fork, then took
> the poker up alongside my head, and knocked me out. (53)

Marie on her raised dais hours later suffers the sisters, even the pitiable
Leopolda, to touch her stigmata: "I smiled the saint's smirk into her
face" (56). But satiric triumph stoops to "the shambles of love," as
Marie forgives the nun's shabby sadism (*Tracks* reveals with a Dickensian touch that they are mother and daughter). A kind of twisted grace
bonds the two for a lifetime. Marie gives her benediction to a resurrection of daily dust: "Rise up and walk! There is no limit to this dust!"
(56).

And there is a man, sweet-toothed Nector, striding uphill with geese
tied to each arm, who finds his wife in this virgin martyr Marie. Nector
subdues the girl-child's wildness, gets caught loving her on the hill

(conceiving Gordie), and then hunkers down to raise broods of kids. He tries to leave Marie for a high-school sweetheart, Lulu Lamartine, and then burns down Lulu's house, only to be brought home by his own daughter to Marie's darkly waxed kitchen floor.

Characters find themselves locked in their pasts, determined by poverty, racism, religion, war on their own soil, the bizarre human condition forever fascinating and confusing—so they reach to one another, laughing, weeping, terrified, needy, murderous, and they touch, crumbling, unable to add up the price or the pieces, powerless to draw the pattern of things together. Lulu's son, Henry Lamartine Junior, an Indian Vietnam veteran, sexually threatens the young Albertine in a city hotel bedroom: "A dark numbing terror had stopped her mind completely. But when he touched her he was weeping" (*LM* 142). Indians, yes, Kashpaws and Nanapush go on in the special ethos of pride and defeat and survival, the estrangement of America's first peoples reserved inside history, clawing their ways home, hanging on, making pies and waxing floors and hunting geese and wiring tractors together, laughing as best they can. Marie gets down on her knees in the kitchen, betrayed by Nector's lustfully comic pursuit of Lulu, as she waxes herself into a domestic corner, only to laugh herself free:

> I felt better as I recognized myself in the woman who kept her floor clean even when left by her husband.
> I had been on a high horse. Now I was kneeling. I was washing the floor in my good purple dress. I never did laugh at myself in any situation, but I had to laugh now. (*LM* 128)

Marie will survive on such self-realizing humor, learn from and accept her mistakes, forgive her husband, and go on living.

These characters exist much like the rest of rural working America, but with that added inflection of pain, desperation, humor, another aboriginal tongue and cultural heritage, and immeasurable enduring strength that is "native" American—the ache of tribal self-definition and the going on in the face of all odds. "Society? Society is like this card game here, cousin," Gerry Nanapush says breaking out of prison. "We got dealt our hand before we were even born, and as we grow we have to play as best as we can" (*LM* 263). This wisdom comes from a political prisoner modeled on Leonard Peltier, a Turtle Mountain Chippewa now serving two consecutive life terms in Marion, Illinois, federal prison on less than circumstantial evidence for murder. Erdrich's fictional deck holds several full houses of such characters.

Comic Cast

The tales track Lipsha's "took-in" fusion of six family lineages and conclude ritually with comic twists in parental recognition. "I could see how his [Gerry's] mind leapt back, making connections, jumping at the intersection points of our lives: his romance with June. The baby given to Grandma Kashpaw. June's son by Gordie. King. Her running off. Me growing up. And then at last June walking toward home in the Easter snow that, I saw now, had resumed falling softly in this room" (*LM* 262). From first to last, beginning to ending snowfall (real and imagined), parts and peoples collate through fourteen tales told by seven mixed-Indian narrators. These voices of clan lineage gather the ghosts of an extended Indian family in the unraveling warp and woof of American history. They all funnel into Lipsha. The novel contextualizes comic detail in the feel of character and situation, where text takes hold as context, such that the narratives speak with a humor, certainly a human presence, that colors the parts discretely. This contextual humor cadences the arc of the story, remaining behind each narrator and within each tale narrated.

The triangle of Marie, Nector, and Lulu represents three comic types, as developed by Frye from the *Tractatus:* the *eiron,* or understater, in Marie (plain dealer); the *bomolocho,* or buffoon, in Nector (matinee idol); and the *alazon,* or overstater, in Lulu (dark lady). Each, too, characterizes a cyclic phase of Frye's comic trinity: Marie integrates families, Nector purges white acculturation, and Lulu renews the Indian vision, as it were, of humans toward one another (especially when Marie helps her to "see" again by the story's end). And in some essential respects, Marie plays the realist in her maternal fusing; Nector, the fool in his noble vanity; and Lulu, the romantic in her sensual celebration, a singular *joie de vivre.*

Marie's story begins in the late winter of French–Indian miscegenation, "the youngest daughter of a family of horse-thieving drunks," Nector says (*LM* 58). She "snares" (her word), or fortuitously seduces, the most handsome Chippewa on the reservation, the vain Nector (Zeus

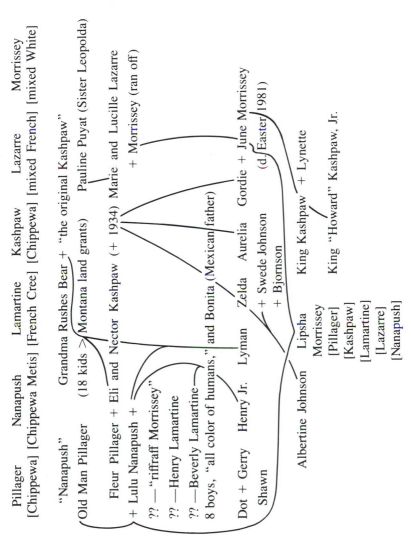

Family trees in *Love Medicine*.

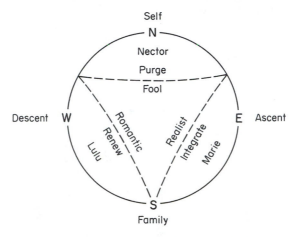

Primary characters and motifs in *Love Medicine*.

of North Dakota) on his geese-laden way to marry Lulu with a French wedding band. Marie is light-skinned enough to pass for poor white, and Indian enough to serve as the Kashpaw matriarch; her maternal role fuses all offspring, from comic birth in early spring, to summer marriage, through many fall children. Lulu's curve joins Marie's roundness here, except that Lulu burns through three marriages, nine fathers of her medley of children, and any number of lovers. She is, indeed, a "lulu" (also short for Louise, suggesting a private joke on the author's name). Thus there's a kind of wild abandon and heroic fatalism in her dark comic passion. Lulu's heated parabola arcs from romance through tragedy to comedy. Lulu's "first" man, when she is a child in the woods, is a dead drifter, for whom she cries all her tears, then laughs at life and thereafter plays at love. In *Tracks* we find that the dead man, Napoleon Morrissey, has been strangled with a rosary by Leopolda, formerly Pauline Puyat, for seducing her—and that Marie is the progeny.

Nector is caught between the two mothers. He is shored up by his stolid wife, Marie—champion potato peeler, floor waxer, saintly forgiver, and perennial adopter. Lulu, his "true love," remains a fiery *femme fatale,* sensual as melting butter on a steamy July afternoon. In some respects, Nector is cast as the comic victim of too much motherly attention (smeared with sentimental adulation for "our Indian") from the white woman artist in the barn, to Hollywood film makers, to being "elected" (that is, drafted) as tribal chairman—"all low pay and no thanks." All in all, he seems a well-meaning man, sharp enough to make tribal deals and play chief, handsome enough to be Hollywood-cast as the dying Indian. Nector remains heroically foolish and divides himself between two women, who outlive him to love each other.

But three is a troubling "sky" number, one shy of earth-based and balanced four to Indian minds. With second- and third-generation métis, then, a quartet complete this trio as narrative foil. They add a fourth type to the comic cast—*agroikos,* or churlish rustic, which Aristotle in the *Ethics* adds to the initial comic trio, so that *eiron* and *alazon* are complemented and completed by *bomolochoi* and *agroikos,* or buffoons and churls.[7] Now we have a whole comic drama: four completes three, balancing the native sense of earth quadrants with the mythic or cosmic triad—and this resolves the generational numerology in seven, the earth–sky resolution of four and three.

An "impure" breed in her own self-description, Albertine opens the novel in spring. She is self-caricatured as "blond, bleak and doomed to wander." This follows June's death as told from a third-person point of view personifying her spirit. In perfect structural balance, third-person omniscience introduces the beginning, double-middle, and concluding sections of the novel. Erdrich thus blocks the fiction in comic symmetry: Chapter 1, "The World's Greatest Fishermen," followed by Albertine's lead-in and chapters narrated by Marie, Nector, and Marie again.

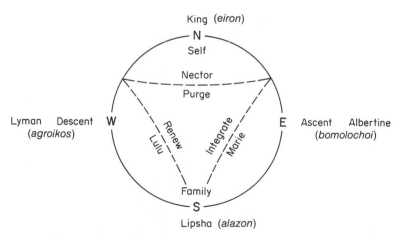

Second-generation characters and motifs in *Love Medicine.*

Chapter 5, "Lulu's Boys," continues the second section with chapters told again by Nector and Marie. Chapter 8, "A Bridge," leads into the third, most unsettling section by Lyman and then Albertine a second time around. The fourth part begins with Chapter 11, "Crown of Thorns," resolved by Lipsha, Lulu (at last!), and Lipsha again.

The narrators set up interwoven points of view, six first-person and eight third-person refractions (in brackets):

Chapter 1, "The World's Greatest Fishermen"	[June M. Kashpaw] and Albertine Johnson (I)
Chapter 2, "Saint Marie"	Marie Lazarre (I)
Chapter 3, "Wild Geese"	Nector Kashpaw (I)
Chapter 4, "The Beads"	Marie Kashpaw (II)
Chapter 5, "Lulu's Boys"	[Lulu Lamartine and Beverly Lamartine]
Chapter 6, "The Plunge of the Brave"	Nector Kashpaw (II)
Chapter 7, "Flesh and Blood"	Marie Kashpaw (III)
Chapter 8, "A Bridge"	[Albertine Johnson and Henry Lamartine Jr.]
Chapter 9, "The Red Convertible"	Lyman Lamartine
Chapter 10, "Scales"	Albertine Johnson (II)
Chapter 11, "Crown of Thorns"	[Gordie Kashpaw and Sister Mary Martin de Porres]
Chapter 12, "Love Medicine"	Lipsha Morrissey (I)
Chapter 13, "The Good Tears"	Lulu Lamartine
Chapter 14, "Crossing the Water"	[Howard Junior] and Lipsha Morrissey (II)

These narrative voices tell the tale as tribal chorus over half a century, the whole humorously grounded in points of view, from the "spirits" humanly conceived to the earthlings who laugh, gossip, and cackle the bonds of a familial home: "Then they were laughing out loud in brays and whoops, sopping tears in their aprons and sleeves, waving their hands helplessly" (*LM* 21). This family laughter absolves, indeed celebrates, outliving childhood pain. Each voice rings clear and resonant, like a pebble in a birch-ringed, rippling pool.

In many respects, Albertine is the collective voice among the women. She, like Grandma Marie, is an understater, a comic heroine. She deadpans the joke on "Patient Abuse" (nursing students accent the first word; Kashpaws, the second). Albertine inherits her Aunt June's love of dance and laughter. Humorously parallel with Lulu's passion, she passes out beside Lipsha in a "comic" vision from too much beer, *vin* from "roses," and beauty under the northern lights. Albertine voices the ragtag integration and "permitted disrespect" that brings the family "home" after June's death; in the city she absorbs the purgative irony of Henry Lamartine's veteran "return." She laughs at Dot in a bar, narrowly escapes mayhem, and tells the renewal story of Shawn's birth in "Scales" (Albertine reappears in *The Beet Queen* and prefigures a future heroine of *American Horse* in Erdrich's tetralogy). Albertine's narratives personally register June's distant love, death, and resurrection, as she carries her aunt's spirit onward.

Her cousin Lipsha (June's son) has the mythic "trembling hand"— fusing all the families, in fact, as orphan cum culture hero. Off-stage shaman, Old Man Pillager is his paternal grandfather, along with his grandmother Lulu Nanapush (married Lamartine) down through his father, Gerry Nanapush. Lucille Lazarre and a "run off" Morissey are his genetic grandparents through June Kashpaw. Psychically and more domestically, Nector Kashpaw figures to be his maternal grandfather, as Marie Lazarre adopts her dead sister's grandson and raises Lipsha among her own. A "took in" saved from drowning, Lipsha grows up with a healing humor. "I know the tricks of mind and body inside out without ever having trained for it," he says, "because I got the touch" (*LM* 189–90). It's the healing medicine of hands-on humor, the deeper touch or feel for the comic life-spirit, even if things don't always work out (a different shaman altogether from the folklore of "witch" doctors and desert gurus).

Lipsha plays his role with male innocence until the very end. A shy, even girlish boy with long eyelashes, he's nonthreatening to feminine senses of nurturing and sensitivity, as opposed to Nector's male naiveté and sexual folly. Nector burns his wick at both ends, whereas Lipsha waits to light his. Lipsha's jokes roll off his tongue understated, if outrageous, as with the bottle of Old Grand Dad between the eyes to announce his father's visitation to the Twin Cities. Or they backfire— the frozen turkey hearts for Grandpa's waning devotion. Or they ring wildly ironic—reporting Nector shouting "HAIL MARIE, FULL OF GRACE" in church to a God going deaf—indeed, to his wife, Marie. Lipsha's jokes resolve with gaming humor worthy of Huizinga's *Homo ludens*—a crimped "perfect family" that wins Lipsha the Firebird, his father's escape, and his own return home. This comic healer comes on a touch earnest, innocent of evil, Christlike in a secular realism that never betrays faith in humanity, no matter how low things get. He's the outsider "took in," the castaway found. His is the ancient story of the orphan adopted and finally reclaimed by true royalty (June and Gerry as queen and king tricksters). In a comic way, Lipsha figures as the "divine child" of ancient myth.

The other two concluding narrators seem to be foils: Lyman (Nector and Lulu's illicit son, whom Lulu saves from the burning house) and Howard Junior, or Little King. Their ironic witness serves as honest check to easy solutions in the broader comic tones of the fiction. Lyman watches a hysterically laughing Henry Junior wade into the Red River and sink, followed by the red convertible's searching headlights, "still lighted even after the water swirls over the back end. I wait. The wires short out. It is all finally dark. And then there is only the water, the sound of it going and running and going and running and running" (*LM* 154). It's a terrible moment of drowning in the river's deeper currents sweeping onward. At the end, Howard's acculturated and mean "existence" in the city brings him to betray his even meaner father, King, when Gerry Nanapush shows up to meet Lipsha on comic paternal grounds (revealing the "slightly fucked" heart, a Nanapush "thing" that will keep Lipsha out of the service). The final scene of *Love Medicine* bizarrely orchestrates two sets of fathers and sons: King Junior, an antinarrator as it were, will survive the winter of urban Indian discontent, but the future promises no renaissance (Aurelia's "pale petunia" homestead for the Kashpaws seems as far away as the aurora borealis). Yet Lipsha has learned the feminist virtues of patience by way of Marie, as well as his grandmother Lulu's bluff. "So I just smiled," Lipsha says playing for his future in King Senior's kitchen, "although my stomach was a churning washer full of dimes" (240).

Lipsha's healing humor, by contrast, incorporates the strengths and transforms the weaknesses of the generation that preceded him. Too much like Nector, he can't shoot straight enough to kill a goose for the shamanic "love medicine" in its monogamous heart. So he buys frozen turkey hearts at the Red Owl market, blesses them himself with holy water, and fatally tries to charm Nector back into Marie's arms. The potion backfires. After Marie's sharp slap on the back to make him swallow, Nector chokes to death on his grandson's made-up medicine, though he seems to die willingly in Lipsha's arms. The slapstick hilarity of the scene fits the characters, as the misfire seems surreally fitting—a dark comic lesson in the courage of good hearts to survive or accept their mistakes, trickster's sins accounted for. Nector dies of his own forked "love" between two women.

Marie is filled with a mother's compassionate humor. Hers is an understated feminine realism in the comic service of bonding, surviving threats, and rebonding her clan family. She's clearly a regenerated Eve with the only bearing crab-apple tree on the reservation. The nuns planted two more after twelve years, she says, but they bear no "crabs." Marie adds firmly, "Mine was established." With "a mouth like a flophouse," Marie has the *eiron*'s role of straight woman who bequeaths her honesty and warmth to a foster grandson, Lipsha.

On the distaff side, the gap-toothed Lulu exaggerates everything as true *alazon*. With her blackberry eyes and feline ways, she teaches Lipsha to play, to tell stories, to crimp cards, to laugh at himself. Lulu is a bit of a witch or shamanness, linked sexually with Lipsha's grandfather Old Man Pillager, the medicine man. With French rouge on her cheeks, she has the "spark," Nector knows only too well, to unwrap the dripping butter on the hottest day in July and go at it in the front seat of her Nash Rambler. She is all action, wasting no words. "It's a damn pretty place," she says on the hill with Nector (correcting the shadowed memory of "paradise lost" when Nector fell into Marie's arms and betrayed Lulu a quarter of a century before). Hers is the sensual acceptance of what is, the positive "yes" of things, after all is said and done. She's fictive sister to the Wife of Bath, Moll Flanders, and Molly Bloom. Lulu can stare down a tribal council as she threatens paternity suits against half the married men (including Nector) when they challenge her homestead. She plays the best and most crooked pinochle in the senior citizens' home, crimping cards with tricks passed on to Lipsha. She's a grandmother worth knowing, if a bit risky to be around.

Nector, finally, seems something of a short-sighted Adam. He thinks he's sharp, but in fact he is just keen and dumb enough to be manipulated his entire life by two women and everyone else's misguided flattery. "I guess," Lipsha says, "you could call him a monument all of himself" (*LM* 191–92). He's something of the archetypal slapstick innocent, an Indi'n Charlie Brown. "Disrobe," the snaggle-toothed white woman orders in her barn. "What robe?" he asks (90). Lipsha looks back later on Grandpa: "some people fall right through the hole in their lives" (Marie reaches through the stigmatic "hole" in her hand to bring him back from Lulu's burning house into her waxed kitchen). His river "branches" between Scylla and Charybdis, Marie and Lulu, sour and sweet. "Call me Ishmael," Nector mugs as a boy reading *Moby-Dick* and vowing to hold his breath to let the current save him from what his mother calls "the great white wail." Significantly so, he eats "too much Milky Way," as Lipsha puts it, and develops diabetes, a disease all too common among Indians. His brain finally snaps with senility, a chosen second childhood of Lulu's "yes," signifying a comic assent regardless of cost (a nod to Molly Bloom in Joyce's *Ulysses*). His grandson concludes, "So I figure that a man so smart all his life—tribal chairman and the star of movies and even pictured in the statehouse and on cans of snuff—would know what he's doing by saying yes. I think he was called to second childhood like anybody else gets a call for the priesthood or the army or whatever" (190–91). Nector teaches his grandson a role of comic salvation, as Lipsha plays the perennial orphan whose innocence blesses him in rebirth.

There is something Dickensian in the humor here, seasoned by Faulkner's comic vison, rich with Shakespearean doublings and popular puns. Critics have seen this as the humanly "spherical" simplicity of Pickwick, a primal innocence or potential good nature in the face of evil, even if the vision darkens as the players age. It's both childlike, evincing faith in human nature, and dramatically sophisticated as comedy. *The Tempest* resolves with such "grace" over exacting justice, and Dilsey's fabled endurance in Faulkner's *The Sound and the Fury* turns on maternal black humor, as imagined by a white southern male novelist.

On the surface, Erdrich's portraits seem cartooned at times—Nector the male simpleton, Marie the strong mother, Lulu the untamed lover. Beneath plotted ripples lie complex "native" currents that strike the reader as convincing. Erdrich's fiction is etched as indelibly American as anything written by Eudora Welty or Flannery O'Connor, and coming fiction promises more. Lipsha and Albertine hold out hope for the future—not just another novel like *American Horse,* but a Native American bisociation of cultural differences for most Americans.

Contraries

The fiction is emplotted, beginning to end, under a fluorescent Dakota night sky. Characters walk endlessly through spring downpours like lake-walking "Jesus" or June bugs that hatch from the opening sketch of a North Dakota "spring" blizzard. It is a country of soggy birch and aspen bottoms, frozen pothole lakes, and migrating birds in the great flyway of America. Geese, cranes, and ducks fly north to south to north again with the seasons, traversing the Canadian border, just west of the white-owned Red River Valley, where the Chippewa lived historically.

The novel's humor works with and against a ground-zero pathos— the sordid, fallen condition of "man" and relatively loyal "woman." Adam and Eve reemerge as mixed-blood Native Americans. Marriages are "on and off again," as with Gordie and June, who conceives Lipsha with Gerry in the "off" times. At June's wake, a mix of beer, pies, laughter, stories, kin insult, and despair settles over stale hunting jokes, King Senior's rage, the sisters' kitchen slander, Albertine's "homecoming," and Lipsha's shy silence.

Outside by the woodpile and winter wheat, Lipsha's voice constructs a "bridge" home for Albertine. "We floated into the field and sank down, crushing green wheat. We chewed the sweet kernels and stared up and were lost. Everything seemed to be one piece. The air, our faces, all cool, moist, and dark, and the ghostly sky. Pale green licks of light pulsed and faded across it. Living lights. Their fires lobbed over, higher, higher, then died out in blackness" (*LM* 34). The fiction's discrete lights form a human whole littered with the clothing, crumbs, twigs, fillings, and broken words of real working lives. "The people" look up at the midnight lights to survive the darkness.

These Kashpaws and Nanapushes and Lamartines remain fiercely "Indi'ns," poor and thick with one another. They no longer speak Chippewa, but a dialect of American red English that could be mouthed nowhere else but here. This proletarian speech is peculiar to America, with tongues rooted in two thousand Native American languages, girdered with German and Latin grammar, patinated with French a millennia ago, and overlaid with colonial English. The idioms are still responsive to regional character and climatic elements and local airwaves. All statements lie understated and yet suggestive as deadpan metaphors. Nector speaks of Marie, his child-virgin-wife martyred and married on the hillside: "The sun falls down the side of the world and the hill goes dark. Her hand grows thick and fevered, heavy in my own, and I don't want her, but I want her, and I cannot let her go" (*LM* 62). First Man, First Woman—the old Adamic ("red earth") story is translated natively from *Paradise Lost*. Reshaping berry pies after a family fight in the kitchen, Albertine works with what she has: "But once they smash there is no way to put them right" (39). When Nector comes back from Lulu's burning house, Marie retrieves him with the lyric courage of the desperate (not to mention Mother Mary reaching out to the damned): "I put my hand through what scared him. I held it out there for him. And when he took it with all the strength of his arms, I pulled him in" (129).

The ends of the stories rise up off the page, soar through the reader's mind, and hang etched and limpid against a canvas of blank space: drowning in spring Turtle Mountain snow with June, dreaming with Albertine under starless North Dakota night skies, musing with Lipsha and Canada geese calling lonely and lyrical overhead, agonizing with Henry Junior hearing human–animal cries in locked bathrooms, wandering with Gordie or June through sleezy rain-soaked beerpiss bars. And still the novel ends in the daily redemption of sunrise, a son driving his fugitive father home along the Canadian border and himself back to Turtle Mountain.

With an intricate sense of humor, Louise Erdrich evinces a woman's compassion, understanding, even acceptance of the forgivably strange violence in human events. Hers is a mother's tolerance, if not affection, for what cannot easily be loved in human nature—petty, mean, senseless, outrageous, sometimes brutishly male and viciously female smallnesses in the face of vast natural forces and the flood of human history.[8] All have a part here, each a position, everyone a perspective in the communal "place to love and be irritated with." The novelist's humor integrates people, place, and circumstance in a feminine web finely woven, holding out for something better, the children's future, mutual tolerance, forgiveness, even love.

And still America surges on, west, south, north, the mixed flotsam and jetsam of the world, smack up against Native Americans, clashing, warring, laughing, intermarrying, digging and cursing and trashing and blessing the land, until a writer like Erdrich comes to the surface, cast up to show us ourselves again. As the poet W. C. Williams says in "To Elsie," she reveals "the truth about us," comically homespun: Americans gone "crazy" back home, intermarrying with "a dash of Indian blood," a dream of September goldenrod, an excreted earth under our feet. In these "isolate flecks," as Williams sees, fallen to earth and sent skyward again—out of these loved, damned, and bastard words in a deeply grounded humor—rise our love medicines, our "native" Americas.

Belonging

> This was the wages of the father meeting up with the son and the
> ghost of a woman caught in the dark space between them.
>
> LIPSHA, in Louise Erdrich, *Love Medicine*

Lipsha bringing "her home" ties down an old American myth, it occurs
to me, and suggests something deeper about Mother Earth than Western
wandering. It is a Native American sense of place-that-we-call-home as
living mother. This belief has to do with where we came from, where
our ancestors are buried, and where we are going to return: "across the
water" of time or history to the earth itself, down into things in the end,
whether we are culturally in motion or in place, migrating or settling
down, on the road out West or just parked in front of the TV. It is a sense
of *be*longing, says Lipsha, the child-who-thought-himself-an-orphan: a
sense of knowing one's mothering place, touching-in with hearth-and-
home, the traditional "woman's place."

So to "bring her home" finally means belonging matrilocally somewhere, the answered longing to *be* someplace. "Belonging was a matter
of deciding to," Lipsha concludes and crimps himself "a perfect family." Or belonging is having that somewhere catch up with you or acci-
dentally realizing that it was always there, as Lipsha does. At the
Canadian border with Lipsha's belated father, a migratory "here" is
suddenly not "away from" home, but carried doubly within him in
motion (as we all were once carried "beneath our mother's heart,"
Erdrich adds in "Where I Ought to Be"). In some true post-Depression
sense, then, it is bringing home *home,* through self-realization within
tribal history. "I drove the tangled highways in a general homeward
direction," Lipsha says inside his mother's Firebird, something of a
mobile native womb at the end.

Indian homing turns on a sense of origin in a real historical place: a
concept of family once or still there, an idea of extended kinship, a call
to a particular land like a geographical magnet—a humor of belonging.
Places and their names, the Cibecue Apache tell Keith Basso, keep the
people in line. Along with their jokes, place-names keep people morally
"at home," literally and figuratively grounded. It has never been easy
homing, from Odysseus lost at sea among sirens, to Ishmael adrift, to
Momaday's Abel running from war-torn Los Angeles toward a "house
made of dawn." Welch's nameless Indian narrator admits the "torture"

of coming home in the hung-over opening of *Winter in the Blood*. Still, this authentic voice knows Montana as his ancestral origin and end:

> It could have been the country, the burnt prairie beneath a blazing sun, the pale green of the Milk River valley, the milky waters of the river, the sagebrush and cottonwoods, the dry, cracked gumbo flats. The country had created a distance as deep as it was empty, and the people accepted and treated each other with distance.
>
> But the distance I felt came not from country or people; it came from within me. I was as distant from myself as a hawk from the moon.[9]

That last image, lyrically emblematic, focuses the Blackfeet story in a cultural icon, hawk against moon. Here the art of ancient winter counts, those eidetic histories drawn on animal skins, images and tells everything. Plains Indian art *is* history, in this instance, primary and primal document. This native image for North America "makes it new," as Pound pressed modernists, renews the eidetic truth native to the land and people, even ironically. This, then, is something tribally old made contemporaneously new.

Integratively so, Leslie Silko closes *Ceremony* with renewed southwestern harmonies: Grandmother Spider's Pueblo patterns orally woven together in the breed-bastard-orphan life of Tayo, now placed among the people, a regionally emergent Indian-Hispanic-Anglo cultural hero:

> The ear for the story and the eye for the pattern were theirs; the feeling was theirs; we came out of this land and we are hers.
>
> In the distance he could hear big diesel trucks rumbling down Highway 66 past Laguna. The leaves of the big cottonwood tree had turned pale yellow; the first sunlight caught the tips of the leaves at the top of the old tree and made them bright gold. They had always been loved. He thought of her then; she had always loved him, she had never left him; she had always been there. He crossed the river at sunrise.[10]

The scene foreshadows Lipsha at the end of *Love Medicine*, indeed, recalls Abel running to conclude *House Made of Dawn*. Tayo's "she" is the immemorial mother, and this bridge joins two banks where his mother, Laura, crossed the river naked at dawn half a life ago, miscegenously impregnated with Tayo. The native message is that southwestern tribal "changes" have taken a century to reveal coherent patterns, genetic blendings, and cultural fusions of Spanish, Indian, and immigrant bloodlines. This America is peopled by many pilgrims, textured with many regional contexts that signify home.

So among Indians, home is rooted in a historical place to belong, culturally responsive among one's people. Return is mandatory. Home includes a particular physical landscape, flora and fauna—all the leggeds and wingeds and roots, the seasons, weather, climate, sun, moon, and starlight at given angles. Its direct line traces genetic lineage or parentage, along with collateral kin, blooded and adopted; its fringes leaf with "bros" and "sisters" who for various reasons are, or say they are, "half," "step," or otherwise. Its trunk roots down beneath the "bloody loam" of earth history, as Williams gauged American culture, to our ancestral "old ways." Its mystical reachings in *Love Medicine* naturalistically shine in the northern lights: "As if they sky were a pattern of nerves and our thoughts and memories traveled across it," Albertine muses under "the drenching beauty" beside cousin Lipsha. "As if the sky were one gigantic memory for us all"—a luminous history always there, consciously seen or not. And here June would be dancing "a two-step for wandering souls. Her long legs lifting and falling. Her laugh an ace" (*LM* 35).

All this, Lipsha learns later through Grandma Lulu, studs "a knowledge that could make or break you." It's an old Oedipal gamble, cognate with Welch's contrary wisdom of Old Man and Old Woman in Blackfeet creation myth, modern as a broken marriage dramatized by Sam Shepard. Frost scanned this formally as the "straight crookedness of a good walking stick," a compelling off-rhythm in slant rhyme. In the northern heart of America, we may find our way "home" through its elision and rediscover communal humor through individual hurt. To quote Dickinson, "To be assisted by Reverse, / One must Reverse have bore—" (no. 910). Long after the delayed-stress veteran, Henry Lamartine Junior, has stepped into a swollen river and drowned, Lulu speaks her son's name softly: "I wanted him to know that he still had a home."

So America's native son or liberty's daughter searches for a cultural triad: cemetery of the past, granary of the present, and schoolyard of the future. These are humanly figured in buried ancestors, working parents, and budding offspring. Such is America's past, present, and future, its historical presence among tenaciously rerooting immigrants. Indians remain more aware of this than any other group in the country, partly because of their "native" consciousness, their tribal definitions as "first" Americans.

At home, most closely, Americans of three generations gather in the kitchen or, until urban conversions, on the porch to be liminally both in and out of nature and civilization. The kitchen still seems the locus of "home," the gathering place, where the women make pies, brew coffee, and talk. This is where Marie waxes her floor, where Nector stumbles back home, where Lipsha plays for family stakes in the Twin Cities. The novel opens in the kitchen, returns here periodically, and closes by the river, which carries everyone home. Americans peel potatoes, bake berry pies, smoke cigarettes, gossip, drink spirits, build up and cut down one another, tell all kinds of stories, and generally "do America" in mother's kitchen.

But we "natives" also love our cars; and we keep traveling after love medicines, in Albertine's black Mustang, June's posthumous blue Firebird, Henry Junior's red Oldsmobile, Lulu's tan Nash Ambassador. And these driving names are drawn mythically from American history: the wild mustang (Spanish *mesteño,* "stray" mixed-blood) or Indian pony; the Aztec bird of fire, as the "winged serpent" of the sun, Quetzalcoatl; or the "old" way "mobile," the heap dad drove about. Add to these auto-mobiles the Thunderbird, the Winnebago, the Chief, the Cherokee, the Pontiac. Indians and wild animals animate our motoring lexicon, along with our sports teams—Redskins and Lynx, Warriors and Wildcats, Seminole and Fury. Apache helicoptors led the antitank advance in our 1991 war in Iraq, the "well rooted" Edenic garden of recent killings.

All this continues a cultural history of the frontier, which butted up against Native American cultures, some like the Pueblos in situ for thousands of years, others like the Navajo newly arrived, and still others like the Lakota seminomadic and carrying home with them for a millennium. For all of us, émigrés and otherwise, it was and is a "quest" for home, a concern for bonding humor, ironic or lyric, and a question of where to sink one's roots. Once rooted, we seek to stay; if dispossessed, we question how to regenerate humor and home. Cherokee women carried plant tubers from Georgia to Oklahoma on the Long March, having stroked the leaves and bark on rooted trees goodbye when they were forced to leave the Southeast.

The native theme of America, then, beyond the denuded loam, might be the ancient origin of culture, the orphan-who-finds-a-family-home. It is the outcast adopted, the long trek back, as Erdrich charts in her novels. The Depression leaves us all with an orphan story in the family.

Erdrich's characters in *The Beet Queen,* even the homely sugar beet, come as transplants; each seems a graft, a foundling or "took in," as all across America, from Thomas Merton to Huck Finn to Humbert Humbert.

But how do Indians find home beyond American homelessness? Perhaps they find it consciously, perhaps mythically through a "second sense," as Nector says of his twin Eli, hunting geese. After the disrobed Nector takes "the plunge of the brave" in the white woman's barn, his forest double Eli still has "an aim I cannot match." Nector trades what Eli shoots, and home is where it always was: *here,* but down in the deeper-loamed, native self. Neglected by her dying mother, June is said to have "sucked on pine sap and grazed grass and nipped buds like a deer" to survive. She is "the child of what the old people called Manitous" (*LM* 65), Marie says when she takes in her sister's daughter (genetic mothers seem to falter where adoptive ones stand fast). This implies something of an old belief about instinct—that Achilles might be natively gifted as a warrior, for example, or as Lyndon Johnson compared politics on Capitol Hill to coyote hunting in Texas: "feelin', smellin', an' knowin'." Getting home "down-home" would seem an American adoptive trick, a backlash against the pretenses, for better or worse, of *Kultur.* "Goes backward, looks forward," the Swampy Cree say of the homing porcupine that backs into its cultural future: *usa puyew, usu wapiw.*[11]

Native Wit

> WONG: You have mentioned that non-Indians often either miss, or choose to ignore, the humor in *Love Medicine.*
>
> ERDRICH: I think that's often the case. In talking to tribal people who've read the book, the first thing they say is, "Oh yes, that funny book." It's not like they self-consciously pick out the humor, but on the whole it's funnier than a lot of critics who read it who were kind of saying this is devastating.
>
> "An Interview with Louise Erdrich and Michael Dorris"

Native wit, to Americanize Freud's *Witz* for the moment, seems our conscious ace in the hole, as Albertine muses of a laughing June twostepping among the northern lights. This wit is an Indian wild card and

American twist on an ancient cultural paradigm, getting-back-home. June's first words, "What's happening? Where's the party?" tell Andy (and us in the novel's first dialogue) that she's game to play, even her last card, going home. Her death brings the family to life in a seriocomic homecoming wake. "I came to play," Gerry echoes June's gambit at the other end of the novel. Trickster father, shaman son, and ingrate brother draw cards for the foxy mother's Firebird: "we have to play as best we can" (*LM* 262–63).

What Mary Douglas might see as lyric cartoons of "permitted disrespect" stretch the Kashpaw clan thin, yet reassemble it, recharge its dynamics, and launch Albertine and Lipsha, in particular, as emissaries of the fiction's future. Gently sad in a "shell" pullover, June parodies a tempted, martyred, and resurrected feminist Jesus Christ (her initials are J. K., sister to J.C.) drinking "Angel Wings" in a North Dakota oilrigger bar just before Easter. Her body now lies under a pink gravestone on the convent hill, but her soul, according to Albertine's "vision" under the aurora borealis, is laughing, singing, and dancing a longlegged two-step in the sky. Just so, the Kashpaw homestead itself, minded now by Aunt Aurelia (sunrise here, too), is painted a peeling lavender. Certainly there's feminine hope in these pastel promises of rebirth, even if the paint peels: the dawn of another character, good joke, or infectious story.

With throaty resilience, June lives out a lyric humor as something of an absentee mother. Hers is a woman's love for the unloved, a singsong reaffirmation through toughness, acceptance, and forgiveness. This humorous resilience implies a woman's willowy ability when down to survive comically by springing back, as Nector first says of Marie on the hill, or if martyred like June, to be remembered well and to have the last laugh on death. Women at the kitchen wake cackle like hens—a laughter that absolves and connects, as it celebrates the survival of pain and folly. Across genders "Dad" grins wolflike in fate's teeth, as with Gerry's trickster wit and body wisdom (Nanapush is a breath away from Nanabush, Manabozho, and Wenebojo, the old Chippewa trickster names). Gerry remains a political martyr, feminine-assisted, with the coyote wiles to get in and out of very tight spots—indeed, to conceive a child under penal guard (*A-ho!* Julia Kristeva).

Still, a mother adds the known constant in the homing equation of Indian humor. Fathers with fists of rotting meat come and go past the dogs, through back doors and windows (Nector must wash his hands with lavender soap before Lulu will let him into bed). Both Lulu and Marie prove to be Lipsha's grandmothers, and after Nector's death Marie puts drops in Lulu's cataracts so that she might see through a mother's gracing tears. An edged forgiveness is the fiction's final word. "Salt or sugar?" Marie riddles Nector earlier with her snap-back mother-sea wit, the "whip singing" watery torsion of a young willow down by the river. This fencing and forgiving, still salty humor is Trickster's blessing as (s)he gambles with our lives. Such humor can be seen in "the look of mothers drinking sweetness from their children's eyes," Lipsha says of Grandma Marie, who adopted his mother, June. He thinks of tenacious dandelions: "a bitter mother's milk. A buried root." Nature's native icon turns out to be a dandelion's bother and blessing outside the senior citizens' home, complemented comically by the beet in Erdrich's next novel.

The dandelion ("lion's teeth" yellowed) is a grafted weed from Europe that blooms golden and seeds white in styptic puffballs, by now a mixed-breed weed to be sure. The dandelion has become as natively hard to root out as crabgrass, yet it ferments a sweet wine, if properly tended, or a tasty salad, as Indians once prepared. So in *Love Medicine* the dandelion's iconic humor—weedy, whip-singing, willowy, unwanted—blooms as a naturalized image of (Native) American resilience. Nector roots them out on the lawn of the senior citizens' home with a two-pronged fork (his comic phallic scepter?). Albertine in early spring finds them when she first receives news of June's death: "a big stretch of university lawn that was crossed by a steam-pipe line of grass—so bright your eyes ached—and even some dandelions" where she lay thinking "of Aunt June until I felt the right way for her" (*LM* 9).

There is a desperate humor at work here, too, the cheek of the damned. The novel bisociatively keys on quick shifts and reversals, from hilarious cartoons to darkly ironic pathos. Henry Junior will not laugh, Lyman says (Henry's emasculated namesake committed suicide on the railroad tracks, while his "real" father, the seductive brother Beverly, a door-to-door urban Indian huckster, left for the city to sell "educational books"). Henry Junior cannot laugh, that is, until he takes his own life by drowning, a cursed death that haunts the land, according to Chippewa legend.

Two characters, Gerry Nanapush and Gordie Kashpaw, serve as doubles toward the novel's end to play out the tragicomic consequences of tricksterism. As counter "twins" to Eli and Nector, their names even chime: Gerry Nanapush and Gordie Kashpaw (something of an off-rhyme twists through "-push" and "Kash'" echoed conversely in "Nana-" and "-paw"). Gordie was conceived on the convent hill by Marie and Nector in the beginnings of Erdrich's fictional time—child of paradise lost for the moment. He grows up playing incestuously with his cousin and elopes to South Dakota (a state border joke?) with June. Keyed to their beginnings, the marriage is more miss than match. When June dies, Gordie starts drinking, drifting, dying inside.

Gerry's mother is Lulu, Marie's double. We gather that his father (always a mystery around Lulu) is Old Man Pillager, the Chippewa shaman of the woods, offstage and never seen. Lulu lets slip later, "no white man has made a jail that could hold the son of Old Man Pillager" (*LM* 225), as she appears to confess who fathered Gerry. From childhood, Gerry acts in the style of trickster's progeny: "He laughed at everything, or seemed barely to be keeping amusement in. His eyes were black, sly, snapping with sparks. He led the rest in play. . ." (84). His Nanapush name calls on the Chippewa trickster, and his size and agility mark him "cat-quick for all his mass" (165). He bruises a drunken cowboy's balls "to settle the question" of "whether a Chippewa was also a nigger" (161). It lands Gerry in prison, where he keeps returning mainly "for breaking out" (160). This reversing, shape-changing, liminal Indi'n stays one step ahead of Officer Lovchik. "So you see," Albertine says, "it was difficult for Gerry, as an Indian, to retain the natural good humor of his ancestors in these modern circumstances" (163). Trickster teaches a cautious empathy, however, for things that go wrong, funny or not. Reverse fate engenders a wily, forgiving, yet ever alert ancestral "good" humor. Gerry does remain manly (conceiving Shawn with Dot in a prison waiting room) and humorously quick-witted in a droll way, until he hides on the wrong reservation and takes the rap for killing an FBI agent at Pine Ridge. So for the moment, he is serving two life sentences in a maximum-security prison where no touching, talking, or engendering is allowed.

"Crown of Thorns" follows "Scales" to connect Gerry with Gordie. Gordie's hands seize alcohol compulsively (trickster motifs of old) as his mind splinters in the wake of June's death. He suffers guilt over hitting June, hallucinating a feminine succubus in alcoholic fascination: "The can was bent at the waist and twisted at the hips like the torso of a woman" (*LM* 173). In this Bergsonian nightmare, where the inanimate and animate merge comically dark, Gordie's world blows a fuse when he overloads his trailer's power circuits. His psyche dissociates: "he both missed June and was relieved to be without her" (176). Nector thought the same of being held by Marie on the hill, conceiving Gordie: "I don't want her, but I want her, and I cannot let her go" (62). This is the classic double bind, a paralytic corner, and Trickster begins playing cruel doubling games as Gordie hits "a tough old doe" with his Malibu. He carries the wrong key (always two contrary keys to things) for his trunk, so he stashes the carcass in the back seat: "because two keys were made to open his one car, he saw clearly that the setup of life was rigged and he was trapped" (179). No doubt this *is* an "opposite think-ing" world, as the Cree way; rather than play it, Gordie freezes and loses the "big one" (he is a failed Golden Gloves boxer). The deer wakes up in his back seat as Gordie drives deliriously to find more drink. "Ears pricked, gravely alert, she gazed into the rearview and met Gordie's eyes" (180). Gordie bludgeons the deer with "a flat-edged crowbar thick as a child's wrist" (180). In delirium tremens, he thinks he has killed June. This tragic Adamic son, haunted by Eve, heads to the convent for Catholic absolution.

   " 'It's been, shit, ten years since my last confession.' He laughed, then he coughed" (*LM* 184). Gordie sobs his story to Sister Mary Martin de Porres of Lincoln, Nebraska. This forty-two-year-old celibate (June's double) plays her clarinet late at night when she can't sleep. An un-hinged "man" appears at her window with a dead deer in the back seat that he thinks is his murdered wife. "At the first sight of it, so strange and awful, a loud cackle came from her mouth." Mary (nominally kin also to "Saint" Marie) swoons in her "passion" over the deer and collapses, only to emerge from the car as the third resurrection of "June" to Gordie's distraught imagination. This sends him howling like a wounded animal into the woods, where next morning the reservation police and Public Health Service orderlies come to take him away.

   The deer's death musk overcomes Sister Mary in a strange consum-mation with sexually religious overtones. The scene registers an epi-phany of dark, delicate, and deeply sensual humor between estranged men and women. Nuns take vows to wed a two-thousand-year-old mar-tyr, and then long for human love late at night; widowed men drink themselves into delirium. "She followed him, calling now, into the apple trees but lost him there, and all that morning, while they waited for the orderlies and the tribal police to come with cuffs and litters and a court order, they heard him crying like a drowned person, howling in

the open fields" (*LM* 188). The sterile "crabs" of the nuns' garden mock
this replay of the Expulsion, while Gordie's drowning—in grief, alcohol, the rain-soaked Dakota winter–spring—fulfills an old Indian
prophesy against those who violate the "mother" earth and must die by
water.

In contrast to such low comic pathos stands Lipsha, Gerry's illicit son
by June. Lipsha seems a bridging child of the future—a parodic "took
in"—a *real* Nanapush–Kashpaw breed who fuses all families, genetic
and adoptive. *Love Medicine* evens out through cross-generational
dyads that balance each generation's triad (diachronic fusion of synchronic imbalance). Marie, Nector, and Lulu in the first generation are
paralleled by Gordie, June, and Gerry in the next. The two triangles
overlap, genders equalize, and the doubled "irrational" triads balance
as in a six-pointed star.

Lipsha in the third generation brings it all together at the center of a
star quilt. This is the seventh "point" in the hexagonal morning star of
understanding, Venus—historically the Star of David or Solomon's
Seal, signifying peace and understanding in Judeo-Christian history, or
the "perning gyres" of cabalistic faith, according to Yeats. A comic
structural perspective, tribally oriented, temporally fuses people who

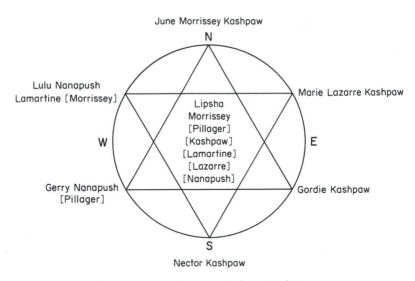

Interconnected characters in *Love Medicine*.

are spatially dislocated by existential individualism (the atomism of the West). Humor reorients tragic *dis*possession. This communal process reconfigurates human time as it is passing in space (Bahktin's "chronotopes" as the living space of human characters). Time-passing outlives time-past. The point here is to move on and "bring her home," set Dad free, point Lipsha toward the sunrise.

Caring for his adoptive grandparents, Lipsha learns the "whip singing" humor of Marie's resilence and Nector's humanness, as Grandpa teases Grandma to "pitch whoopee" again:

> "And you got no more whoopee to pitch anymore anyhow!" she yelled at last, surprising me so my jaw just dropped, for us kids all had pretended for so long that those rustling sounds we heard from their side of the room at night never happened. She sure had pretended it, up till now, anyway. I saw that tears were in her eyes. And that's when I saw how much grief and love she felt for him. And it gave me a real shock to the system. You see I thought love got easier over the years so it didn't hurt so bad when it hurt, or feel so good when it felt good. I thought it smoothed out and old people hardly noticed it. I thought it curled up and died, I guess. Now I saw it rear up like a whip and lash.
>
> She loved him. She was jealous. She mourned him like the dead.
>
> And he just smiled into the air, trapped in the seams of his mind. (*LM* 192)

These late-blooming arts to counter sadness—laughter, love, and language—compel Lipsha to a comic "medicine" that backfires, yet the joke seems timely to Nector's going. Lipsha learns something from Nector bellowing in church to a God growing deaf:

> Our Gods aren't perfect, is what I'm saying, but at least they come around. They'll do a favor if you ask them right. You don't have to yell. But you do have to know, like I said, how to ask in the right way. That makes problems, because to ask proper was an art that was lost to the Chippewas once the Catholics gained ground. Even now, I have to wonder if Higher Power turned it back, if we got to yell, or if we just don't speak its language.
>
> I looked around me. How else could I explain what all I had seen in my short life—King smashing his fist in things, Gordie drinking himself down to the Bismarck hospitals, or Aunt June left by a white man to wander off in the snow. How else to explain the times my touch don't work, and farther back, to the old-time Indians who was swept away in the outright germ warfare and dirty-dog killing of the whites. In those times, us Indians was so much kindlier than now.

We took them in.

Oh yes, I'm bitter as an old cutworm just thinking of how they done to us and doing still.

So Grandpa Kashpaw just opened my eyes a little there. Was there any sense relying on a God whose ears was stopped? Just like the government? I says then, right off, maybe we got nothing but ourselves. And that's not much, just personally speaking. I know I don't got the cold hard potatoes it takes to understand everything. (*LM* 195)

In order to snare back Grandpa's affection, Lipsha dreams up the love medicine of eating geese hearts (like some coyotes, geese mate for life). This recalls Nector mounting the hill with wild geese, Marie "barreling" into his arms, and the maculate conception of Gordie. Lipsha talks to himself waiting in the sloughs for honkers; he recalls funny stories about a cousin named "Wristwatch" and misses his only shot. He buys frozen turkey hearts at the Red Owl store (the winged totems multiply) still with "faith in the cure," a "belief against the odds" of comic failure. "Faith might be stupid," Lipsha reasons, "but it gets us through." Did "anyone ever go and slap an old malpractice suit on God? Or the U.S. government?" It's the comic spirit humanly brought to earth, a sense of ending humor, a belief in futurity. Indians know this one cold.

Where "the Father" at the convent would defer, Sister Mary Martin "blesses" the makeshift cure by telling Lipsha "just be yourself." So he sprinkles holy water on the turkey hearts with his own "touch," the wise fool's best trick. Back home with the potion, Nector teases Marie, tonguing a turkey heart and spitting it out, so she (by now a large woman) slugs him and he chokes to death. Grandpa dies voluntarily in Lipsha's arms, worn out chewing on tough bird hearts: "He waved at me, grinned, and then the bobber went under" (*LM* 208). With the grace of "terrible understanding" that his intellect centers in his heart (like the snapping turtle still alive, Nector says, when its head is chopped off), Lipsha learns an opposite lesson about mortality, charity, and his own native humor: "your heart's position. You wear your life like a garment from the mission bundle sale ever after—lightly because you realize you never paid nothing for it, cherishing because you know you won't ever come by such a bargain again. Also you have the feeling someone wore it before you and someone will after" (213–14). For a novel framed between the deaths of June and Nector, this is a "took-in" faith and means for celebrating—indeed, caring for—survival.

> All the blood children and the took-ins, like me, came home from Min-
> neapolis and Chicago, where they had relocated years ago. They stayed with
> friends on the reservation or with Aurelia or slept on Grandma's floor. . . .
>   The family kneeling down turned to rocks in a field. It struck me how
> strong and reliable grief was, and death. Until the end of time, death would
> be our rock.
>   So I had perspective on it all, for death gives you that. All the Kashpaw
> children had done various things to me in their lives—shared their folks with
> me, loaned me cash, beat me up in secret—and I decided, because of death,
> then and there I'd call it quits. If I ever saw King again, I'd shake his hand.
> Forgiving somebody else made the whole thing easier to bear. (210–11)

Lipsha sends Grandpa's ghost to "Look up Aunt June" (*LM* 213). He
confesses the "truth" about the "fake" medicine to Grandma, but
stresses that Nector loves and doesn't blame her. "It's true feeling, not
no magic," he confesses, and she gives back her love to him.

> Yet a look came on her face. It was like the look of mothers drinking
> sweetness from their children's eyes. It was tenderness.
>   "Lipsha," she said, "you was always my favorite."
>   She took the beads off the bedpost, where she kept them to say at night,
> and she told me to put out my hand. (214)

Lipsha's own tears take him from Lulu's cataracts to his mother June
and father Gerry, tying up the novel with a dandelion blessing from a
"perfect family":

> The earth was full of life and there were dandelions growing out the window,
> thick as thieves, already seeded, fat as big yellow plungers. She let my hand
> go. I got up. "I'll go out and dig a few dandelions," I told her.
>   Outside, the sun was hot and heavy as a hand on my back. I felt it flow
> down my arms, out my fingers, arrowing through the ends of the fork into the
> earth. With every root I prized up there was return, as if I was kin to its secret
> lesson. The touch got stronger as I worked through the grassy afternoon.
> Uncurling from me like a seed out of the blackness where I was lost, the
> touch spread. The spiked leaves full of bitter mother's milk. A buried root. A
> nuisance people dig up and throw in the sun to wither. A globe of frail seeds
> that's indestructible. (215)

Blessed by his mother's rosary, Lipsha digs with his grandfather's comically forked tool, drawing the bisociated earthly energies back from
dandelion roots that soak up the sun's power.

Dandelion tenacity at the fiction's end, humorous to be sure, may represent bonding and survival, tolerance and stubbornness among collateral Indian kin. It also surprises and comically inverts through its homely symbolism. This coding implies the "permitted disrespect" and comic license of trickster tales the world over, barroom jokes, kitchen slander, sibling rivalry, parental mystery, tall yarns, and traveling salesman stories, where near insult is enjoyed—indeed, nurtured—in order to season a home for all.

Coming on Home

> . . . if our relationships are ever going to be human, and not just play-by-numbers, men have to follow women into the woods and women likewise. There must be an exchange, a transformation, a power shared between them. Living in empty country, the woods to me have always been a place of mystery, a shelter. That's where we have to go to find each other.
>
> "Interview with Louise Erdrich"

The novel's double coda, "The Good Tears" and "Crossing the Water," blesses the past with healing waters. This end anticipates things to come, more stories and storytellers, comic futurity. Lulu, dark earth mother with blackberry eyes, enters late as a narrator, à la Molly Bloom in *Ulysses*. She's worth the wait. Lulu lets "in the world" and loves wholly with "wild and secret ways." Three times married and many more times romanced, this contemporary Pocahontas is Ms. Trixter, coyotess par excellence. Her "true love" Nector "dawdled" a bit too long, as men will, and she found herself elsewhere, marrying "a riffraff Morrissey for hurt and spite" (*LM* 217). She defends her "lonesome knob of prairie" against all men who visit her front door and back window. "I can beat the devil himself at cards," she says, "because I play for the sheer amusement" (220). Lulu is *Homa ludens* at her best, pure player. "She might be soft and sweet as marshmallows," Lipsha warns, "but in her biceps there was torsion steel" (242). She survives the fires and floods of time, only more bald and somewhat blind with cataracts, pausing by Nector transfixed at the candy machine (his "Milky Way" station in life). Lulu finally looks up to see Marie putting mothering tears in her eyes. It's a sister to sibling tenderness. The rivals mourn Nector's passing together: "It was the first time I saw exactly how another woman felt," Lulu says (236). Lilith "knows" Eve here, over Adam's fall, and the two women become one, two Marys joined, cross-lovers beloved. This is a true feminism—love of the feminine, minus the antimasculine skew. Lulu knows the world for what it is: "dreamstuff," our "mortal illusions." Thus she plays it for all she's worth, as Huizinga speaks of "*il*-lusion" intelligently "in-play" among humans.

"Crossing the Water" strikes a final chord of an old blues hymn—going home. The controlling motif of the fiction flows home through rivers and lakes, the currents in things, downpours, blizzards, drownings, tears, baptisms, rebirths. Consciousness is liquidly dense. The Chippewa are washed in "the water monster, Missepeshu," a word that absorbs the fiction's familial white and red tributaries, "Morrissey" and "Kashpaw," in the métis confluence suggesting Mississippi (*LM* 194). It seems another of Manabozho's fictionalized tongue twisters.

"Howard," or King Junior, opens the last chapter from an acculturated breed's perspective—the existential "I" in primary school. This disturbing portent of self-realization, a false narrative ascent, quickly gives way to Lipsha in King Senior's "long dark closet" of a Twin Cities apartment. He feels "like a beggar at the table of life" playing five-card stud for Lucky Charm marshmallow bits. In the middle-distance, Little King watches cartoons of Wiley Coyote getting blown up on TV.

Earlier Lulu tells Lipsha about Gerry and June, his real father and mother. Although he is a bastard, at least his mother did not try to drown him in a gunnysack (probably King's stepbrother sarcasm). This make-or-break knowledge (going to meet the man at the crossroads, even to marry his queen) casts an old Oedipal joke, potentially tragic, that smacks Lipsha between the eyes as a tossed empty of Old Grand Dad.

> "I want to meet my dad," I said aloud.
> An old Sioux vet who said he was at Iwo Jima with Ira Hayes passed me a bagged flask of whiskey underneath the sign PLEASE DON'T DRINK HERE. THIS IS **YOUR** LOBBY. I took a long pull, slugged it down. Then I started crying. That is, tears came out. I made no sound.
> "It often has that effect on me too, boy," the old man said. "It cleans you out."

So I let the tears fall, my hands shredding the bag, until the face of Old
Grand Dad was revealed and the clerk told us to take it outside. . . .
  "Ira's favorite brand," said my friend, gazing tenderly at the empty bottle.
"What the hell."
  As he walked away he threw it over his shoulder, and it hit me smack
between the eyes. (*LM* 247)

With this slapstick sign, Lipsha heads "onward in my quest." This son
would "get down to the bottom of my heritage" (248), as Erdrich plays
with the *Roots* rage that began in the late 1970s in America. The scene
may also parody Welch's grandfather scene in *Winter in the Blood*
(what's in the old man's pants, the horse's fart, laughing recognition). In
Love Medicine Lipsha learns that his irregular heartbeat keeps him out
of the military that once warred against Indians. This "fucked" heartbeat also bonds Lipsha to Old Man Pillager, the Chippewa shaman,
through the cardsharps Gerry and his mother, Lulu. The Nanapushes
know how to crimp cards and play for the highest stakes. Trickster's
lessons arrive indispensably—the twists, doublings, and opposite think-
ings of survival, occasionally winning, outliving the losing. One can
never think to have won it all, to sit back and coast, or not still to lose
(the "contingent" reality that Richard Preston identifies in a Cree traditional worldview). Lipsha can play, as Lulu does, *for* the playing, and
not lose for the losing, since "the sheer amusement" comes after she
confronts death at an early age, only to come back for more. There's a
"marked" deck of mortal "men" in this card-game world, Lulu knows
as well as any woman—and this is her grandson's crossed heritage, to
play as he will.
  So Lipsha in the end decides to grow up (he can no longer "afford"
Adamic or Indian innocence): "Belonging was a matter of deciding to.
Through many trials I had seen this to be true. I decided I belonged,
whether or not King thought I did. I was a real kid now, or halfway real.
I crimped myself an ace" (*LM* 255). Lipsha chooses to play a game he
must play, a comedy of survival. His chosen card is the one-eyed jack of
hearts with "a banana peel" in his hand, a contemporary bicultural
clown—an Indi'n Chaplin, Will Rogers, and Charlie Hill rolled together. They play, and wait—for Dad.
  By now, Gerry Nanapush, according to the local news, has grown
two inches and added seventy more pounds. He is at-large, "dangerous," and coming home, wherever that is. Gerry enters Trickster-

fashion by the skylight shaft and looms over "the dirtiest kitchen table in Minnesota," his son and cellmate, and a marked deck of cards. Father faces son for the first time, and the canine grin tells all: "His grin flashed now, wolf white and sharp, in his big placid face. Until he grinned like that he looked asleep. Suddenly he tossed his hair back and bust out laughing" (*LM* 259–60). Gerry "knows" his son by Lulu's system of card crimping, Trickster's semiotics as it were (as the old riddles tell us our family origins, back to Odysseus's scar on his thigh and the living marriage bedpost as sign to his wife, Penelope). The Nanapush clan carries the "touch" together, healing, playing, signing the world.

In good *Homo ludens* fashion, the card game must be played for "real stakes," June's Firebird. The novel ends where it begins, in the kitchen, as Lipsha deals himself a straight high run of hearts, a royal flush, or "perfect family" (*LM* 264). Even Dad is amazed. Then the police bang on the door, Little King betrays his father (Freudian microjoke), and Lipsha contemplates "the wages of the father meeting up with the son and the ghost of a woman caught in the dark space between them" (265). This classical wedge opens the way home, as Gerry vanishes and Lipsha grabs his mother's car keys "to freedom." With Dad hidden in the trunk, "I drove the tangled highways in a general homeward direction," reversing the agony of Gordie's martyred doe in the back seat (266).

Lipsha remembers the "key" that Gordie left home and rebirths his father from the Firebird trunk, "curled up tight as a baby in its mother's stomach" (*LM* 267). A right-hand turn to Canada will take Gerry "home" to another wife and child (an exiled play paradigm of Lipsha, June, and Gerry), but not quite "free." Redemption remains comically ironic, at best, since it must be realistic, and Trickster's fantasies give way to necessary lessons about American freedom. Whether Dad killed the "smokey" is too deep a mystery to be known. "I'm sorry but I just don't trust to write down what he answered, yes or no. We have entered an area of too deep water" (269). It's the conditional reality of Indian–white interactions, still a liminal zone where the buckskin stretches thin. The border is always to be played seriously, since life, death, family, and future are the stakes.

Father and son exit bonded as "cons." Lipsha has figuratively gone AWOL, though he hasn't yet been inducted. But "this odd thing with our hearts," a murmur that marks Nanapush men, grants Lipsha comic pardon from war. As with all heroic clowns, oddity sets him apart, exonerates him, and distinguishes him as Gerry's son. So he sets his father "free" (as can be) and turns back home across the Red River border, stopping on the bridge above the "dark, thick, twisting river" below (*LM* 271). June's death in the snowstorm, Henry Junior's drowning, Gordie's alcoholism, Nector's grin going under with the bobber: these losses bring Lipsha home of necessity to the comic realism of mortality. This is an Indian humor of hearth and home deep as the Red River's current in the mother earth. *Love Medicine* finally seems a fiction for us to accept, love, even celebrate our lapses and irritations over what-is, the way things are in (Native) America.

Native wit, then, relates to love "medicines"—the aches, pains, passions, or losses of bonding. It seasons many modern odysseys—the drives, accommodations, failures, and sacrifices of re-rooting. Our loves may be matters of good "medicine" or luck or simply the good-will-of-necessity where mutual needs transcend betrayals. So we love the "family" in various forms, from Lulu's wild brood of nine genetically freckled kids, to Zelda and Aurelia's abstemious kitchens, to June's wayward love, to Marie's home-for-strays. There is no "pure" America, but truly a pluralistic one for "took ins." A compassionate woman talks at the center, and a man lurks somewhere on the edges of the clearing. These mixed-Indian love medicines would seem universal matters of passion and procreation, the mysteries of attraction and off-spring of various unions, along with questions of how we all tolerate the goings-on in our "new land," our old garden.

Such medicine of love could be an issue of religion, of belief and disbelief, sacred to secular lives in this unsettled land, newly Christianized, anciently ceremonialized. There are many gods around. At Turtle Mountain, the Convent of the Sacred Heart crowns the hill, and Old Man Pillager "spells" the woods: Sister Leopolda's repressed rage, to Sister Mary Martin's clarinet calls through the night, to frozen turkey hearts from the Red Owl store as palliative for Grandpa's ailing passion, to Lipsha's healing "touch." None is infallible. These cures touch us, whether we are lonely, deranged, or wildly pathetic. Healing rituals may encompass deep faith all the way to surreal pranks on religion. Native gods know when we're playing.

At home the American-sensical middle ground ends the-way-things-are and, contrariwise, as they must be when we don't like them. This kind of no-nonsense reality inversely calls for an antidote, a joke, a ritual, or a vision: June's laugh, Lipsha's cure, Albertine's "drenching beauty" of the northern lights. Death is a bond here, a reason to forgive or to administer motherly drops to blurred visions, "the milk of human kindness." We are all, finally, not only natives by birth or adoption, but mixed-blood American daughters and sons, mothered collectively by our Maries with grace, fathered by ludic Tricksters, loved by Lulus shamelessly, counseled by our kin with common virtues that Gonzalo called "gentle/kind" in *The Tempest*.

We talk ourselves home; some write the way. Old storytelling to present-day chatter at family gatherings, river to kitchen, comprise the texts and contexts, the foods and feuds and reconciliations of our tales. These are our homes and humors in the verbal tongue and tissue we call American culture. All this, in this good land, voices our "nature" at large, what the Lakota back home call *Takuskanskan,* or "What Moves-moves," our commonly blessed, native America.

7

Red Gods, Blue Humors: James Welch

I like to warp reality a little.

JAMES WELCH, *Four Winds*

Purgatorial Jive

Punctuated with scatological humor, *Winter in the Blood* (1974) cuts across "field and stream" Montana with unflinching irony, unrelieved by pity or sentimentality. A decade later *Love Medicine* could be lyric, even epiphanal (transcendent of male violence and female pathos), but James Welch's first novel suffered its masculine "vision" comically dark.

Where did Welch inherit this contrary humor? It can be mistaken for bitterness, misread as depression, misconstrued to be offensively masculine (it is an understatement to say that feminist readers do not take to the book). This Blackfeet-fathered son seems to come by his humor natively, from tricksters of old to AIMsters of late. Reviewing Duane Niatum's updated *Harper's Anthology of 20th Century Native American Poetry* (1988), Louis Owens notices "unmistakable threads of common Indian experience" among contemporary native writers: "Close and exact attention to environment; consciousness of a heritage passed down through a precarious and evolving oral tradition; a heightened awareness of myth; a frequent and often bone-dry humor; the inevitable anger."[1] All these criteria surface in Welch. His "bone-dry" humor twists surrealist, given the torque of Montana reality, or a character's intake of spirits on a sweltering day. Ironic humor—a bisociative mode that does not so much take as straddle sides—tracks back to the 1960s, when countercultural movements and pan-Indian resistances were shaking the country. While AIM protesters occupied Alcatraz or took their military stand at Wounded Knee, Arthur Kopit's play *Indians,* first performed in 1968, toured Europe and America. A surreal *Tempest* (Buffalo Bill Cody as ironic Prospero), the play was reworked in England with assistance from the Royal Shakespeare Company. *Indians* dramatized Buffalo Bill in limbo, visited by ghosts of warriors such as Sitting Bull, Gall, Sweet Grass, and Geronimo. As an absurdist anticeremonial to Cody's Wild West spectacle, *Drama of Civilization,* which played New York's Madison Square Garden in the 1880s, Kopit's *Indians* assumed an exorcist role in 1969, the year *House Made of Dawn* won the Pulitzer. Momaday's 1971 review of *Indians* and Deloria's first two books in the *New York Review of Books* was ironically placed next to an ad for the documentary film *Interviews with My Lai Veterans,* about the massacre of Vietnamese civilians by U.S. soldiers.

Momaday heard Buffalo Bill's stuttering first word, "Ah," as the "very syllable" of American anguish in Kopit's *Indians.* "For all his waiting," Momaday saw only too well, "the Indian of today earns less, suffers more ills, and lives a shorter life than anyone else in this country."[2] Then what keeps the people going? Puzzling over "a catalogue of ethnic jokes" in Deloria's *Custer Died For Your Sins,* Momaday pressed for more "real" information about the "essential humor" of Indians, a "profound gaiety of vision and delight" that prefaces humor and presages renewal. "Beneath the surface of anger there are the currents of recovery and resolve."

Momaday's *House Made of Dawn* opened bicultural eyes with a veteran native homecoming where Abel murders the white Indian in himself. This self-reflexive purgation was offset by the urban dark humor of a parodic priest, John "Big Bluff" Tosamah. Then in *Ceremony* (1977) Silko retold the story of soldiers coming home to self-destruction or reinitiation into the Pueblo. And in *The Woman Who Owned the Shadows* (1983), Paula Allen recorded a feminist variant, the life-story of Ephanie Atencio, a veteran "woman-woman," or lesbian, daughter of the Keres matrix, Yellow Woman. More recently, Michael Dorris has fictionalized three generations of Northwest Indian women leaving for the city and coming back to Montana in *A Yellow Raft in Blue Water* (1986). These comings home gather in Erdrich's three novels to date and constellate the generic Native American novel today.

Dorris and Erdrich's *The Crown of Columbus* (1991) appears to be their au courant quincentennial homecoming. But it was Welch's first novel, *Winter in the Blood,* telling the "truth" boldly, sparely, dark comically, that drew praise from the novelist Reynolds Price as a "perfect novel."[3] Old Blackfeet and Gros Ventre storytellers had seasoned his stage; Hemingway and Steinbeck would have envied his lean, candid craft and finely ironic humor.

The Creation, according to Blackfeet genesis myths, smacks of a surreal jester's joke, ironic with a bite. Recorded from George Bird Grinnell, through Clark Wissler and John Ewers, down to Malcolm McFee, the hilariously realistic story of Na'pi and Kipi'taki shapes Blackfeet worldviews. If, as in the case of the Blackfeet, a culture's primary deity, the Creator sun (*God* as it were), proves a clown, the world certainly seems dangerously comic, for better or worse. Yet dialogue between "first" man and "first" woman began innocently, playfully enough:

> There was once a time when there were but two persons in the world, Old Man and Old Woman. One time, when they were travelling about, Old Man met Old Woman, who said, "Now, let us come to an agreement of some kind; let us decide how the people shall live." "Well," said Old Man, "I am to have the first say in everything." To this Old Woman agreed, provided she had the second say.[4]

If "first" man, an Adamic harlequin, gets the initial dialogical word, "first" woman, a witty Eve, gets the last. She is not so naive as he, though they end tragicomically bonded in loss. Old Man and Old Woman make up things as they are, including human beings. Thinking everything should be easy, he proposes ridiculous constructions—vertical eyes and mouth, ten fingers on each hand, and convenient navel pubes for sex. She, ever practical and "realistic," counters with functional advice to "right" things. In this crosswise dialogue, Old Woman planes vertically slanted eyes, halves the number of fingers, and hides the sexual parts. A little difficulty, she reasons, will keep people honest, caring, and compassionate. This creation myth records a dialectical humor, wildly cartooned in the generative marriage of sun and moon:

> So they went on until they had provided for everything in the lives of the people that were to be. Then Old Woman asked what they should do about life and death; should the people always live, or should they die? They had some difficulty in agreeing on this; but finally Old Man said, "I will tell you

what I will do. I will throw a buffalo-chip into the water, and, if it floats, the people die for four days and live again; but, if it sinks, they will die forever." So he threw it in, and it floated. "No," said Old Woman, "we will not decide in that way. I will throw in this rock." (*Mythology* 21)

At this point, serious comic inversions prove painful. This cross-comic couple sets up binary "orders" of reality that must be *played out*—that is, Adamically given and ironically lived.

The spirit of Trickster infuses god, fool, superhero, and devil all rolled into one. His comically begotten son, Na'pi-as-Adam, teeters between mythic and "real" worlds. This liminal swing leaves the human condition precariously unstable, as Blackfeet thinking projects the contrary give-and-take of a conditional reality never quite within grasp. Thus people delude, dream, or "create" themselves, Freud says, such that comic displacement answers a "fallen" bondage to reality.

After a time Old Woman had a daughter, who died. She was very sorry now that it had been fixed so that people died forever. So she said to Old Man, "Let us have our say over again." "No," said he, "we fixed it once." (*Mythology* 21)

The unalterable problem is that people play for keeps, Huizinga argues, the human stake in all games: the rules have been fixed. So Old Man and Old Woman partner as reality's fools. He plays romantic naif, the old *alazon*. She assumes the role of realistic *eiron*, playing off his foolish dreams. The marriage is overshadowed by a surrealist frame that brackets their comic dialogue.

Alazon's naiveté is countered by *eiron*'s bivalence, Frye contends, and their dialogic irony generates that secondary shift in meaning where the surface of things, an illusory wish, is complected by further depth. Simplistic appearance is doubled by multiplex reality. In Blackfeet terms, comic irony weds Na'pi and Kipi'taki, male and female, clown and confidante. This paradigm results in a dialogue, even an argument, about the way things might be, but nevertheless *are*. It's a dialectic of romantic possibility and realistic probability. In short, this Blackfeet creation myth spins a Western twist on "opposite thinking," as the Cree trust in *tipikochiyetim*. All things live in their opposites, play out their inversions, are known by their distortions, gain power through their contraries. Cartooning, in this sense, may be an inverse surface art of encoding the "deeper structure" of things (Dickens or Rabelais as Western masters, trickster myths as native contexts). These comic twists can prove humorously wise to survivors of hard times or tragically fatal to those who fail.

Funky Indi'ns

> I resent you once told me how I'd never know
> what being Indian was like. All poets do. Including
> the blacks. It is knowing whatever bond we find we find
> in strange tongues.
>
> RICHARD HUGO to ROBERTA WHITEMAN,
> "Letter to Hill from St. Ignatius"

In his twenties, James Welch toyed with the idea of being a writer as he majored in business at the University of Montana. Welch saw poetry simply as a "diversion" until he was twenty-five.[5] Then, studying verse under Richard Hugo, he caught fire and decided "to give writing a good shot." Hugo had left Yale to fish, teach, and write in Montana near his birthplace. He wrote to "Jim" Welch, a.k.a. "Chief Boiling Whiskey," from Browning:

> I spent this night, the only white
> in the Napi Tavern where the woman tending bar
> told me she's your aunt. A scene of raw despair. Indians
> sleeping on the filthy floor. Men with brains scrambled in wine.
> A man who sobbed all night, who tried in strangled desperation
> to articulate the reason. And the bitterest woman I've seen
> since the Depression.[6]

This homeless child of the Depression—bombardier over Italy in World War II, escapee from 1950s American materialism, critic of Ivy League aesthetes—in mid-life crisis headed back to "wilderness" Indians for ironic redemption. Comic *alazon* to dire *eiron,* his mixed American motives staked out a contrary modernist range. Hugo wrote to Roberta Hill (who later married the Arapaho artist Ernie Whiteman) from Ignatius, Montana:

> Chant to me in your poems
> of our loss and let the poem itself be our gain. You're gaining
> the hurt world worth having. Friend, let me be Indian. Dick.
>
> ("Letter to Hill from St. Ignatius," *31 L*)

Hugo, along with such poets as Lawrence, Neihardt, Austin, and Williams, felt that the legacy of the "Indian" is our native heritage and American "gain." Grief bonds him native, his wit ironically edged to survive. He chants blank verse as a maudlin, motherless boy of the West, childless child of his own loneliness, who scribbles postwar lyric blues searching for home. Perhaps Leslie Fiedler caught the 1960s drift when he saw the "return" of the vanishing American in countercultural desperations to legitimize male origins. On the other side, Hugo "opened up the world of writing to me," Welch remembers, a "first real" and finally "main influence. . . . It wasn't something you had to be a genius to do, or wear a black cape," but come to simply and naturally, "an ordinary person with a certain amount of imagination, a certain ability with language."

The latter seems the key, for Welch carved out an idiomatic voice whose muscular rhythms, sculpted images, succinct dialogue, and descriptive concisions marked him as a gifted prose poet, American as well as Native American. He came to writing as a new "breed" positively "between" cultures, effectively bicultural. In the style of Steinbeck and Hemingway, he told the truth about what he knew; ancestral stepson to Na'pi, he skewed "reality" just enough to leave a surreal mark. Welch portrayed scenes of devastation that left others speechless, hopelessly sentimental, or sadly dead-ended. He called a halt to the noble savage, the schizoid Western stereotypes that went back to Amerigo Vespucci's cannibals. Then, too, Welch cinched up the slack in Indian writing, countering Momaday's hypnotic prose rhythms and purling parallelisms.

As an American Indian, Welch felt and negotiated the distance between two estranged worlds, the intercultural chasm splitting national and ethnic senses of self. His writing straddled proper diction and pantribal idiom, artistic imagery and working detail. This red English tongue gave him a new verbal medium, and tribal identity seeded his story. Many "others" of other races and walks of life were acting accordingly, from Langston Hughes's earlier "blues" poetry, to black voter registration in the South, to war protestors in the heartland, to hippies on the West Coast, to the women's movement in the Northeast. A kind of regional nationalism began raising issues of race and gender voiced in local tongues. Welch spoke for a generation of dispossessed Indian young who argued that America must make some pluralist readjustments, indeed, some global revisions of its Western "manifest" destiny among "men."

In 1967, the artist Fritz Scholder painted the first of his "Indian Series" in Santa Fe: "monster Indians, Indians on horses," he said, "the Dartmouth Portraits and the American Portraits along with contemporary Indians in Gallup and most recently, the Indian postcards."[7] Indian pop made its comically serious debut. "Also in the course of the last ten years, I have painted butterflies, women, vampires, dogs, cats, and the Sphinx and pyramids," he added with no small irony. "I'm not an Indian painter," Scholder said at UCLA in 1982, "I'm an Indian who paints."[8] The freedom to play off images permitted the artist a certain disrespect necessary to modernist craft and imagination. At that symposium, he admonished Momaday and several hundred Indian scholars, "Don't paint 'Indians'—paint what you see." A few howled back to protest his success painting Indians. It was good coyote theater.

The cliché of "Indian" was crumbling for Indi'ns. Scholder's polychromatic cartoon humor (*Indian Postcard #1*), his cutting sense of truth and ironic bisociation (*Cowboy Indian*), his realism (*Indian with Beer Can*), his delightful sense of bicultural play (*Indians in Transition*), his native pain (*Dog and Dead Indian*) with historical tragedy (*Portrait of a Massacred Indian*) and nationalist irony (*Last Indian with a Flag*), and his surrealist sense of resurrection (*Indian Power*), all focused into a self-portrait, *Laughing Artist*. This self-cartooned, grinning Fritz folded his arms (Indian-style) and laughed back at America in cowboy boots, turquoise-buckled jeans, denim workshirt, and long dark hair. Welch published *Winter in the Blood* in the same year, 1974.

Bad Jokes

"What are you looking up here for? The joke's in your hand."
JAMES WELCH, *Winter in the Blood* (urinal graffiti)

Winter in the Blood takes place in a concentrated Montana time–space, late summer's heat, as its cold subtext draws on a century of Indian–white dispossession. The "opposite-thinking" pretext is genetically "winter in the blood," a fiery freeze encoded inversely in plains Indian veins. Welch's novel germinates from a fall "spring," as it were, that ends in the rainy mud of the death of Bird the cow pony, the burial of the narrator's grandmother, and "a joker playing a joke" on us all.[9]

All we know of the narrator's name comes in the belated memory of

Fritz Scholder (Luiseño), *Laughing Artist* (1974).
(Courtesy of Fritz Scholder)

his father "peeing what he said was my name in the snow" on their way
to visit the hermit grandfather, Yellow Calf (*WIB* 161). Half a life later,
our piss-named narrator limps home with a wounded knee and black eye
in the same ditch where his brother Mose was killed by a passing drunk.
And here his father froze to death. The almost autistic narrator—nameless character for faces that have gone under, family names that ghost
stones and bones—is mute witness to the winter irony of Montana
native life. He survives as "No Name," trapped nominally like a latter-
day Odysseus ("No Man" in the cannibal monster's cave) in intercultural uncertainty. We cannot so much "name" him as in some
estranged way shadow his consciousness: he is the voice behind the
voiceless, the silent irony or sad joke that outlives suffering. "A circle
of Styrofoam hung from the top point of the cross," No Name says of
the grave of Mose, a brother–prophet in bondage. "From the bottom of
the circle, pointing down, a piece of wire wrapped in green, and, below
that, a faded paper flower barely visible in the weeds. There was no
headstone, no name, no dates. My brother" (143). Ironic bearer of
God's commandments, Mose has been reduced to shards, the bad grammar and sacred irony of a sad joke, as with the other Christian names in
the tale: Teresa, the virgin martyr; Amos, the apocalyptic duck; John
"First Raise," the deceased father.

The thirty-two-year-old protagonist goes on a vision quest of sorts, as
William W. Thackeray detailed in *MELUS* in 1980.[10] His Cree
girlfriend Agnes, old tribal enemy from the Northeast, absconds with
his rifle and razor, cartoon phallic fetishes. No Name comes home twice
to his grandmother's rocking catatonia (another tongue and time) with a
black eye, bloody nose, and wounded knee (a bad Sioux joke from the
1890 massacre), broken at the primal scene of his brother Mose's death.
His nominally sainted mother, Teresa, stands in her kitchen silent, sarcastic, or simply "bitchy"—a comically negative gender label in the
novel, as in "poor son-of-a-bitch" and "bastard," working codes for
Adamic man in his fallen condition. The traditional family, including
cross-sexual bonds, has acculturatively broken down over the last century. No Name needs a name badly, and home has been reconfigured
since his widowed mother married Lame Bull, a "breed" mock father.

Distance thus seems the key to No Name's existence. "I was as
distant from myself as a hawk from the moon" (*WIB* 2). Hawklike, he
circles a landscape as relentlessly horizontal as the "big" sky rolling
overhead. His tribal clan is decimated. The deserted "Earthboy" home-

stead, where Welch was a youngster, remains a ghostly acreage around a barbed-wired graveyard. His family ground is denuded—father and brother dead, matriarch remarried to a squat comic farmer. His mother tags all Indian men as "fools," dead husband and son foremost, as Old Woman still pesters Old Man. No Name hears a surreally flattened language of cowboy Indian idioms spoken into a cold northwesterly or smoke-blue bar. He survives a fragmented self-identity ravaged by boozing, balling, brawling, wanderlust, and prolonged pubescent trickery. "That's another thing the matter with these Indians," Lame Bull kvetches of his hired hand, just cold-cocked and fired for quitting. "They get too damn tricky for their own good" (30).

By the end of his odyssey of boilermakers, bad jokes, broken promises, bent noses, and broads, No Name comes "home" purgatively. This contrary sense of the traditional *nostos*—a purgative stage of comic integration and renewal—tallies with the second criterion of Frye's model: the communal scapegoating of winter's pain to prepare for spring. No Name exorcises an Indian agony to turn historical soil for reseeding. He finally recognizes his blind hermit grandfather, Yellow Calf, as Na'pi of old, a Montana Indian Tiresias. His trusty gelding falls back dead while trying to rescue a spinster cow from the mud (perhaps a totemic parody of the 1883 Winter of Starvation, when No Name's grandfather "saved" his widowed grandmother). The story ends with No Name burying his nameless grandmother, daughter of Kipi'taki, now "planted" in the mother earth with her parodic "medicine" pouch. He goes off to find his girlfriend and propose a questionable marriage, as the story teeters on comic rebirth (Grandma's fall burial and crème-de-menthe "spring" on Agnes's teeth).

The novel turns dead center on an anonymous old man in a straw hat and green gabardines (ironic spring in fall?) chuckling "heh heh" three times, rolling a smoke, striking a kitchen match on his fly, and pitching facedown in a bowl of oatmeal. "Deader'n a doornail," No Name tells the "airplane man" in the Legion Club (opening the next chapter). This novel cartoons a magic realism gone mad, as our deadpan antihero heads to the men's room for relief. "*What are you looking up here for?*" graffiti greets him over the urinal. "*The joke's in your hand.*" Bad joke, surreal scenario.

Winter in the Blood opens with a poetic shard broken off from "Riding the Earthboy 40," the title poem of Welch's 1971 collection. Its shifting template casts unstable, surrealist dream shadows.

Bones should never tell a story
to a bad beginner. I ride
romantic to those words,
those foolish claims that he
was better than dirt, or rain
that bleached his cabin
white as bone. Scattered in the wind
Earthboy calls me from my dream:
Dirt is where the dreams must end.

The volume of poetry—serious verse play, for sure, with poetic coding
that dissolves as it forms—begins with a foxy shaman and nervous
coyote; it closes with a revised W. C. Fields one-liner, "Never Give A
Bum An Even Break." Welch's poetic rhetoric seems an indecipherable
plain(s) style, the complex codex of "simple" country observations,
anything but simple. A bisociative dark field, dirt versus dreams, car-
tographs the exterior and interior landscape of the opening half-poem. It
is unsettlingly comic, disturbingly strange, painfully candid. Referents
come hard, harder to decipher. Only a fool would insist that he "knew"
how to read the poetic codices.

Will Welch's prose, then, prove broken-poetic? Its grainy realism and
disillusioned romance seem uneasily glued by a split comic vision. We
see *through* one layer of "reality" (the heart's innocent desires) to a
counterlayer of truths (the mind's descent to bones and dirt) into palimpsests of infinite layerings. To see, to know, to laugh earlier tripled an
etymological paradigm of humor: here it is important, purgatively, that
we "see through" things in unresolved perspectives, that we know by
contrary points of view. The Adamic–Earthboy's "bones" tell a dream
of loss, disillusion, and death (back to the "clowny" Blackfeet Na'pi,
the poem's missing referent). In this decreative fall, dirt counters the
naif's dreams.

The novel reworks old mortal myths. By the end, a grandfather's
"Adam's apple" has twice bobbed in silent spasms of laughter, familial
jokes too much for words. The poetic fragment that opens the fiction
closes on a triple slant rhyme that doesn't quite settle (wind / dream /
end). This "off" rhyming drives the point home that slant is all: we ride
the "Earthboy 40" (quarter-section) falling off. The rhyme tries to bind,
as it should, but can't; and so we start the novel from the fallen ground
of a near rhyme. Twenty years back Mose died by the highway, as his

younger brother broke his knee. We end the story with No Name chthonically stuck up to his crotch in the mud, Grandma "planted" in the earth, Bird dead, girlfriend Agnes gone. Maybe the time has come for reconstruction, sprouting back, after such purgative suffering; maybe not. The existentially resurrected cowboy-Indi'n-trickster plans to "ride" the earth again, find Agnes and propose marriage, settle down and raise a family. It might be Nector of *Love Medicine* brought back to life, younger, leaner, an Algonkian native farther west, still the American "Indian" Adam. The "red earth" First Man of Juedo-Christian history stands next to Na'pi of Blackfeet genesis.

So Welch within a modernist context writes a darkly humorous Montana novel, if comic at all, in a world soured by historical catastrophe. The Indian perspective, as Erdrich has observed, is postapocalyptic: the worst has already occurred with removal, declared federal war, genocide, absolute poverty, and almost total decimation of the original populations. "Native" American survival is tantamount to Viktor Frankl walking out of the German death camps with self-determinant humor.[11]

Welch's fiction touches on sexual and alcohol abuse (hardly just an Indian problem), dispossession, betrayal, pain, and death, to note but a few wintry blues in a work of ironic distances. Critics have pointed to the humor, dark red for sure, but most circle it warily like a pile of road apples along the highway to higher tribal totems (animal imagery, traditional subtexts, feminist shadowings, and alienation, for example, as in the 1978 *American Indian Quarterly* issue on *Winter in the Blood*). Andrew Horton in this symposium issue argues for a "bitter comic" vision (132). Alan Velie reduces the definition of "a comic novel" to "a funny book," reasoning tautologically over Welch's humor "from raucous farce to subtle satire" (143). In the transcribed discussion that followed six papers presented in Chicago in December 1977, Carter Revard notes a mixture of "tragedy and comedy, somewhat squashed together. . . . [T]hings go together there which are both funny and kind of horrifying" (159–60).

In this vein, John Hawkes addresses his own postwar American fiction in the mid-1960s: "I don't mean to apologize for the disturbing nature of my fiction by calling it comic." Hawkes's aim is never to let the reader "think that the picture is any less black than it is or that there is any easy way out of the nightmare of human existence." His humor, instead, engages a world gone berserk after two world wars, the Korean "conflict," and Vietnam. Euroamerica seems shadowed with a sense of dark comic apocalypse, and for some this fall mandates a change in Western "man's" direction:

> As I say, comedy, which is often closely related to poetic uses of language, is what makes the difference for me. I think that the comic method functions in several ways: on the one hand it serves to create sympathy, compassion, and on the other it's a means for judging human failings as severely as possible; it's a way of exposing evil (one of the pure words I mean to preserve) and of persuading the reader that even he may not be exempt from evil; and of course comic distortion tells us that anything is possible and hence expands the limits of our imaginations. Comic vision always suggests futurity, I think, always suggests a certain hope in the limitless energies of life itself.[12]

A modern protagonist wakes up unheroically in a world where the "comic" offers no escape, so he salvages what he can, bound by hunger, sex, dislocation, and distortion. He finds himself victim of postwar stress and veteran of death. Dark humor is his last line of defense.

Welch's narrative opens on an off-color line: "In the tall weeds of the borrow pit, I took a leak and watched the sorrel mare . . . " By the end of the novel, No Name recalls his father "peeing what he said was my name in the snow" in the same ditch (*WIB* 182). Pissing in the white "borrow" pit where "earth"(boy) has been dredged to crown a blacktop highway signals a subtext of comic excretion. No Name evacuates in the deserted Earthboy ditch, where a "rectangle of barbed wire" imprisons the family graves. As prefigured in the red mare, he's "coming home" to the Indian women—his tough-love mother, cigar-store grandmother, and runaway girlfriend from an enemy tribe.

There is a war at home among the sexes. On a quest home, our hung-over Indian "hero" stands in for Eliot's Fisher King or Hemingway's emasculated lover, Jake Barnes. Grandma plots to murder the Cree magazine reader, as a century ago Blackfeet women terrorized their cross-tribal competition. And John First Raise earlier dreamed of killing female elk in the Little Rockies; bull meat would be "tough and stringy," he knew from experience. "Fool," Teresa chides her son and husband (a mock Oedipal triangle). Throughout the novel, the comic male totem of a pheasant cock "full of twists" struts, crows, and scratches foolishness in the brush (*WIB* 9). Inversely, Belva Long Knife caricatures the mother as a castrating warrior woman. At spring brand-ings, she chews roasted calf testicles and stares down the cowboys around the campfire.

So women reduce to a "fierce mother," and shrewd men play "dumb" son. Their conversations parody "talk" as parabolic cul de sacs. Half-swacked mutter and sexual come-on constitute the mismatched monologues of bar dialogue. A wandering white "father" thinks he recognizes his "daughter" in a Montana saloon:

> "But I've seen you before, somewhere else. My memory is like a steel trap." He narrowed his eyes. "Bismarck? North Dakota?"
> She shook her head.
> "Minneapolis?"
> She blew a smoke ring at the mirror.
> "That's funny. You sure it wasn't Chicago?"
> "I've never been there. I might be from the West Coast."
> "That's it! Seattle!" His elbow bounced off my ribs. "Ha, you see?"
> "Seattle?" I asked.
> "I wouldn't be from Seattle for all the rice in China." She counted some coins on her tray. "Now, Portland might be different—they've got roses there."
> "My mother raises morning glories," I said.
> "Los Angeles?"
> "I hate morning glories. I hate anything to do with morning."
> "But that's just the name. They bloom in the evening too—. . ." (*WIB* 49)

These skewed exchanges go nowhere, littered with distracted or lost referents, non sequiturs, and evasions, like a series of W.C. Fields sarcasms. What masks as thought moves in contrapuntal directions, at angular intersections of characters' lives. Everything seems a crooked way in, a twisted syntax of ironic distance and spatial displacement.

The skeletal family of two men and a woman, a comic triangulation, carry on a triadic "dialogue" that forks absurdly in the wake of Grandma's death:

> "She passed away," Teresa said, setting down the sack of groceries.
> "What did you do to your nose?" Lame Bull said.
> Teresa looked at him. "It was a merciful death."
> "No, seriously, what did you do to your nose?"
> "Where is she now?" I said.
> "We took her to Harlem." Teresa began to put the canned goods in the cupboard.

"Somebody busted me one," I said to Lame Bull. "How come? Why don't we just bury her here, where the rest of them are?"

"She was a fine woman," Lame Bull said.

"Because they have to fix her up. They'll make her look nice. And Father Kittredge will want to say a few words over her." (*WIB* 133–34)

These cubist semiotics splay all directions in common. Talk splinters in a strangely circular plot as words stray, minds slide, voices fade, tongues stutter. Our "hero" barhops, rolls redheaded drunks in the john, pisses in the ditches, humps and slaps women in hotel rooms or trailers (never "love" at home), swears crudely and cracks bad jokes, fights and farts, gets drunk, passes out, and wears a Levi jacket over his T-shirt. He ends pretty much where he began, going home.

Why do we stay with him, even like him a little? Although not exactly an ideal or a noble savage, he is surely as convincing a coyote as national icons like James Dean, Elvis Presley, and Mick Jagger (though a parodied "real" man sans razor and rifle). Yet Welch "sees through" the mask of American braggadocio, a Zane Grey idol caricatured. As trickster texts for centuries have taught Indians, things always have two or more eyes and ears, arms and legs, voices and minds. These are ancient human cautions and humors, an old contingent realism of survival in a world composed mostly of "others." In Welch's fiction, "Ace" and "sport" tag men satirically in bars, restrooms, hayfields, fishing streams, and the endless bedroom pursuit of women. Welch does not play Indian naively here; this is a real cartoon of American manhood, beneath which runs a critical set of lessons.

"That's one thing you learn about men—" says the barmaid in Malta to our questionable hero, "you don't joke with them unless you mean business" (*WIB* 50). Comedy is the bottom line, the bond taken seriously. Play sets the hook, seriously surreal, the come-on of need and hunger *played* for keeps, as far as keeping anything goes in a land where loss is the bonding denominator. Metonymy (literally "change" the "name" substitution) scores the barroom text as slant cousin of *logos*.

The two suits watched her.

"Nice little twitch," said the first suit. His red necktie had worked its way out of his coat.

"Yes," said the second suit. "I wouldn't mind a little bit of that myself."

"Ah, but she would wear you out. You can tell by the hips."

"My wife has hips like that and it's all I can do to stay in bed with her."

"My wife has hips like that," I said, "but she has smaller breasts."

"Small breasts are best," said second suit. "My wife has big breasts and they just get in the way. What you can't get in your mouth is wasted anyway."

"My wife has breasts that hang down to her knees and her nipples are too dark."

"Pink nipples are easily the best," I said.

"My wife is dead," said the man who had torn up his airplane ticket. (50–51)

Men without women belly up to the bottom line of this novel, where "dirty" bar talk and bad jokes end with the worst joke of all, a common death saved for last.

The wonder of the fiction, indeed, is that No Name still "rides" the "Earthboy 40." Uneasy on Bird's saddle in the end, he rescues a wild-eyed cow stuck in the mud, her calf bawling in the distance (the novel's parental paradigm). The modern Earthboy is still swearing and kicking comically, still upright, still joking off-color, still telling the story:

What did I do to deserve this? Goddamn that Ferdinand Horn! Ah, Teresa, you made a terrible mistake. Your husband, your friends, your son, all worthless, none of them worth a shit. Slack up, you sonofabitch! Your mother dead, your father—you don't even know, what do you think of that? A joke, can't you see? Lame Bull! The biggest joke—can't you see that he's a joke, a joker playing a joke on you? Were you taken for a ride! Just like the rest of us, this country, all of us taken for a ride. Slack up, slack up! This greedy stupid country— (*WIB* 169)

Such de-famation spins heroism and referent horizons around. It sets idealism askew on real edges of comic unknowing and angles away from romance. Maybe this cowboy will drink crème de menthe with his girlfriend in the end, propose on the spot, settle down, and start a family; so the cycle will go around another generation. It's an age-old fantasy, torqued by reality and history, worthy of Blackfeet creation myths.

Thus Welch's novel modernizes the ancient comic dialogues of Na'pi and Kipi'taki in "making things up" the way they are, the way they just may be, as we resist. Death turns on a joke between buffalo chip and stone on the waters of time, and momentary survival is ironically comic. "No, we fixed it once," Old Man says with a last word out of turn.

There's a deadly twist in human history, a dialogue of differings that cannot be unsaid, necessitating a dark sense of humor to negotiate survival, or any hope of celebration, however provisional.

Crude Comic Pop

Welch's world is ironically rife with gender complaints, sexual disparities, and misunderstandings between men and women. "Bitch" and "ditch" explode as pivotal concepts in the fiction. Women seem bitches; men sons-of-bitches, if not bastards. As lifelong trickster "cocks" or immature "cow*boys,*" men remain estranged from disapproving mothers. No Name's lovers are *M*-coded matrons marshaled ironically as the barmaid from Malta, Malvina, and Marlene. The women are rightly irritated; everyone is fiesty, tricky, restless. These seem the dialects and dialectics of the homeless, where "bitch" and "ditch" soon operate as verbs: "to ditch" things, or to evacuate and dredge, and "to bitch," or to disparage our "ditched" common condition.

These homely, potentially comic monosyllables burst as purgative phonemes. Comic pops and negative undercuttings risk putting a reader off, but also get attention. All the unprintables (phonemic shorties)— shit, tit, suck, turd, piss, and the censored *f* and *c* words—seem to spring from debased tongues and bruised hearts, a fallen language of love. But the fiction is essentially comic, a parody of Mickey Spillane tough guys fingering guns in bars and mauling women, though No Name does not force himself on anyone. The "airplane man," the three seductions, his own "family"—all these more or less constellate around him, and he passively suffers their provisional bonding. Why is such offense funny? With crafted release it taps a libidinous fount of exiled energy, Trickster's underground reservoir. The fiction comically privileges risk and defies repression. It tolerates deviance by inversely proving societal behavior. Stretching the buckskin comically thin, *Winter in the Blood* might be considered a realist's test of "permitted disrespect." And this is the point with the basics of dark comedy: a play with pain, the humor in hurt. The potential offense charges the joke, teases the norm, and gambles on picking up the audience's attention, even negatively. To play "dirty" and get away with it is an offbeat, especially postmodern art.

Crafted confusion reigns in this fiction. "I couldn't tell if it was fear or love or lust," No Name, his hands shaking in a bar by the end, says of pursuing Agnes. "Maybe it was a kind of love" (*WIB* 113). What kind of love is a "kind" of love? It is certainly confused, possibly unreal, definitely laced with dirty signals and "blue" humors in a land where blue jeans and a working man's "blues" may be the common de-nominator, if not the national dress and folk song. American plain speech similarly codes small and (in)significant details: lint on a comb, a tuft in a bus driver's ear, the hairs in Grandma's facial mole. A fly drowning in wine on the kitchen table focuses the novel's lowest comic totem at the "marriage reception" celebrated with Fritos and a wine "made of roses" by stepfather, remarried mother, and quizzical son.

American "blues" lend an interethnic perspective. Ralph Ellison saw black blues as a way of living by and through pain, indeed, "squeezing from it a near-tragic, near-comic lyricism."[13] "My only sin / Is in my skin / What did I do / To be so black and blue?" Louis Armstrong sang at Carnegie Hall in 1947. As Freud argued of the transformative power of humor or Viktor Frankl learned of survivalist laughter in the death camps, perspective is, ironically, all. Reading contraries provides a variable index to intercultural shades of humor, and Welch mixes many offbeat blues together.

Whereas Erdrich can play with the lyric humor of the oilman Andy "peeling" a blue Easter egg (rebirth?) for June in a sleazy bar across the Dakota border, Welch gets down lower with jerking-off jokes, tits and ass and crap talk, malfunctioning farm machinery, a typist's complaints, the "short" hand of everyday working America from a female skew, or come-on women from a man's point of view. Erdrich holds out with a mother's grace, even bonding or rebonding—in a word, integrating— as Welch just hangs on. Malvina's whiskey-perfumed bedroom, for example, smells little like the lavender-soaped bed where Lulu enter-tains Nector, after he washes the smell of rotting meat from his hands. Welch's men do not wash their hands, but handle and abuse their wom-en coarsely. So people try their best not to feel. Perhaps women and men in Erdrich and Welch are cut, after all, from the same Indian cloth of comic families, even single affairs, but they register different female and male perspectives on "love." Lulu is at home, after all, when Nector comes to visit, and he is not exactly a sexual stranger. Malvina picks up No Name for a night and tells him the next morning, "Beat it." The differences between the fictions seem gender-based between ideal and real projections of the world. *Love Medicine* appears integrative in a feminist moral sense, while *Winter in the Blood* seems purgative in a male candid sense.

The comedy in *Winter in the Blood* does not come easily, nor is it always on the surface. Teresa isn't vocal with her laughter, regardless of any humor she harbors. Although none too celebrative of her small gains from husband to husband, she is characterized by a "clear bitter look, not without humor, that made the others of us seem excessive, too eager to talk too much, drink too much, breathe too fast" (*WIB* 134– 35). Kipi'taki's granddaughter stands her ground against men as braggarts, fools, and clowns. Teresa adds an ethnic firmness to an ancient mother-right: the "privileged license" to silence fools with her withering, not altogether humorless, look. This is a comic vision from way down, deadpan, satiric, understated. It's a not-to-be-fooled-with mother wit that knows when to bite or bite its tongue.

Knowledge in the novel arrives relative, culturally variable, often darkly comic. Mary Douglas discusses the social contexts that code when we "know" to laugh, the permitted license or privileged offense. In the novel, such "play" with pain seems to germinate a surrealism slanted beyond mimesis, where Welch sketches cartoons with fictive surfaces. The text plumbs the depths of things, base and basic, the bottom of modern human existence, and asks us to bounce back for more, another one-liner, one more one-night stand, joke, drink, or breath. It's trickster stuff. At least we go on going on—to the point, cathartically, that Welch has purged his fictive Indian scene by exposing false sentiment, amoral abuses, male folly, and female fractiousness. *Winter in the Blood* is a bold comic experiment in realistic fiction.

John First Raise drank and joked with white men, then charged them twenty bucks for knowing where to kick their hay balers awake. He told them stories and "made them laugh until the thirty-below morning ten years ago we found him sleeping in the borrow pit across from Earthboy's place," where the novel opens (*WIB* 6). This dead-drunk father, Indian wit, and barroom raconteur is planted in a wooden-marked grave still sinking; baptized by winter-in-the-blood, John "First Raise" lies unrisen. It's a different tale altogether from June walking home "across the water," resurrected in Albertine, or Gerry sprung free by his son Lipsha, border brother to No Name.

If men prove loquacious wanderers, drunks, and "no good Indians," according to the remarried widow in this fiction, her own first husband is doomed to die stuporous in a frozen snowbank: "a blue-white lump in the endless skittering whiteness" (*WIB* 19). Yet the poetry of such concise, rhythmic description is as clipped and skillful, eidetic and memorable, Freud might note, as a masterful joke or visionary dream. So, too, if sons are paternally condemned to search for parentage, family, love, and home in the Great American Desert of a modernist wasteland, then their mothers, grandmothers, daughters, and female lovers look on with dark comic sarcasm—an ironic nod to old taboos about sexual division, feminist castrators in the visage of Belva Long Knife with the campfire boys. "He was a wanderer—" Teresa tells No Name of his father, "just like you, just like all these damn Indians" (20). She prefers the whitewashed company of off-reservation priests and burly half-breed farmers.

Welch gives us a desacralized humor that grounds Montana Indians and excretes bad spirits with Swiftean satire. The spinster cow is stuck in the mud with a stream of "crap down her backside," and Bird takes a "walking crap" on the way to Yellow Calf's hermitage. No Name pisses in the ditch, and the carsick professor's daughter vomits in the roadside bushes. The bar "swamper" goes to the back room "to bleed my lizard." These candid, low bodily functions cleanse through elimination. So, too, laughter here (basely akin to belching or breaking wind) opens a closed psyche or anatomy as a comically negative release. It may be Freud's joking bottom line described in *Witz* as "the economy in the expenditure of effect."

All the novel's revelations come as excreted bursts, basely comic, evacuant. During the narrator's first adult visit, Yellow Calf coughs up a "spasm of mirth or whatever" when No Name chides him about keeping a woman around. Lame Bull roars and falls over backward in his kitchen chair, returning from his honeymoon with Teresa. The "airplane man" explodes with an absurdist laugh at the bar waitress, whom he claims as his lost daughter, then plunges through the swinging saloon doors into the night. A swayback twenty-three-year-old horse farts his "instant of corruption" when No Name realizes he is standing before his grandfather laughing. It may be laughter that racks the throat, but still transcends pain, a blue paean of survival.

Despite the losses, characters come around and stick around to laugh, albeit discordantly. There's evidence of equestrian mockery: "Old Bird shuddered, standing with his hindquarters in the dark of the shed. He lifted his great white head and parted his lips. Even from such a distance I could see his yellow teeth clenched together as though he were strain-

ing to grin at us" (*WIB* 14). Such horsy humor leers through the fall
mask of plains history, as a blind old hunter faces his grandson across
century-old winters of starvation: "watching his silent laughter as
though it was his blood in my veins that had told me," No Name says
near the novel's end.

This fiction documents a genetic, cultural, and historical "winter" in
blood. It tracks the government's near extermination of the buffalo,
reservation roundups of prisoners of war, and one-quarter of the Blackfeet dead in the 1883 Winter of Starvation, when the people were forced
to camp by their traditional enemies, the Gros Ventre or "Gut" people,
literally "Big Bellies." Here a young Blackfeet widow mated liminally
for life with a teenage hunter who brought her meat to survive. At the
other end of three generations along the Milk River, polluted purple in
the stifling late-summer Montana heat, our thirsting, rutting narrator
finds his native heritage written like blood script from a land of endless
distances and dispossessed peoples.

Laughter in this novel can be taken as an absurdist cry of survival.
Trickster's old yelp, the comic bark of *Canis latrans,* offers no sign that
things are any easier to bear than they ever were; but then again, No
Name yowls at the moon his own way, bucks the odds, sees the grains of
salt in his sweat, and licks the dirt from his wounds. No Name continues
to sharpen his wits on real stones, on disillusions that strip men of
illusions. Laughter of this kind, a dark wit, is homeopathic medicine.
We suffer a "cockeyed" earth, a blind grandfather tell us— "Of course
men are the last to know" (*WIB* 68)—but it's never too late or little. The
survival of the next generation may depend on such lowly knowledge.

In a biologically purgative sense, laughter is analogous to animal
cries or barks above the threat of catatonia. It rumbles out of grounded
thoughts under stunned silence. Laughter here is a sign of primal in*sight*
into and through acculturated confusion. In *Winter in the Blood* the
Oedipal epiphany, comically dramatized, comes as scatological closure,
an Indian variant on Dante's descent into and out of Satan's anal hell:

A mosquito took shelter in the hollow of his cheek, but he didn't notice. He
had attained that distance. "To be an old dog like myself, the only cycle
begins with birth and ends in death. This is the only cycle I know."

I thought of the calendar I had seen in his shack on my previous visit. It
was dated 1936. He must have been able to see then. He had been blind for
over thirty years, but if he was as old as I thought, he had lived out a lifetime

before. He had lived a life without being blind. He had followed the calendar,
the years, time—
  I thought for moment.
  Bird farted.
  And then it came to me, as though it were riding one moment of the
gusting wind, as though Bird had had it in him all the time and had passed it
to me in that one instant of corruption.
  "Listen, old man," I said. "It was you—you were old enough to hunt!"
But his white eyes were kneading the clouds.
  I began to laugh, at first quietly, with neither bitterness nor humor. It was
the laughter of one who understands a moment in his life, of one who has
been let in on the secret through luck and circumstance. (*WIB* 158)

Our comic *under*standings—and cathartic laughter—resonate the
thunder of imminent storms, echo the rumble of a horse's guts, and ride
"the gusting wind." Comic insight is flatulently reduced to a chthonic
trope. This is a parodic wisdom especially modern, consciously antiheroic, grounded in a real world.

  Human fate thus erupts naturally "with neither bitterness nor
humor," sparked by a horse fart that accents "the laughter of one who
understands a moment in his life." During this lowly revelation, the
lesson breaks through civilized niceties to say in so many words:

This is your grandfather, you fool, and this Ancient Fool, another grandson
of Old Man Na'pi, will teach you something about surviving winter in the
blood. Pity's a bitch. Montana is Montana, mountainous and scant. This is
called Glacier County for good reason, and winters are hell. They have never
been easy anywhere, even before the white man. History, too, is tricky. You
have no say over your genetic family or fate, Mister Indi'n. Your mate will be
a matter of choice, perhaps endurance at times, even betrayal, disease, or
death, but it doesn't stop there. Things go on. Children come and go. The
thunder calls rain that seeds the earth. Burials can bring rebirths, even sprin-
kled with graveyard humor when life ends.

Or so the monologue might go.
  Welch's surreal story ends with Grandmother's requiem and dark
comic closure borrowed from *Hamlet:*

The old lady wore a shiny orange coffin with flecks of black ingrained
beneath the surface. It had been sealed up in Harlem, so we never did find out
what kind of makeup job the undertaker had done on her.

The hole was too short, but we didn't discover this until we had the coffin halfway down. One end went down easily enough, but the other stuck against the wall. Teresa wanted us to take it out because she was sure that it was the head that was lower than the feet. Lame Bull lowered himself into the grave and jumped up and down on the high end. It went down a bit more, enough to look respectable. (*WIB* 174)

Dante called the comic cycle "divine" through his descent into hell, purgation, and paradisaic reascension: the promise of dawn, spring, and renewal by way of purgative loss in the face of all odds. And Viktor Frankl revised his scientific lifework rising out of the death camps with a sense of "paradoxical intention" that crystallized in logotherapy:

> Such a procedure, however, must make use of the specifically human capacity for self-detachment inherent in a sense of humor. This basic capacity to detach one from oneself is actualized whenever the logotherapeutic technique called "paradoxical intention" is applied. At the same time, the patient is enabled to put himself at a distance form his own neurosis. Gordon W. Allport writes: "The neurotic who learns to laugh at himself may be on the way to self-management, perhaps to cure." (*MSM* 197)

Perhaps No Name, detached nominally and distanced psychically, finds his way home through certain comic red blues. When we reverse the "contrary" twice, we're back where we started.

Indi'n Ends?

Humans do not survive forever. Hardly a "divine" perspective, Welch's novel is grounded, lowly enough, in day-to-day ironic realities. It is a desacralized world, for better or worse, where the gods give way to secular survival, and the dead are buried with bizarre comic relief. Humor here, dark as it may be and fallen miserably, roots both vision and hallucination in reality, whether drunk in a Harlem bar, fasting on a Montana vision quest, fantasizing romance along the Milk River, or face to face with Old Man himself in the ditch. Comedy sets up a countervoice and countervision to the dream state. Its double thinking educates us in reversals, in warped psychic mirrors and perceptual twists. We learn to keep from playing out the folly of the hapless "other": white "airplane man" on the lam, Randolph Scott grinning "cruelly" from memory's billboard, or Doris Day drunk with her toe stuck in a bottle. Dark red humor rakes this compost for spring renewal. In other words, the dark comic view of whites and Indians helps us not to mistake the illusion, or play, or mask, or movie for America's given reality. If we can see and accept truth through the fictional real, a grainy irony may help us to play the game better, or as best we can, fully conscious of our foolish parts and allotted cartoons. We must be willing to forget and forgive and go on, mistakes or no. Trickster's absolution, low as he gets, is wintry grace. We learn from Old Man to break through the crust of a parched earth, pray to a choked sky, loosen a blocked spirit, listen to a silenced culture, and relearn a lost lineage. This is the dilemma for contemporary man wastelanding, from Welch's Montana, to Eliot's London, to Frazer's ancient Egypt, where our modernist myths collate back into the *Vedas,* or so a Western humanist education today would have it.

Thus a comic *de*basement is necessary, a "fall" to inform us through the winter of "spring," a death to bring us to life. Through the realism of il-lusion, as Huizinga shows, a novel cannot "lie." Its words may be illusory constructs, unreal in some sense perhaps, but not untrue. The fiction plays out our environmental, biological, cultural, or psychic slips—and offers purgative catharsis, a displacement that re-places us. We re*member* with Indians and re*turn* to the old lessons, still current. Some concept of the "fortunate" (Native) American fall creates a living paradox, a death-to-life lesson. This disillusion is integral to realization of a fuller life.

In our time, Viktor Frankl saw man as swine and saint in Nazi Germany. When Frankl begged an Auschwitz cell mate to help protect his lifework, a manuscript hidden under his coat, the prisoner hissed one word, "*Scheiss,*" and turned away. "Our generation is realistic, for we have come to know man as he really is. After all, man is that being who has invented the gas chambers of Auschwitz; however, he is also that being who has entered those gas chambers upright, with the Lord's Prayer or the *Shema Yisrael* on his lips" (*MSM* 213–14). For those who outlive genocidal terrors, ironic survival has become a bisociative way of life: "Thus the illusions some of us still held were destroyed one by one, and then, quite unexpectedly, most of us were overcome by a grim sense of humor. We knew that we had nothing to lose except our so ridiculously naked lives. When the showers started to run, we all tried very hard to make fun, both about ourselves and about each other. After

Navajo rodeo clown. (Photograph by Kenji Kawano)

all, real water did flow from the sprays!" (24). Frankl discovered dark humor in the death camps as "another of the soul's weapons in the fight for self-preservation . . . an ability to rise above any situation, even if only for a few seconds. I practically trained a friend of mine who worked next to me on the building site to develop a sense of humor. I suggested that we would promise each other to invent at least one amusing story daily, about some incident that could happen one day after our liberation" (68). "Apart from that strange kind of humor," Frankl recalls, "another sensation seized us: curiosity" (24). Curiosity sparks improvisation and futurity—what can and could happen, apart from what has fallen. In this respect, a bisociative sense of irony connects winter with spring, as it oils the lock between darkest night and dawn's door. Such modernist humor tunes the contrary fork of Blackfeet views in *Winter in the Blood*.

"Suffering ceases to be suffering in some way at the moment it finds a meaning," Frankl notes, "such as the meaning of a sacrifice" (*MSM* 179). Frankl saw our fall and resurrection as "paradoxical intention"; Blackfeet Cree cousins call it "opposite thinking." For James Welch, red blues seem a purgative pain and passage through an inherited "winter in the blood." Space curves cyclically, as No Name comes home, to Malta, to Havre, to home again. Time recurs as kinship, father and mother, or stepfather ironically reborn, or brother remembered. Ancient reciprocities with animals—horses, birds, fish—return totemically. These gains emerge through a dark comedy of losses where laughter is excretive and regenerative. And the horse's fart epiphanizes recognition: to dream, to damn, to joke the hurt out. Tenderness is hardbitten and hard-won from a grainy ironism. This complex comic position seems both modernist and mythological, Euroamerican and Native American, as registered in Indian art today.

8

Comic Accommodations: Momaday and Norman

INTERVIEWER: "Why do you suppose that Indian humor has been so little recognized by the majority culture? And so little understood?"

MOMADAY: "It's probably been kept a secret. It's one of the strongest elements of language within Indian cultures. . . . Humor is really where the language lives, you know. It's very close to the center, and very important."

N. SCOTT MOMADAY, in Charles L. Woodard, *Ancestral Voice*

Serious Play

We have brought the earth.
Now it is time to play;
As old as I am, I still have the feeling of play.
KO-SAHN, in N. Scott Momaday, *The Way to Rainy Mountain*

"It seems to me that the humor in your writing is underexamined critically," Charles Woodard says to N. Scott Momaday in *Ancestral Voice*. "Yes, I think it may be difficult to perceive some of my humor because it is understated, and it doesn't always come off as humor."[1] For a novel laden with pain, *House Made of Dawn* is counterbalanced not with Erdrich's nurturing humor or the plains cut of Welch's winter, but in a lyrically tempered irony. The novel's sense of personal tragedy is mediated by a tribal sense of ceremony and historic renewal, the rebirth of spring from winter. "We may call it the drama of the green world," Northrop Frye writes of Shakespearean comedy, "its plot being assimilated to the ritual theme of the triumph of life and love over the waste land."[2] *House Made of Dawn* cyclically dramatizes Frye's paradigm of a "comic" spring: integration (coming home), purgation (of racism, war, and death), inverse renewal (the dawn of a new cycle). Despite sufferings, the fiction projects the "able" resurrection of Cain's slain brother, struggling to regain a native place in his grandfather's fields. This Adamic vision prefigures a generation of American Indians reemergent from older traditions.

"I most admire those whose primary concerns are proportion, design, and symmetry," Momaday says of Indian artists. "They understood the intricate patterns of the universe. In the Indian world, an understanding of order is paramount . . . " (*AV* 170). With "appropriate" design, Momaday's style and authorial stance turn on parallelism. His prose generates conjunctively from a principle of reduplication, or variation and contrast, in the continual balancings of ongoing tradition: "Abel was running. He was alone and running, hard at first, heavily, but then easily and well." The syntax is accretive, as it builds from simple to compound statement, adverbally colored, then visually descriptive. "The road curved out in front of him and rose away in the distance. He could not see the town. The valley was gray with rain, and snow lay out upon the dunes." Words swell in sequences, compound, pause, then flow into parallel rhythms, always returning to a declarative horizon note. "It was dawn."

In oral cultures, each generational voice hinges on the edge of extinction, Momaday observes in the essay "The Man Made of Words." Tribal peoples hold dialogues with the animal world in an extended kinship that calls for mutual survival (some say that animals created language so people could talk with them; others believe that Trickster had a hand in this). Early on, a young Abel walks to the edge of the Valle Grande, one of the world's largest calderas, to witness "golden eagles, a male and a female, in their mating flight. They were cavorting, spinning and spiraling on the cold, clear columns of air, and they were beautiful."[3] (Eagles and Indians seem to embody the deepest folkloric myths of North America.) The binary dualism of Pueblo thought registers as the gender pairing of eagles in mating flight. Momaday's iambic syntax pairs phonemes, balances phrases, cadences sentences, and moves on imitating a vision of the eagles in flight. "The male followed, and Abel watched them go, straining to see, saw them veer once, dip and disappear" (*HMD* 20). The narrative explores, suspends, and swoops forward in celebration of words-in-motion, as nothing is left at rest, all ceremonially cadenced. Gerunds link noun and verb states, "things" and their generative acts. There is no lost movement in this organic formalism.

The pan-tribal systems of "four winds," "roads," or "directions"— from the Navajo "holy winds" to Black Elk's four-part sacred hoop with four-leggeds, two-leggeds, roots, and wingeds—fuse into a south-western metaphysics. This quartered system projects tribal reciprocity between temporal and typic actors, human and animal characters. The word "character," conveniently enough, suggests both a written sign and a human actor; and in this Indian context, actor means animal-person, totemically answered by person-as-animal. So, too, Momaday's mixed-blood tribal fusions—Kiowa, Cherokee, Pueblo, Anglo, and Navajo—align genetics and cultures toward mutual exchange. Such complementarity implies the ideal or "sacred" reciprocity so charac-teristic of pan-Indian thinking: interdependent life-forms in a nurturing mother earth beneath a protective father sky. In *House Made of Dawn* the quadripartite system, as well, encompasses four modes of thinking: dramatic (action), pathetic (affection), mythic (ideation), and totemic (representation). In the manner of Lévi-Strauss, we realize a four-by-four or pan-Indian, as it were, deep "comic" structure:

CHARACTERS	MALE	FEMALE	OLD ONES	PRIESTS
DRAMATIC	Abel [Ben]	Angela	Francisco [Mariano]	Tosamah
PATHETIC	Vidal	Milly [Carrie]	"Daddy"	Padre Olguin [Martinez]
MYTHIC	Juan Reyes	Porcingula and "Pony"	Josie and Aho	Fray Nicholás [Santiago and Porcingula]
TOTEMIC	Horse	Fish	Bears and wolves	Eagle and rooster
PARODIC	Snake	Grunion	Guinea pig	Pigeon
TYPES	*ALAZON* (protagonst)	*AGROIKO* (rustic)	*BROMOLOCHO* (buffoon)	*EIRON* (ironist)

As these phyla suggest, Momaday's stylistic parallelism shows up in characters doubling, tripling, and quadrupling (double doubling) in bal-anced directions simultaneously. The structure also draws on Frye's four

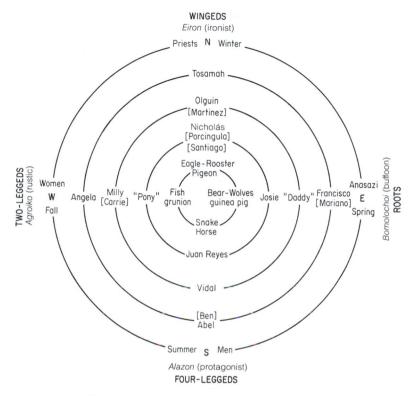

Concentric characters in *House Made of Dawn.*

"characters" from Aristotle's discussion of comedy (*alazon, agroiko, bromolocho, eiron*).[4] The grid configurates in concentric "sacred hoops." Abel is the focal protagonist, shadowed by his Navajo friend, Ben Benally, narrator of the book's third section in Los Angeles. Abel's affair with Angela in Jemez, New Mexico, leads toward Milly in the city, as it reaches back into Abel's past with Josie and Ben's first passion with the Navajo seductress "Pony." Sensuality here implies the possibility of renewal deeply embedded in nature, a male–female fecundity interconnecting all beings.

In this novel, male is identified sexually with horses, antisexually with snakes (the albino's tongue writhes and his lips are scaly in the sexual homicide; the sadistic cop, Martinez, is known as "Culebra," the Spanish word for "snake"). The feminine seems as fluid as water beings and associated with fish, paraodically with grunion (dancing their tails into the sand on southern California beaches after summer full moons, laying eggs to be fertilized by the males). The "old ones," or Pueblo-named Anasazi, appear in Abel's grandfather Francisco, Milly's dirt-farmer "Daddy," and Tosamah's grandmother Aho with the Jemez woman Old Josie, who clowns to bring Abel out of catatonic grief when his mother dies. These anciently "rooted" beings are totemically embodied in the bear and its sacrifice for the people, as well as the timber wolves that shadow Francisco's first bear hunt. The wolves welcome Francisco with the canine humor of *Homo ludens*. *"And at the same time he saw the dark shape sauntering among the trees, and then the others, sitting all around, motionless, the short pointed ears and the soft shining eyes, almost kindly and discreet, the gaze of the gray heads bidding only welcome and wild good will"* (*HMD* 180). In the City of Angels, animals are reduced to pigeons and a dead guinea pig named Vicenzo (ironic "victory"). Back at Jemez, the Anasazi speak through Francisco, who teaches his grandsons, Vidal and Abel, the sunrise contours of the land: *"The larger motion and meaning of the great organic calendar, the emergency of dawn and dusk, summer and winter, the very cycle of the sun and of all the suns that were and were to come. And he knew they knew, and he took them with him to the fields and they cut open the earth and touched the corn and ate sweet melons in the sun"* (*HMD* 178).

In the fourth phylum, we come upon the visionaries, imagined through the mating flight of eagles and the mythic sacrifice of the rooster, Santiago. These are parodied in the urban pigeons of central Los Angeles, where noon is always dark and the sun never shines. Indians subsist in the downtown basements and tenement halls of this house made of darkness.

A priest's journals provide historical background and intercultural fragments for the last century of Jemez–white acculturation. With the conquering Spanish, Fray Nicholás (Francisco's "father") bequeaths a questionably celibate priesthood to Padre Olguin, who arrives in Jemez from Mexico when Abel stumbles home drunk from the German front. Seven years later, Father Olguin strains to "understand" when Francisco dies in early spring of 1952 (on Momaday's own birthday, February 27, the date that the fourth and final section of the novel, "The Dawn Runner," opens in Walatowa). The Jemez children, as nature's festive fools in ludic agon, mock Fray Olguin, the Catholic "father":

Out of the corner of his good eye he saw a child leap out of the way and fall.
The child rolled over and laughed. Suddenly the walls of the town rang out
with laughter and enclosed him all around. . . . Then in the ebbing pitch and
rock that followed, as the cloud of dust and laughter drew down upon him, he
saw the cradleboard fixed to the wagon. . . . The muscles twitched under the
fat and the head turned slowly from side to side in the agony of sad and
helpless laughter. Then the wall of dust descended upon the face, and the
cries of the children became a shrill and incessant chant: "Padre! Padre!
Padre!" (*HMD* 69–70)

Questions of paternity riddle the fiction—Francisco's priestly father
Nicholás, Abel's unknown father, Milly's "Daddy," Angela Grace St.
John's offstage husband and child. These patriarchal gaps are set against
a child's longing for mother love and nurturing humor—Old Josie,
Angela, Milly, "mother earth" in Pueblo myths.

Broken women seek to rebond with lost men. Old Josie, a surrogate
mother and lover, clowns and cries and tries to teach Abel to laugh
again, after his consumptive mother and brother die:

Francisco clicked his tongue and said that his grandsons ought to be left
alone, but fat Josie just lifted her leg and broke wind, sneering the old man
away. And the children huddled against her and laid their heads on her great
brown arms. And the week after Vidal was buried, Abel went to her for the
last time as a child, and Francisco never knew. She crossed her eyes and stuck
out her tongue and danced around the kitchen on her huge bare feet, snorting
and breaking wind like a horse. She carried her enormous breasts in her
hands, and they spilled over and bobbed and swung about like water bags,
and her great haunches quivered and heaved, straining against her ancient,
greasy dress, and her broad shining face cracked in a wonderfully stupid,
four-teeth-missing grin, and all the while tears were streaming from her eyes.
(*HMD* 106–7)

Josie seems sister to Faulkner's Dilsey or Williams's Elsie. Sexually and
scatologically comic, Josie survives as a woman with essential love for
Abel: she is his surrogate "mother," first lover, and matriarchal clown
in a story that turns on pain toward comic renewal.

The "dawn" can be felt behind Abel's suffering, back through "time
immemorial," as the Pueblos say. The village children mock the
"Padre"; old ones click their tongues; the Navajo come as desert
coyotes to the Pueblos; Francisco forces a smile to bring home a drunk-

en grandson; Milly laughs continually in resistance to her urban displacement from Oklahoma, where Indians were relocated a century
back; Tosamah cracks wry jokes and lyricizes his Oklahoma origins;
and at the novel's end, indeed its beginning, Abel sings voiceless renewal blessed with ashes, pollen, and rain as he runs "home" toward
the sunrise in early spring. In traditional terms, this implies ceremonial
and historical promise of rebirth. The Navajo night-song of "pollen,"
the Pueblo ashes on the snow, and the warming rain on Abel's skin
recall an endless cycle of death and resurrection. They reach back
through ancient phoenix myths, Egyptian to Aztec to Pueblo, about
cyclical rebirth from ashes. This faith lies embedded in human–animal
evolution for thirty thousand or more years, a Pueblo "ladder" in the
Sangre de Cristo canyons. This chain of being is crowned with ancient
animal tricksters: "Coyotes have the gift of being seldom seen; they
keep to the edge of vision and beyond, loping in and out of cover on the
plains and highlands. And at night, when the whole world belongs to
them, they parley at the river with the dogs, their higher, sharper voices
full of authority and rebuke. They are an old council of clowns, and they
are listened to" (*HMD* 55).

Like a carnival pack of gypsies, the Navajos come to Jemez to trade:
"the children of the town would run out to see, to stand at the fences
and cheer and chide; there would be an old enactment of laughter and
surprise. The end of the train would be brought up by fools, in a poor
parody of pride" (*HMD* 66). This laughter is both welcome and warning, a kind of ritual gossip defining tribal boundaries. It is significant
that the children, natural inheritors of the culture, should be the ones "to
stand at the fences and cheer and chide." Earlier (later in time actually)
Francisco greets Abel, who has come home drunk on a bus from World
War II: "Tears came to his eyes, and he knew only that he must laugh
and turn away from the faces in the windows of the bus" (13).

Milly tries to relocate Abel in Los Angeles. Characterized by "sob-
bing laughter" (*HMD* 112), she seems a needy Oklahoma emigrant of
the Depression who has lost her only daughter and her dust-bowl father.
Laughter is a sign of last defense and, paradoxically, of her faith in
living: "she was always laughing," Ben says. "She was talking to him
and laughing, and her laughter was real and ringing" (99). And Abel
embraces her as a lost child come home thirsting for mother's milk: "He
held one of her breasts with the tips of his fingers, so lightly and

carefully that it might have been a bead of rain, and sucked it for a long time" (100).

Abel embodies the famished Indian protagonist, no less than Welch's No Name or Silko's Tayo, seeking home in a modern wasteland. The sexual plot gives men, through women, a survivalist choice of comic over tragic perspectives. In this narrative, fertile silence, procreative darkness, and flowing consciousness suggest feminine mysteries. For Pueblos, water equates with cyclically renewable life: mother's milk, rain and snow, runoff irrigation for the fields, baptism, purification, and birth through seminal fluids. After Josie, Milly acts as Abel's fallen mother, in contrast with sex between Abel and Angela (possibly a "scarlet letter" parody of a white woman longing for Lawrentian renewal with a dark Adamic man, shadowed as carnal knowledge with a bear "blue-black and blowing"). Angela plays the pregnant virginal child who detests her white fetus and comes to Jemez for healing waters, a pseudo-1960s vision of the Zen "nothing beyond." She seduces her dark woodcutter, and the moment before consummation Abel "was dark and massive above her, poised and tinged with pale blue light. And in that split second she thought again of the badger at the water, and the great bear, blue-black and blowing" (*HMD* 62). With both Angela and Milly (and back through Josie, Abel's first mother–seductress), sex seems an attempt at procreative reunion, both purgative and naturalistically comic. Sexuality is a natural ceremony of the body—a play beyond pain, a pleasure with suffering at its core. It appears a separation that adjoins—"the deep cleavage between," the narrator says of Abel's affair with Milly (101).

In the narrative, laughter and sexuality cross as sources of recessed power, indeed, necromancy. Ben recalls a scene in Los Angeles, which triggers the memory of his first sexual encounter with a girl named Pony:

> When Milly heard that, the way he told it, she got so tickled she didn't know what to do. She couldn't stop laughing, and pretty soon we had to laugh, too. And then she got the hiccups, and that just made it worse. We almost laughed ourselves sick. We were just sitting there shaking and the tears were coming out of our eyes and we were acting like a bunch of damn fools, I guess, and we didn't care. She was pretty when she laughed.
> *There was a girl at Cornfields one summer. . . .*

> *Pony, they called her, and she laughed, and her skin was light and she had*
> *long little hands and she wore a dark blue velveteen blouse and a corn-*
> *blossom necklace with an old najahe like the moon and one perfect powder-*
> *blue stone. . . . (HMD 151)*

These sensual scenes flash back to Francisco's primal love for Porcingula, daughter of a witch, *"laughing and full of the devil,"* who
mocks Francisco's origins, *"had he not been sired by the old consump-*
tive priest?" (184). She gives herself to both Francisco and Mariano,
the rival Francisco conquers in the dawn race. *"She laughed and wept*
and carried his child through the winter. . . . The child was stillborn,
and she saw that the sight of it made him afraid, and it was over. The
shine came again upon her eyes, and she threw herself away and
laughed" (185). This bewitched daughter bears the name of the Catholic
Indian saint, Porcingula, whose festival complements the Feast of Santiago. The old myths rattle like skeletons behind the contemporary plot.

The albino as tragic native caricature threatens a tribal festive humor.
After flagellating Abel with the sacrificial rooster in the Feast of Santiago, Juan Reyes offers a deadly embrace outside a bar at night:

> Now and then the white men laughed, and each time it carried too high on the
> scale and ended in a strange, inhuman cry—as of pain. It was an old wom-
> an's laugh, thin and weak as water. . . . And throughout Abel smiled; he
> nodded and grew silent at length; and the smile was thin and instinctive, a
> hard, transparent mask upon his mouth and eyes.
>   . . . Then he closed his hands upon Abel and drew him close. Abel heard
> the strange excitement of the white man's breath, and the quick, uneven
> blowing at his ear, and felt the blue shivering lips upon him, felt even the
> scales of the lips and the hot slippery point of the tongue, writhing. He was
> sick with terror and revulsion, and he tried to fling himself away, but the
> white man held him close. The white immensity of flesh lay over and
> smothered him. He withdrew the knife and thrust again, lower, deep into the
> groin. (*HMD* 77–78)

The ritual murder of the albino would seem to purge a caricatured
"whiteness" from the Indian world (Jemez has a high incidence of
albinism). Festivals of sacrifice antecede this purgation: the rooster,
horse, and hero of the Santiago legend; the Navajo clowns; the children
mocking the "father" (a patriarchal trio including Francisco with a bad

leg, Padre Olguin with a bad eye, and Juan Reyes or "King John," parodically connected with Angela Grace "St. John").

Natural cycles finally win out, as witchery spells itself. Evil caricatures its own, purges itself, implodes within closed tragic forms. Here, laughter mocks sadness, and however darkly comic, it opens what Bakhtin (discussing Rabelais's "grotesque realism")[5] calls the "merry loophole" of possibilities beyond natural distortions. The albino's Indian–Anglo ambiguity, his physical pain and psychic suffering, his strangely ageless virility and grotesque power, point toward evil as a given to be accepted by Francisco. This grandfather is "saint" or "brother" of the animal-man in Christian legend. That is, through Francisco's traditional Pueblo eyes, the grotesque is acknowledged and forgiven: "He was too old to be afraid. . . . [E]vil had long since found him out and knew who he was. He set a blessing upon the corn and took up his hoe. . . . And where he had stood the water backed up in the furrow and spilled over the edge. . . . Above the open mouth, the nearly sightless [albino's] eyes followed the old man out of the cornfield, and the barren lids fluttered helplessly behind the colored glasses" (*HMD* 64). To adapt Pueblo terms to Christian myth, the story replays good and evil in the garden, Adam transcending Satan through love of his work and corn "children."

Trickster Be with Us

> "I used to listen to Tosamah. He's a clown, and you have to laugh at some of the things he says. But you have to know how to take it, too. He likes to get under your skin; he'll make a fool out of you if you let him."
>
> BEN BENALLY, in N. Scott Momaday, *House Made of Dawn*

"The Longhair," the first of the four sections in *House Made of Dawn*, ends as Francisco works alone in his fields. The albino has been disemboweled, and Abel will be imprisoned for seven years for ritual murder (recalling a 1952 case in which the Felipe brothers were accused of killing Nash Garcia, a New Mexico state trooper). In section 2, "The Priest of the Sun," toiling grandfather and grotesque albino dissolve to a caricatured city priest, the Reverend John "Big Bluff" Tosamah of the

Holiness Pan-Indian Rescue Mission, Los Angeles. Tosamah's mission features a signboard that is postscripted, "Be kind to a white man today."

Such downbeat Indian jokes riffle a mixed lexicon of Tosamah's "conviction, caricature, and callousness." This multivalent mode comes through the authorial voice of a novelist who, after he finished writing *House Made of Dawn* in July 1968, signed himself, successively, "Irving Mad Buffalo," "Horace Gall," and "Irv Bitter Bison" in letters to Gus Blaisdell, the New Mexico editor who championed Momaday's *The Way to Rainy Mountain* against dismissive literary critics and anthropologists.[6] Navarre Scott "Totsotoah" Momaday seems to stand an inflection away from John "Big Bluff" Tosamah. The word *Totsotoah* in Kiowa means "Red Bluff," Momaday's second Kiowa name after Tsoai-talee, or Rock-tree Boy. These mixed namings point toward what Pueblo clowns call "talking backward," jumbling their codes comically, as clowns find contrary "logic" and outrageous gaming in reversals.[7] "Tosamah is my mouthpiece in a certain way," Momaday admitted to Charles Woodard. "Just between you and me and several million readers, I think Tosamah is perhaps the most interesting character in the novel. He certainly was an interesting character to develop. He fascinates me. I like him and dislike him deeply" *(AV* 124).

Tosamah is a self-reflexive parodist. Through the official peyote text of "Saint John" in the Native American Church, he exposes the white "fall" into language, schemes of Big Ideas masked rhetorically (deconstructive jive from an Indian point of view). He self-parodies Momaday's own high regard for the sacred bond of the "Word." Preaching the "Word," Tosamah is netted in his own caricatured web for Anglo rhetoricians: "The fat was *John's* God, and God stood between John and the Truth. . . . He made it soft and big with fat. He was a preacher, and he made a complex sentence of the truth, two sentences, three, a paragraph" *(HMD* 86–87). John Tosamah's sermons swell "full of sound and meaning, signifying nothing," as the narrative appropriates Shakespeare, Faulkner, and Momaday's own Kiowa grandmother in *The Way to Rainy Mountain.*

This clown of mixed tongues, then, is liminal priest, Indian Saint John of skid row sidewalks. He is both part of the problem (white self-reflexivity) and perceptive of intercultural complexity. Tosamah defers to Momaday's grandmother as native storyteller, to the Sun "Dance" as divinely comic ceremony, to the "*word*" as primal voice and child's redemptive play. "The Word did not come into being, but *it* was. It did not break upon the silence, but *it was older than the silence and the silence was made of it*" (*HMD* 91). As binary L.A. priest and comic shaman, rapping about Aho in Oklahoma and "Saint" John two thousand years back, Tosamah plays Momaday's acculturated surrogate in a city of eighty thousand relocated Native Americans (just down the coast from Santa Barbara, where Momaday wrote *House Made of Dawn*).

The combined characters of Abel and Tosamah pose a case of doubly encoded author. Abel is the Jemez "other" to the Kiowa–Oklahoma Momaday, who was himself estranged as a teenager in Jemez, foreign to men such as the Pueblo Abel and the Navajo Ben. In a double twist, Abel is an outsider "took in," as Lipsha says in *Love Medicine*— bastard by an unknown father. Tosamah comes on as the corrective caricaturist to Abel's sacrificial role, finally completed in the dawn run. Traditional Indian is "permitted" disrespectful laughter through a licensed trickster, as Tosamah chants Anglicized healing songs from the Navajo, together with the other relocated Indians in the city of angels: "Restore my feet for me, / Restore my legs for me, / Restore my body for me, / Restore my mind for me, / Restore my voice for me" (*HMD* 134). Tosamah is clown-priest, Saynday of the city, mythic trickster who first pulled the Kiowas from the hollow log of tribal history. He cobbles and reconstructs reality as best he can, offsetting Abel's deadly seriousness.

Momaday redeems this liminal clown privately, as the self-parody encodes a comic artistry. It serves to redirect Abel toward the eastern sunrise (Tosamah's satire in part drives Abel east from the western city), purging his pain, integrating him into an extended Indian family (Milly, a mother; Ben, a Navajo brother to replace Vidal; Tosamah, a resurrected comic "father"), and renewing his life inversely through his grandfather's death. Thus Tosamah plays Momaday's Kiowa kinsman, his comic double, a contrary cousin.

Trickster is liminally essential to this renewal and survival. Jarold Ramsey, in *Coyote Was Going There* and, more particularly, in *Reading the Fire*, generates a multidimensional definition of the Indian trickster:

> . . . an imaginary hyperbolic figure of the human, irrepressibly energetic and apparently unkillable, whose episodic career is based upon hostility to domesticity, maturity, good citizenship, modesty, and fidelity of any kind; who in Freudian terms is mostly id, a little ego, and no superego; who is given to

playful disguises and shape-changing; and who in his clever self-seeking may accomplish important mythic transformations of reality, both in terms of creating possibility and in terms of setting human limits. From a structural standpoint, Tricksters are important mediative figures.[8]

As street-smart con man, Tosamah survives Los Angeles and ministers through "grandfather" peyote: "that little old woolly booger turns you on like a light, man. Daddy peyote is the vegetal representation of the sun" (*HMD* 101). John Tosamah figures as a native jive artist: child of the 1960s, contrary and recreant, refusing to grow up in the eyes of the Great White Father. In Ramsey's neo-Freudian terms, his *ego* is that of a displaced, single man in the city, the existentially omnipresent "I" of Western history. Resistant to white acculturation, he talks back tribally. His Beverly Hills "sister," a Wannabe shamanic coyotess, can be distantly heard in the parodic Angela Grace St. John. John's *superego* lies far back with the "old ones," Aho's mythic Kiowa tales in Oklahoma or Francisco's traditional Pueblo past in Jemez. And Tosamah's *id* is the pure appetite of a compulsive shape-changer, boundary-hopper, and rule-breaker (author in disguise, Charlie Hill of darker Hollywood). In Geza Roheim's terms, this trickster–clown transforms into tribal hero, supported for millennia by a cultural superego that permits license, experimentation, and adaptation within traditional norms.

The character of Tosamah as contemporary trickster channels comic theories into ludic oxymoron. Huizinga's freeing play is his release from Abel's heaviness, as Freud argues of discharge through humor. He satirically tests the pan-tribal limits of Douglas's "permitted disrespect." As Turner's liminal shaman between tribe and town, he combines Radin's all-faces figure, Jung's "oldest" archetype of chronos in chaos, Koestler's doubling bisociation, and Lévi-Strauss's mediative *bricoleur* (reality's handyman). Finally, he personifies Konrad Lorenz's transformer of hostility, a comic fight-or-flight shaman wielding Frankl's comic will to survive.

At the close of *On Aggression,* Lorenz foregrounds the "heaven-sent gift" of humor, "a faculty as specifically human as speech or moral responsibility." The Austrian ethologist theorizes that "laughter probably evolved by ritualization of a redirected threatening movement," deflecting aggression. As such, laughter "forms a bond and simultaneously draws a line."[9] It is a sign of strength and a signal for negotiation—that is, a signal not to use that strength violently (bearing the "fangs" in order to bypass combat, a significant evolution in animal–human intelligence). Biology supports Lorenz's psychology: "When pompousness is abruptly debunked, when the balloon of puffed-up arrogance is pricked by humor and bursts with a loud report, we can indulge in uninhibited, refreshing laughter which is liberated by this special kind of sudden relief of tension. It is one of the few absolutely uncontrolled discharges of an instinctive motor pattern in man of which responsible morality wholly approves" (*OA* 295). Lorenz redirects humanist attention toward jokes, aphorisms, riddles, and humor at large among others. "Laughter never makes us uncritical," Lorenz warns against conversion, "while enthusiasm abolishes all thought of rational self-control" (294). "It is my firm belief that a man sufficiently gifted with humor is in small danger of succumbing to flattering delusions about himself because he cannot help perceiving what a pompous ass he would become if he did. I believe that a really subtle and acute perception of the humorous aspects of ourselves is the strongest inducement in the world to make us honest with ourselves, thus fulfilling one of the first postulates of reasoning morality" (296). Deconstructive *contradiction* may be a modernist comic key to bicultural honesty: speaking "against" the grain, or Cree "opposite thinking" as decreative play, teaches an audience more than one side to things. "Sufficient humor," Lorenz concludes, "may make mankind blessedly intolerant of phony, fraudulent ideals. Humor and knowledge are the two great hopes of civilization" (298). An imaginative play of mind is their proving ground.

Thus Trickster functions as transformer precisely because his comic (dis)charge arcs across separate modes of a joking equation: both metamorphosis and mystery are enacted in narrative humor. In "bisociated" play, things are funny when we "see," but humorous too when we remain in the dark, illuminated by what we do not "know." We remain open to laughing at the unknowable across the played division. "Humor is the best of lie-detectors," Lorenz counsels (*OA* 295). Satire, Lorenz argues, is "a poem aimed at prevalent vices and follies." As such it seems "the right sort of sermon" when "militant enthusiasts" would distort truth through skewed ideologies (295). Tosamah in this regard seems more critical to Abel's regeneration than most readers have seen.

Momaday's humor is embedded in the narrative "way" toward sunrise. He has an old storyteller's faith that the human voice will carry us through the worst, toward the truth, into a better world. Bakhtin found such trust in the comic *heteroglossia* of fictive voices from Dickens to Dostoyevsky to Rabelais:

> Out of the doorways he [Francisco] passed came the queer, halting talk of old fellowship, Tanoan and Athapascan, broken English and Spanish. He smelled the odor of boiled coffee, and it was good. He cared less for the sweet smell of piki and the moist, broken loaves of sotobalau, the hot spicy odors of paste and posole; for old men do not hunger much. Better for their novelty were the low open fires of the wagon camps, the sweet fat which dripped and sizzled on the embers, the burned, roasted mutton, and the fried bread. And more delicious than these was the laden air that carried the smoke and drew it out in long thin lines above the roofs, swelling in advance of the rain. . . . [T]he old man had an ethnic, planter's love of harvests and of rain. And just there on the obsidian sky, extending out and across the eastern slope of the plain, was a sheer and perfect arc of brilliant colors. (*HMD* 71–72)

The rainbow is an ancient sign of native trust, comically akin to religious faith without dogma. Here Trickster keeps the priest grounded in reality, the grandfather in touch with his growing plants and children. This is where the artistic clown reminds the people how comically wrong and oddly right humans can be.

Seeing Cree

> "It helps to listen in on people talking," Pelly said. "Hang around the porch." . . .
> "How much do, you get?" he said, pointing to his head.
> "How much?" I said.
> "How much Cree?" he said. "Words—which?"
>
> HOWARD NORMAN, *The Northern Lights*

Without compass or stars a person lost in the wilderness eventually comes full circle. Perhaps this wanderer tracks the eye's arc or the earth's curve, or leans into the slightly lopsided gait of *Homo ludens*. This means circling back home, sooner or later, by virtue of natural laws. It is a given among bipeds bound to the earth, erratic evidence of the homing rotation of all things. Gray whales find their way from Alaska to Mexico and return. Monarch butterflies are tagged from

Maine flying to their origin in Mexico. Salmon go back to spawn and die where they were born, and snow geese fly from Canada to the Gulf of Mexico and home again. So, too, with humans: the circularity in mythic narrations, the return to basics, the reintegrative homecoming. This comic curve, a humorous paradigm, finally grounds erratic behavior.

A full generation separates *House Made of Dawn* (1968) from Howard Norman's *The Northern Lights* (1987)—a nineteen-year renaissance of American Indian literatures. Narrative has shifted from Momaday's impressionism to Norman's pointillist realism, as modern fiction tightens stylistically from William Faulkner to Raymond Carver. Looking back through Norman's novel to Momaday, American Indian literature has thickened the canon. Momaday, Silko, Welch, and Erdrich have garnered international distinctions, and Norman's first novel was nominated in 1988 for a National Critics Circle Book Award. Americans are coming home these days, seeking rootedness and rebirth, often by way of "native" America.

Our North and South Americas seem in the throes of cultural renewal. Northrop Frye posits this renaissance as a final stage of comic myth. Constance Rourke would trace the growth of American humor from immigrant pioneers on the frontier, to colonized peoples asserting independence, to global interdependencies. We have had wireless evidence of this interethnicity—thousands of tongues in the air—for almost a century, and now our common survival faces ecological and nuclear imperatives. Natively, all would locate a homeland and heritage; ideally, most would share resources and goods. The majority would live out their lives in relative peace. Collaboration seems the key to a "native" American future. No more drunken Injun Joe, Indian-giver decoys, or "honest Injun" ploys. No more wild-man neoprimitivism, squaw misogyny, warrior violence, or buckskin separatism.

If Abel—victim of wars and Euroamerican acculturations of five centuries, martyred victor through his own people's suffering—strained and in some respects was broken into going home, Noah Krainik, the non-Indian narrator of *The Northern Lights,* tries inversely to find home with mixed-blood Canadian Cree in the village of Quill, Manitoba. His mother, Mina, goes cabin-fever crazy with omens of the Ark in the North, and Anthony, Noah's errant father, deserts the family to become a bush hermit. After an orphaned cousin, Charlotte, comes to live with Mina, Noah seeks solace in the company of Sam and Hettie, a mixed-

blood couple in Quill. Here his best friend, Pelly, an abandoned Indian
who lives with Sam and Hettie, sketches villagers and learns circus
tricks on a mail-order unicycle.

Pelly breaks through the ice and drowns while performing stunts on
his unicycle. Hettie goes distraught with grief. Mina and Charlotte,
tired of waiting for Anthony's return, relocate in the neocolonial city of
Toronto. Noah eventually joins them to help run the Northern Lights
movie house, where Mina long ago met Anthony. There Noah befriends
an ambidextrous Cree named Levon, whose homeless family moves
into the projection booth. Finally, Anthony returns to a cold reception
and backs out again, and the Krainiks are left in the city with relocated
Indians. At the end, Noah imagines Pelly's ghost behind an ice-skating
radio personality, Fabian Bennet, who promises to send Hettie and Sam
greetings on his radio program, "Great Books."

Noah's story hangs between the rich lyricism of *Love Medicine* and
the lean naturalism of *The Beet Queen*. This seems a "breed" fiction
suspended between red and white psyches, leaning interculturally toward the former from the unrest of the latter. Here the botanical concept
of "grafting" could be an example of a new cultural paradigm. Indians
and Euroamericans have intermixed for half a millennium, to the extent
that the great majority of Indians today, as the Canadians say, are métis
(no less "Indi'n" for that). It is a concept similar to *mestizo* in South
America, where "Spanish" more accurately means mixed-blood Indian. Norman describes a woman in the North: "Pelly's aunt Hettie was a
stout, lively Cree woman who had married Sam when she was eighteen
and he was twenty-four. Mixed Indian–white marriages had taken place
in the region for centuries. In Quill they were neither advocated nor
discouraged, but more or less tolerated with varying degrees of hope or
doubt."[10] This mix is America's reality across the demographic spectrum where myths are interculturally portable. Indians adapted to such
importations as Christianity and English, not to mention horses and
basketball; and Euroamericans at one time or another, certainly as children, "play Indian." Aside from "wild" longings, all yearn to locate a
native home, life-style, and mythos in America. And most Indians
struggle to acculturate to new "American" ways. In *The Northern
Lights* natives on both sides appear plurally dislocated, commonly seeking a locus.

American ethnocentrisms face both ways over the Buckskin Curtain,
and the time has come to recognize a more positive paradigm of collab-

oration across xenophobic frontiers. "You don't write off all the white people," Betonie tells Tayo in *Ceremony,* "just like you don't trust all Indians." The notion that we are all in this *together* may be the most plural, indeed democratic concept in America. We will survive collaboratively or perish separately. It finally boils down to choices: a bloody history of Western existential heroics or the comic accommodations of pan-tribal humor.

Some options survive in good trickster fashion. Norman's Cree translations in *The Wishing Bone Cycle* (1976) and *Where the Chill Came From* (1982) distinguish him delightfully, even strangely. He is a gifted bicultural translator in American Indian studies, inheriting a tradition that Franz Boas and his students began a century ago. With graduate work in zoology and folklore, and flexibility in a dozen or so languages, this young writer translates interdependent life-forms through brilliant bricolage: linguistic anthropology, intercultural folklore, biocultural ethnography, poetic translation, and now cross-cultural fiction. His bisociative art bridges "North" America—that is, Canadian-American cultures too long separated.

Clipped Talk

> "It's right you learn to speak it, but keep in mind a white man can't think in Cree."
> I was immediately taken by Hettie's language, the sound of it. The way certain phrases went from long vowels to abrupt, almost slurred consonants, then quickly to a final vowel. Phrases that emanated from so deep a hollow in the throat that they seemed like whispers. The shifts in cadence and inflection, and the travels, within a single sentence, from scratchy monotones to lilting, buoyant strains.
>
> HOWARD NORMAN, *The Northern Lights*

The Northern Lights encapsulates an essential story about a "spice-box place" of northern people. "Odd things brought people close." Noah phrases the generative formula for the fiction, "The Cree took from Christian teachings only what they felt was strange, humorous, or useful." An odd trinity of human imperatives: sex may embrace all three, food comes close, and religion remains inspired by spirits "strange, humorous, or useful":

"Noah," Levon said, mulling the name over. "He's the one, took a bunch
of animals, out on a boat, eh? Had a lot of 'em to eat. Ate some he'd never
ate before. More went out on his boat, than came back. Ate two of each.
Even ate snake. Wandered a long time, long time."
    "Is that how you heard it?"
    "Yeah, my grandmother. She got it from, some preacher, the story. Is how
she told it."
    "I heard it a different way. But yours makes better sense."
    "Where you from, that you know some language?"
    "Quill—north Manitoba."
    "Me—I'm from North Knife. Was."
    "I know where it is."
    "Yeah? Was." (*NL* 194–95)

Levon's lost home in North Knife encodes the story of the James Bay
Hydro-Electric Project: "Was." As detailed in Boyce Richardson's
Strangers Devour the Land (1976), this early-1970s venture, undertaken
by the government of Quebec for economic reasons, was a planned
disaster that flooded hundreds of tribal villages, disrupted countless
game migrations, and destroyed historical, religious, and burial sites.
How all this happened in our time is told personally through the people
forced from their native homelands into city slums.

Not without incisive humor: "Pelly was Quill's only circus ever,"
Noah says in *The Northern Lights* (37). This mixed-Cree, as an abandoned clown on a unicycle, dramatically focuses the story. Things work
backward. Grief-ghosts show up at village dances when a hermit is
invited not to attend, only to emerge as the errant father Anthony. The
pain in the North, then, coexists with a survivalist humor, as
Wichikapache the trickster counters the ravenous Windigo, cannibal of
winter. This is "opposite thinking," as the Cree say; anything can
happen. Two unexpected deaths begin the story: Pelly breaking through
the ice on Paduola Lake and Wilfred the mail pilot crashing into a tree.
Like a zigzag unicycle ride, the narrative then backs up and comes
forward, charting Noah Krainik's double sense of family.

Norman's storytelling is richly veined with intercultural play, where
the ordinary to one mind seems strange to another. Native humor remains a character's stay against loss. Noah's makeshift family of mother, son, and cousin bonds in the face of betrayal, as teasing stepsiblings
develop a "cautious deference" toward love. Finally, the fiction implies, the splits between cultures can be comically bridged, admitting

the differences, playing out the congruities. What cannot be translated is left to faith in the "other," general good humor, or simply trust. The storytelling "draws" a reader in with Pelly's precise detail:

> Pelly sketched away. I turned off the radio. Then he drew a picture of me turning off the radio. Then a self-portrait: Pelly sitting in a corner, sketching. Pelly Bay.
> It has since haunted me, how his name referred to water. (*NL* 18)

Person, incident, picture, and self-portrait overlay a resonant narrative context. The telling is deeply penetrant and powerfully currented: a fluid, dense medium of northern consciousness, simple and basic as water. The book gives us its watery northern world, includes us, finally encompasses us in a terrain that is strangely enticing, both "over" and "out" there. The novel cherishes what the North *is,* without unnecessary embellishment.

> "Einert, my good man," he said. "It was brave of you to smother your beloved phonograph to save the store. To save us all from certain death by fire. You're a brave, brave man, Einert. Poor, poor old phonograph, going to be as rusty as . . . as . . . as a phonograph left out in the snow, is what it'll be as rusty as. That, and nothing else. It is what it is." (17–18)

The talk captures voices original to northern people and places:

> "We'll need a tent," he said.
> "Sure, in case it rains."
> "I'll paint posters. You can hand 'em out."
> "Go down to Winnipeg, maybe."
> "Drive around in the truck. Names on the side. Girls."
> "Let's practice some more." (*NL* 31)

Not even an "I said" or a "Pelly said." Comically clipped, this dialogue seems a kind of chiseled semiology—a landscape, a language, a mixture of tongues and peoples and histories. Their "signs" show only tips of coded communication in a cold climate, where actions do the talking, and there is no facility or time for wasted words (winter breathing is stiff reckoning this far north). Here a whole cosmos of substructures and interconnections determine meanings: one must *read* things closely. The style is characterized by roving commas, idiosyncratic synapses in thought, syntactic suckholes, vast cultural slippages, and linguistic distances. It's an essential story of the North, its peoples and many languages, that reifies northern reality in words and acknowledges where words stop short. The patois of tongues is syncopated and suspended in odd ways. Sam "worried that her [Hettie's] real sorrow would get lost between languages" (97). A fine humor warms this winter, a sunrise beyond the dark chill:

> The pilot's name was Moses Dog Toussaint. He was part Cree Indian, part French Canadian, more on the Cree side, with closely cropped black hair, a round face, and a gap-toothed smile. I had not flown with him before. In the roughest turbulance he hummed in a monotone as if to steady the plane. "We, should . . . mmmm . . . hmmmmm . . . mmmmm . . . get there, soon." He also spoke with pauses between syllables as unpredictable as the choppiness of the air. . . .
> "Coffee, I get, now," Moses said. "See you, later, sometime, eh?" (13)

A reader listens hard to be alert, awake, quick, and yet not too much in a hurry. Alert as men crossing a winter stream, Lao-tzu once said of the homing "way" in China. As an elder and two boys set out hunting, the dialogue is critically edged with comic wisdom:

> "Down—that way," Job said, nodding south. "Then—to a river, small. Then—to a river, bigger. Trap's out there."
> "That's about as much of the future as he's likely to mention," Pelly said. "Don't talk about what you're *going* to do when you get back. Job says talking about the future insults the land. Makes it seem like we think there's no dangers that could kill us. Animals are always listening in, too. They won't give themselves up on a hunt, if they think we're taking it for granted that there'll be plenty to eat. It's best to think just about what's in front of you. That's what Job says." (*NL* 76–77)

This essential wishing-bone talk or "luck" talk, as Noah says of the Cree propensity to gamble, or "play fate," is how Huizinga sees *Homo ludens,* comic at heart, naturally humorous. The narrative feels like erratic spurts of activity in a snowy plain, where only rustlings break God's slow game of checkers.

And when the dramatic action snaps, as it does at the end of the first chapter, it's quick and decisive, though somehow "known" or even sensed and predicted. The details of Pelly's death come word of mouth after a prolonged buildup. The understated story, the inevitable tragedy of death, is mixed with comic survival. At the age of fourteen, Noah hears Hettie's voice crack on the wireless: "Listen, Sam is all broken. He's sat down. He can't talk. Listen, some bad news, from here. I can hardly say it. An accident. On the pond. Pelly went through. Fell through. He gathered us, for watching his tricks. Everybody. Was there. On the unicycle he was. Sam and me we had chairs waiting for us special in the snow. We sit in them. We have blankets. On our laps. Especially at us Pelly is waving. He did tricks. Funny ones. Then he did going backward" (*NL* 43). And that's it: *tipikochiyetim,* as the Cree say, "opposite thinking," life and death. Just so, Kwakwu the porcupine "goes backward, looks forward" backing into his burrow, *usá puyew, usu wapiw.* Only poor Pelly forgot to look down, or if he did, accepted the plunge.

This story is freshly played out for all its pain. We learn about the hard things up north—suckholes, accidents, alcohol, fathers going strangely away—and still the family comes back to the Northern Lights in Toronto, and keeps the movie house lit up in comic futurity. The fresco in Noah's Toronto theater recalls Albertine's epiphany in *Love Medicine*: "Most of the figures, even the kneeling Indians, gazed skyward, so that the cumulative effect was a worshipful moment of awe at the display of aurora borealis on the dome" (*NL* 178). This comic promise is emblemized in a special kind of northern rainbow on the ceiling, the afterglow of Francisco's vision of Jemez in *House Made of Dawn*, "a sheer and perfect arc of brilliant colors" (*HMD* 72).

The Northern Lights makes us aware of the "wireless," globally intertextual world we live in: "Often when I woke the radio was still on, and I'd hear maritime weather reports, soccer games from South America, an orchestra from Amsterdam, wheat surveys from Saskatchewan, a soprano trilling up the scale in London, medical advice from Boston" (*NL* 35). The narrative makes its way across the page and seeps into the reader's consciousness, where its memory glows like night-lights, the afterimage of a 1930s movie. Humor, lyric grace, encapsulated characterization, focused point of view—all this from a time when movies, radio talk shows, readings from books, and stories among people came to a finely tuned point. Such storytelling is vulnerable to interruption and busy static from the "civilized" world outside.

This book seems narrated from an older time. It carries Chekhov's clear lines, almost an allegorical style of characterization that makes a reader think of Gogol (the Father, the Mother, the Boy, the Friend, the adoptive Sister, the . . .). And yet its "magic," if you will, comes across somehow timeless and expressly modern, as in Márquez or Kundera or Calvino. The plot has versatility, surprise, and a startling capacity for wonder. Noah's story seems modernly "schooled" ("cut," Pound said) and locally attuned to the rural ways of an older time and place, the Indi'n ways of another culture that still exists outside Euroamerican history. Mariya Ludovic, a Yugoslav in Toronto, footnotes Noah, "That definitely not a city boy talking." "Guess not," he defers (*NL* 190). And in the Cree English we get fragments focused, set apart, disjointed but tangibly clear: "Want, to be a *student*?" Levon asks Noah. His ambidextrous Cree surname, Makowisite, sets up a bicultural log: "Uses both, each good as each."

Anthony and Charlotte guess each other to sleep, dialectically making things up. Such displaced comic play underlies the inventive formula for the fiction:

> "Where's it raining?" he asked into the dark.
> Charlotte guessed. "London, England," she might say. No matter which city she named, she was always correct.
> "Right," Anthony said. "Now, who is it raining on?"
> "An old woman, but she doesn't have a raincoat on."
> "Wrong. It's raining on a man and a woman, talking with each other. She's holding an umbrella."
> "They're trying to figure out where to have supper."
> "No, they're not. They're arguing about something."
> "No, they get along fine. They just can't figure out where to eat."
> "That's the reason they can't get along. They should just go to a place, sit down, and have a good supper. Instead, they're out in the rain, arguing."
> "Yes, they should just get inside."
> "Now, what are their names?" (*NL* 46)

The dialogue recalls a microlyric reality in the mode of magic realism.[11] Right/wrong . . . No, they're not . . . No, they get along fine . . . That's the reason . . . Yes, they should . . . Now, what are their names? As in Erdrich's *The Beet Queen*, minimal, telling details grace a spare, often cold landscape where everything stands out surreally against a gaping winter backdrop. It's something akin to Williams's red wheelbarrow glistening in the rain, against our vast, unsatisfied need to "know" what is going on ("So much depends on"). A minimalist poetics of the North operates here, as coded jokes tie the whole story together. In the beginning, Anthony and Mina court in the Toronto lobby of the Northern Lights theater, an improvisational date to a movie they never saw. A generation later, the narrative rewinds the film and runs things backward to a new start with Anthony's final exit. These emplotted jokes spark like funny tics dreamed up to keep mind and body warm by a traveler walking through a frozen tundra.

All the action comes arrestingly understated—Pelly on his unicycle, then drowned, the news transmitted by radio in the opening lines (the magic and doom of "wireless" news). Anthony comes and goes bizarrely like the "airplane man" in Welch's *Winter in the Blood* or some would-be Windigo who cannot quite make it back to humanity. Charlotte calls her stepbrother "dummy" in loving letters from the new Toronto "home." Cree life in Quill radiates around the storekeeper and his snow-smothered radio on New Year's Eve. The dance that didn't. . . . All these surprises are blended into a perfectly straightforward narrative, a kind of Nick Adams, Nick Carraway, or Huck Finn farther north than anyone has yet gone in American fiction. Adamically pure and yet penetrant, it is as though the cold, isolation, and vast distances make things and peoples count more, each breath, each trapped beaver, each rabbit pelt in winter, each song in the spring or on the radio, each person or village. The novel gently places us down in the city, where Cree indigents like Levon "hunt" for nickels in rental machines and stadiums. His family survives on the mud hens along city docks or on the breed goldfish–carp in the parks at night. In this city, the "awkward guest" Anthony—no longer Father—enters and exits, by now on the edge of derangement, an urban bag man (no longer shaman or forest hermit asked "not" to attend the dance). He silently comes in and out carrying his empty French-horn case, like a movie played to the end, then rewound to get the reel ready again. "You'll see—he comes and goes," his wife says early on (*NL* 55).

So this is the North: its severities, beauties, and daily ludic survivals, given the contraries of a climate that reverses itself between momentary well-being and deadly exaction. The dramatic tension turns on yes/no sets of dialogue, countering northern forces in nature, not necessarily opposing, but certainly not blowing in the same direction all the time. The story comes out tense and entertaining with contraries of people, male/female, young/old, well/ill, domestic/estranged, tribal/self-ostracized. And there's always another point of view, another tribal talk, an emotion or a thought as yet unanticipated. The novel unravels a continuous story, images crystallizing from plain things, "ending" with a character on ice skates whom Noah has heard on the radio for twenty years reading "Great Books."

Cultural multiplicities bunch together in this lucid story with so many layers and facts: fish, home interiors, radio shows, dances, shy courtings, contrary flirtings, marriages that don't work (and some that do), daily talks and nontalks. All the mélange of the Far North (French, Finnish, Cree, Ojibwa, Norwegian, Russian, and countless others) concatenates the dialogue. The story grows like an icicle on the eave of a modest forest home—clear, glistening in the sun, chilly, tapering to a comic point. A nub, a perception, a punch line is always working on the reader—its crystalline form and living motion melt like ice on a hot stove, as Frost said of a poem, finding a way home.

Daily details keep life going. Back at Quill, Noah remembers: "We mostly *heard* the animals, at night, anyway. Porcupines mewed, called in high-pitched cackles or staccato coughs, and gnawed at our outhouse. The caribous snorted like pigs or emitted guttural bellows, forced gusts of breath through their nostrils when they foraged near our house, kicking away snow to find ground cover. Occasionally we heard the echoing shriek of a lynx or the industrious scraping of its claws on a branch" (*NL* 56). This is the art of fine ethnographic writing, the imaginative craft of expert zoology. Hettie cooks up dumplings of bear fat and water, as she sings Cree songs of the seasons:

> Many of the songs she knew evoked birds, weather, and seasons, especially winter. "Others leave, you stay. Raven." That was another one. "One day you're walking on leaves, ptarmigan. The next on snow." Or: "Duck, you got caught! Sudden ice." (35)

The diction is elliptically thick. Traditionally the moon-months tell seasonal times descriptively: "chimney smoke was our windsocks" during "rimey moon," or, as the Cree say, *Yekewutinoowepsim*. Temporality gets even more complicated, as nature imitates the "art" of nature in a migration of decoys. Sam's carved ducks go south by plane, via the storekeeper Sohms, and then they're brought back north by Anglo hunters to decoy ducks flying south! The novel tells "how a direction—in this case, *north*—took on a character in the imagination of people" (106). A single-sentence paragraph summarizes the half-year season: "Winter might be seven months long" (36). And this dominant northern season carries its own jokes:

> "Put your hands down around your peckers," Sam would say, demonstrating. "They'll warm up fast. Do I have to tell you that every time?" he would laugh. (36)

It's a survivor's joke (learned from Trickster) against real frostbite. Noah remembers being introduced to bivalent tongues in Quill:

> "Genius, pure and simple," Sam said. "Now he'll know if he's indoors or out in two languages."
> I sat down at the table. Hettie poured me a cup of tea. "*Nepesu,*" she said. "*Nunaskwonowin,*" I said haltingly.
> Hettie shook her head. "Taste first," she said. "Then if, you like, it, speak." (*NL* 72)

This could be the epigraph to the book: taste, listen, speak later. Talk after testing things. And let the tongue lie quiet for a minute before the teeth clatter. The initial silence is telling, a significant waiting. *Mewewin,* pure *mewewin,* Cree sing out, the lyric "gift" not easily come by. Savor the taste, test it, figure it out. Such is a gratuitous, lyrical form of humor shared by tribal peoples, though not often talked about.

There is a critical insistence here, during times of danger, on not talking, a nonspeech about speech. Levon speaks for Indians another way in Toronto:

> "Park cop, bastard, knows my face. Caught me once. One night. . . ."
> "What'd he do when he caught you?" I whispered.
> "No fuckin' talk," he said, his voice strained. (*NL* 208)

"I don't want to talk about it," Noah writes to Charlotte of his hermit Old Man (141). Such could be an antitext behind the text, especially where city dangers or forest spirits are concerned. Those who know express a wise fear of saying the wrong thing.

> "Maybe—yes," Job said, a look of consternation crossing his face as he stared into the woods. "Maybe now, they turn over our canoe. Maybe now, they laugh, so loud, till"—he covered his ears with his hands—"we are deaf. Maybe, they just fly the bear trap, somewhere else." (78)

Job's caution is not paranoia or superstition, but a keenness—an alertness to "Maybe," a conditional epistemology where the Cree live expectantly, without certainty, as Richard Preston shows in *Cree Narrative* (1975). Spirits "do anything—for a smoke," Sam says. Such fear of talk keeps listeners alert, aware of control's limits, honest about luck. Job tells Noah, "A person who has bad luck in hunting gets to eat right along with everyone else" (214). The moral resurfaces in the Toronto slums. "Luck was a complicated thing—it carried from village to village, was deft at reversals, often occurring as swiftly as a boy dropping through the ice" (112). No more need be said. Poor Pelly.

> Levon looked at me. "Make up what you want," he said. "But what we got—it's right in front of you. No problem." (*NL* 215)

The northern lights still shine in the end, like Silko's stars in *Ceremony,* or the sunrise in *House Made of Dawn,* or the aurora borealis in *Love Medicine.* They give tricksters reason to keep on going on. The narrative closes gently with the "ghost" of Pelly comically resurrected in Fabian Bennet on skates in Toronto, to begin at the end and go back again. The pattern follows Anthony in and out of the theater, entering in reverse, from the beginning with Mina, finally "seen" for who he is by everyone in the makeshift family. None particularly wants to face his unhappy "ghost" in the flesh. Each fears the other will go over the edge seeing this derelict dad (he's been "jacking" the family around, Levon puts it).

But by the end Mina rests contented, Charlotte is being tutored, Levon and his Cree family are running the projection booth for the film *The Magnificent Seven,* an early-1960s Western. The story closes in parabolic curve, touching down in the city, where so many have migrated from the country. "This goddamn city, like to kill you in ways, if you let it," Levon says of relocation (*NL* 203). So the people live "closed up" in one-room "homes" or movie projection booths, scavaging parks, ravines, and railroad tracks for muddy fish, ground squirrels, and poached ducks. The radio programs for this urban hunting ground are "Lights Out," "Great Men of Vision," and "Great Books." A struggle for equilibrium shadows city life, as Noah says. "Perhaps it was like learning to ride a unicycle, keeping perfectly balanced despite fierce crosswinds. Walking down Palmerston Avenue, I drew strength from thoughts of that kinship" (234).

So Quill is a real fantasy of the past for natives. "Was," Levon says, though the possibility lingers that Fabian Bennet will say hello to Hettie on "Great Books." Noah closes the story sketching his radio hero ice-skating in a public Toronto rink: "He calmly pushed off in a long stride, his hands clasped behind his back. His movements were simple, but as he rounded the far end of the rink my thoughts took another turn, and I saw a figure fly into an expert zigzag, halt, perform a counterclockwise spin. I heard my lone applause echo against the domed, star-filled sky above Quill" (*NL* 236). Something simple lingers about the story. It hangs as a chert of the contemporary nuclear family: the clear telling of a single narrator and his small band of mother, adopted sister, even errant father and adoptive Indi'ns. The orphaned Charlotte writes to Noah, *"it's who's ever right in front of me, that's who my family is"* (168). Pelly is neglected by his parents, Charlotte is abandoned, and Noah's father goes nuts, while his mother remains mildly obsessed with the Ark and the Flood. Like Lipsha in *Love Medicine,* they're all "took-ins." The narrative feels immensely, comically complex, interweaving Cree and white points of view, gathering the telling details of all these lives:

> Finally Sohm said, "There's a Bible passage about evidence of things not seen."
>
> He had offered this as proof that the very things that draw people closer or estrange them most severely cannot always be defined. Yet I had the feeling, as we left the store, that every person there took home the same conclusions they had arrived with, and that the dance would drift down into Quill's memory in all those varied interpretations. (117)

"Ghosts," perhaps, give people a way to think about their losses—multiplicities of views on events that estrange or draw folks together—death, luck, spirits, love, mystery, beauty, truth. And no one understands it all, certainly.

This Noah narrator and his Ark of a novel entice readers north: the people, "natives" all, birds and animals that survive the "Flood" of contemporary history in the James Bay catastrophe, Levon's family no longer where their village "was." That's all. A drunken father, a persistent mother—Noah and his wife. Adoptive kin, Cree and otherwise, a boy and a girl paired as siblings, the "lost" Indian brother Pelly, and the receding natural home for us all (the wilderness as our old home back there . . .). The advancing flood of time and civilization. Mortality. Not that everything is that bad: the family is still more or less intact, growing up into the city, though dad is lost in the alleys, and the Cree live in the projection booth. Levon can "hunt" the parks and bingo games at the Salvation Army for a living. It's definitely an "ending" that brings to a close an older way of life, even if Fabian Bennet says hello to Hettie in Quill on the radio.

There is a disquieting denouement to all this. We don't want to end it, to let go, to face the music of time. How long can Noah hum a few bars of Stravinsky's *Rite of Spring* from childhood memory and survive the streets of Toronto? When will he light out for the territories? Will *The Magnificent Seven* gun down the bad guys who threaten the village (has south come north?) Will the noise of the machines drown out the sounds of chipmunks screaming at night in the park? Will Noah forget how to catch and silence ducks with a twist of their necks? How hungry will our modern tenement heroes become before going back north or coming farther south? Is Toronto, or any city, an alternative to that precious and lonely freedom "out"doors in Quill?

Indians think about these things and try to keep a sense of humor. Lakota friends and families back home shake their heads. Something is slipping away, perhaps. Native American humor helps us understand and cope with a world no easier than it's ever been. Americans must play this game together, for keeps. *Hetchetu aloh!*

Coda

And from this it appears how very precarious and explosive a joke is, and in how many different ways it can manage to misfire. . . .
    A joke is not a thing to be mauled and tinkered and revamped and translated about like an old trunk, from one nation, race, tribe, family, generation, or language, into another. It is a chemical gem, a delicate and precarious contexture of non-affinitive qualities, likely to go off at the touch of a feather in appropriate circumstances, or to lie flat and mute as a pancake if discomposed or mismanaged.

                                        MAX EASTMAN, *The Sense of Humor*

Socrates at the *Symposium*'s festive end, with sunrise cocks crowing after an all-night discourse, tells Aristophanes and Agathon that the "genius" of comedy and tragedy is the same. At this odd moment—the others are asleep, drunk, or gone home—the remaining two listeners sit bemused, if befogged. It may be a sign of Plato's humor, a parodic overtone to his master's theorizing and unresolved brilliance. It may also be true, a bisociative insight. "You have noticed that the truth comes into this world with two faces," Black Elk says. "One is sad with suffering, and the other laughs; but it is the same face, laughing or weeping. When people are already in despair, maybe the laughing is better for them; and when they feel too good and are too sure of being safe, maybe the weeping face is better for them to see."[1]
    "Humor in its adult state is thus seen to be somewhat like electricity," Max Eastman concludes, "and to possess two currents, a negative and a positive." An audience indulges and judges simultaneously in comic contexts, finds joking satisfaction *in* disappointment, Eastman argues. We go away from humor thinking, refreshed, amused, if not puzzled.

Rather than tragically end-stopped, the comic tone is one that mixes "imaginative sympathy," Eastman says, with "corrective hostility." This may mean making the best of a bad thing. Sir Thomas More, addressing the executioner on a shaky scaffold, is said to have requested, "Help me to ascend—I will shift for myself coming down."[2]

Consistent with Frye's paradigm, Erdrich's fiction integrates Americans on the contemporary red-white frontier, while Welch's novels purge a wintry pain. Momaday's vision renews our "native" sense of America, as Norman's narrative fuses Indian and Anglo concerns. These writers represent hundreds of others, from Fonseca's Coyote paintings, to Craig's intercultural cartoons, to Trudell's pop shaman blues, to Deloria's seriously comic social science. The inverse distance between Momaday and Norman over two decades, *House Made of Dawn* to *The Northern Lights,* spans the fictional range of a Native American renaissance. Momaday is an Oklahoma mixed-blood Kiowa educated in the best Anglo schools, tutored by Yvor Winters at Stanford, a Guggenheim scholar and Fulbright lecturer in Moscow, the first Indian recipient of a Pulitzer. Norman is a third-generation Russian émigré schooled among northern storytellers, tutored by Cree such as Jacob Nibènegenesábe, Samuel Makidemewabe, and Sarah Greys.

Bicultural intelligence speaks best for America today, leading to collaborative renewal on both sides—quick wit, native art, natural craft—coming across stylistic differences, lush to lean prose, dramatic tension to comic promise. The vision travels from the Far North to the Southwest deserts on the tensile strength of surviving humor, bonding interculturally. Indi'n humor evinces the courage to survive through Trickster's iconic scavenging, to play with terrible odds, to endure and like it. A fictive cast from Lipsha and No Name, through John Tosamah and Noah Krainik, shows the curiosity to explore extraordinary corners of reality, the quickness to survive on less than convention, the luck to net more than average rewards. Others may want to investigate the humor in other Native works, such as Momaday's *The Ancient Child* (1989), Erdrich's *Tracks* (1988), Welch's *Fools Crow* (1986), Hogan's *Mean Spirit* (1990), Dorris and Erdrich's *The Crown of Columbus* (1991), Silko's *The Almanac of the Dead* (1991), Owens's *Wolfsong* (1991), Young Bear's *Eagle Heart Child* (1992), Naranjo-Morse's *Mud Woman* (1992), or Simon Ortiz's short fiction. And novels now in press or manuscript—Paula Allen's "Raven's Road," for example—surely portend uncharted bends, rapids, and poolings in this current I've called

Indi'n humor. These will be works for further reflection and refinement. "Humor is a wild thing, quick on its wings," Eastman warns (*SH* 110). Paradigms of Indi'n humor should be approached interculturally and intertextually in an interdisciplinary field of serious Western play— Acoma to Austria; psychology to biology; Koestler, Babcock, and Kristeva to Welch, Hogan, and Whiteman. The innovative, vitalist energy must be savored, respected, played out, and treated with delicate discipline as well as genuine delight.

Freud's sense of the precisionist wit vital to the psyche's "humor" sparkles in *The Northern Lights*, twin star to *Love Medicine*. Both novels are steeped in Huizinga's free play of human intelligence. The two-ply nature of seriously artistic comedy, as Koestler demonstrates in *Insight and Outlook*, surfaces in a tragicomic fiction such as *House Made of Dawn*, which seems a bisociative bonding of dark and light, a contrasting of agony and ceremonial rebirth. Beneath the dual planes of pain and play—where an artist suffers reality and finds release in transforming humor—resonate palimpsests of comic possibility (hence "northern lights" in both Erdrich and Norman, along with cleansing rain in *Winter in the Blood*, and the sunrise metaphor that permeates Silko's *Ceremony* and Native American ritual that cyclically concludes *House Made of Dawn*).

"The reports of my death are grossly exaggerated," Mark Twain wrote from London in response to New York newspaper stories of his demise. Such, too, is the survivalist humor of the once lamented "vanishing" Indian. Konrad Lorenz's faith in interspecies "humors" could reasonably save us all.

Threats to our human future have not vanished. Problems, pains, even perversities still salt Indi'n–Anglo relations. When I wrote to colleagues asking for examples of Indian joking, Ward Churchill replied, "Q: How do you keep white women in South Dakota from chewing their toenails? A: Make 'em wear shoes."[3] He posited that humor relieves tension when Indi'ns confront non-Indians, what Eastman feels to be the "shock absorber" aspect of joking. A Creek– Cherokee working with South Dakota Sioux, Churchill found that such humor "tends to be 'inside,' and might be viewed as sexist, racist and all that . . . but is really designed to keep folks with ample reason to do so from going off the deep end; hence, it is in its way *anti*-racist, etc." He added: "Q: What's the fastest animal on 4 legs in North America? A: A dog getting out of Pine Ridge."

Vine Deloria, Jr., wrote to me a second time, just as I was finishing this manuscript: "On the witness stand at the Robideau–Butler trial in Cedar Rapids I was being harassed by a prosecutor who was trying to appear liberal in front of the jury. He said, 'I don't want to insult you by calling you an Indian because we all know you people are only called Indians because Columbus was looking for India.' So quick as I could I said: 'It's a good thing they weren't looking for Turkey.' "[4] And Deloria passed on a global Indi'n *heyoka* joke, in time for the Seoul Summer Olympics: "The Sioux–Korean Diet Exercise Book—101 Ways to Wok Your Dog."

Intertribal barbs are part of the Indi'n bargain. "Q: What do you get when you cross a Navajo and a sheep?" Ward Churchill queried. "A: Retarded sheep." Certainly there's a degree of defensive meanness in drawing the tribal lines between "us" and "them," as Basso shows among the Apache. Jokes stretch across the fissures that separate and mix peoples. Grandma Rushes Bear's pun on the "Great White Wail" in *Love Medicine* comically plays back the lament of "Lo! the poor Indian" in Pope's *An Essay on Man*. Still, having fun with tribal disconnections makes their dissonance into something more than snarled warnings to the "others." In fact, such play or humor indulges the negative charge positively, reversing its field to include rather than exclude "them." As with Marie and Lulu to Nector in a peacetime *Love Medicine*, Millie and Angela in *House Made of Dawn* seem feminine counterparts to Abel's war-torn male psyche. Ironically enough, Tosamah chooses the interethnic mix of the City of Angels, as Gerry Nanapush is forced underground from the Twin Cities. And Noah bonds with Pelly in *The Northern Lights*, while Levon's Cree family lives in the Krainik's Toronto theater booth and projects *The Magnificent Seven*.

These poised disconnections and connections energize the comic context. Douglas and Basso detail how "disrespect" is permitted to "stretch" or hyperbolize across ordinary limits. Such humor tests family, clan, and tribal resilience—to reinforce communal kinship, to weed out or exorcise or "release," as Freud has it (economically), the libidinous life-force common to us all. Red English here is a language special to itself, intertribally inventive, joking, connecting, stretching lines, acculturating on its own terms to persistent Anglo pressures.

In his 1988 letter, Deloria claims boldly: "There are two kinds of people in this world: Indians and those that want to be. There are two kinds of Indians in this world: The Sioux and those who want to be. And there are two kinds of Sioux in this world: The Oglalas and the rest who know better." Indi'n humor is the pan-tribal plus in all this. It signals a spirit of renewal with teeth to mark the enemy and bark him out. It evinces a humanity to integrate with allies. It keeps a faith in renewal. Thus tribal humor stitches the frayed cross-cultural fabric of multiethnic America. "I don't know what's bothering those Indians," Deloria reports Custer quizzing his last sunrise. "They seemed to be having a good time at the dance last night."

Hopi child clown. (Photograph by Owen Seumptewa, Hopi)

Appendix A
Reservation Jokes

This checklist was generated around Pine Ridge Reservation and received in the Alliance, Nebraska, American Indian Center, April 1972 (mailed from the Northwest Nebraska Community Action Council, P. O. Box 746, Chadron, NE).

Being Indian Is

Being Indian is . . . .
Having over 700,000 brothers and sisters!

Being Indian is . . . .
Feeling Grey Wolf, Thunder Chief, Smoke Walker are more beautiful names than Smith, Jones, Brown or Johnson.

Being Indian is . . . .
Watching John Wayne whip 50 of your kind with a single shot pistol and a rusty pocket knife on the late show.

Being Indian is . . . .
Having at least a dozen missionaries from 12 different faiths trying to save your heathen soul every year.

Being Indian is . . . .
Fighting with the U.S. Army to save your country from the evils of communism and against the U.S. Army on your reservation to keep the Corps of Engineers from stealing all of your land.

Being Indian is . . . .
Owning land and not being able to rent, lease, sell or even farm it yourself without BIA approval.

Being Indian is . . . .
Having every third person you meet tell you about his great grand-mother who was a real Cherokee princess.

Being Indian is . . . .
Having 9 out of 10 people tell you how great they believe Jim Thorpe, Squanto, Tonto and Little Beaver are.

Being Indian is . . . .
Belonging to a particular tribe that is the best of the 300 or more that still exist.

Being Indian is . . . .
Being broke all summer because you try to make every Pow-Wow around.

Being Indian is . . . .
Having the greatest grandparents in the world.

Being Indian is . . . .
"Graduating" from a reservation high school and not being able to read an 8th grade English book from your white urban friends' school.

Being Indian is . . . .
Going to the PHS hospital with a blood clot in your head and having the young doctor diagnose your problem as hepatitis, prescribing APC's and rest as a cure.

Being Indian is . . . .
Loving "frybread" and corn soup.

Being Indian is . . . .
Having your non-Indian spouse dancing in full regalia at your tribal Pow-Wow.

Being Indian is . . . .
Not laughing at your children when they mispronounce words in your tribal tongue.

Being Indian is . . . .
Telling "Tricky Dicky" Nixon to put his money where his mouth is.

Being Indian is . . . .
Never drinking *alone*.

Being Indian is . . . .
Knowing the Great Spirit.

Being Indian is . . . .
Having a Christian missionary tell you it is wrong to believe in more than one Divine Being, then listen to him tell you about God, Jesus Christ, the Holy Ghost, the Virgin Mary, St. Joseph, St. Patrick, St. Christopher, St. Francis, etc., etc.

Being Indian is . . . .
Paying 15 or 20 bucks apiece for eagle tail feathers.

Being Indian is . . . .
Knowing the so-called "Peyote Cult" is probably a better way of worshipping the Great Spirit than any other Christian way or denomination.

Being Indian is . . . .
Trading your surplus commodities to a local farmer (who used them for hog feed) in exchange for fresh eggs, butter, milk, etc.

Being Indian is . . . .
Respecting your elders who have earned it.

Being Indian is . . . .
Masking your emotions in times of stress.

Being Indian is . . . .
Never giving up the struggle for survival.

Being Indian is . . . .
To have your liberal white friends continually urging you to do as your black brothers have done.

Being Indian is . . . .
Meeting at least two dozen anthropologists before you're 21.

Being Indian is . . . .
Having a "whitey" of the opposite sex tell you how they *think* you could really turn them on.

Being Indian is . . . .
Having the option of joining at least three dozen Indian Unity organizations.

Being Indian is . . . .
Having at least one alcoholic relative put the touch on you once a day.

Being Indian is . . . .
Having high salaried BIA, PHS, OEO, HEW and DOL white-collar bureaucrats tell you how much money is being *spent on Indians* these days.

Being Indian is . . . .
Having your teenage child come home from school and ask you about "the strange beliefs" of Indians that her/his teacher mentioned in school today.

Being Indian is . . . .
Waiting (impatiently) for the new Tecumseh, Osceola, Crazy Horse, and Geronimo to appear.

Being Indian is . . . .
Missing work at least two days a month because so many of your friends and relatives are dying.

Being Indian is . . . .
Living on borrowed time after your 44th birthday.

Being Indian is . . . .
Having your all Indian school team playing against 7 men on the basketball court, 15 men on the football field, and 12 men on the baseball diamond.

Being Indian is . . . .
Listening to all the middle class Tontos and Uncle Tomahawks tell you we must do things the "American Way."

Being Indian is . . . .
Watching your daughter give away her only pair of overshoes to her friend because she only has to walk six blocks to school and her friend lives in the country.

Being Indian is . . . .
Having white do-gooders continue to do for you instead of with you.

Being Indian is . . . .
Never making quick evaluations of people, but reserving judgement until their actions show what kind of people they really are.

Being Indian is . . . .
Feeding anyone and everyone who comes to your door hungry, with whatever you have.

Being Indian is . . . .
Feeling the stares of all the "whiteys" in any public place you walk into.

Being Indian is . . . .
Punching a "honkie" in the mouth for calling you a "Blanket-ass Injun."

Being Indian is . . . .
Wheeling and dealing to beat your black and brown brothers to "Whitey's" guilty complex dollars which are dangled before you and the blacks and Chicanos.

Being Indian is . . . .
Calling your kinsmen "Apples" for selling out their Indianness for the white man's values. Red on the outside; white on the inside.

Being Indian is . . . .
Not rioting in the streets, but occupying godforsaken places like Alcatraz, Mt. Rushmore, the New York-Canadian bridge, etc.

Being Indian is . . . .
Cutting off your cast after two weeks because it's in the way and isn't needed anyway.

Being Indian is . . . .
Having your friends and relatives accuse you of being a traitor if you earn more than $6,000 a year, wear a tie and white shirt, drive a car less than three years old and have a three bedroom home.

Being Indian is . . . .
Having heard your grandparents, parents and yourself say "When we get our land claims payment" then suddenly realize you are hearing your children use the phrase also.

Being Indian is . . . .
Sad.

Being Indian is . . . .
Tough.

Being Indian is . . . .
Hard.

Being Indian is . . . .
To cry.

Being Indian is . . . .
To laugh.

Being Indian is . . . .
Great.

Being Indian is . . . .
Beautiful.

Being Indian is . . . .
Forever!

AMERICAN INDIAN PRESS ASSOCIATION

NEWS SERVICE

Room 306, 1346 Connecticut Avenue, N.W., Washington, D.C. 20036
FEATHERS - S274   DIRECTOR: Charles E. Trimble (202) 293-9054

HORSEFEATHERS
AIPA Light Feature

MILITANT MORSEL: After the recent Bureau bust of 24 AIM and NIYC activists in Washington, D.C., these items were overheard: "Well," said AIM's Russell Means, "I guess now they can call us the D.C. Dirty Two Dozen." . . . Said a veteran of Alcatraz and the statue-painting in New York, at a late-night meeting with Louis Bruce: "There's more room here in the Commissioner's office than in my entire house" . . . Seneca Laura Wittstock, one of Washington's tiniest and most popular tribespeople, had to chuckle when she discovered that her arresting police officer was named none other than George Washington.

*

AMERICAN INDIAN DAY, celebrated on Sept. 24 this year, was marked by high absenteeism among Indian children in the Great Lakes area while the National Congress of American Indians was deluged with calls from concerned school boards. At the BIA, meanwhile, Louis Bruce telecast a Native message over NBC-TV's "Today Show" and Bureau personnel discussed the flying of tribal flags on BIA poles. Quipped one sardonic activist: "Why not have a National Indian Day? They have their Christopher Columbus Day—and he's just a guy who got lost twice."

*

A PETITION has been submitted by the National Indian Youth Council to the Federal Communications Commission to deny broadcast license renewal to Albuquerque station KGGN-TV on several grounds. KGGN gives almost no coverage to the 78,000 Indians in its viewing area, says NIYC; of the station's 76 employees, none are Indians; the station embodies a "lack of involvement" with the two-state Indian community; and it telecasts stereotyped news of the region's Indians, their lives, and in particular their religious ceremonials, charges NIYC. KGGN has a month to reply to the FCC.

*

A BURIAL SITE approximately 5,000 years old has been discovered in Clay County in northern Mississippi. At first lawmen were suspicious that skeletal remains found near Starkville, Miss., indicated foul play, but a Mississippi State professor laid their fears to rest. The site is an ascending knoll soaring above nearby rivers. Study indicates the age-old community had an average lifespan of 30 years, engaged in trading with nearby tribes, and occupied the location continuously for perhaps four millennia.

*

ARIZONA DATSUN DEALERS have trained 15 Apaches, Cherokees, Hopis, Navajos and Papagos in a special two-week course in automotive service and guaranteed employment for those enrolled in the course as service personnel.

*

THE ALCATRAZ TRIBE has now scattered around the country. Among its foremost members, Sioux John Trudell is employed as youth coordinator by Oklahomans for Indian Opportunity (OIO) in Norman, Okla. La Nada Means is working on her own reservation at Ft. Hall, Ida., in the area of individual legal rights against nagging reservation injustices.

*

LAGUNA PUEBLO, one of New Mexico's 19 adobe and sandstone historic pueblo villages, calls its own suburbs which dot major highway arterials such names as Philadelphia, Boston and New York. Uranium discovered and mined in Laguna country provides the puebloans an opportunity to construct new dwellings—and most are choosing the traditional adobe and sandstone, outside of which invariably appear conical ovens for the baking of bread.

*

IN BROOKLYN on Sept. 25, New York City Deputy Mayor Timothy W. Costello dedicated space provided by the city for the first American Indian service center set up on the Eastern Seaboard. Uniquely an urban experience, all the services, facilities and space in the building on 4201 Fourth Ave. at 42nd St. will be made available to all Indian organizations and interested individuals.

*

INDIAN DRAFT RESISTANCE is the topic of a special publication by the Native American Free University at P.O. Box H, Yelm, Wash. 98597. Entitled "Winning the Peace," the special issue (suggested donation is $2.00) focuses on pre-induction and post-induction requests for conscientious objector classification, documents of appeals and supportive contemporary religious statements from several Indian Nations.

*

HANAY GEIOGAMAH, Oklahoma playwright, says he is interested in running for the position of intertribal chairman of the Five Spaced Out Tribes of Oklahoma. That tribal association reportedly is negotiating with the Five Sophisticated Tribes and the Five Paralyzed Tribes in neighboring counties.

*

LOST TRIBES: Has anyone heard lately from the vegetarian Hominies of Wisconsin, or the mysteriously vanished Eeries of New York, or two missing pueblos? One of the missing pueblos is the Yacoma Pueblo of the Pacific Northwest, and the other is the Pueblo de San Marijuana, one of the Seven Cities of Acapulco Gold.

*

NORBERT HILL, an Oneida councilman who is gentlemanly but candid, suggests that the powers-that-be in Washington responsible for the setback of the Commissioner's new Indian team in the Bureau "kiss the south end of an equine quadruped."

REAGAN STATUE COMMITTEE
NATIONAL GALLERY
WASHINGTON, D.C.

Dear Friend:

We have the distinguished honor of being on the committee to raise five million dollars for the placing of a statue of Ronald Reagan in the Hall of Fame in Washington, D.C. We were in a quandary as to where to place the statue. It was not wise to place it beside the statue of George Washington, who never told a lie, nor beside the statue of Richard Nixon, who never told the truth, since Reagan can never tell the difference.

We finally decided to place it beside the statue of Columbus, the greatest Republican of them all. He left not knowing where he was going and upon arriving did not know where he was; he returned not knowing where he had been and he did it all on borrowed money.

If you are one of the fortunate people who has any money left after paying taxes, we will expect you to make a generous donation to this project.

Very sincerely,

Reagan Statue Committee

P.S. It is said that President Reagan is considering having the Republicans change their party emblem from an elephant to a condom because it stands for inflation, protects a bunch of pricks, halts production, and gives a false sense of security while one is being screwed.

Appendix B
Teaching Indi'n Humor

Cultural Worldviews of Native America
"Indi'n Humor"

Kenneth Lincoln   M200B Am. Ind. St.
Rolfe 3127   M266 English
Friday 9-12   ID# 43622
Winter 1991   Office Hours:
                                                        Friday 12-1
                                                        Rolfe 4314

What do American Indians laugh about (today and yesterday)?
What are the ludic details of some 500 cultures indigenous to the United States,
   laughing all the way across the Bering Straits (which direction) some 40,000
   years?
Why is Trickster still kicking? whom? in what forms?
What's funny about contemporary Indian affairs, apart from fiascos?
How is Indian humor a tribal and political tool?
What's comic about pain? history? words, gods, animals (particularly coyote,
   loon, jay, raven, rabbit, deer or spider), priests, lovers, losers, leaders, he-
   roes, and artists?
Where is the hurt in Indian humor, and why? Why does humor help?
How do human beings survive best?

"One of the best ways to understand a people is to know what makes them
   laugh."
                              —Vine Deloria, Jr., *Custer Died For Your Sins*

1/11   Red Humor
           Vine Deloria, Jr., *Custer Died For Your Sins*
           Harry Fonseca's Coyote Series (in-class slides)
1/18   Holy Fool
           Richard Erdoes & John Fire, *Lame Deer Seeker of Visions*
           Rec: Mary Douglas, "The Social Control of Cognition:
               Some Factors in Joke Perception," *Man* 3 (1968): 361–76
1/25   Cultural Mirrors
           Keith Basso, *Portraits of the "Whiteman"*

        Rec: Clifford Geertz, "From the Native's Point of View" in
        Local Knowledge
2/1   "Opposite Thinking"
        Howard Norman, trans., *The Wishing Bone Cycle* (or *The Northern
        Lights*)
        Rec: Paul Radin, "The Nature and Meaning of Myth" in *The Trick-
        ster*
2/8   Code-Switching Poetics
        Luci Tapahonso, *A Breeze Swept Through*
        Rec: Paula Gunn Allen, Intro and "Grandmother of the Sun" in
        Sacred Hoop
2/15 Song-Poetry & Tribal Play
        A. Grove Day, *The Sky Clears*
        Rec: Dennis Tedlock, "The Analogical Tradition. . ." in *The Spo-
        ken Word*
2/22 No Name Blues
        James Welch, *Winter in the Blood*
        Rec: Welch chapter in K. Lincoln, *Native American Renaissance*
3/1   Fem Indi'n Humors
        Louise Erdrich, *Love Medicine*
        Rec: Preface to ppbk. NAR
3/8   Sacred Play
        N. Scott Momaday, *The Ancient Child* or *House Made of Dawn*
        Rec: Momaday chapter in NAR
3/15 Powwow
        Oral Reports on Research
3/18 "All My Relatives"
        Term Papers Due

. . . 15-20 pages of applied ideas and particularized research, generated by
the course readings and discussions, focused on some aspect of Indi'n Humor.
This research could examine a given tribe, a specific region, a given body of
texts, a special set of rituals, a cycle of myths, an analytical problem or approach to Indian cultures (*de*construction?), a chosen author's works, or anything else that stimulates creative and useful thought in the field (cartoons,
political caricatures, "49" songs, parodies—Vincent Craig, John Trudell, T. C.
Cannon, Floyd Westerman, et. al.).

**The course grade will be a combination of each student's discussion,
class presentation, short writing assignments, and (most importantly) term
paper.**

"Humor, all Indians will agree, is the cement by which the coming Indian
movement is held together. When a people can laugh at themselves and laugh at

others and hold all aspects of life together without letting anybody drive them to extremes, then it seems to me that that people can survive."—Vine Deloria, *Custer*

ho!

Recommended readings on reserve:
American Indian Studies Library, 3214 Campbell, Vee Salabiye (Ms. Generokee)

> Johan Huizinga, *Homo Ludens*
> Clifford Geertz, *Local Knowledge*
> Kenneth Lincoln, *Native American Renaissance*
> Selected Essays (Douglas, Radin, Allen, Tedlock, et. al.)

Requirements: a sense of humor, skin "five thumbs thick" (old Iroquois formula for a leader), some intelligence, love for work, and a handful of anticigars. No joking.

Lincoln's Laws:

> Never argue with a fool. People might not know the difference.
> Never play leapfrog with a unicorn.
> A Smith & Wesson beats four aces.
> Anything good in life is either illegal, immoral, or fattening.
> The other line always moves faster.
> The light at the end of the tunnel is the headlamp of an oncoming train.

Appendix C

Interview with Hanay Geiogamah

Geiogamah Interview, July 29, 1988, Los Angeles:

Hanay Geiogamah took an hour away from editing UCLA's *American Indian Culture and Research Journal* to sit at an outdoor cafeteria table on campus and talk with me about his playwriting. A Kiowa born in Oklahoma in 1945, Geiogamah made his mark in 1972 when the La Mama Experimental Theater Club in New York produced *Body Indian,* assisted by Ellen Stewart and starring the American Indian Theater Ensemble.

Hanay is six feet tall and full-bodied, with a healthy expression of bemused surprise. He talks with an actor's sense of crafted animation. Around us mockingbirds struck up occasionally, and the lunch crowd was noisily filtering in, so trays, chairs, and pots were clanging here and there. We had chatted earlier about Indian humor and art, but not about his plays. Three of some dozen are available in *New Native American Drama* (Norman: University of Oklahoma Press, 1980).

KL: Are these Kiowa words in *Body Indian?*

HG: Yes.

KL: And it's supposed to be in Oklahoma?

HG: Yes. In *Body Indian:* Part Two [not in the anthology] they're standing in front of an Oklahoma City mission. They have no money or anything, and they want to get arrested and thrown in jail, so they'll have a place to sleep and something to eat. So these Indi'ns are standin' there actin' like they're drunk. They have enough wine in their little bottle to dab themselves and smell drunk. An' they see a cop car comin', so they start staggering—in order to get in jail.

KL: I have Sioux friends in Nebraska who did that especially in winter—to get a warm meal!

HG: It worked alright on the stage.

KL: You say that there were scenes in *Foghorn* that were cut out?

HG: You see the whole thing was staged as a lobotomy of the projected head. It

326

was really crazy. I'm almost embarrassed to even talk about it [mutual laughter]. It shows how simplistically stupid I was at the time. We wanted to set it on Alcatraz. We wanted it to be a statement of militancy, an expression of "We know what you snake-eyes think of us." So *Foghorn* started out with this little fight scene among the people on Alcatraz, and then this foghorn came on—you know, towards the end the authorities were turning on those foghorns to harass the Indi'ns. So the surrealism took over immediately, and they had this dynamite to blow up the foghorn. There's a black-out scene with this huge head, the big mouth-like thing open. Instead of dynamiting the head, they began to perform a kind of lobotomy on the head; each of those scenes was being removed during the operation. But that was such a cockamaney device that the more I saw it, the sillier it seemed to me, so we just took it all out.

We still had to have some kind of connecting through-line, so we had them start on Alcatraz. We did a choreographed thing that encompassed all of the stuff that had been removed, and did a kind of symbolic thing at the beginning, which is in there now. So the Indi'ns start out on Alcatraz with these visuals that helped them to go into the play—they landed back in America, taking off on Columbus. Remember it starts with Columbus's guide. It worked out that way—ending at Wounded Knee.

KL: Wounded Knee 1973 was going on when you were going to Germany. Did German actors or playwrights work with you?

HG: We met a number of people in the German theater. They were too mesmerized to really talk about anything real we were doing. Everybody said, "This is Brecht."

KL: Did you go over to the Brecht Theater?

HG: They invited us to come to the Berliner Ensemble. They sent a message to us in West Berlin to come there. So we were their guests for a whole day at the theater. We didn't have a workshop, just a visit. We were just like Indi'n bumpkins. These were the ultrasophisticated, Brechtian-actor, ensemble people. They were the real, real, real thing—they knew theater history, many things of classical theater. We were just neophytes, new actors. We weren't really equipped to have the kind of dialogue or exchange that we could now. If that happened now, I certainly would be more versed in Brecht. But I knew some of him.

KL: Before we had this conversation, I was guessing that you had been over to the Brecht Theater. I think *Foghorn* has a surreal sense of play, hilarity, the jokes, all with a cultural and political context.

HG: Well I had read some Brecht. There was a person named Wilford Leach, who was the artistic director at La Mama, a professor at Sarah Lawrence. He was helping me in the early stages of our development of *Foghorn*. He was staging it for us. Leach helped me understand the Brechtian applications that were coming into the play. That whole kind of attitude—it's almost an attitude more than anything really real, or actually happening. I read the Martin Esslin book on Brecht [*Brecht, The Man and His Work* (1960)] about that time. Mainly I paid attention to the chapter in there called "The Brechtian Theater," which talked about how he uses all the alienation devices. I was in my mid-twenties—more involved in the hustle of getting a theater together, rather than absorbing this kind of thing. I realized, intuitively felt, that what was really interesting about Brecht was the attitude, rather than having the titles go across the stage—everything that constitutes that alienation thing seemed corny to me.

KL: You put in directions saying it should be played gaily and with a light effect, so that the seriousness will find its own way through. That's very Brechtian, such as *Threepenny Opera* music—a kind of celebration, at the same time there are real hard things to deal with here.

HG: Yeah, that's the same thing as with *Body Indian*. The whole thing with humor. . . . I was thinking about this last night, after I read over your précis for the *Indi'n Humor* manuscript. I was trying to pull out—the same thing that you were doing. It's like humor is such a pervasive thing, and yet it's evasive for Indi'ns. An interesting thing happened to me as a just-beginning-to-function-artist-person: I realized the incredible power of humor. Before that I had just been a Kiowa person growing up. From the humor point of view, the Kiowas have a very, very rich sense of humor, very complete, very satirical, very scatological, very screwball, loony, and yet all somehow controlled. You go around Kiowas, like you go to our fair, and you get around a bunch of Kiowas, and they're always laughing, always laughing.

KL: Is Saynday the trickster behind that?

HG: Well, I think that the Kiowas are likely aware of Saynday, but not so much in a formalistic sense. I think you can informally believe that there's a little bit of Saynday in you, without there being some kind of holy stuff, or spiritual stuff, or anything like that. You know, coyote's in me, or something . . . with the Kiowa thing, you say that you've got some Saynday in you. But you understand what they mean—all Kiowas have some Saynday in them.

KL: And all actors.

HG: Oh definitely, Dionysius and Saynday definitely are related. All this humor was just loose, all this humor was just blowing into the air, very little direct, formalistic use. But then, when I did *Body Indian*, I just sat down and wrote *Body Indian*. I had to write a play. I knew what I wanted to write about. I pushed it to the limit—I delayed writing until I absolutely *had* to write the play.

I was working for Louis Bruce at the BIA at that time. It was two days before I had to take the script up to New York, and I said, "I have to write this damn play, I have to do it." So I sat down at my typewriter and I wrote most of it in one burst. It's not that long. The process was immediate. I found this out later: when you try to be funny, it's not. When it's really happening, then there it is, the humor comes on intact. At the time I didn't know I was writing anything funny. I'm writing this [lowers his voice conspiratorially] *pronunciamento* on alcoholism and Indi'ns workin' each other over. I had seen a lot of that in the BIA. I had seen Indi'ns functioning in many ways as their own enemy, screwin' each other, so I understood the metaphor that I was going with. I had no idea that it would work. I had no idea of the humor that was just there in a situation, whether I saw it as humor or not.

So we got the play rehearsed—it wasn't coming' off as funny. It was just us—nobody to react off of it. We all thought that we were doing a big tragedy. We were playing it that way. So then we got it into La Mama. The place was just packed with Indi'ns. From the very thing when that lady gets up off the bed, "Achhh," people just started laughing and laughing and laughing—

KL: So the audience recast your play?

HG: Yeah, the audience laughed all the way through the crazy thing. And I was standing with Ellen Stewart, scared for other reasons as well [whispers]: "They're not 'sposed to be laughing. It's not 'sposed to be funny." They kept laughing, then I cooled off and realized these laugh lines that were there, zinging. Then it got *un*funny, toward the end it just stopped—

KL: With the leg?

HG: Yes, when all that started there was no more laughing—after Howard tells the story of the D.T. chickens in the jail. When the story stopped, the laughing stopped, and they all realized what's happened. It's like it all came together. I said to myself, "I really have to try to figure this out." I didn't think it was a comedy. I wasn't sophisticated enough at the time to understand what comedy is, such a complex thing, fabulously complex. I realized that I had written a tragicomedy, and the comedy part was really comic. So, I started backin' off on it and tryin' to figure out what the hell I had done.

KL: Why do you think there is laughter where you didn't expect there to be? What were you touching that you didn't even know?

HG: I thought that I was just writing about an alcoholic setting. I guess for me all the humor had gone out of that—out of my experiences and my trafficking in the alcoholic aspects of life. It would sometimes cease to be funny to me. I had sometime since stopped finding the humor in it, or seeing that there was anything funny about this. I was writing a serious play, but the whole humor was in something unknown to me.

KL: Freud thinks that laughter means you can handle a situation: I understand it, it's real, it hurts, but I refuse to be defeated by it, in fact, I'll *play* it out.

HG: Yeah, I think all of that is encompassed in *Body Indian*. Then later, when I was able to talk to people who had seen the play, they had to laugh 'cause it was one of the only ways they could deal with the play itself. That play was just so damn graphic it was just really . . . it was staged to the graphic max, just horrifying, absolutely incredible, a horrifying-looking play, just a mind-blowing thing.

KL: Did you take any heat from Indi'ns for going that far?

HG: Oh, yeah, but for myself I was prepared for that. I was aware, even at that younger age, that there's always gonna be some Indi'ns that are gonna attack you, always, always. I did not feel that when the play apparently presented itself as a success, I didn't feel that I had to apologize for anything. I realized that there were just real problems, real things with Indi'ns that needed to be brought to their attention—

KL: —people weren't talkin' about it—

HG: —the hypocrisy that Indi'n brotherhood, Indi'n love, all this Indi'n kind of thing . . . to me was a hypocrisy that I felt very strongly about, 'cause I had seen it, experienced it, and believed in every part of my mind and my heart that it was a real thing. The really pernicious part was that so many Indi'ns did it without really knowing it, without really understanding what they were doing to each other. So that conviction helped me to deal with the few people who were critical of the play, but there were only a few, not that many. It didn't become a problem for the company.

KL: Have you ever performed *Body Indian* on reservations?

HG: Oh, yeah, we even debated whether the kids on reservations could come to it. The kids loved it just as much as anybody else. They understood at their own level what was going on. I don't think that they understood the symbolic inner workings of the leg, all that kind of thing, the railroad— They actually weren't able to translate those metaphorical implications, but they could feel what was there.

KL: Horrible things like the railroad tragedy happened to Pine Ridge Sioux when I was a kid. Or maggots in a man's leg wounds when he was dead drunk. Tragicomic situations seem to draw the line: either we can push on the Wounded Knee pain, keep sucking on the tragedy, or turn it around, which seems to be what this play's doing. Turn it around so people look at it. What about the stage directions just before the end? You say Bobby turns with a "sardonic smile." How do you read that? It seems to me the play's final icon.

HG: Yeah, he's face-down, and it's almost like a jack-in-the-box that pops up. It's like the smile on a clown, a painted-on smile. The clown is a figure of humor and mirth, but you look at the clown and you see that it's just something that is there. By that point all his feelings and everything are completely choked and parched out of him. When a lot of Indi'ns are at that point of extreme exposure, they smile. I don't know if you've ever seen that happen.

KL: Yeah, I have seen it, and it's not just Indians. They say it happens when people are hung or tortured to death—a final grimace, *risus sardonicus* doctors call it. It's defiance of one's own suffering, refusal, in some way—

HG: Yeah, also too, jus' keeping going— Bobby realizes that he let this happen to him.

KL: He's taking responsibility.

HG: Yeah, he's taking responsibility for himself. It's a smile that—sort of like inward and outward as well.

KL: The pained smile is some kind of understanding that the play is trying to bring through here: now you *see*. It's a ground zero for Indi'n humor, a choice to start exercising options, or it's all over.

HG: Yeah, alright, and that's where he's at. He's clean now, he's been cleaned out, cleansed, with no Christian iconography or anything. It's just clean, it's over, start over. So he says hello to himself, there's nobody else there for him.

KL: Take it down to the bottom, where counselors talk about tough love.

HG: Also, too, in that there's a certain kind of commonplace, at least for me— it wasn't like some intellectually removed concept or some attitude. I knew all of those people. All Indi'ns know those people. The situation is right there, or it was in '73. It's not necessarily removed. So with that, the tragedies of your life, you can even joke at them, you can laugh at them, you can try to get something humorous out of them. It's part of the arsenal that you can draw from the tribal thing. Accept it.

KL: Why do you think you felt the dark humor at that time, with Wounded Knee going on in '72–'73, and the ultra high serious, the Russell Means syndrome—warriors and all that? I sense something else here—an ability to play with and to caricature one's own, as a way to bring tribal people to their senses without having to die.

HG: Yeah, if Russell had to die, he wouldn't like it, you know. Those poor people that got killed at Wounded Knee martyred themselves for a fifty percent cause, a half-baked, inchoate cause. The whole thing was to me unnecessary, the way that they zealously let it get out of control. I think that Indi'ns always have the capacity to look at themselves. Indi'ns know themselves, and that's part of the sardonic thing that's in Bobby Lee's life. They know what the hell they're doin', what they're capable of, and they know their weaknesses, they know their strengths. The part where they fail themselves is in knowing their strengths. They haven't grasped how to activate them in this terribly new world the past four hundred years, at least not in the right kind of way—instead of *mis*activiating them in the sense of militancy, and racism, reverse racism, and blame, blame, blame. Of course we've lived through a tragedy, there's no doubt about that, but the capacity to renew oneself, and to heal oneself, and to take care of oneself is always there, always has been there.

KL: How about in the obverse way of that, the sense of keeping the good times going, which seems to be a theme of the 49s and powwows. In a way, Indi'n humor or "good times" can translate into alcoholism.

HG: That's the lack of control, the lack of a formalistic sense of responsibility. You can only go so far, instead of being driven to it—casually speeding—let it all hang out, go, go, go, go, go. I think that excessiveness is something particular to the contemporary Indi'n character that wasn't there before.

KL: In the trickster stuff, there's an argument that trickster plays out the crazy stuff, breaks all the rules to show the rules. I theoretically understand that, but I'm not sure in practice just how it works.

HG: Yeah, we came up with some of that when we dealt with *Coon Cons Coyote* [Melville Jacobs's translated Nez Perce tale] which is in the original *Shaking the Pumpkin* anthology. We just took that and staged it. I went through a lot of other coyote stuff to strengthen that coyote, and just rejected all of it, the more graphic stuff. There was no way that you could stage that, without getting accused of being sensationalist, or just doing this bawdiness for the sake of it. You know, there was this vaginal blood and all that, an awful lot of it, especially in the plateau coyotes. That excessiveness in the stories themselves, the tales that had been handed down, could not come into the theater. We did not think that that was something that could cross over into the theater. I mean, yes, we could do the farting, some comic bestial sodomy, because all of that is like in the satyr plays of Aristophanes and other works. But some of it was just not, just wouldn't go—wouldn't go in '73 when we first did that, and it still won't go.

KL: Did you hear bawdy trickster stories when you were growing up?

HG: No, no.

KL: I've always wondered about the authenticity of those parts.

HG: The Kiowa would not ever tell them—just now and then, when there were the boys, guys, something even approaching pornographic.

KL: People wonder why Momaday never brought Saynday into his work.

HG: They moved him out of Oklahoma at an early age. Saynday lives around Carnegie and Hobart, and he doesn't really live out there in New Mexico. Somebody else lives out there, his brother or sister—

KL: Striped *Koshares* [sharp laughter]. I mentioned before the theater of the '60s, Kopit, Marquis de Sade, and Brecht. Given a Euroamerican setting in

Berlin to do *Foghorn,* what makes this peculiarly or particularly Indi'n, as opposed to stuff that Europeans were already seeing?

HG: I think I understand that: it's the way we do it. The whole thing was performed with Indi'n actors, forms and styles we have codified to some extent. All acting is basic for everybody, vocal projection and all of that. There are universals that apply to everybody. But there are also things that apply to Indi'ns. There are things that you can do with your body, your voice, your timing, your expression that are universal within the Indi'n world. It's like Jewish shtick, Jewish humor. An Indi'n guy couldn't successfully do a Jewish comedy thing. There are things about it that are Jewish and give it its Jewish humor spin. The same with Indi'n actors. So you can do Brecht, you can do any kind of theatrical thing, you Indianize it.

KL: Is it like the lip thing Siouxs do?

HG: Yeah, all of that, body gestures, lip gesturing. You will recognize and understand almost all of it, how these things incorporate themselves into a rehearsal process.

KL: With the dozen people or so in the troupe, do they interplay, interact, add lines? You just get them going, so it's very much a group creativity?

HG: That's the way *49* was. I just wrote the script.

KL: *49* seems to be up-beat in the three anthologized plays. It's as though the anthology comes through to the singing and dancing Indian-style as celebrating, as 49s and powwows are.

HG: There's some hard shit in *49* too. The girl gets killed, the cops. There's some sad things there, that poor little guy runnin' around not really knowing the songs. . . .

KL: But it seems an Indi'n resistance, in the sense of Indi'n unity defying the cops, as though that is what they're gonna hang on to.

HG: That just comes straight from the 49 in Oklahoma City or Anadarko. All one had to do was attend 49s and see this shit happen, then just work it so you can stage it. All that—I've seen the police come in with helicoptors, police dogs, overkill, sheriffs. You'll notice that in all those plays there's a kind of control thing, Night Walker, and in *Foghorn* too—something manipulative which to me is like the Indi'n . . . however rowdy and raucous Indi'ns are, there's always some control thing going deep within. And that umbilical control line also attaches itself to the humor as well. So you can see the excessiveness of Indi'n humor, but very rarely will you see it go completely wacko, sicko.

KL: Do you think that's a part of a tribal identity?

HG: Yeah, keepin' you attached to the tribal thing. I cannot make too terribly much of a fool of myself. I can be goofy, bawdy, kookoo, and all this other stuff, and some people will think of me as witty and funny, but I cannot go too far, all the way out. Like Lenny Bruce pushes all the way over. Indi'ns have their inner control thing (this is my theory, probably mostly bullshit) but it's like for myself, sometimes I let myself just be too sensitive. I'll say something too excessive, or else it's misunderstood. And I become very sensitive when I do that. When it's not funny to the other person, you come off as being hard, cold, cruel.

KL: Do you know the phrase "permitted disrespect" from Mary Douglas?

HG: Yeah.

KL: She's arguing that in tribal situations where we know each other, especially in family situations, that teasing is a way of exploring and establishing boundaries. We permit that license. But Keith Basso in *Portraits of the "Whiteman"* cites Apaches about the point where the comic buckskin breaks—

HG: Indi'ns are very, very good at intuitively sensing when they're nearing that breaking point. So there's an eternal dignity to it, eternal, that attaches itself to the tribal identity. That force keeps you from going over. At the same time you can watch stuff like that and people love it. You can take the humor and use it as something purposeful and useful and instructive and helpful, but you have to learn how to do it.

KL: The other side to that, the debit side, would be a kind of Indi'n red pride that would keep people from talking about things—hard, stiff, nonresilient. I've seen people back home who've gone through so much trouble that they lose it up here in the head. They just can't laugh.

HG: That's one of the saddest things to see the Indi'ns who can't laugh. I've always thought that a lot of those people have been somehow BIAized, or they work for Indi'n health, or somebody conned them about what "really" matters in life, and they forgot. They let go of that innate Indi'n sense in life that not everything is serious, dead-on. There are some parts in life where you can have fun, otherwise then what the hell is it all about? An' you can see the Indi'ns who have had it blanched out of them. That's sad, very sad; humorless people anywhere are sad people. Now there's an inverted kind of humor—

KL: Contrary kind of stuff, where you turn it around, talk upside-down, talk back?

HG: Yeah, that inverted humor is the one that's hot right now. You have to be careful with that warrior stuff.

KL: In terms of where you've come over fifteen years, have you been writing more?

HG: Yeah, I have a whole new collection to be published, a musical comedy called *War Dancers,* which is really, really funny, I think. Reading it, I giggle and laugh at it. I became less afraid, I should say, of comedy, and realized that there are limitations and you have to understand them and not be so afraid of them that you are gingerly going around on tiptoes. You can't do that, there has to be spontaneity, or else you're writing jokes, a Neil Simon kind of thing.

KL: Do you think in terms of the social, historical crises of the '60s and early '70s, that the urgency of that behind us may free you up to play, in a sense that this is play that will be more liberating?

HG: Yeah, I've thought about that. Now what can I do?

KL: I thought in *Foghorn* when the actors finally got to the Wild West Show with the peace pipe song, the 1943 "Pass the Peace Pipe," that it must have been like a chorus line.

HG: That really was, it was just absolute—

KL: That's kind of the peak of the play?

HG: Yeah, then the surrealism comes in at Wounded Knee in being arrested—

KL: But the idea of pure song and dance in the play, celebration of being together—

HG: That's the high point, it just breaks loose. The audience loved *Foghorn*. The actors would really get into it. We'd turn the sound up just as loud as we could without breaking the limits. We had the visuals as big as we could magnified in zoom reverse. Everything was just wild, absolutely wild, and it got wilder and wilder. It doesn't matter whether the structure of the play is ramshackle or not. That's what was going on.

KL: One thing I came to this morning was about the oral tradition, as it were (if I could ever figure out what that meant). It never did depend on the holy script, as writing does, but on improvisational play and creativity. The energy released by people playing is not even verbal. Words are some of it, but a lot simply turns on bodies dancing to musical tones.

HG: Yeah, that found its way into the actors. They were doing it in a subliminal manner when they got to impersonate Lady Bird Johnson or the Lone Ranger—the animation that you would see them giving to these things was just a buoyancy you would see coming out. I think a lot of Indi'ns identified with roles in the play—it's just such a compendium of silly little stereotypes. I think vicariously a lot of Indi'ns were playing the Lone Ranger, along with the actors, playing the First Lady, playing that nun, playing the school-teacher. Once again, the hardest scene, the cruelest scene is the schoolteacher scene, and the audience just laughed, and laughed, and laughed. She couldn't hardly get her lines out. That was just recognition.

KL: So with all this, how would you try to boil down the term Indi'n humor? The tribal norms of play, the present sense of pain?

HG: I see the Indi'n capacity for humor as a blessing. And I see it as one of the fundamental miracles of our lives. It's a miraculous thing that's pulled us through so much. It's a force that's part of religion. I don't see religion so much as just being our bundles or our prayers. It's everything from the past that we've brought forward with us, our memories, ancestors, especially that, all of these things are religion to me—singing, dancing, stories, suffering, all of that. And respect and caring for each other. So in that sense humor is definitely a part of religion. I truly believe that the older Indi'ns laughed, and laughed, and laughed. I remember my dad's maternal grandfather with a big, bellowing Kiowa laugh—so I know that they laughed. However hard their lives were, there always had to be something funny. You've always got to try to balance everything, know where that factor fits into the way that you conduct your life.

KL: So this may have been something in terms of survival? pre-white? ancient?

HG: Oh, yeah, otherwise why bother? What the hell do you want to live for if you can't laugh? I wouldn't want to live if I couldn't laugh. I've tried to experience all kinds of humor, you know, black humor, sardonic humor, Jewish humor. It's all basically the same thing—touching on survival. Survival means your life, and your life is your religion. It's all there, not a God like that up there, I don't believe that. And I don't think that the old Indi'ns believed in that sense.

KL: So jokes are like skewed prayers bringing things back down?

HG: Yeah, and the people who do them, the priests, are the keepers of that faith. And unfortunately not every Indi'n has a sense of humor, an operative sense of humor; but I think that all understand what is being laughed about or joked with or treated humorously. They all understand, though they may have lost their capacity to respond. I wish everybody could read the Joseph Campbell treatise on religion—his whole idea of religion is so affirming in artic-ulating what I had instinctively intuited.

KL: Are there clown priests among Kiowa?

HG: No, not like Sioux *heyokas.* The most recent keeper of our medicine bundles, the ten grandmothers, now nine (one of them burned up in a house)—he was the most religiously significant person in our tribe. This old man was the principle keeper of six grandmother medicine bundles in his house, a power-packed place; yet this man understood, he was completely responsible, aware of his duties, functions, responsibilities to the tribe. This is how I try to understand and accept it; he was aware of every tragedy, every silliness. He had a capacity for laughing, giggling, every old Indi'n joke, self-stereotype, that laughing concept, he was aware of all of it. He knew that Indi'ns could make fun of having lice, commodities, beat-up cars, being thrown in jail, and drunkenness and laziness, all of these things. And at the same time he had the responsibility for maintaining the dignity, the harmony, all— He made no big deal out it. That was one of the fundamental things I've learned in my life, from knowing this man—he didn't make a big deal out of everything. No Crow Dog type of Indi'n myths, I have this property, or this right. The old man was totally unpretentious. Totally . . . humble. And yet with the profound capability to understand all of this. He didn't bat an eye.

KL: A good actor?

HG: He didn't bat an eye. So to me it's like a small miracle if you can bring laughter into somewhere, it's a blessing.

Notes

(Pre)amble

1. *Los Angeles Times,* Sunday Calendar, 20 May 1990.
2. John Lowe, "Theories of Ethnic Humor," *American Quarterly* 38 (1986): 449.
3. Larry Wilde, *The Complete Book of Ethnic Humor* (Los Angeles: Pinnacle Books, 1978), 18, 25.
4. Julian Steward, "The Ceremonial Buffoon of the American Indian," *Papers of the Michigan Academy of Science, Arts, and Letters* 14 (1931): 187–207.
5. James Howard, "The Dakota Heyoka Cult," *Scientific Monthly* 78 (April 1954): 254–58.
6. Gary Witherspoon, *Language and Art in the Navajo Universe* (Ann Arbor: University of Michigan Press, 1977), 184.
7. Paula Gunn Allen, letter to author, 29 February 1988.
8. Clifford Geertz, *Local Knowledge: Further Essays in Interpretive Anthropology* (New York: Basic Books, 1983), 70.
9. This pronunciation may have something to do with a relative absence of double vowel structures in Native American languages (Paul Kroskrity, October 1988).
10. Wsevolod W. Isajiw, "Definitions of Ethnicity," *Ethnicity* 1 (1974): 111–24.
11. Anthony Mattina, *The Golden Woman: The Colville Narrative of Peter J. Seymour,* trans. Anthony Mattina and Madeline de Sautel (Tucson: University of Arizona Press, 1985), 9. The introductory materials are reprinted in Mattina, "North American Indian Mythography: Editing Texts for the Printed Page," in *Recovering the Word: Essays on Native American Literature,* ed. Brian Swann and Arnold Krupat (Berkeley and Los Angeles: University of California Press, 1987).
12. Henry Louis Gates, Jr., has some postmodernist things to say about African-American "signifyin(g)" *difference* in *The Signifying Monkey: A Theory of African-American Literary Criticism* (New York: Oxford University Press, 1988).
13. Charles L. Woodard, *Ancestral Voice: Conversations with N. Scott Momaday* (Lincoln: University of Nebraska Press, 1989), 112–13.
14. John (Fire) Lame Deer and Richard Erdoes, *Lame Deer, Seeker of Visions: The Life of a Sioux Medicine Man* (New York: Simon and Shuster, 1972), 45.
15. Charles Berlitz, *Native Tongues* (New York: Putnam, 1982), 314.
16. John Wideman, "The Black Writer and the Magic of the Word," *New York Times Book Review,* 24 January 1988, 28.
17. Toni Morrison, "Unspeakable Things Unspoken: The Afro-American Presence in American Literature," *Michigan Quarterly Review* 28 (Winter 1989): 11.
18. Toni Morrison, *The Bluest Eye* (New York: Holt, Rhinehart and Winston, 1970), 45.
19. Hanay Geiogamah, *New Native American Drama: Three Plays* (Norman: University of Oklahoma Press, 1980), 7.

20. Leslie Silko, "Language and Literature from a Pueblo Indian Perspective," in *English Literature: Opening Up the Canon*, ed. Leslie A. Fiedler and Houston A. Baker (Baltimore: Johns Hopkins University Press, 1981), 71.

21. William Leap at American University has been investigating the intercultural sociolinguistics of pidgin American Indian languages. See his *Papers in Southwestern English: Studies in Southwestern Indian English* (San Antonio: Trinity University, 1977) and *Language Renewal among American Indian Tribes: Issues, Problems, and Prospects* (Roslyn, Va.: National Clearinghouse for Bilingual Education, 1982), edited with Robert N. St. Clair. Richard and Mary Jo Malancon write on 1915 Indian English spoken at Haskell Institute: "The English spoken by many American Indians in the United States differs from standard English expression in specific and demonstrable ways. Descriptive research has shown that Indian English is not a single language variety but a set of varieties each using English vocabulary but operating off of an Indian language structural base" (Leap, *Studies* 143).

22. N. Scott Momaday, *House Made of Dawn* (New York: Harper Perennial, 1977, 104–5.

23. Vincent Crapanzano, *The Fifth World of Forster Bennett: Portrait of a Navajo* (New York: Viking, 1972), 83.

24. In a related cultural context, "black speech is not simply faulty English," Wideman adds, "but a witness to a much deeper fault, a crack running below the surface, a fatal flaw in the forms and pretensions of so-called civilized language" ("Black Writer" 28).

25. Frank Marcus, Taos Pueblo fire chief, quoted in Nancy Wood, *Taos Pueblo* (New York: Knopf, 1989), 41.

Chapter 1

1. The most engaging tribal people I've known laugh the heartiest—Al Logan Slagle (Cherokee), Mark Monroe (Lakota), Paula Gunn Allen (Laguna Pueblo), Alfonso Ortiz (San Juan Pueblo), Vee Salabiye (Navajo), Vine Deloria, Jr. (Lakota), Duane Champagne (Turtle Mountain Chippewa), Hanay Geiogamah (Kiowa), Mike Kabotie (Hopi), Barney Bush (Shawnee–Cayuga), Harry Fonseca (Maidu), Rebecca Tsosie (Yaqui). The Lone Wolf and Monroe families, originally from Pine Ridge and Rosebud Sioux Reservations, now Alliance, Nebraska (and now many more surnames and extended families), took me in as a kinsman to share their hurt and humor—Grandpa "Buffalo" Bill, Lulu and the irrepressible George Lone Wolf (our local *heyoka*), the two Connies, Butch, Mark, and all the cousins and kids. The Sioux medicine men Dawson No Horse, John Fire, and Lawrence Antoine were some of the wisest stand-up clowns I've known. Jenny Lone Wolf of my hometown served Indian people as a family healer through her eighties, a quietly powerful woman of humor. Grandma Jenny gave me good reason to laugh at myself and with her many families. Like her "took-in" grandson, Sonny Boy, I was encouraged to feel at home, despite the ethnic handicap.

2. Vine Deloria, Jr., *Custer Died For Your Sins: An Indian Manifesto* (New York: Macmillan, 1969), 167.

3. Cited in Robert D. Pelton, *The Trickster in West Africa: A Study of Mythic Irony and Sacred Delight* (Berkeley and Los Angeles: University of California Press, 1980).

4. Constance Rourke, *American Humor: A Study of the National Character* (1931; Garden City, N.Y.: Doubleday, 1953).

5. "Let Us Examine the Facts," in *Native American Testimony, An Anthology of Indian and White Relations: First Encounter to Dispossession*, ed. Peter Nabokov (1978; New York: Harper & Row, 1979), 153–55. This collection as a whole best illustrates the range of American Indian oratory "at the forest's edge," though a reader could draw from several dozen others.

6. Greg Sarris, "The Verbal Art of Mabel McKay," (Ph.D. diss., Stanford University, 1989).

7. UCLA sociologist Duane Champagne, personal conversation, spring 1988.

8. Alicia Suskin Ostriker, *Stealing the Language: The Emergence of Women's Poetry in America* (Boston: Beacon Press, 1986).

9. Hélène Cixous, "The Scene of the Unconscious," in *The Future of Literary Theory*, ed. Ralph Cohen (New York: Routledge, 1989), 12.

10. Max Eastman, *The Sense of Humor* (New York: Scribner, 1921), 20.

11. Janet Cliff, UCLA doctoral student in folklore and mythology, brought this intercultural gaming text to my attention in her study of Navajo gambling. See her 1990 doctoral dissertation, "Lucidity: A Model for Understanding Play and Games." Also see her "Navajo Games," *American Indian Culture and Research Journal* 14 (1990): 1–81.

12. Arthur Koestler, *Insight and Outlook: An Inquiry into the Common Foundations of Science, Art, and Social Ethics* (New York: Macmillan, 1949), xiii, 38.

13. Northrop Frye, *Anatomy of Criticism* (Princeton, N.J.: Princeton University Press, 1957), 172.

14. Leslie Silko, "Language and Literature from a Pueblo Indian Perspective," in *English Literature: Opening Up the Canon*, ed. Leslie A. Fiedler and Houston A. Baker, Jr. (Baltimore: Johns Hopkins University Press, 1981), 70.

15. Laura Coltelli, "Interview with Leslie Marmon Silko," in *Winged Words: American Indian Writers Speak*, ed. Laura Coltelli (Lincoln: University of Nebraska Press, 1990), 146–47.

16. We "see" to "know" the humorous twists in things, as in the etymological daisy chain woven by Koestler: English "wit" < German *wissen* or to "know" < Old English *witan* or to "know" < Latin *videre* or to "see" and Greek *eidon* or "saw" < and Sanskrit *Veda* or sacred "knowledge" (*IO* 15).

17. "Interview with Jim Pepper," *Caliban* 5 (1988): 167.

18. Sigmund Freud, *Jokes and Their Relationship to the Unconscious*, trans. and ed. James Strachey (New York: Norton, 1960), 14.

19. Michel Foucault, *The Order of Things: An Archaeology of the Human Sciences* (New York: Vintage Books, 1970), 72.

20. Barbara Babcock, "Ritual Undress and the Comedy of Self and Other," in *A Crack in the Mirror: Reflexive Perspectives in Anthropology*, ed. Jay Ruby (Philadelphia: University of Pennsylvania Press, 1982), 187–203.

21. Stephen Trimble, "Brown Earth and Laughter: The Clay People of Nora Naranjo-Morse," *American Indian Art Magazine* 12 (Autumn 1987): 58–65.

22. See Barbara Babcock, Guy Monthan, and Doris Monthan, *The Pueblo Storyteller* (Tucson: University of Arizona Press, 1986).

23. Dennis Tedlock, *The Spoken Word and the Work of Interpretation* (Philadelphia: University of Pennsylvania Press, 1983), 329–31.

24. The conventional formula for a right triangle's hypoteneuse configurates as $\sqrt{3^2 + 4^2} = \sqrt{5^2}$. Since the square root of 3 represents the first numerical "surd" or radical (indivisible) number, the equation cannot be reduced to root particles. By definition and application, the formula must remain combinational or bisociational—that is, parallel structures with squared, then "rooted" results. There is a certain playful kind of poetic form in such an equation: all to say, by way of experiential methodology and extended metaphor, that context determines text, as wave pattern shapes particle in position. A given minim of any joke is meaningless out of sequential context, or so Mary Douglas extends Freud to show the cultural continuum of a given joke.

25. Vine Deloria, Jr., letter to author, 16 June 1988.

26. See Friedrich Nietzsche, *The Gay Science: With a Prelude in Rhymes and an Appendix of Songs*, trans. Walter Kaufmann (1882; New York: Random House, 1974).

27. Barbara Babcock, "Arrange Me into Disorder: Fragments and Reflections on Ritual Clowning," in *Rite, Drama, Festival, Spectacle*, ed. John J. MacAloon (Philadelphia: University of Pennsylvania Press, 1984).

28. Hayden White, *Metahistory: The Historical Imagination in Nineteenth-Century Europe* (Baltimore: Johns Hopkins University Press, 1973).

29. Julia Kristeva, *Tales of Love*, trans. Leon S. Roudiez (New York: Columbia University Press, 1987), 73.

30. Georges Bataille, *Guilty*, trans. Bruce Boone (San Francisco: Lapis Press, 1988), 95.

31. Julia Kristeva, *The Kristeva Reader*, ed. Toril Moi (New York: Columbia University Press, 1986), 50.

32. Julia Kristeva, "The Pain of Sorrow in the Modern World: The Works of Marguerite Duras," *PMLA* 102 (March 1987): 138–52.

33. Hélène Cixous and Catherine Clement, *The Newly Born Woman*, trans. Betsy Wing (Minneapolis: University of Minnesota Press, 1986), 33.

34. Thomas E. Mails, *Fools Crow* (Garden City, N.Y.: Doubleday, 1979), 8.

35. Sigmund Freud, "Humour," *International Journal of Psychology* 9 (1928): 1–6.

36. Don C. Talayesva, *Sun Chief: The Autobiography of a Hopi Indian*, ed. Leo W. Simmons (New Haven, Conn.: Yale University Press, 1942), 41.

37. William Hazlitt, "On Wit and Humor," quoted in Paul Cline, *Fools, Clowns, and Jesters* (La Jolla, Calif.: Green Tiger Press, 1983), 33.

38. Stanley Vestal, "The Works of Sitting Bull: Real and Imaginary," *Southwest Review* 19 (April 1934): 265–77.

39. Stanley Vestal, *Sitting Bull: Champion of the Sioux. A Biography* (1932; Norman: University of Oklahoma Press, 1956), 240–41.

Chapter 2

1. Sigmund Freud, "Humour," *International Journal of Psychology* 9 (1928): 6.

2. Wallace H. Black Elk and William S. Lyon, *Black Elk: The Sacred Ways of a Lakota* (San Francisco: Harper & Row, 1990), 48.

3. John (Fire) Lame Deer and Richard Erdoes, *Lame Deer, Seeker of Visions: The Life of a Sioux Medicine Man* (New York: Simon and Schuster, 1972), 19.

4. Mary Douglas, "The Social Control of Cognition: Some Factors in Joke Perception," *Man* 3 (1968): 361–76.

5. J. Anthony Paredes, letter to author, 17 February 1988.

6. "So Says Buffy Sainte-Marie" (interview by Leroy Woodson, Jr.), *Los Angeles Times Magazine*, 20 April 1986, 20.

7. Geoffrey H. Hartman, "The State of the Art of Criticism," in *The Future of Literary Theory*, ed. Ralph Cohen (New York: Routledge, 1989), 100.

8. Joseph Epes Brown, "The Wisdom of the Contrary: A Conversation with Joseph Epes Brown," *Parabola* 4 (February 1979): 57.

9. "The Great Vision," in *Black Elk Speaks: Being the Life Story of a Holy Man of the Oglala Sioux*, trans. John Neihardt (1932; New York: Pocket Books, 1972).

10. Geoff Sanborn, "Unfencing the Range: History, Identity, Property, and Apocalypse in *Lame Deer, Seeker of Visions*," *American Indian Culture and Research Journal* 14 (1990): 39–57.

11. Richard Erdoes to Geoff Sanborn, 8 April 1991, *American Indian Culture and Research Journal* 15 (1991/1992): 163–165.

12. Barbara A. Babcock, "Introduction," *The Reversible World: Symbolic Inversion in Art and Society*, ed. Barbara A. Babcock (Ithaca, N.Y.: Cornell University Press, 1978), 14.

13. Victor Turner, *Forest of Symbols* (Ithaca, N.Y.: Cornell University Press, 1967), 184.

14. Frances Densmore, *Teton Sioux Music*, Smithsonian Institution Bureau of American Ethnology, Bulletin 61 (Washington, D.C.: 1918; New York: Da Capo Press, 1972), 158.

15. Johan Huizinga, *Homo Ludens: A Study of the Play-Element in Culture* (1938; Boston: Beacon Press, 1955), 28.

16. Martin Heidegger, in *On the Way to Language* (1959: New York: Harper & Row, 1971), traces such "playful thinking" back to Hermes, the winged messenger as god of science, eloquence, and cunning, from whom we derive hermeneutics, or techniques of interpretation.

17. Sigmund Freud, *Jokes and Their Relationship to the Unconscious*, trans. and ed. James Strachey (New York: Norton, 1960).

18. Jean Lande, "Paul Klee," in *"Primitivism" in Twentieth Century Art: Affinity of the Tribal and the Modern*, ed. William Rubin (New York: Museum of Modern Art, 1985), 2:487.

Chapter 3

1. Rayna Green, "Playing Indian: An American Obsession" (Lecture delivered at University of California, Los Angeles, 4 May 1987).

2. Cf. William Carlos Williams's mythic seeds of American history, *In the American Grain*, 2nd ed. (New York: New Directions, 1956).

3. Harper & Row in June 1988 contracted with Louise Erdrich and Michael Dorris for a story about a Columbus manuscript rediscovered by an Indian heroine. On the promise of a five-page outline, Erdrich and Dorris sold the idea of a novel to be published in 1990

and netted $1.5 million, with a $750,000 advance, according to news reports. *The Crown of Columbus* was published in April 1991.

4. Keith H. Basso, *Portraits of "The Whiteman": Linguistic Play and Cultural Symbols Among the Western Apache* (Cambridge: Cambridge University Press, 1979), 46–47.

5. Bill Hess, "A Navajo Laughs," *Nations* 1 (1981): 18.

6. Keith H. Basso, " 'Stalking with Stories': Names, Places and Moral Narratives among the Western Apache," in *Text, Play, and Story,* ed. E. M. Bruner. Proceedings of the American Ethnological Society (Washington, D.C.: American Ethnological Society, 1983), 41.

7. Jaime de Angulo, *A Jaime de Angulo Reader,* ed. Bob Callahan (Berkeley: Turtle Island Foundation, 1979), 186.

8. Jaime de Angulo, *Indians in Overalls* (San Francisco: Turtle Island Foundation, 1973), 220.

9. Via Frazer's thirteen volumes of *The Golden Bough,* Jesse Weston's Grail mythology in *From Ritual to Romance,* and the linguistic anthropology of Franz Boas and Edward Sapir, among others, as reviewed in the early 1920s in the American periodical *The Dial,* where Eliot published letters home from London.

10. Johann Herder, "From a Correspondence on Ossian and the Songs of Ancient Peoples," in *Symposium of the Whole,* ed. Jerome Rothenberg and Diane Rothenberg (Berkeley: University of California Press, 1983), 7.

11. Hayden White, *The Wild Man Within,* ed. Edward J. Dudley and Maximillian E. Novak (Pittsburgh: University of Pittsburgh Press, 1973).

12. Dylan Thomas, *Portrait of the Artist as a Young Dog* (New York: New Directions, 1940), 11–12 (italics added).

13. Elias Canetti, *The Conscience of Words,* trans. Joachim Neugroschel (New York: Seabury Press, 1979), 241.

Chapter 4

1. Awaited by no less than President Reagan and Secretary of the Interior James Watt, as reported by Daniel Shorr, "Reagan Recants His Path from Armageddon to Detente," *Los Angeles Times,* 3 January 1988, 5.

2. Peter Nabokov, "Return to the Native," *New York Review of Books,* 27 September 1984.

3. *Los Angeles Times,* 1 June 1988, pt. 1, 14.

4. Suzan Shown Harjo, "American Indians: Target of Neglect," *Miami Herald,* 5 June 1988, 6C.

5. See Jarold Ramsey, *Reading the Fire: Essays in the Traditional Indian Literatures of the Far West* (Lincoln: University of Nebraska Press, 1983), and Kenneth Lincoln, *Native American Renaissance* (Berkeley and Los Angeles: University of California Press, 1983).

6. John Trudell and Jesse Ed Davis, "Baby Boom Che," aka *Grafitti Man,* The Peace Company Album, 1986.

7. Anne Wright, ed., *The Delicacy and Strength of Lace: Letters Between Leslie Marmon Silko and James Wright* (St. Paul, Minn.: Graywolf Press, 1986).

8. William Bright, "The Natural History of Old Man Coyote," in *Recovering the*

Word: Essays on Native American Literature, ed. Brian Swann and Arnold Krupat (Berkeley and Los Angeles: University of California Press, 1987), 346.

9. Gary Snyder, "The Incredible Survival of Coyote," in *The Old Ways* (San Francisco: City Lights Books, 1977), 68.

10. Peter Blue Cloud, "Coyote's Discourse on Power, Medicine and Would-Be Shamans," *Coyote's Journal,* ed. James Koller, "Gogisgi" Carroll Arnett, Steve Nemirow, and Peter Blue Cloud (Berkeley: Wingbow Press, 1982), 57.

11. Dell Hymes, "5-Fold Fanfare for Coyote," in *Coyote's Journal,* ed. Koller et al., 82–83.

12. Barre Toelken, "Poetic Retranslation and the 'Pretty Languages' of Yellowman," in *Traditional Literatures of the American Indian,* ed. Karl Kroeber (Lincoln: University of Nebraska Press, 1981), 90.

13. Bright, citing Francois Leydet's *The Coyote,* in "Natural History of Old Man Coyote," 354.

14. Bright, citing a study by R. D. Andrews and E. K. Borgess, in "Natural History of Old Man Coyote," 351.

15. Isabel Foreman, "Coyote, Coyote," *impact: Albuquerque Journal Magazine,* 18 February 1986, 8.

16. Harry Fonseca, interview with Margaret Archuleta, November 1985, in "Coyote: A Myth in the Making: A Ten-Year Retrospective of Harry Fonseca" (M.A. thesis in American Indian Studies, University of California, Los Angeles, 1987).

17. Harry Fonseca, taped interview with Craig D. Bates, 15 November 1985, quoted in Archuleta, "Coyote."

18. Frank La Pena and Craig D. Bates, comps., *Legends of the Yosemite Miwok,* illustrated by Harry Fonseca (Yosemite, Calif.: Yosemite Natural History Association, 1981), quoted in Archuleta, "Coyote."

19. Paul Radin, *The Trickster: A Study in American Indian Mythology* (1956; New York: Shocken, 1972), 169.

20. Jarold Ramsey, ed., *Coyote Was Going There: Indian Literature of the Oregon Country* (Seattle: University of Washington Press, 1977), xxv.

21. Barry Lopez, *Giving Birth to Thunder, Sleeping with His Daughter: Coyote Builds North America* (Kansas City, Mo.: Sheed Andrews and Mc Meel, 1977), xiv–xv.

22. Harry Fonseca, letter to author, 15 January 1991.

23. Fritz Scholder, *Indian Kitsch: The Use and Misuse of Indian Images* (Flagstaff, Ariz.: Northland Press, 1979), 4.

24. Joy Gritton, a UCLA doctoral candidate in art history, is researching this Indian tourist business: "It was amidst the post-war affluence of the Eisenhower age, however, that the tourist industry became a leading source of income in such Western states as Arizona, New Mexico, Wyoming, and Montana. Americans hit the road in unprecedented numbers. Paid vacations, usually consisting of three weeks or more, were included in 95 percent of labor contract agreements. Between 1945 and 1960, 15,000 new motels and hotels were built in the West and conditions in parks such as the Grand Canyon, Yellowstone, and Mesa Verde became so crowded that the number of visitors had to be restricted. Indian communities became leading 'attractions.' 'Harvey Detours' offered limousine tours of the pueblos, guided by the infamous 'Harvey Girls,' and the Southern Pacific Railway featured motor trips to cliff dwellings" ("Painted Images of the Tourist in the Plains and Southwest" [University of California, Los Angeles, manuscript, 1985]).

25. Barbara Babcock, "'A Tolerated Margin of Mess': The Trickster and His Tales Reconsidered," in *Critical Essays on Native American Literature*, ed. Andrew Wiget (Boston: Hall, 1985), 153–85.

26. Frank La Pena, "Coyote: A Myth in the Making: An Interview with Harry Fonseca," *News from Native California* 1 (November–December 1987): 18–19.

27. Harry Fonseca, "Contemporary American Indian Art: Diversity in Tradition" (Lecture delivered at the University of California, Los Angeles, 6 May 1986).

28. Harry Fonseca, in *Terra* 25 (November–December 1986): 16.

29. Lawrence Beck, "Lawrence Beck," in *3d Biennial Native American Fine Arts Invitational* (exhibition catalogue) (Phoenix: Heard Museum, 1987).

30. Robert D. Pelton, *The Trickster in West Africa: A Study of Mythic Irony and Sacred Delight* (Berkeley and Los Angeles: University of California Press, 1980), 18.

31. Gerald Vizenor, *Darkness in Saint Louis Bearheart* (St. Paul, Minn.: Bookslinger, 1978), vii.

32. Vizenor defends his fictive license in the Coltelli interviews: "there are people who are very offended by a scene of a woman having sex with dogs. All right. I answer it in two ways: first of all, you misread it, if you're offended. So it's the way you read it— that's your problem." It appears that one's own point of view rules here, despite social norms, any sense of boundaries, or common taste, tribal or otherwise. "My second statement, to somebody who finds fault with that," Vizenor goes on, "is you'd better reread it and then tell me what's wrong with a human being loving an animal. What's wrong with that is Judeo-Christian, not tribal. That doesn't mean that tribal people are sleeping with animals, I don't mean that, but in the story there isn't anything wrong with it. I thought it was a very sensous act of love. I was turned on by it myself. I thought it was cosmically erotic; it was mythically connected, sexually and culturally, and I just think it's a wonderful scene. And on a constellation blanket, no less!" ("Interview with Gerald Vizenor," in *Winged Words: American Indian Writers Speak*, ed. Laura Coltelli [Lincoln: University of Nebraska Press, 1990], 175–76).

33. Gerald Vizenor, *Griever: An American Monkey King in China* (Normal: Illinois State University, 1987), 34.

34. Barre Toelken, "The 'Pretty Language' of Yellowman: Genre, Mode, and Texture in Navaho Coyote Narratives," *Genre* 2 (September 1969): 211–35, and revised version in *Smoothing the Ground*, ed. Brian Swann and Arnold Krupat (Berkeley and Los Angeles: University of California Press, 1983).

35. Gerald Vizenor, ed., *Summer in the Spring: Ojibwe Lyric Poems and Tribal Stories* (Minneapolis: Nodin Press, 1981), 37.

36. Gerald Vizenor, *The Trickster of Liberty: Tribal Heirs to a Wild Baronage* (Minneapolis: University of Minnesota Press, 1988), ix–x.

37. Robert Gish, review of *The Trickster of Liberty*, by Gerald Vizenor, *American Indian Culture and Research Journal* (1988): 85–88. See also Elémire Zola's criticisms in the revised *I Letterati e Lo Sciamano: L'Indiano nella letteratura americana dalle origini al 1988* (Venice: Marsilio Editori, 1989).

38. Hanay Geiogamah, interview with author, 29 July 1988 (see Appendix C).

39. Hanay Geiogamah, *New Native American Drama: Three Plays* (Norman: University of Oklahoma Press, 1980), xxiv.

40. See Tom Hicks's video satire, *Return of the Country*, where white "savage"

children in an inverse Indian-Anglo America must burn their Bibles and forsake heathen ways.

Chapter 5

1. Paula Gunn Allen, personal conversation, September 1990.

2. See George Forgie's *Patricide and the House Divided* (New York: Norton, 1979) for a psychohistorical study of Abraham Lincoln's day, when sons killed one another in the inherited wake of their "fathers" killing the British grandfathers.

3. Beth Brant, "Coyote Learns a New Trick," in *Living the Spirit: A Gay American Indian Anthology,* ed. Will Roscoe (New York: St. Martin's Press, 1988), 163–66.

4. Mary Crow Dog, with Richard Erdoes, *Lakota Woman* (New York: Grove Weidenfeld, 1990), 131.

5. James Wright to Leslie Silko, 18 December 1979, in *The Delicacy and Strength of Lace: Letters Between Leslie Marmon Silko and James Wright,* ed. Anne Wright (St. Paul, Minn.: Graywolf Press, 1986).

6. Laura Coltelli, "Interview with Paula Gunn Allen," in *Winged Words: American Indian Writers Speak,* ed. Laura Coltelli (Lincoln: University of Nebraska Press, 1990), 22.

7. Alicia Suskin Ostriker, *Stealing the Language: The Emergence of Women's Poetry in America* (Boston: Beacon Press, 1986).

8. Susan Sontag, *Styles of Radical Will* (New York: Farrar, Straus & Giroux, 1969), 204.

9. Paula Gunn Allen, *The Sacred Hoop: Recovering the Feminine in American Indian Tradition* (Boston: Beacon Press, 1986), 222, 243, 223.

10. Rebecca Tsosie (Yaqui descent) put it so in a seminar paper on feminist Indian writers: "The women poets of today, both Indian and non-Indian, speak from a 'Trickster' point of view: through their travels and their impressions they show us the 'promise' the pain and the humor that is a part of being a woman, alive in America. And we, as women, are intimately associated with life in its simplest forms: we feel the unborn child twitch inside our bellies; each birth is a triumph for us, whether it is our own child, or a small new lamb, or even the first soft green of a young corn plant struggling through the soil.

"It is to the common feelings of life that I speak, for they are the threads of the tapestry that binds us all together as women—as wives, mothers, daughters and lovers.

"In the lonesome first light of a Kansas City dawn, I can hear the hollow whistle of the trains coming and going. I can see their lights—the lights that for Joy Harjo's Noni Daylight are the 'motion of time that she could have / caught / and moved on / but (instead) chose to stay / in Kansas City' (*She Had Some Horses* [1982]). These are the lights that flicker through the poems of these women, and allow us to travel on dream trains through the lives of many American women. This is how we travel on, passing through the rebirth of dawn" ("Changing Women: American 'Native' Poets" [University of California, Los Angeles, manuscript, 1985], 2–3).

11. Paula Allen, interview with Franchot Ballinger and Brian Swann, *MELUS* 10 (Summer 1983).

12. UCLA anthropologist Johannes Wilbert, personal conversation, 1987.

13. Viktor Frankl, *Man's Search for Meaning,* rev. ed. (New York: Washington Square Press, 1985), 24.

14. Paula Gunn Allen, " 'The Grace That Remains'—American Indian Women's Literature," *Book Forum* 5 (1981): 376–82.

Chapter 6

1. Louise Erdrich, *Love Medicine* (New York: Holt, Rinehart and Winston, 1984), 34–35.

2. Louise Erdrich, "Where I Ought to Be: A Writer's Sense of Place," *New York Times Book Review,* 28 July 1985, 24.

3. Jan George, "Interview with Louise Erdrich," *North Dakota Quarterly* 53 (Spring 1985): 242.

4. Louise Erdrich, *The Beet Queen* (New York: Holt, 1986), 45.

5. "Studs Terkel Hour" (KCRW, Los Angeles), 19 April 1987.

6. Sherman Paul, "Ethnopoetics: An 'Other' Tradition," *North Dakota Quarterly* 53 (Spring 1985).

7. Northrup Frye, *Anatomy of Criticism* (Princeton, N.J.: Princeton University Press, 1957), 172.

8. In describing the land disputes at the White Earth Chippewa Reservation in Minnesota, Erdrich and Dorris conclude: "The debate continues—in Washington and St. Paul and Naytahwaush—between disgruntled antagonists often related by blood or geography. As in a family, each position, though contradictory to all others, is persuasive, wrenching. There are no wild-eyed profiteers here, no evil geniuses; the authors of the turn-of-the-century deals that caused this mess are dead and mostly forgotten. None of the cliches seem to apply: the state is liberal, sensitive, the tribal government efficient, the protestors idealistic, the non-Indians salt-of-the-earth people whose complaint is with policy, not race. It's nothing personal, everyone seems to proclaim" (Louise Erdrich and Michael Dorris, "Who Owns the Land?" *New York Times Magazine,* 4 September 1988, 65).

9. James Welch, *Winter in the Blood* (New York: Harper & Row, 1974), 4.

10. Leslie Marmon Silko, *Ceremony* (New York: Viking, 1977), 255.

11. See the discussion of Howard Norman's *The Wishing Bone Cycle* entitled "Trickster's Bones," in Kenneth Lincoln, *Native American Renaissance* (Berkeley: University of California Press, 1983), 127–29.

Chapter 7

1. Louis Owens, review of *Harper's Anthology of 20th Century Native American Poetry,* edited by Duane Niatum, "The Book Review," *Los Angeles Times,* 21 February 1988, 8.

2. N. Scott Momaday, "Bringing on the Indians," *New York Review of Books,* 8 April 1971.

3. Reynolds Price, Review of *Winter in the Blood*, by James Welch, *New York Times Book Review*, 10 November 1974, 1.

4. Clark Wissler and D. C. Duvall, *Mythology of the Blackfoot Indians*, Anthropological Papers of the American Museum of Natural History (New York: The Trustees, 1908), 2: pt. 1, 19.

5. Taped interview, April 1985, American Audio Prose Library.

6. "Letter to Welch from Browning," in Richard Hugo, *31 Letters and 13 Dreams* (New York: Norton, 1977), 42.

7. *Fritz Scholder: Major Indian Paintings 1967–1977* (Santa Fe: Wheelwright Museum, n.d.).

8. Fritz Scholder, "Sharing a Heritage" (Lecture delivered at American Indian Arts Conference, University of California, Los Angeles, May 1982).

9. James Welch, *Winter in the Blood* (New York: Harper & Row, 1974), 169.

10. William W. Thackeray, " 'Crying for Pity' in *Winter in the Blood*," *MELUS* 7 (Spring 1980): 61–78.

11. Viktor Frankl, *Man's Search for Meaning*, rev. ed. (New York: Washington Square Press, 1985).

12. John Hawkes, "John Hawkes: Interview," *Wisconsin Studies in Contemporary Literature* 6 (Summer 1965): 145–46.

13. Ralph Ellison, "Richard Wright's Blues," in *Shadow and Act* (1964; New York: Vintage Books, 1972), 78.

Chapter 8

1. Charles L. Woodard, *Ancestral Voice: Conversations with N. Scott Momaday* (Lincoln: University of Nebraska Press, 1989), 128.

2. Northrop Frye, *Anatomy of Criticism* (Princeton, N.J.: Princeton University Press, 1957), 182.

3. N. Scott Momaday, *House Made of Dawn* (New York: Harper Perennial, 1977), 20.

4. "The context of *eiron* and *alazon* forms the basis of the comic action, and the buffoon and the churl polarize the comic mood" (Frye, *Anatomy of Criticism,* 172).

5. Katerina Clark and Michael Holquist, *Mikhail Bakhtin* (Cambridge: Harvard University Press, 1984), 318.

6. See Kenneth Lincoln, "Tai-Me to Rainy Mountain," *American Indian Quarterly* 10 (Spring 1986): 101–17.

7. Louis A. Hieb, "Meaning and Mismeaning: Toward an Understanding of the Ritual Clown," in *New Perspectives on the Pueblos*, ed. Alfonso Ortiz (Albuquerque: University of New Mexico Press, 1972), 163–95.

8. Jarold Ramsey, *Reading the Fire: Essays in the Traditional Indian Literature of the Far West* (Lincoln: University of Nebraska Press, 1983), 27.

9. Konrad Lorenz, *On Aggression*, trans. Marjorie Kerr Wilson (New York: Harcourt Brace Jovanovich), 293.

10. Howard Norman, *The Northern Lights* (New York: Summit Books, 1987), 22.

11. See the contrary talkings of Haitians comically arguing "rhum" in Norman's

earlier Ananse translations, in Paulé Bartón, *The Woe Shirt: Caribbean Folk Tales* (Great Barrington, Mass: Penmaen Press, 1980).

Coda

1. John G. Neihardt, trans., *Black Elk Speaks: Being the Life Story of a Holy Man of the Oglala Sioux* (1932; New York: Pocket Books, 1972), 159–60.

2. Max Eastman, *The Sense of Humor* (New York: Scribner, 1921), 94.

3. Ward Churchill, letter to author, 1 February 1988 (ellipses in original).

4. Vine Deloria, Jr., letter to author, 16 June 1988.

Selected Bibliography

Adams, Alexander B. *Sitting Bull: An Epic of the Plains*. New York: Putnam, 1973.

Allen, Paula Gunn. "Autobiography of a Confluence." In *I Tell You Now: Autobiographical Essays by Native American Writers*, edited by Brian Swann and Arnold Krupat, 141–54. Lincoln: University of Nebraska Press, 1987.

———. *The Blind Lion*. Berkeley: Thorp Springs Press, 1974.

———. *A Cannon Between My Knees*. New York: Strawberry Press, 1981.

———. *Coyote's Daylight Trip*. Albuquerque: La Confluencia, 1978.

———. " 'The Grace that Remains'—American Indian Women's Literature." *Book Forum: "American Indians Today—Thought—Literature—Art"* 5 (1981): 376–82.

———. Interview with Franchot Ballinger and Brian Swann. *MELUS* 10 (Summer 1983): 1–25.

———. *The Sacred Hoop: Recovering the Feminine in American Indian Traditions*. Boston: Beacon Press, 1986.

———. *Shadow Country*. Native American Series, no. 6. Los Angeles: American Indian Studies Center, University of California, Los Angeles, 1982.

———. *Skins and Bones*. San Francisco: West End Press, 1988.

———. *Star Child*. Marvin, S.D.: Blue Cloud Quarterly, 1982.

———. *The Woman Who Owned the Shadows*. San Francisco: Spinsters Ink, 1983.

———. *Wyrds*. San Francisco: Taurean Horn Press, 1987.

———, ed. *Spider Woman's Granddaughters: Short Stories by American Indian Women*. Boston: Beacon Press, 1989.

———, ed. *Studies in American Indian Literature. Critical Essays and Course Designs*. New York: Modern Language Association, 1983.

American Indian Quarterly 4 (May 1978). Symposium issue on *Winter in the Blood*.

Apte, Mahadev L. *Humor and Laughter: An Anthropological Approach*. Ithaca, N.Y.: Cornell University Press, 1985.

Archuleta, Margaret. "Coyote: A Myth in the Making." *Terra* 25 (November–December 1986): 13–20.

———. "Coyote: A Myth in the Making: A Ten-Year Retrospect of Harry Fonseca." Master's thesis, University of California, Los Angeles, 1987.

Astrov, Margot, ed. *American Indian Prose and Poetry: An Anthology.* 1946. Reprint. New York: Capricorn, 1962.

Austin, Mary. *The American Rhythm.* New York: Harcourt, 1923.

Babcock, Barbara. "Arrange Me into Disorder: Fragments and Reflections on Ritual Clowning." In *Rite, Drama, Festival, Spectacle,* edited by John J. MacAloon. Philadelphia: University of Pennsylvania Press, 1984.

―――. "Ritual Undress and the Comedy of Self and Other." In *A Crack in the Mirror: Reflexive Perspectives in Anthropology,* edited by Jay Ruby, 187–203. Philadelphia: University of Pennsylvania Press, 1982.

―――. " 'Those, They Called Them Monos': Cochiti Figurative Ceramics, 1875–1905." *American Indian Art Magazine* 12 (Autumn 1987): 50–57, 67.

―――. " 'A Tolerated Margin of Mess': The Trickster and His Tales Reconsidered." In *Critical Essays on Native American Literature,* edited by Andrew Wiget. Boston: Hall, 1985.

―――, ed. "Introduction." *The Reversible World: Symbolic Inversion in Art and Society.* Ithaca, N.Y.: Cornell University Press, 1978.

Babcock, Barbara, Guy Monthan, and Doris Monthan. *The Pueblo Storyteller.* Tucson: University of Arizona Press, 1986.

Bakhtin, M. M. *The Dialogic Imagination.* Translated by Caryl Emerson and Michael Holquist. Edited by Michael Holquist. Austin: University of Texas Press, 1981.

―――. *Rabelais and His World.* Translated by Helen Iswolsky. Cambridge, Mass.: MIT Press, 1965. Reprint. Bloomington: Indiana University Press, 1984.

―――. *Speech Genres and Other Late Essays.* Translated by Vern N. McGee. Edited by Caryl Emerson and Michael Holquist. Austin: University of Texas Press, 1986.

Bandelier, Adolf F. *The Delight Makers.* 1890. Reprint, with an introduction by Stefan Jovanovich. New York: Harcourt Brace Jovanovich, 1971.

Bartón, Paulé. *The Woe Shirt: Caribbean Folk Tales.* Translated by Howard Norman. Great Barrington, Mass.: Penmaen Press, 1980.

Basso, Ellen B. *In Favor of Deceit: A Study of Tricksters in an Amazonian Society.* Tucson: University of Arizona Press, 1987.

Basso, Keith H. *Portraits of "The Whiteman": Linguistic Play and Cultural Symbols Among the Western Apache.* Cambridge: Cambridge University Press, 1979.

―――. " 'Stalking with Stories': Names, Places and Moral Narratives among the Western Apache." In *Text, Plan, and Story,* edited by E. M. Bruner, 19–55. Proceedings of the American Ethnological Society. Washington, D.C.: American Ethnological Society, 1983.

―――. *Western Apache Language and Culture: Essays in Linguistic Anthropology.* Tucson: University of Arizona Press, 1990.

Bataille, Georges. *Guilty.* Translated by Bruce Boone. Venice, Calif.: Lapis Press, 1988.

Bataille, Gretchen M., and Kathleen Mullen Sands. *American Indian Women: Telling Their Lives.* Lincoln: University of Nebraska Press, 1984.

Bataille, Gretchen M., and Charles L. P. Silet, eds. *The Pretend Indians: Images of Native Americans in the Movies.* Ames: Iowa State University Press, 1980.

Bauman, Richard. *Verbal Art as Performance.* Prospect Heights, Ill.: Waveland Press, 1977.

Beck, Lawrence. "Lawrence Beck." In *3d Biennial Native American Fine Arts Invitational* (exhibition catalogue). Phoenix: Heard Museum, 1987.

Beckett, Samuel. *Watt.* 1953. Reprint. New York: Grove Press, 1959.

Benjamin, Walter. *Illuminations.* Translated by Harry Zohn. 1955. Reprint. London: Collins, 1973.

Bergson, Henri. "Laughter" (1899). In *Comedy,* edited by Wylie Sypher, 61–190. Garden City, N.Y.: Doubleday, 1956.

Berkhofer, Robert F., Jr. *The White Man's Indian: Images of the American Indian from Columbus to the Present.* New York: Random House, 1978.

Berlitz, Charles. *Native Tongues.* New York: Putnam, 1982.

Bernheimer, Richard. *Wild Men in the Middle Ages: A Study in Art, Sentiment, and Demonology.* Cambridge, Mass.: Harvard University Press, 1952.

Bevis, William. "Native American Novels: Homing In." In *Recovering the Word: Essays on Native American Literature,* edited by Brian Swann and Arnold Krupat, 580–620. Berkeley: University of California Press, 1987.

Bibeau, Don, Carl Gawboy, and Naomi Lyons. *Everything You Ever Wanted to Ask About Indians: But Were Afraid to Find Out!* Saint Cloud, Minn.: North Star Press, 1971.

Billington, Ray Allen. *Land of Savagery, Land of Promise: The European Image of the American Frontier in the Nineteenth Century.* New York: Norton, 1981. Reprint. Norman: University of Oklahoma Press, 1985.

Blackburn, Thomas C., ed. *December's Child: A Book of Chumash Oral Narratives.* Berkeley: University of California Press, 1975.

Black Elk, Henry, Kate Blue Thunder, Irene Clairmont, and Christine Dunham. *Buckskin Tokens: Contemporary Oral Narratives of the Lakota.* Edited by R. D. Theisz. Aberdeen, S.D.: North Plains Press, 1975.

Black Elk, Wallace H., and William S. Lyon. *Black Elk: The Sacred Ways of a Lakota.* San Francisco: Harper & Row, 1990.

Blue Cloud, Peter. "Coyote's Discourse on Power, Medicine and Would-Be Shamans." In *Coyote's Journal,* edited by James Koller, "Gogisgi" Carroll Arnett, Steve Nemirow, and Peter Blue Cloud, 49–57. Berkeley: Wingbow Press, 1982.

———. *Elderberry Flute Song: Contemporary Coyote Tales.* Trumansburg, N.Y.: Crossing Press, 1982.

Boen, Elenore Smith. *Return to Laughter.* 1954. Reprint. Garden City, N.Y.:
    Doubleday, 1964.
Brandon, S. G. F. *A Dictionary of Comparative Religions.* New York: Scribner,
    1970.
Brant, Beth. *A Gathering of Spirit: Writing and Art by North American Indian
    Women.* Exp. ed. San Francisco: Sinister Wisdom, 1984.
Bright, William. "The Natural History of Old Man Coyote." In *Recovering the
    Word: Essays on Native American Literature,* edited by Brian Swann and
    Arnold Krupat, 339–87. Berkeley: University of California Press, 1987.
Brinton, Daniel. *The Myths of the New World.* Philadelphia: McKay, 1868.
Brotherston, Gordon. *Image of the New World: The American Continent Por-
    trayed in Native Texts.* London: Thames and Hudson, 1979.
Brown, Joseph Epes. "The Wisdom of the Contrary: A Conversation with
    Joseph Epes Brown." *Parabola* 4 (February 1979): 54–65.
————, ed. *The Sacred Pipe: Black Elk's Account of the Seven Rites of the
    Oglala Sioux.* 2d rev. ed. Baltimore: Penguin Books, 1971.
Bruchac, Joseph, III, ed. *Survival This Way: Interviews with American Indian
    Poets.* Tucson: University of Arizona Press, 1987.
Burns, Diane. *Riding the One-Eyed Ford.* New York: Strawberry Press, 1981.
Bush, Barney. *My Horse and a Jukebox.* Native American Series, no. 4. Los
    Angeles: American Indian Studies Center, University of California, Los
    Angeles, 1979.
Caillois, Roger. *Man, Play, and Games.* Translated by Meyer Barash. New
    York: Free Press, 1961.
Camus, Albert. *The Myth of Sisyphus, and Other Essays.* Translated by Justin
    O'Brien. New York: Knopf, 1955. Reprint. New York: Vintage Books,
    1959.
Canetti, Elias. *The Conscience of Words.* Translated by Joachim Neugroschel.
    New York: Seabury Press, 1979.
Carpenter, Carole Henderson. "Morrissean—The Artist as Trickster." *art mag-
    azine 46* 11 (November–December 1979): 55–59.
Cixous, Hélène. "The Scene of the Unconscious." In *The Future of Literary
    Theory,* edited by Ralph Cohen. New York: Routledge, 1989.
Cixous, Hélène, and Catherine Clement. *The Newly Born Woman.* Translated
    by Betsy Wing. Minneapolis: University of Minnesota Press, 1986.
Clark, Katerina, and Michael Holquist. *Mikhail Bakhtin.* Cambridge, Mass.:
    Harvard University Press, 1984.
Clements, William. "The Ethnic Joke as Mirror of Culture." *New York Folklore*
    12 (1986): 87–97.
Cliff, Janet Marion. "Ludicity: A Model for Understanding Play and Games."
    Ph.D. diss., University of California, Los Angeles, 1990.
————. "Navajo Games." *American Indian Culture and Research Journal* 14
    (1990): 1–81.

Clifford, James. "On Ethnographic Authority." *Representations* 1 (Spring 1983): 118–46.

———. *The Predicament of Culture: Twentieth-Century Ethnography, Literature, and Art.* Cambridge, Mass.: Harvard University Press, 1988.

Clifton, James A., ed. *The Invented Indian. Cultural Fictions and Government Policies.* New Brunswick, N.J.: Transaction, 1990.

Cline, Paul. *Fools, Clowns, and Jesters.* La Jolla, Calif.: Green Tiger Press, 1983.

Cohen, Ralph, ed. *The Future of Literary Theory.* New York: Routledge, 1989.

Coltelli, Laura, ed. *Winged Words: American Indian Writers Speak.* Lincoln: University of Nebraska Press, 1990.

Connell, Evan S. *Son of the Morning Star: Custer and the Little Big Horn.* New York: Harper & Row, 1985.

Conover, Ted. *Coyotes.* New York: Random House, 1987.

Cook, Albert. *The Dark Voyage and the Golden Mean: A Philosophy of Comedy.* 1949. Reprint. New York: Norton, 1966.

Cooley, Jim. "A Vision of the Summer Plains: The Photography of Horace Poolaw." *Four Winds* 3 (Summer 1982): 66–72.

Cousins, Norman. *Anatomy of an Illness as Perceived by the Patient: Reflections on Healing and Regeneration.* New York: Norton, 1979.

———. *Head First: The Biology of Hope and the Healing Power of the Human Spirit.* New York: Penguin Books, 1989.

Craig, Vincent. Cartoons. *Apache Scout,* 1977–1978.

Crapanzano, Vincent. *The Fifth World of Forster Bennett: Portrait of a Navajo.* New York: Viking Press, 1972.

———. *Tuhami: Portrait of a Moroccan.* Chicago: University of Chicago Press, 1980.

Cronyn, George W. *The Path on the Rainbow: An Anthology of Songs and Chants from the Indians of North America.* New and enl. ed. Foreword by Kenneth Lincoln. New York: Liveright, 1934; New York: Ballantine, 1991.

Crowder, Jack L. *Stephannie and the Coyote.* Bernalillo, N.M., 1969.

Crow Dog, Mary, with Richard Erdoes. *Lakota Woman.* New York: Grove Weidenfeld, 1990.

Culp, James. *Hopi Songs of the Fourth World.* New York: New Day Films, 1988. Videocassette.

Davis, Douglas M., ed. *The World of Black Humor: An Introductory Anthology of Selections and Criticism.* New York: Dutton, 1967.

De Angulo, Jaime. *Indians in Overalls.* San Francisco: Turtle Island Foundation, 1973.

———. *Indian Tales.* New York: Hill and Wang, 1953.

———. *A Jaime de Angulo Reader.* Edited by Bob Callahan. Berkeley: Turtle Island Foundation, 1979.

Dearborn, Mary V. *Pocahontas's Daughters: Gender and Ethnicity in American Culture.* New York: Oxford University Press, 1986.

De Beauvoir, Simone. *The Second Sex.* Translated and edited by H. M. Parshley. New York: Knopf, 1952.

Deloria, Vine, Jr. *Behind the Trail of Broken Treaties: An Indian Declaration of Independence.* New York: Dell, 1974.

————. "Custer Died For Your Sins." *Playboy,* August 1969, 131–32, 172, 175.

————. *Custer Died For Your Sins: An Indian Manifesto.* New York: Macmillan, 1969.

————. *God Is Red.* New York: Grosset and Dunlap, 1973.

————. *We Talk, You Listen: New Tribes, New Turf.* New York: Delta, 1970.

DeMallie, Raymond, ed. *The Sixth Grandfather: Black Elk's Teachings Given to John G. Neihardt.* Lincoln: University of Nebraska Press, 1984.

Densmore, Francis. *Teton Sioux Music.* Smithsonian Institution Bureau of American Ethnology, Bulletin 61. Washington, D.C., 1918. Reprint. New York: Da Capo Press, 1972.

Dinnerstein, Leonard, Roger L. Nichols, and David M. Reimers. *Natives and Strangers: Blacks, Indians, and Immigrants in America.* 2d ed. New York: Oxford University Press, 1990.

Dobie, J. Frank. *The Voice of the Coyote.* Boston: Little, Brown, 1949. Reprint. Lincoln: University of Nebraska Press, 1961.

Dorris, Michael. "The Cowboy and the Indians: Reagan's Patronizing Remarks Add Insult to Injury." *Los Angeles Times,* 12 June 1988, Book Section, 5.

————. *A Yellow Raft in Blue Water.* New York: Holt, 1987.

Dorris, Michael, and Louise Erdrich. *The Crown of Columbus.* New York: HarperCollins, 1991.

Douglas, Mary. *Natural Symbols. Explorations in Cosmology.* New York: Pantheon, 1970.

————. *Purity and Danger: An Analysis of Concepts of Pollution and Taboo.* London: Routledge & Kegan Paul, 1966.

————. "The Social Control of Cognition: Some Factors in Joke Perception." *Man* 3 (1968): 361–76.

Drinnon, Richard. *Facing West: The Metaphysics of Indian-Hating and Empire Building.* New York: New American Library, 1980.

Dudden, Arthur Power, ed. *American Humor.* New York: Oxford University Press, 1987.

Dudley, Edward J., and Maximillian E. Novak, eds. *The Wild Man Within.* Pittsburgh: University of Pittsburgh Press, 1973.

Dunn, Dorothy. "Awa Tsireh: Painter of San Ildefonso." *El Palacio,* April 1958, 107–15.

Eastman, Max. *The Sense of Humor.* New York: Scribner, 1921.

Eco, Umberto, Gian Paolo Cesarani, and Beniamino Placido. *La Riscoperta dell'America*. Rome: Laterza, 1984.

Eisen, George. "Coping in Adversity: Children's Play in the Holocaust." In *Meaningful Play, Playful Meaning*, edited by G. A. Fine. Association for the Anthropological Study of Play, vol. 11. Champaign, Ill.: Human Kinetics, 1987.

Ellison, Ralph. "Change the Joke and Slip the Yoke." In Ralph Ellison, *Shadow and Act*, 45–59. 1964. Reprint. New York: Vintage Books, 1972.

———. "Richard Wright's Blues." In Ralph Ellison, *Shadow and Act*, 77–94. 1964. Reprint. New York: Vintage Books, 1972.

Enck, John J., Elizabeth T. Forter, and Alvin Whitley, eds. *The Comic in Theory and Practice*. New York: Appleton-Century-Crofts, 1960.

Erdrich, Louise. *Baptism of Desire*. New York: Harper & Row, 1989.

———. *The Beet Queen*. New York: Holt, 1986.

———. "Interview with Louise Erdrich," by Jan George. *North Dakota Quarterly* 53 (Spring 1985): 240–46.

———. *Jacklight*. New York: Holt, Rinehart and Winston, 1984.

———. *Love Medicine*. New York: Holt, Rinehart and Winston, 1984.

———. "Mister Argus." *Georgia Review* 39 (Summer 1985): 379–90.

———. *Tracks*. New York: Holt, 1988.

———. "Where I Ought to Be: A Writer's Sense of Place." *New York Times Book Review*, 28 July 1985, 1, 3–4, 23–24.

Erdrich, Louise, and Michael Dorris. "An Interview with Louise Erdrich and Michael Dorris," by Hertha D. Wong. *North Dakota Quarterly* 55 (Winter 1987): 196–218.

———. Interview. "Bill Moyers' World of Ideas." Public Affairs Television. 14 November 1988.

———. "Who Owns the Land?" *New York Times Magazine*, 4 September 1988, 32–35, 52–53, 57, 65.

Esslin, Martin. *Brecht, The Man and His Work*. Garden City, N.Y.: Doubleday, 1960.

Evans-Pritchard, Deirdre. "How 'They' See 'Us': Native American Images of Tourists." *Annals of Tourism Research* 16 (1989): 89–105.

Farrer, Claire R. *Play and Inter-Ethnic Communication: A Practical Ethnography of the Mescalero Apache*. New York: Garland, 1990.

Felheim, Marvin. *Comedy: Plays, Theory, and Criticism*. New York: Harcourt, Brace & World, 1962.

Ferrero, Pat. *Hopi Songs of the Fourth World*. New York: Videocassette. New Day Films, 1988.

Fiedler, Leslie. *The Return of the Vanishing American*. New York: Stein and Day, 1969.

Fiedler, Leslie, and Houston A. Baker, eds. *English Literature: Opening Up the Canon*. Baltimore: Johns Hopkins University Press, 1981.

Fire, John (Lame Deer), and Richard Erdoes. *Lame Deer, Seeker of Visions: The Life of a Sioux Medicine Man*. New York: Simon and Schuster, 1972.

Fonseca, Harry. "Artist in Profile: Harry Fonseca," by Barbara Littlebird. *Four Winds*, Winter 1981.

———. "Contemporary American Indian Art: Diversity in Tradition." Lecture delivered at University of California, Los Angeles, 6 May 1986.

———. "Coyote: A Myth in the Making. An Interview with Harry Fonseca," by Frank La Pena. *News from Native California* 1 (November–December 1987): 18–19.

———. "Coyote: An Interview with Harry Fonseca," by Lorenzo Baca. *News from Native California* 4 (Spring 1990): 31. Excerpted from Fall 1983 video.

———. *Coyote: Thirteen Lithographs and a Poem*. Sacramento: Limestone Press, 1984.

———. "Coyote, Coyote!" by Isabel Foreman. *impact: Albuquerque Journal Magazine*, 18 February 1986, 4–9.

———. "Harry Fonseca." Washington, D.C.: American Indian Arts and Crafts Board, 1976.

———. Interview. November 1985. In "Coyote: A Myth in the Making: a Ten-Year Retrospect of Harry Fonseca," by Margaret Archuleta. Master's thesis, University of California, Los Angeles, 1987.

———. Interview with Craig D. Bates. 15 November 1985. In Margaret Archuleta, "Coyote: A Myth in the Making: A Ten-Year Retrospect of Harry Fonseca." Master's thesis, University of California, Los Angeles, 1987.

———. "An Interview with Harry Fonseca," by Lorenzo Baca. Fall 1983. Video.

———. "Coyote." *Terra* 25 (November–December 1986): 16.

Forgie, George. *Patricide and the House Divided*. New York: Norton, 1979.

Foucault, Michel. *The Archaeology of Knowledge and the Discourse on Language*. Translated by A. M. Sheridan Smith. New York: Pantheon Books, 1972.

———. *The Order of Things: An Archaeology of the Human Sciences*. Translated by Michel Foucault. New York: Vintage Books, 1970.

———. *This is Not a Pipe*. Translated and edited by James Harkness. Berkeley: University of California Press, 1982.

Frankl, Viktor. *Man's Search for Meaning*. Rev. ed. New York: Washington Square Press, 1985.

Frazer, Sir James. *The Golden Bough*. 13 vols. Cambridge, 1890.

Freeman, Robert. *For Indians Only*. San Marcos, Calif., 1980.

Freud, Sigmund. "Humour." *International Journal of Psychology* 9 (1928): 1–

6. Reprinted in *Sigmund Freud: Collected Papers,* edited by James Strachey, 5: 215–21. London: Hogarth Press, 1950.

——. *The Interpretation of Dreams.* 3d ed. Translated by A. A. Brill. London: Allen and Unwin; New York: Macmillan, 1932.

——. *Jokes and Their Relationship to the Unconscious* (1905). Translated and edited by James Strachey. New York: Norton, 1960.

——. *Totem and Taboo: Some Points of Agreement Between the Mental Lives of Savages and Neurotics.* Translated by James Strachey. New York: Norton, 1950.

Friedan, Betty. *The Feminine Mystique.* New York: Norton, 1963.

Fritz Scholder: Major Indian Paintings 1967–1977. Sante Fe: Wheelwright Museum, n.d.

Frye, Northrop. *Anatomy of Criticism.* Princeton, N.J.: Princeton University Press, 1957.

Gates, Henry Louis, Jr. *The Signifying Monkey: A Theory of African–American Literary Criticism.* New York: Oxford University Press, 1988.

——, ed. *"Race," Writing, and Difference.* Chicago: University of Chicago Press, 1985.

Geertz, Clifford. "Deep Play: Notes on the Balinese Cockfight." *Daedalus* 101 (1972): 1–37.

——. *Local Knowledge: Further Essays in Interpretive Anthropology.* New York: Basic Books, 1983.

——. *Works and Lives: The Anthropologist as Author.* Stanford, Calif.: Stanford University Press, 1988.

Geiogamah, Hanay. *New Native American Drama: Three Plays.* Norman: University of Oklahoma Press, 1980. Includes *Body Indian, Foghorn,* and *49.*

Giago, Tom. "Nothing Can Top Indian Joke Session." In *Notes From Indian Country,* 1: 237–38. Pierre, S.D.: State Publishing, 1984.

Gill, Don. "The Coyote and the Sequential Occupants of the Los Angeles Basin." *American Anthropologist* 72 (1970): 821–26.

Gish, Robert. Review of *The Trickster of Liberty: Tribal Heirs to a Wild Baronage,* by Gerald Vizenor. *American Indian Culture and Research Journal* 12 (1988): 85-88.

Glancy, Diane. *One Age in a Dream.* Minneapolis: Milkweed Editions, 1986.

Gleason, William. " 'Her Laugh an Ace': The Function of Humor in Louise Erdrich's *Love Medicine.*" *American Indian Culture and Research Journal* 11 (1987): 51–73.

Green, Rayna. *Native American Women: A Contextual Bibliography.* Bloomington: Indiana University Press, 1983.

——. "Native American Women: Review Essay." *Signs: Journal of Women in Culture and Society* 6 (Winter 1980): 248–67.

————. "The Only Good Indian: The Image of the Indian in American Vernacular Culture." Ph.D. diss., Indiana University, 1973.

————. "Playing Indian: An American Obsession." Lecture delivered at University of California, Los Angeles, 4 May 1987.

————, ed. *That's What She Said: Contemporary Poetry and Fiction by Native American Women*. Bloomington: Indiana University Press, 1984.

Greenburg, Andrea. "Form and Function of the Ethnic Joke." *Keystone Folklore Quarterly* (Winter 1972): 144–61.

Greenfield Review: American Indian Writings 9, nos. 3, 4 (1981).

Gritton, Joy. "The Institute of American Indian Arts and the Modern Indian Art 'Movement': The Planted Roots of Resistance." Department of Art History, University of California, Los Angeles, 1987. Manuscript.

Guardini, Romano. *The Church and the Catholic, and The Spirit of the Liturgy*. Translated by Ada Lane. New York: Sheed and Ward, 1940.

Harjo, Joy. "Santa Fe" and "Deer Dancer." *Ploughshares* 15 (Winter 1989–90): 100–2.

————. *She Had Some Horses*. New York: Thunder's Mouth Press, 1983.

————. *What Moon Drove Me to This?* 1978. Reprint. New York: Reed, 1979.

Harjo, Joy, and Stephen Strom. *Secrets from the Center of the World*. Sun Tracks Series, vol. 17. Tucson: University of Arizona Press, 1989.

Harjo, Suzan Shown. "American Indians: Target of Neglect." *Miami Herald*, 5 June 1988, sec. C.

Hartman, Geoffrey H. "The State of the Art of Criticism." In *The Future of Literary Theory*, edited by Ralph Cohen. New York: Routledge, 1989.

Haslam, Gerald. "American Indians: Poets of the Cosmos." *Western American Literature* 5 (Spring 1970): 15–29.

————. "American Oral Literature: Our Forgotten Heritage." *English Journal* 60 (September 1971): 709–23.

————. "The Light that Fills the World: Native American Literature." *South Dakota Review* 11 (Spring 1973): 27–41.

————. "Literature of the People: Native American Voices." *CLA Journal* 15 (December 1971): 153–70.

Hassan, Ihab. *The Postmodern Turn. Essays in Postmodern Theory and Culture*. Columbus: Ohio State University Press, 1987.

Hawkes, John. "John Hawkes: Interview." *Wisconsin Studies in Contemporary Literature* 6 (Summer 1965): 145–46.

Heidegger, Martin. *On the Way to Language*. Translated by Peter D. Heitz. 1959. Reprint. New York: Harper & Row, 1971.

Hess, Bill. "A Navajo Laughs." *Nations* 1 (1981): 14–20.

Hickerson, Nancy Parrott. *Linguistic Anthropology*. New York: Holt, Rinehart and Winston, 1980.

Hicks, Bob. *Return of the Country*. American Film Institute Master's Thesis Film. Los Angeles, 1984. Videocassette.

Hieb, Louis A. "Meaning and Mismeaning: Toward an Understanding of the Ritual Clown." In *New Perspectives on the Pueblos,* edited by Alfonso Ortiz, 163–95. Albuquerque: University of New Mexico Press, 1972.

Hogan, Linda. *Calling Myself Home.* Greenfield Center, N.Y.: Greenfield Review Press, 1978.

———. *Eclipse.* Native American Series, no. 6. Los Angeles: American Indian Studies Center, University of California, Los Angeles, 1983.

———. *Mean Spirit.* New York: Atheneum, 1990.

———. *Seeing Through the Sun.* Amherst: University of Massachusetts Press, 1985.

Horn, Patrice. "Eskimo Humor—More than a Laughing Matter." *Psychology Today,* March 1974, 14, 88.

Horton, Andrew. "The Bitter Humor of *Winter in the Blood." American Indian Quarterly* 4 (May 1978): 131–39.

Howard, James. "The Dakota Heyoka Cult." *Scientific Monthly* 78 (April 1954): 254–58.

Hubbard, Patrick. "Trickster, Renewal and Survival." *American Indian Culture and Research Journal* 4 (1980): 113–24.

Hugo, Richard. *31 Letters and 13 Dreams.* New York: Norton, 1977.

Huizinga, Johan. *Homo Ludens: A Study of the Play-Element in Culture.* 1938, 1944. Reprint. Boston: Beacon Press, 1955.

Hymes, Dell. "5-Fold Fanfare for Coyote." In *Coyote's Journal,* edited by James Koller, "Gogisgi" Carroll Arnett, Steve Nemirow, and Peter Blue Cloud, 82–83. Berkeley: Wingbow Press, 1982.

Isajiw, Wsevolod W. "Definitions of Ethnicity." *Ethnicity* 1 (1974): 111–24.

Jennings, Francis. *The Invasion of America: Indians, Colonialism, and the Cant of Conquest.* Chapel Hill: University of North Carolina Press, 1975.

Kabotie, Mike. *Migration Tears.* Native American Series, no. 7. Los Angeles: American Indian Studies Center, University of California, Los Angeles, 1987.

Kafka, Franz. *Amerika.* Translated by Edwin Muir. New York: New Directions, 1946.

Kerouac, Jack. *Desolation Angels.* New York: Coward-McCann, 1965.

Kinsella, W. P. *The Fencepost Chronicles.* Boston: Houghton Mifflin, 1986.

———. *The Moccasin Telegraph and Other Stories.* New York: Penguin Books, 1983.

Klein, Allen. *The Healing Power of Humor: Techniques for Getting Through Loss, Setbacks, Upsets, Disappointments, Difficulties, Trials, Tribulations, and All that Not-So-Funny Stuff.* Los Angeles: Tarcher, 1989.

Kluckhohn, Clyde, and Dorothea Leighton. *The Navajo.* Rev. ed. Garden City, N.Y.: Doubleday, 1962.

Koestler, Arthur. *Insight and Outlook: An Inquiry into the Common Foundations of Science, Art and Social Ethics.* New York: Macmillan, 1949.

Koller, James, "Gogisgi" Carroll Arnett, Steve Nemirow, and Peter Blue Cloud, eds. *Coyote's Journal*. Berkeley: Wingbow Press, 1982.

Kopit, Arthur. *Indians*. New York: Hill and Wang, 1969.

Kristeva, Julia. *The Kristeva Reader*. Edited by Toril Moi. New York: Columbia University Press, 1986.

―――. "The Pain of Sorrow in the Modern World: The Works of Marguerite Duras." Translated by Katharine A. Jensen. *PMLA* 102 (March 1987): 138–52.

―――. *Powers of Horror*. Translated by Leon S. Roudiez. 1980. Reprint. New York: Columbia University Press, 1982.

―――. *Tales of Love*. Translated by Leon S. Roudiez. New York: Columbia University Press, 1987.

Kroeber, Karl. *Traditional Literatures of the American Indian: Texts and Interpretations*. Lincoln: University of Nebraska Press, 1981.

Krupat, Arnold. *For Those Who Come After: A Study of Native American Autobiography*. Berkeley: University of California Press, 1985.

La Farge, Oliver. *Laughing Boy*. 1929. Reprint. Cambridge, Mass.: Riverside Press, 1957.

La Pena, Frank. "Coyote: A Myth in the Making. An Interview with Harry Fonseca." *News from Native California* 1 (November–December 1987): 18–19.

La Pena, Frank, and Craig D. Bates, comps. *Legends of the Yosemite Miwok*. Illustrated by Harry Fonseca. Yosemite National Park, Calif.: Yosemite Natural History Association, 1981.

Lawrence, D. H. *Mornings in Mexico*. 1927. Reprint. London: Heinemann, 1956.

―――. *Studies in Classic American Literature*. New York: Seltzer, 1923.

Leap, William L. "The Study of American Indian English: An Introduction to the Issues." In *Papers in Southwestern English: Studies in Southwestern Indian English,* edited by William L. Leap, 3–22. San Antonio: Trinity University, 1977.

Leap, William, and Robert N. St. Clair, eds. *Language Renewal among American Indian Tribes: Issues, Problems, and Prospects*. Roslyn, Va.: National Clearinghouse for Bilingual Education, 1982.

Lévi-Strauss, Claude. *The Savage Mind*. 1962. Reprint. Chicago: University of Chicago Press, 1966.

―――. *Totemism*. Translated by Rodney Needham. 1962. Reprint. Boston: Beacon Press, 1963.

Lewis, Paul. *Comic Effects. Interdisciplinary Approaches to Humor in Literature*. Albany: State University of New York Press, 1990.

Leydet, Francois. *The Coyote: Defiant Songdog of the West*. San Francisco: Chronicle Books, 1977.

Lincoln, Kenneth. "Caliban Again." *Kenyon Review* 9 (Winter 1987): 90–109.

———. "Indians Playing Indians." *MELUS* 16 (Fall 1989–1990): 91–98.

———. "Heroic Lies: Ollie North and the Ghost of Custer." *Caliban* 5 (1988): 109–21.

———. "A MELUS Interview: Hanay Geiogamah." *MELUS* 16 (Fall 1989–1990): 69–81.

———. "Indi'n Humor." *Caliban* 3 (1987): 114–18.

———. *Native American Renaissance*. Berkeley: University of California Press, 1983.

———. "Tai-Me to Rainy Mountain." *American Indian Quarterly* 10 (Spring 1986): 101–17.

Lincoln, Kenneth, with Al Logan Slagle. *The Good Red Road: Passages into Native America*. San Francisco: Harper & Row, 1987.

Lips, Julius E. *The Savage Hits Back: Or, The White Man Through Native Eyes*. London: Lovat Dickson, 1937.

Littlebird, Barbara. "Artist Profile: Harry Fonseca." *Four Winds*, Winter 1981.

Lopez, Barry Holstun. *Giving Birth to Thunder, Sleeping with His Daughter: Coyote Builds North America*. Kansas City, Mo.: Sheed Andrews and McMeel, 1977.

Lord, Albert B. *The Singer of Tales*. New York: Atheneum, 1974.

Lorenz, Konrad. *On Aggression*. Translated by Marjorie Kerr Wilson. New York: Harcourt Brace Jovanovich, 1966.

Lowe, John. "Theories of Ethnic Humor: How to Enter, Laughing." *American Quarterly* 38 (1986): 439–60.

Luckert, Karl W. *Coyoteway: A Navajo Holyway Healing Ceremonial*. Tucson: University of Arizona Press; Flagstaff: Museum of Northern Arizona Press, 1979.

McNickle, D'Arcy. *Native American Tribalism: Indian Survivals and Renewals*. 1973. Reprint. New York: Oxford University Press, 1979.

Mails, Thomas E. *Fools Crow*. Garden City, N.Y.: Doubleday, 1979. Reprint. New York: Avon Books, 1980.

Makarius, Laura. "Le Mythe du 'Trickster'." *Revue de l'histoire des religions* 175 (1969): 17–46.

———. "Ritual Clowns and Symbolic Behavior." *Diogenes* 69 (1970): 44–73.

Malotki, Ekkehart. *Gullible Coyote Una'ihu: A Bilingual Collection of Hopi Coyote Stories*. Tucson: University of Arizona Press, 1985.

Marcus, George E., and Michael M. J. Fischer. *Anthropology as Cultural Critique: An Experimental Moment in the Human Sciences*. Chicago: University of Chicago Press, 1986.

Marriott, Alice. *Saynday's People: The Kiowa Indians and the Stories They Told*. Lincoln: University of Nebraska Press, 1963.

Martin, Calvin, ed. *The American Indian and the Problem of History*. New York: Oxford University Press, 1987.

Marx, Karl. *Capital: A Critical Analysis of Capitalist Production*. Translated by

Samuel Moore and Edward Aveling. Edited by Friedrich Engels. London: Swan Sonnenschein, 1903.

Matthiessen, F. O. *American Renaissance: Art and Expression in the Age of Emerson and Whitman*. New York: Oxford University Press, 1941.

Matthiessen, Peter. *Indian Country*. New York: Viking Press, 1984.

Mattina, Anthony. *The Golden Woman: The Colville Narrative of Peter J. Seymour*. Translated by Anthony Mattina and Madeline de Sautel. Tucson: University of Arizona Press, 1985.

———. "North American Indian Mythography: Editing Texts for the Printed Page." In *Recovering the Word: Essays on Native American Literature*, edited by Brian Swann and Arnold Krupat. Berkeley: University of California Press, 1987.

Mechling, Jay. " 'Playing Indian' and the Search for Authenticity in Modern White America." *Prospects* 5 (1980): 17–33.

Meeker, Joseph W. *The Comedy of Survival: In Search of an Environmental Ethic*. 2d ed. Los Angeles: Guild of Tutors Press, 1980.

MELUS: Native American Literature 12 (Spring 1985).

Merquior, J. G. *Foucault*. 1985. Reprint. Berkeley: University of California Press, 1987.

Moi, Toril, ed. *French Feminist Thought: A Reader*. London: Blackwell, 1987.

Momaday, N. Scott. *The Ancient Child*. New York: Doubleday, 1989.

———. "Bringing on the Indians." Review of *Indians*, by Arthur Kopit; *Custer Died For Your Sins* and *We Talk, You Listen*, by Vine Deloria, Jr.; and *Man's Rise to Civilization as Shown by the Indians of North America from Primeval Times to the Coming of the Industrial State*, by Peter Farb. *New York Review of Books*, 8 April 1971, 39–42.

———. *House Made of Dawn*. New York: Harper & Row, 1968.

———. *The Names*. New York: Harper & Row, 1976.

———. *The Way to Rainy Mountain*. 1969. Reprint. Albuquerque: University of New Mexico Press, 1976.

Monro, D. H. *Argument of Laughter*. 1951. Reprint. Notre Dame, Ind.: University of Notre Dame Press, 1963.

Morreal, John. *Taking Laughter Seriously*. Albany: State University of New York Press, 1989.

———, ed. *The Philosophy of Laughter and Humor*. Albany: State University of New York Press, 1990.

Morson, Gary Saul. *Bakhtin: Essays and Dialogues on His Work*. Chicago: University of Chicago Press, 1986.

Nabokov, Peter. "Return to the Native." *New York Review of Books*, 27 September 1984.

———, ed. *Native American Testimony. An Anthology of Indian and White Relations: First Encounter to Dispossession*. 1978. Reprint. New York: Harper & Row, 1979.

Naranjo-Morse, Nora. *Mud Woman: Poems From the Clay.* Tucson: University of Arizona Press, 1992.

Neihardt, John G., trans. *Black Elk Speaks: Being the Life Story of a Holy Man of the Oglala Sioux.* 1932. Reprint. New York: Pocket Books, 1972.

Niatum, Duane. *Carriers of the Dream Wheel: Contemporary Native American Poetry.* New York: Harper & Row, 1975.

————, ed. *Harper's Anthology of 20th Century Native American Poetry.* San Francisco: Harper & Row, 1988.

Nichols, John D. " 'The Wishing Bone Cycle': A Cree 'Ossian'?" *International Journal of American Linguistics* 55 (1989): 155–78.

Nietzsche, Friedrich. *The Gay Science: With a Prelude in Rhymes and an Appendix of Songs.* Translated by Walter Kaufmann. 1882. Reprint. New York: Random House, 1974.

Nisbet, Alec. *Konrad Lorenz.* New York: Harcourt Brace Jovanovich, 1976.

Norman, Howard. *The Northern Lights.* New York: Summit Books, 1987.

————, trans. *Where the Chill Came From: Cree Windigo Tales and Journeys.* San Francisco: North Point Press, 1982.

————. trans. *The Wishing Bone Cycle: Narrative Poems from the Swampy Cree Indians.* New York: Stonehill, 1976. 2d ed., expanded to include "Who Met the Ice Lynx" and "Why Owls Die with Wings Outspread." Santa Barbara: Ross-Erikson, 1982.

Norris, Christopher. *Deconstruction: Theory and Practice.* 1982. Reprint. New York: Methuen, 1985.

northSun, nila. *Diet Pepsi and Nacho Cheese.* Fallon, Nev.: Duck Down Press, 1977.

Norwood, Vera, and Janice Monk, eds. *The Desert Is No Lady: Southwestern Landscapes in Women's Writing and Art.* New Haven, Conn.: Yale University Press, 1987.

Olson, Elder. *The Theory of Comedy.* Bloomington: Indiana University Press, 1968.

Ong, Walter J. *Orality and Literacy: The Technologizing of the Word.* London: Methuen, 1982.

Ortiz, Alfonso. "An Indian Anthropologist's Perspective on Anthropology." *Indian Historian* (1970): 11–14.

————, ed. *New Perspectives on the Pueblos.* Albuquerque: University of New Mexico Press, 1972.

Ostriker, Alicia Suskin. *Stealing the Language: The Emergence of Women's Poetry in America.* Boston: Beacon Press, 1986.

Owens, Louis. Review of *Harper's Anthology of 20th Century Native American Poetry,* edited by Duane Niatum. *Los Angeles Times, Book Review,* 21 February 1988, 8.

————. *Wolfsong.* Albuquerque: West End Press, 1991.

Paredes, J. Anthony. "Plains Indian Clowns: A Typological Study." Master's thesis, University of New Mexico, 1964.

Paul, Sherman. "Ethnopoetics: An 'Other' Tradition." *North Dakota Quarterly* 53 (Spring 1985): 37–44.

Paulson, Ronald, ed. *Satire: Modern Essays in Criticism.* Englewood Cliffs, N.J.: Prentice-Hall, 1971.

Pearce, Roy Harvey. *Savagism and Civilization: A Study of the Indian and the American Mind.* Rev. ed. of *The Savages of America* (1953). Berkeley: University of California Press, 1988.

Pelton, Robert D. *The Trickster in West Africa: A Study of Mythic Irony and Sacred Delight.* Berkeley: University of California Press, 1980.

Pepper, Jim. "Interview with Jim Pepper." *Caliban* 5 (1988): 150–71.

Peyer, Bernd, ed. *The Elders Wrote: An Anthology of Early Prose by North American Indians, 1768–1931.* Berlin: Dietrich Reimer Verlag, 1982.

Pokagon, Simon. "The Future of the Red Man." *Forum* 23 (1897): 698–708.

Potts, L. J. *Comedy.* New York: Capricorn Books, 1966.

Preston, Richard. *Cree Narrative: Expressing the Personal Meaning of Events.* National Museum of Man Mercury Series. Canadian Ethnology Service Paper, no. 30. Ottawa: National Museum of Canada, 1975.

Price, Reynolds. Review of *Winter in the Blood,* by James Welch. *New York Times Book Review,* 10 November 1974, 1.

Radcliffe-Brown, A. R. "On Joking Relationships." *Africa* 13 (1940): 195–210.

Radin, Paul. *The Trickster: A Study in American Indian Mythology.* 1956. Reprint. New York: Shocken Books, 1972.

Ramsey, Jarold. *Reading the Fire: Essays in the Traditional Indian Literatures of the Far West.* Lincoln: University of Nebraska Press, 1983.

———, ed. *Coyote Was Going There: Indian Literature of the Oregon Country.* Seattle: University of Washington Press, 1977.

Richardson, Boyce. *Strangers Devour the Land: A Chronicle of the Assault upon the Last Culture in North America, the Cree of Northern Quebec, and their Last Primeval Homelands.* New York: Knopf, 1976.

Ricketts, Mac Linscott. "The North American Indian Trickster." *History of Religions* 5 (1965): 327–50.

Robinson, Terry. *Tough Fry Bread. A Collection of Cartoons.* New Orleans: Written Heritage, 1990.

Roessel, Robert A., Jr., and Dillon Platero, eds. *Coyote Stories of the Navajo People.* Rough Rock, Ariz.: Navajo Curriculum Center Press, 1974.

Roheim, Geza. "Culture Hero and Trickster in North American Indian Mythology." In *Selected Papers of the International Congress of Americanists,* edited by Sol Tax. Vol. 3. Chicago: University of Chicago Press, 1952.

Roscoe, Will, ed. *Living the Spirit: A Gay American Indian Anthology.* New York: St. Martin's Press, 1988.

Rose, Wendy. *Lost Copper.* Morongo Indian Reservation: Malki Museum Press, 1980.

————. *What Happened When the Hopi Hit New York.* New York: Contact II, 1982.

Rosen, Kenneth, ed. *The Man to Send Rain Clouds: Contemporary Stories by American Indians.* New York: Random House, 1974.

Ross, A. C. *Mitakuye Oyasin: "We Are All Related."* Ft. Yates, N.D.: Bear, 1989.

Rothenberg, Jerome, ed. *Shaking the Pumpkin: Traditional Poetry of the Indian North Americas.* Garden City, N.Y.: Doubleday, 1972.

Rothenberg, Jerome, and Diane Rothenberg, eds. *Symposium of the Whole: A Range of Discourse Toward an Ethnopoetics.* Berkeley: University of California Press, 1983.

Rourke, Constance. *American Humor: A Study of the National Character.* 1931. Reprint. Garden City, N.Y.: Doubleday, 1953.

Ryden, Hope. *God's Dog: A Celebration of the North American Coyote.* 1975. Reprint. New York: Penguin Books, 1979.

Said, Edward W. *Orientalism.* New York: Random House, 1978.

Sainte-Marie, Buffy. "So Says Buffy Sainte-Marie," by LeRoy Woodson, Jr. *Los Angeles Times Magazine,* 20 April 1986, 20–22, 32.

Salabiye, Velma S. "Humor and Joking of the American Indian: A Bibliography." *American Indian Libraries Newsletter* 10 (Fall 1986): 2–4. See Humor and Joking of the American Indian: a Bibliography.

Sanborn, Geoff. "Unfencing the Range: History, Identity, Property, and Apocalypse in *Lame Deer, Seeker of Visions.*" *American Indian Culture and Research Journal* 14 (1990): 39–57.

Sarris, Greg. "On the Road to Lulsel: Conversations with Mabel McKay." *News from Native California* 2 (September–October 1988): 3–6.

————. "The Verbal Art of Mabel McKay." Ph.D. diss., Stanford University, 1989.

Sayre, Robert F. "Trickster." *North Dakota Quarterly* 53 (Spring 1985): 68–81.

Schaeffer, Neil. *The Art of Laughter.* New York: Columbia University Press, 1981.

Scholder, Fritz. *Indian Kitsch: The Use and Misuse of Indian Images.* Flagstaff, Ariz.: Northland Press, 1979.

————. "Sharing a Heritage." Lecture delivered at American Indian Arts Conference, University of California, Los Angeles, May 1982.

Seals, David. *The Powwow Highway.* New York: Penguin Books, 1979.

Sekaquaptewa, Emory. "Clown Story." *Suntracks: An American Indian Literary Magazine* 5 (1979) 1–2.

Sherzer, Joel, and Anthony C. Woodbury, eds. *Native American Discourse:*

Poetics and Rhetoric. Cambridge Studies in Oral and Literate Culture. Cambridge: Cambridge University Press, 1987.

Shipley, William. "Mountain Maidu and the Art of Translation." *News from Native California* 2 (November–December 1988); 12–16.

Shorr, Daniel. "Reagan Recants His Path from Armaggedon to Detente." *Los Angeles Times,* 3 January 1988, Opinion Section, 5.

Silko, Leslie Marmon. *Ceremony.* New York: Viking Press, 1977.

————. *The Delicacy and Strength of Lace: Letters Between Leslie Marmon Silko and James Wright.* Edited by Anne Wright. St. Paul, Minn.: Graywolf Press, 1986.

————. *Laguna Woman.* Greenfield Center, N.Y.: Greenfield Review Press, 1974.

————. "Language and Literature from a Pueblo Indian Perspective." In *English Literature: Opening Up the Canon,* Selected Papers from the English Institute, 1979, n.s., vol. 4, edited by Leslie A. Fiedler and Houston A. Baker, Jr., 54–72. Baltimore: Johns Hopkins University Press, 1981.

————. *Storyteller.* New York: Seaver Books, 1981.

Sjöö, Monica, and Barbara Mor. *The Great Cosmic Mother: Rediscovering the Religion of the Earth.* San Francisco: Harper & Row, 1987.

Skeels, Dell. "The Function of Humor in Three Nez Perce Indian Myths." *American Imago* 11: 249–61.

Slotkin, Richard. *The Fatal Environment: The Myth of the Frontier in the Age of Industrialization, 1800–1890.* Middletown, Conn.: Wesleyan University Press, 1985.

Smith, Barbara, ed. *Home Girls: A Black Feminist Anthology.* New York: Kitchen Table, Women of Color Press, 1988.

Smith, John. *The Generall Historie of Virginia, New England & the Summer Isles.* 1624.

————. *New England Trials.* 1622.

Smith, Juane Quick-to-See. Preface to *Women of Sweetgrass, Cedar and Sage: Contemporary Art by Native American Women.* (exhibition catalogue). New York: Gallery of the American Indian Community House, 1985.

Smith, Patricia Clark, with Paula Gunn Allen. "Earthy Relations, Carnal Knowledge." In *The Desert Is No Lady: Southwestern Landscapes in Women's Writing and Art,* edited by Vera Norwood and Janice Monk. New Haven, Conn.: Yale University Press, 1987.

Snyder, Gary. *Axe Handles.* San Francisco: North Point Press, 1983.

————. *Earth House Hold: Technical Notes and Queries to Fellow Dharma Revolutionaries.* New York: New Directions, 1969.

————. "The Incredible Survival of Coyote." In Gary Snyder, *The Old Ways, Six Essays.* San Francisco: City Lights Books, 1977.

————. *Turtle Island.* New York: New Directions, 1974.

Sollors, Werner. *Beyond Ethnicity.* New York: Oxford University Press, 1986.

————, ed. *The Invention of Ethnicity.* New York: Oxford University Press, 1989.

Sontag, Susan. *Styles of Radical Will.* New York: Farrar, Straus & Giroux, 1969.

Spencer, Robert F. *Forms of Play of Native North Americans.* St. Paul, Minn.: West, 1977.

Spinden, Herbert Joseph. "Indian Artists of the Southwest." *International Studio* 95 (February 1930): 49–51, 86.

Stedman, Raymond William. *Shadows of the Indian: Stereotypes in American Culture.* Norman: University of Oklahoma Press, 1982.

Steward, Julian H. "The Ceremonial Buffoon of the American Indian." *Papers of the Michigan Academy of Science, Arts, and Letters* 14 (1931): 187–207.

Strouse, Jean. "In the Heart of the Heartland." Review of *Tracks,* by Louise Erdrich. *New York Times Book Review,* 2 October 1988.

Swann, Brian, and Arnold Krupat, eds. *I Tell You Now: Autobiographical Essays by Native American Writers.* Lincoln: University of Nebraska Press, 1987.

————. *Recovering the Word: Essays on Native American Literature.* Berkeley: University of California Press, 1987.

————. *Smoothing the Ground: Essays on Native American Oral Literature.* Berkeley: University of California Press, 1983.

Sypher, Wylie, ed. *Comedy.* Garden City, N.Y.: Doubleday, 1956.

Takaki, Ronald, ed. *From Different Shores: Perspectives on Race and Ethnicity in America.* New York: Oxford University Press, 1987.

Talayesva, Don C. *Sun Chief: The Autobiography of a Hopi Indian.* Edited by Leo W. Simmons. New Haven, Conn.: Yale University Press, 1942.

TallMountain, Mary. *The Light on the Tent Wall. A Bridging.* Native American Series, no. 8. Los Angeles: American Indian Studies Center, University of California, Los Angeles, 1990.

————. *There Is No Word for Goodbye.* Marvin, S.D.: Blue Cloud Press, 1982.

————. "*You Can* Go Home Again: A Sequence." In *I Tell You Now: Autobiographical Essays by Native American Writers,* edited by Brian Swann and Arnold Krupat, 1–13. Lincoln: University of Nebraska Press, 1987.

Tapahonso, Luci. *A Breeze Swept Through.* Albuquerque: West End Press, 1987.

————. *One More Shiprock Night.* San Antonia: Tejas Art, 1981.

————. *Seasonal Woman.* Santa Fe: Tooth of Time Books, 1982.

Tedlock, Dennis, trans. *Finding the Center: Narrative Poetry of the Zuni Indians.* 1972. Reprint. Lincoln: University of Nebraska Press, 1978.

————. *The Spoken Word and the Work of Interpretation.* Philadelphia: University of Pennsylvania Press, 1983.

————, trans. *Popul Vuh: The Mayan Book of the Dawn of Life.* New York: Simon and Schuster, 1985.

Terkel, Studs. "Studs Terkel Hour" (radio program). KCRW, Los Angeles, 19 April 1987.

Thackeray, William W. " 'Crying for Pity' in *Winter in the Blood.*" *MELUS* 7 (Spring 1980): 61–78.

Todorov, Tzvetan. *The Conquest of America: The Question of the Other.* Translated by Richard Howard. New York: Harper & Row, 1984.

————. *Mikhail Bakhtin: The Dialogical Principle.* Translated by Wlad Godzich. Vol. 13, *Theory and History of Literature.* Minneapolis: University of Minnesota Press, 1984.

Toelken, Barre. "Poetic Retranslation and the 'Pretty Languages' of Yellowman." In *Traditional Literatures of the American Indian,* edited by Karl Kroeber. Lincoln: University of Nebraska Press, 1981.

————. "The 'Pretty Language' of Yellowman: Genre, Mode, and Texture in Navaho Coyote Narratives." *Genre* 2 (September 1969): 211–235.

Towers, Robert. "Roughing It." Review of *Tracks,* by Louise Erdrich. *New York Review of Books,* 10 November 1988, 40–41.

Trimble, Stephen. "Brown Earth and Laughter: The Clay People of Nora Naranjo-Morse." *American Indian Art Magazine* 12 (Autumn 1987): 58–65.

Trudell, John. *Living in Reality: Songs Called Poems.* Los Angeles: Commonwealth, 1982.

Trudell, John, and Jesse Ed Davis. "Baby Boom Che." In *aka Grafitti Man.* The Peace Company Album, 1986.

Trudell, John, and Kenneth Lincoln. Interview. "Mid-Morning Los Angeles," KTLA-TV, 14 January 1988.

Tsosie, Rebecca. "Changing Women: American 'Native' Poets." University of California, Los Angeles, December 1985. Manuscript.

Turner, Victor. *The Forest of Symbols.* Ithaca, N.Y.: Cornell University Press, 1967.

Velie, Alan R. *Four American Indian Literary Masters.* Norman: University of Oklahoma Press, 1982.

————. "Indians in Indian Fiction: The Shadow of the Trickster." *American Indian Quarterly* 8 (Fall 1984): 315–29.

————. "*Winter in the Blood* as Comic Novel." *American Indian Quarterly* 4 (May 1978): 141–47.

Vendler, Helen. *Part of Nature, Part of Us: Modern American Poets.* Cambridge, Mass.: Harvard University Press, 1980.

Vespucci, Amerigo. *Mundus Novus.* 1503.

Vestal, Stanley. "The Hollywooden Indian." *Southwest Review* 21 (July 1936): 418–23.

———. *Sitting Bull: Champion of the Sioux. A Biography.* 1932. Reprint. Norman: University of Oklahoma Press, 1956.

———. "The Works of Sitting Bull: Real and Imaginary." *Southwest Review* 19 (April 1934): 265–77.

Vizenor, Gerald. *Crossbloods: Bone Courts, Bingo, and Other Reports.* Minneapolis: University of Minnesota Press, 1990.

———. *Darkness in Saint Louis Bearheart.* St. Paul, Minn.: Bookslinger, 1978. Reprinted as *Bearheart: The Heirship Chronicles.* Minneapolis: University of Minnesota Press, 1990.

———. *Griever: An American Monkey King in China.* Normal: Illinois State University Press, 1987, 1990.

———. *Warriors of Orange.* Minneapolis: Film in the Cities, 1984. Videocassette.

———. *Interior Landscape: Autobiographical Myths and Metaphors.* Minneapolis: University of Minnesota Press, 1990.

———. *The People Named the Chippewa: Narrative Histories.* Minneapolis: University of Minnesota Press, 1984.

———. "Trickster Discourse." *Wicazo Sa Review* 5 (Spring 1989): 2–7.

———. *The Trickster of Liberty: Tribal Heirs to a Wild Baronage.* Minneapolis: University of Minnesota Press, 1988.

———, ed. *Narrative Chance: Postmodern Discourse on Native American Indian Literatures.* Albuquerque: University of New Mexico Press, 1980.

———, ed. *Summer in the Spring: Ojibwe Lyric Poems and Tribal Stories.* Minneapolis: Nodin Press, 1981.

Volborth, Judith. "Night Songs." In *Thunder-Root: Traditional and Contemporary Native Verse.* Native American Series, no. 3. Los Angeles: American Indian Studies Center, University of California, Los Angeles, 1978.

Walker, Nancy A. *A Very Serious Thing: Women's Humor and American Culture.* Minneapolis: University of Minnesota Press, 1988.

Wallace, Ronald. *God Be with the Clown: Humor in American Poetry.* Columbia: University of Missouri Press, 1984.

Walsh, Marnie. *A Taste of the Knife.* Boise, Idaho: Ahsahta Press, 1976.

War Cloud, Paul. *Sioux Indian Dictionary.* Pierre, S.D.: State Publishing, 1968.

Warren, Robert Penn. *Chief Joseph of the Nez Perce, Who Called Themselves the Nimupu—"The Real People."* New York: Random House, 1982.

Weatherford, Jack. *Indian Givers: How the Indians of the Americas Transformed the World.* New York: Crown, 1988.

Welch, James. *The Death of Jim Loney.* New York: Harper & Row, 1979.

———. *Fools Crow.* New York: Viking Press, 1986.

————. Interview, April 1985. American Audio Prose Library, Columbia, Mo.

————. *Riding the Earthboy 40*. New York: World, 1971. Reprint. New York: Harper & Row, 1976.

————. *Winter in the Blood*. New York: Harper & Row, 1974.

Welsford, Enid. *The Fool: His Social and Literary History*. New York: Farrar & Rinehart, 1935.

White, Hayden. *Metahistory: The Historical Imagination in Nineteenth-Century Europe*. Baltimore: Johns Hopkins University Press, 1973.

————. "The Wild Man Within." In *The Wild Man Within*, edited by Edward J. Dudley and Maximillian E. Novak. Pittsburgh: University of Pittsburgh Press, 1973.

Whiteman, Roberta Hill. *Star Quilt*. Minneapolis: Holy Cow! Press, 1984.

Wideman, John. "The Black Writer and the Magic of the Word." *New York Times Book Review*, 24 January 1988.

Wiget, Andrew, ed. *Critical Essays on Native American Literature*. Boston: Hall, 1985.

Wilde, Larry. *The Complete Book of Ethnic Humor*. Los Angeles: Pinnacle Books, 1978.

Willeford, William. *The Fool and His Scepter: A Study of Clowns and Jesters and Their Audience*. Evanston, Ill.: Northwestern University Press, 1969.

Williams, Robert A., Jr. "Gendered Checks and Balances: Understanding the Legacy of White Patriarchy in an American Indian Cultural Context." University of Arizona College of Law, 1990. Manuscript.

Williams, Walter L. *The Spirit and the Flesh: Sexual Diversity in American Indian Culture*. Boston: Beacon Press, 1986.

Williams, William Carlos. *In the American Grain*. 2d ed. New York: New Directions, 1956.

Wimsatt, W. K., ed. *The Idea of Comedy, Essays in Prose and Verse: Ben Jonson to George Meredith*. Englewood Cliffs, N.J.: Prentice-Hall, 1969.

Wissler, Clark, and D. C. Duvall. *Mythology of the Blackfoot Indians*. Anthropological Papers of the American Museum of Natural History, vol. 2. New York: The Trustees, 1908.

Witherspoon, Gary. *Language and Art in the Navajo Universe*. Ann Arbor: University of Michigan Press, 1977.

Woodard, Charles L. *Ancestral Voice: Conversations with N. Scott Momaday*. Lincoln: University of Nebraska Press, 1989.

Woodson, LeRoy, Jr. "So Says Buffy Sainte-Marie." *Los Angeles Times Magazine*, 20 April 1986, 20–22, 32.

Wright, Anne, ed. *The Delicacy and Strength of Lace: Letters Between Leslie Marmon Silko and James Wright*. St. Paul, Minn.: Graywolf Press, 1986.

Ybarra-Frausto, Tomás. "*Rasquachismo:* A Chicano Sensibility." Stanford

University. Manuscript to be published 1992 in *CARA* catalogue, UCLA Wight Gallery Exhibit.

Zenner, Walter P. "Jokes and Ethnic Stereotyping." *Anthropological Quarterly* 43 (1970): 93–113.

Zitkala-Sa. *American Indian Stories.* 1921. Reprint. Lincoln: University of Nebraska Press, 1985.

Humor and Joking of the American Indian: A Bibliography

The following bibliography was compiled by Velma S. Salabiye for a class on Indian humor at UCLA as part of English 190: Literature and Society, "Indi'n Humor." The citations reflect the various studies regarding Indian humor. It is a compilation of citations gleaned from various sources. It is not comprehensive; it does not include Clown, Coyote, or Trickster figures. It is intended to serve as a beginning bibliography for further research.

Ultimately, somewhere in regarding the published literature, one *can* discover—Indians *do* laugh, Aye!—V.S.S.

(First published in the *American Indian Libraries Newsletter* 10, no. 1 [Fall 1986]: 2–4.)

Basso, Keith H. *Portraits of "The Whiteman": Linguistic Play and Cultural Symbols Among the Western Apache.* Cambridge: Cambridge University Press, 1979.

Bibeau, Don, Carl Gawboy, and Naomi Lyons. *Everything You Ever Wanted to Ask About Indians: But Were Afraid to Find Out!* Saint Cloud, Minn.: North Star Press, 1971.

Brown, Paula. "Changes in Ojibwa Social Control." *American Anthropologist* 54 (1952): 57–70.

Burton, Henrietta K. "Their Fun and Humor." *Indians at Work* 3 (1935): 24.

Churchill, Ward. "Charlie Hill: The Lenny Bruce of Native America." *Shantih* 4 (1979): 57–58.

Codere, Helen. "The Amiable Side of Kwakiutle Life: The Potlach and the Play Potlatch." *American Anthropologist* 58 (1956): 334–51. Response from V. Barnouw in *American Anthropologist* 59 (1957): 532–35.

Cuppy, Will. *The Decline and Fall of Practically Everybody.* New York: Holt, 1950.

Deloria, Vine, Jr. "Indian Humor." *Custer Died For Your Sins: An Indian Manifesto.* New York: Macmillan, 1969, 146–67.

Densmore, Frances. "The Words of Indian Songs as Unwritten Literature." *Journal of American Folklore* 63 (1950): 450–58.

Dorson, Richard M. "Comic Indian Anecdotes." *Southern Folklore Quarterly* 10 (1946): 113–28.

Easton, Robert. "Humor of the American Indian." *Mankind* 2 (1970): 37–41.

Edmunds, R. David. "Indian Humor: Can the Red Man Laugh?" In *Red Men and Hat-Wearers: Viewpoints in Indian History: Papers from the Colorado State University Conference on Indian History, August, 1974,* edited by D. Tyler, 141–53. Boulder, Colo.: Pruett, 1976.

Foster, George M. *A Summary of Yuki Culture.* Berkeley: University of California Press, 1944.

Freeman, Robert. *For Indians Only.* Escondido, Calif.: Brinck Lithography, 1971.

———. *Rubber Arrows.* Escondido, Calif: A & L Litho, 1989.

———. *War Whoops and All that Jazz.* San Marcos, Calif.: Palomar, 1974.

Geiogamah, Hanay. *New Native American Drama: Three Plays.* Norman: University of Oklahoma Press, 1980.

Gifford, Edward W. *The Kamia of Imperial Valley.* Washington, D.C.: Government Printing Office, 1931.

Hess, Bill. "A Navajo Laughs." *Nations* 1 (1981): 14–20.

Hill, Willard W. *Navajo Humor.* Menasha, Wis.: Banta, 1943.

Holden, Madronna. " 'Making All the Crooked Ways Straight': The Satirical Portrayal of Whites in Coast Salish Folklore." *Journal of American Folklore* 89 (1976): 271–93.

Horn, Patrice, et al. "Eskimo Humor—More than a Laughing Matter." *Psychology Today,* March 1974, 14, 88.

Howard, James H. "Peyote Jokes." *Journal of American Folklore* 75 (1962): 10–14.

Jacobs, Melville. "Humor and Social Structure in Oral Literature." In *Culture in History; Essays in Honor of Paul Radin,* edited by S. Diamond, 181–89. New York: Columbia University Press, 1960.

Levine, Stuart. "Our Indian Minority." *Colorado Quarterly* 16 (1968): 297–320.

Long Lance, Chief Buffalo Child. "Indians of the Northwest and West Canada." *Mentor* 12 (1924): 3–40.

Miller, Frank C. "Humor in a Chippewa Tribal Council." *Ethnology: An International Journal of Cultural and Social Anthropology* 6 (1967): 263–71.

Opler, Morris E. "Humor and Wisdom of Some American Indian Tribes." *New Mexico Anthropologist* 3 (1938): 3–10.

Osborne, Ralph, ed. *Who Is the Chairman of This Meeting? A Collection of Essays.* Toronto: Neewin, 1972.

Parker, Arthur C. "How Indians Cracked Their Jokes." In *The Indian How Book.* Garden City, N.Y.: Doubleday, 1946, 132–40.

Parsons, Elsie C. "Micmac Folklore." *Journal of American Folklore* 38 (1925): 55–133.

Preston, W. D. "Six Seneca Jokes." *Journal of American Folklore* 62 (1949): 426–27.

Price, John A. "Stereotyping by Indians." *Native Studies: American and Canadian Indians.* Toronto: McGraw-Hill Ryerson, 1978, 217–25.

Richardson, Boyce. *Strangers Devour the Land: A Chronicle of the Assault Upon the Last Coherent Hunting Culture in North America, the Cree of Northern Quebec, and Their Last Primeval Homelands.* New York: Knopf, 1976.

Skeels, Dell. "A Classification of Humor in Nez Perce Mythology." *Journal of American Folklore* 67 (1954): 57–63.

Trimble, Charles, et al. *Shove It, Buster. We'd Rather Have Our Land! A Candid Look at Modern Indian History in the Making.* Denver: American Indian Press, 1971.

Voegelin, C. F. "Pregnancy Couvade Attested by Term and Text in Hopi." *American Anthropologist* 62 (1960): 491–94.

Wallace, William J. "The Role of Humor in the Hupa Indian Tribe." *Journal of American Folklore* 66 (1953): 135–41.

Wardenaar, Leslie A. "Humor in the Colonial Promotional Tract: Topics and Techniques." *Early American Literature* 9 (1975): 286–300.

Watkins, Floyd C. "James Kirk Paulding: Humorist and Critic of American Life." Ph.D. diss., Vanderbilt University, 1952.

Wilson, Alan, and Gene Dennison. *Laughter: The Navajo Way.* Vol. 1. Gallup: University of New Mexico Press, 1970.

Witt, Shirley H., and Stan Steiner. "Indian Humor." In *The Way: An Anthology of American Indian Literature,* edited by Shirley H. Witt and Stan Steiner, 73–77. New York: Knopf, 1972.

Index

Adam and Eve, 122, 180, 233, 257, 264–65, 281, 287, 289

Agroikos (rustic), 29, 227, 282–83

Alazon (imposter), 29, 78, 94, 224, 257, 258, 282–83

Alcatraz, occupation of, 167, 168, 255

Allen, Paula Gunn, 7, 9, 25, 64, 172, 177, 179, 181–85 passim, 189–93 passim; "Raven's Road," 310; *The Sacred Hoop*, 24, 181, 205, 206; *The Woman Who Owned the Shadows*, 255

Almanac of the Dead (Silko), 310

"America" (Ginsberg), 137

American Humor (Rourke), 53, 213, 220, 295

American Indian Movement (AIM), 26, 175

American Indian Theater Ensemble, at La Mama, 162

American Museum of Natural History, 61

American Rhythm, The (Austin), 121, 220

Amerika (Kafka), 108

Anatomy of an Illness (Cousins), 34

Anatomy of Criticism (Frye), 18, 23, 29, 30, 31, 205, 280–81, 295

Ancestral Voice (Woodard), 3, 12, 280

Ancient Child, The (Momaday), 178, 310

Aquash, Annie Mae, 174

Archuleta, Margaret, 139

Aristotle, 29

Armstrong, Louis, 270

Austin, Mary, 107; *The American Rhythm*, 121, 220

Ax Handles (Snyder), 113

Azbill, Henry Ke'a'a'la, 138

Babcock, Barbara, 42, 66; on *The Delight Makers*, 37; with Helen Cordero, 38; on "reversible field" of

comedy, 55; *The Reversible World*, 70; "A Tolerated Margin of Mess," 142

Bachelard, Gaston, 8

Bakhtin, Mikail, 44, 65, 79, 85; "chronotopes," 245; *heteroglossia*, 294; *Rabelais and His World*, 167

Bandelier, Adolf, 38; *The Delight Makers*, 37

Banks, Dennis, 128

Barlow, Joel: "Hasty Pudding," 124

Barth, John: *The Sotweed Factor*, 167

Baseball, as played by Navajo, 28

Basso, Keith, 40, 42, 66, 235, 312; with Nick Thompson, 102–3; *Portraits of "The Whiteman,"* 92–98 passim

Bataille, Georges, on laughter, 44

Bates, Craig, 139

Beans, Billy, 97

Bear, The (Faulkner), Sam Fathers in, 112

Beauvoir, Simone de, 180

Beck, Lawrence, 152–53

Beet Queen, The (Erdrich), 213–18 passim

Benjamin, Walter: *Illuminations*, 33

Bergson, Henri: "Rire," 26, 81

Berkhofer, Robert, 42, 90; *The White Man's Indian*, 122

Bernheimer, Richard: *Wild Man in the Middle Ages*, 10

"Bessie Dreaming Bear" (Walsh), 16

Beyond Ethnicity (Sollors), 13

Big Foot, 61

"Bisociation" (Koestler), 28, 35, 39, 42, 71, 73, 79, 81, 93, 167, 190, 220, 254, 279, 293, 311

Bissonette, Pedro, 174

Black Elk, Nicholas: *Black Elk Speaks*, 21, 58, 67, 74, 79, 104